Accolades for the first edition

"For a B&B breakfast at home, check out *Rise & Dine*."
— *Food & Wine*

"The most tantalizing recipes shared by America's B&B innkeepers."
— *Bed & Breakfast*

"Armchair travelers and kitchen magicians will delight in this packed volume. This book is a must for breakfast lovers as well as travel enthusiasts."
— *Country Almanac*

"Bed and breakfasts serve up some winning brunch ideas. A source of B&B recipes is a new book titled *Rise & Dine: Savory Secrets from America's Bed & Breakfast Inns*."
— *Chicago Tribune Syndicate*

"*Rise & Dine* is a delightful collection of breakfast treats."
— *Charlotte Herald*

"It is hard to find a really good breakfast-recipe book. This qualifies. One wonders about the fist fights over Best Ever Chocolate Chip-Banana Muffins." — *Metro Menus*

"A positive contribution to the B&B industry and good breakfasts everywhere. *Rise & Dine* makes the grade from the toughest testers: other innkeepers." — *The Inn Times*

"A good read for the armchair gourmet." — *Inn Marketing*

"Contains quite an array of tantalizing items. Recipes are appealing, easy to follow even for novice cooks, and require ingredients that are readily available. Many are do-ahead, making them good choices for entertaining."
— *Yellow Brick Road, The Bed & Breakfast Newsletter*

"Innkeepers know how to make the biggest muffins, the fluffiest pancakes, the heartiest omelets. And their recipes have been collected in *Rise & Dine*."
— *Newspaper Enterprise Association*

"A handy guide for the cook who likes to travel."
— *Virginian Pilot*

"Breakfast is the most important meal. *Rise & Dine* features recipes from some 100 US bed and breakfasts."
— *The Toronto Sun*

"This book reveals breakfast secrets of the pros."
— *The Montreal Gazette*

A Benjamin Franklin Award finalist

*Dedicated
to my parents,
Lorraine and Perry.
After all — you made me!*

Rise & Dine

AMERICA

Savory Secrets from
America's Bed & Breakfast Inns

MARCY CLAMAN

Callawind
Publications Inc.

MONTREAL, CANADA

Other B&B cookbooks from Callawind Publications:

Rise & Dine Canada: Savory Secrets from Canada's Bed & Breakfast Inns by Marcy Claman
Breakfast at Nine, Tea at Four: Favorite Recipes from Cape May's Mainstay Inn by Sue Carroll

Rise & Dine America: Savory Secrets from America's Bed & Breakfast Inns

Copyright © 1998 by Callawind Publications Inc. This second edition is an expansion and revision of a work originally published as *Rise & Dine: Savory Secrets from America's Bed & Breakfast Inns.*

Cataloguing in Publication Data
Claman, Marcy, 1963–
    Rise & dine America : savory secrets from
America's bed & breakfast inns

Includes index.
ISBN 1-896511-09-0

    1. Breakfasts.   2. Brunches.   3. Afternoon teas.
4. Bed and breakfast accommodations—United States—
Directories. I. Title.   II. Title: Rise and dine America.

TX715.C57 1998   641.5′2   C97-901141-8

Copyediting: Tracy Fairchild / Cover illustration and design: Shari Blaukopf / Indexing: Christine Jacobs

10 9 8 7 6 5 4 3 2 1

Printed in Canada
All product/brand names are trademarks or registered trademarks of their respective trademark holders

Callawind Publications Inc.
    3383 Sources Boulevard, Suite 205, Dollard-des-Ormeaux, Quebec, Canada H9B 1Z8
    2083 Hempstead Turnpike, Suite 355, East Meadow, New York, USA 11554-1730
    E-mail: info@callawind.com   http://www.callawind.com

Contents

Acknowledgments

A heartfelt thank you goes out to all the bed & breakfast inns appearing in this book for allowing me to publish your recipes, and especially for your continued encouragement.

Thank you to Tracy Fairchild for all your wise editorial guidance, food knowledge, and inspiring enthusiasm. Are you a breakfast lover yet?

Many thanks to Shari Blaukopf for designing and illustrating the cover of my dreams and providing artistic guidance.

My family and friends have been a constant source of inspiration from the beginning. I thank you all for helping me test recipes and giving me the feedback I needed to make this book the best it could be.

To Lenny, thanks for being the best breakfast partner I could ever hope for.

Introduction

What's a bed & breakfast inn? *It's a charming home-away-from-home that includes a heavenly breakfast, warm ambiance, hospitable innkeepers, and the interesting company of other guests. When was the last time you enjoyed such comforts at your average hotel or motel?*

I'm a true breakfast lover and, while driving in the countryside on our honeymoon, my husband Lenny and I came upon an oh-so-quaint and inviting B&B. Too good to pass up, we signed on for a trial stay and the promise of a memory-making breakfast. We weren't disappointed (even today I remember those wonderful apricot pancakes!). And so began our initiation to the charm and culinary delights of B&B travel.

Some years later, winding our way home from yet another B&B stay (with an unforgettable homemade apple strudel still on my taste buds), I was struck with the idea of combining a B&B cookbook and travel guide in one. This idea became the original, best-selling *Rise & Dine: Savory Secrets from America's Bed & Breakfast Inns*.

I was delighted at the success of the first edition and I'm so pleased to be able to bring out this new edition. It features totally updated and expanded B&B travel information from all 50 states and the District of Columbia, convenient lay-flat binding, and, of course, even more delectable and easy guest-tested recipes than ever.

B&Bs chosen for the book come from a variety of sources: my own personal experience, recommendations from family and friends, and recommendations from various publications and travel guides devoted to B&B travel. In turn, these B&Bs are asked to share their savory secrets for breakfast, brunch, and afternoon tea — recipes that hit the spot with their guests day in and day out.

If this book whets your appetite for exploring America's B&Bs, use it as a guide to your travels — whether you're interested in cozying up to a roaring fire at a picture-postcard, Austrian-style chalet, enjoying a whimsical stay in an authentic 1923 red caboose, or regaling in the 19th-century splendor of a restored Queen Anne mansion. Since B&Bs are like people (no two are alike!), I've tried to represent as many different B&B experiences as possible — from rustic to ultimate luxury.

Whatever your taste in culinary adventures or your budget, you're bound to find a B&B or two in this book that fits perfectly. For your information, each recipe is accompanied by a description of the contributing B&B, along with a guide to cost for double occupancy per night (excluding taxes) in US dollars. Please note that rates are current as of this book's printing and are subject to change without notice.

$ = under $50 $$ = $50 – $89 $$$ = $90 – $120 $$$$ = over $120

Here's to many memorable B&B meals and travel adventures — right from your kitchen table!

— Marcy Claman

Index of B&Bs

Beverages & Cereal

Apple-Cranberry Breakfast Pudding

"This recipe is my own creation and one of my guests' favorites. I've even had requests for it from as far away as Germany and Australia. After I spoon a healthy dollop of sour cream topping over the steaming pudding, it looks like a breakfast sundae!" — Anne Stuart

4 cups skim milk
¾ cup brown sugar, firmly packed
½ teaspoon salt
6 ounces golden raisins
2 cups large-flake rolled oats
4 – 5 Red Delicious apples, cored, sliced thin, but not peeled
1 cup fresh cranberries, halved
1 cup chopped pecans, walnuts, or almonds
Non-fat sour cream
Cinnamon sugar

Preheat the oven to 350°F. Combine the milk, ½ cup of the sugar, and salt in a microwave-safe large bowl. Heat in the microwave oven until very hot but not boiling (about 6 – 8 minutes on high). To this mixture, add the raisins, oats, apples, cranberries coated with the remaining ¼ cup of brown sugar (by shaking both in a plastic bag), and nuts. Mix well. Put into a stoneware serving/cooking bowl and bake for 30 minutes. Stir before serving. Top each serving with a dollop of non-fat sour cream sweetened with cinnamon sugar. *Yield: 8 – 12 servings.*

Annie's Bed and Breakfast

Anne and Larry Stuart
2117 Sheridan Drive
Madison, Wisconsin 53704
Tel/Fax: (608) 244-2224
$$$ – $$$$

ABOUT THE B&B

Opened April 1985 as Madison's first bed and breakfast inn, Annie's is a rustic cedar shake and stucco house in a quiet neighborhood overlooking the beautiful valley of Warner Park, a block away from Lake Mendota's eastern shore. Tall green spruces, shaggy birch trees, and extensive gardens surround the house, gazebo, and lily pond to frame views of meadows, water, and woods. Luxury, getaway accommodations include two comfortable two-bedroom suites filled with antiques and little surprises and a sumptuous whirlpool for two in a room by itself, surrounded by mirrors, lush plants, and music. Awake to Annie's famous homemade full country breakfast, then visit museums, art galleries, theaters, shopping malls, State Street, the University of Wisconsin campus, Olbrich Botanical Gardens, the Farmer's Market, and more. Warner Park nature trails, bicycle-jogging path, tennis courts, swimming beach, and boat docks are just outside the back door. Innkeepers Anne (an artist) and Larry (a financial planner) enjoy nature, art, architecture, literature, music, and people.

SEASON

all year

ACCOMMODATIONS

two suites with private baths

Thornrose House at Gypsy Hill

Suzanne and Otis Huston
531 Thornrose Avenue
Staunton, Virginia 24401
Tel: (540) 885-7026
Fax: (540) 885-6458
www.shenwebworks.com:
8001/thornrose
$$

ABOUT THE B&B

Thornrose House is a turn-of-the-century Georgian Revival with a wraparound veranda and nearly one acre of gardens with Greek colonnades. It is adjacent to the 300-acre Gypsy Hill Park with facilities for tennis, golf, swimming, and summer band concerts. Breakfast begins with the house specialty of Bircher muesli, a Swiss concoction of oats, fruit, nuts, and whipped cream. This is followed by an ever-changing menu of hot entrées and fresh baked muffins and breads. Fireplaces in the sitting room and dining room warm you on chilly mornings and winter evenings, while a baby grand piano invites you to share your musical talents. Thornrose House is conveniently located in the heart of the Shenandoah Valley, which offers hiking, biking, antique hunting, historical museums, summer theater, and numerous fine restaurants.

SEASON

all year

ACCOMMODATIONS

five rooms with private baths

Bircher Muesli

"In 1895, Swiss physician Dr. Bircher-Benner concocted this combination of fruit and cereal and, to demonstrate its nutritional value, fed it three times a day to children with rickets. Our own data confirms its value, because we haven't had a single case of rickets break out amongst our guests since we've been serving it!"
— Suzanne Huston

1 cup large-flake rolled oats
⅓ cup golden raisins
Milk
1 apple, peeled, cored, and grated
Juice of ½ lemon
Chopped fruit of the season
2 large spoonfuls whipped cream or vanilla yogurt
⅛ cup sliced almonds, toasted

Soak the oats and raisins overnight in the refrigerator in just enough milk to cover. In the morning, add the grated apple, lemon juice, and fruit. Fold in the whipped cream and top with the almonds. *Yield: 4 servings.*

Breakfast Granola

4 cups large-flake rolled oats
1 cup powdered non-fat milk
1 cup wheat germ
½ cup chopped almonds or peanuts
1 tablespoon ground cinnamon
1¼ cups brown sugar, firmly packed
¼ cup warm water
¾ cup vegetable oil
2 teaspoons vanilla
½ cup raisins (optional)

Preheat the oven to 200°F. Combine the oats, powdered milk, wheat germ, almonds, and cinnamon. In a separate bowl, mix the sugar, water, oil, and vanilla together. Combine with the oat mixture and mix well. Bake on a large cookie sheet, stirring every 30 minutes or until dry (about 2 hours). Cool and mix in the raisins if you like — or leave plain. Store in an airtight container. *Tip:* There are 281 calories per ½ cup serving. *Yield: 8 cups.*

Circa 1843
Est. 1986

The Blushing Rosé B&B

Ellen and Bucky Laufersweiler
11 William Street
Hammondsport, New York 14840
Tel: (607) 569-3402
Fax: (607) 569-3483
$$

ABOUT THE B&B

*I*n the heart of the wine country, The Blushing Rosé is a pleasant hideaway for honeymooners, anniversary couples, and romantic trysters alike. Whether you spend your day driving, hiking, biking, or just plain relaxing, The Blushing Rosé is the ideal haven at which to end your day. Arise to the wonderful aroma of fresh-baked granola and whole grain bread, and begin your day with a special breakfast. The inn itself has an ambiance of cozy, 19th-century America. There are four spacious guest rooms each with a sitting area and private bath. Air conditioning and ceiling fans are among some of the amenities offered. This B&B is located on the southern tip of Keuka Lake, one of New York's famous Finger Lakes.*

SEASON

May 1 to November 30

ACCOMMODATIONS

four rooms with private baths

Captain Ezra Nye House

Elaine and Harry Dickson
152 Main Street
Sandwich, Massachusetts 02563
Tel: (800) 388-2278 or (508) 888-6142
Fax: (508) 833-2897
E-mail: captnye@aol.com
$$$

ABOUT THE B&B

A sense of history and romance fills this 1829 Federal home, built by the distinguished sea captain, Ezra Nye. Located in the heart of historical Sandwich Village, Captain Ezra Nye House is within walking distance of Sandwich Glass and Doll museums, Thornton Burgess Museum, Shawme Lake, fine dining, and antique shops. Heritage Plantation, the marina, an auction house, as well as Cape Cod Bay and Canal are nearby. Activities also include whale watching or a day at the beach. The inn was chosen one of the top 50 inns in America, one of the five best on the Cape, and was Cape Cod Life magazine's readers' choice as best bed and breakfast on the upper Cape. It has been featured in Glamour, Toronto Life, and Innsider magazines. A full breakfast is served each morning, and specialties include walnut goat cheese soufflé, peach kuchen, or baked French toast. Harry's interests include golfing and collecting Chinese export porcelain, while Elaine is an avid cyclist and enjoys yoga.

SEASON

all year

ACCOMMODATIONS

six rooms (including one suite) with private baths

Cape Colada

1 pineapple, peeled and cored
5-ounce can cream of coconut*
1 small ripe banana
6 ice cubes
10 cranberries, halved

This is a key ingredient in piña coladas and should be available in cans in the liquor department of your supermarket.

Purée the pineapple, cream of coconut, peeled banana, and ice cubes in a blender. Pour into 6 wine glasses and garnish with a few halved cranberries. *Tip:* This drink is very good with a French toast breakfast. *Yield: 6 servings.*

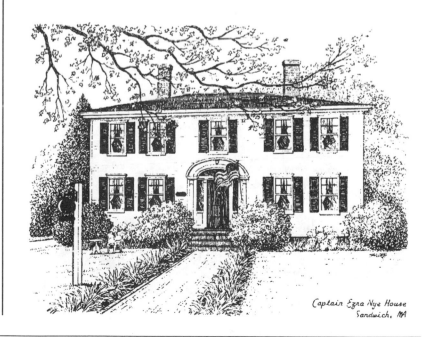

Captain Ezra Nye House
Sandwich, MA

Fruit Frappé

(*Recipe from* A Baker's Dozen Breakfast Favorites.)

"This recipe of ours was featured in the 'You Asked for It' column of Gourmet *magazine several years back."* — Susan Vernon

2 cups small ice cubes (to fill the blender ⅓ full)
1 cup papaya nectar
¾ cup pineapple juice
½ ripe banana
About ⅓ cup frozen blackberries or raspberries (not packed in syrup)
1 tablespoon cream of coconut*

*This is a key ingredient in piña coladas and should be available in cans in the liquor department of your supermarket.

In a blender, blend the ice cubes, papaya nectar, pineapple juice, peeled banana, berries, and cream of coconut at high speed until smooth.
Yield: 4 – 6 servings.

Casa de las Chimeneas
Bed & Breakfast Inn

Susan Vernon
Box 5303, 405 Cordoba Road
Taos, New Mexico 87571
Tel: (505) 758-4777
Fax: (505) 758-3976
E-mail: casa@newmex.com
$$$$

ABOUT THE B&B

Written up by many magazines, newspapers, and guidebooks over the years, *Casa de las Chimeneas (House of Chimneys Inn) has earned an enviable reputation for luxurious accommodations and delicious breakfast fare. Only a short walk from Taos's historic plaza, this hacienda-style B&B is set off from the town by seven-foot adobe walls. The grounds of this oasis are adorned with lovingly tended gardens, featuring more than 2,400 bulbs and countless perennials. Each guest room features a pueblo-style fireplace, private bath, and a private entrance, plus special attention to detail — such as lace-trimmed linens and hand-painted bathroom tiles. Common areas feature regional art, tiled hearths, French doors, and traditional ceiling beams (called "vigas"). The Southwestern influence is also felt at the Casa's breakfast table, where house specialties include huevos rancheros with green chili stew and blue corn pancakes with fresh berries. Innkeeper Susan Vernon is an avid gardener and enjoys sharing her love of horticulture.*

SEASON

all year

ACCOMMODATIONS

six rooms (including one suite)
with private baths

Saltair
Bed and Breakfast

Nancy Saxton and Jan Bartlett
164 South 900 East
Salt Lake City, Utah 84102
Tel: (800) 733-8184 or (801) 533-8184
Fax: (801) 595-0332
$$ – $$$

ABOUT THE B&B

Listed on the National Register of Historic Places, this 1903 Victorian house is the oldest continuously operating B&B in Utah and has hosted many dignitaries. The comfortably elegant house is furnished with period antiques, handmade quilts, and highlighted with wood and beveled glass. Room amenities include fresh flowers, saltwater taffy, terry cloth robes, and down comforters. Guests enjoy a warming fire in the parlor, a summer breeze on the front porch swing, or a Salt Lake starlit night in the B&B's hot tub. Breakfast may include cereal and yogurt, fruit, coffee or tea, a hot entrée, and a fruit smoothie. Located in a friendly residential neighborhood, Saltair is one mile west of the University of Utah, the historic downtown Salt Lake area, Temple Square, and the Utah Symphony Concert Hall, and is near Utah Jazz basketball, museums, theaters, and shopping. Seven ski resorts are 35 minutes away, while canyons for hiking and mountain biking are 10 minutes away.

SEASON

all year

ACCOMMODATIONS

two rooms with private baths;
three rooms with shared bath

Fruit Smoothie Drink

"Try as many combinations of fresh fruit and juice concentrates as you like — but always use a banana!" — Nancy Saxton

1 banana
1½ cups vanilla yogurt
½ of 12-ounce can frozen mixed fruit juice concentrate (Welches
    brand recommended)
1 tray of ice cubes
Fresh fruit (optional)

Place the peeled banana, yogurt, fruit juice concentrate, ice cubes, and fruit in a blender. Add water until it reaches the top of the blender. Cover and blend to liquefy. *Yield: 5 servings.*

Granola Supreme

14 cups large-flake rolled oats
¾ cup sunflower seeds
3 cups chopped roasted nuts (pecans, walnuts, almonds, or mixture
   of these)
4 cups fresh wheat germ (not toasted)
3 cups grated fresh coconut
¾ cup sesame seeds
2 cups brown sugar
1½ cups cold water
1 tablespoon vanilla
1½ cups vegetable oil
1½ teaspoons salt

Milk, yogurt, or soy milk

Preheat the oven to 275°F. Mix the oats, sunflower seeds, nuts, wheat
germ, coconut, sesame seeds, and sugar. In a separate bowl, mix the
water, vanilla, oil, and salt. Combine both mixtures, stirring thoroughly
(add more water if necessary). Bake 45 – 60 minutes, stirring as needed.
Don't brown too much. Serve with milk, yogurt, or soy milk.
Yield: 20 – 25 servings.

Natural
Bed & Breakfast

L. Marc Haberman
3150 East Presidio Road
Tucson, Arizona 85716
Tel: (520) 881-4582
Fax: (520) 326-1385
$$

ABOUT THE B&B

As much a private retreat as a B&B, the Natural B&B offers visitors natural, whole foods served in a non-toxic, non-allergenic environment, professional therapeutic massages, and health consultation services. Wake to a full vegetarian breakfast and spend your day horseback riding in the beautiful Tucson desert or visiting the Sonora Museum (only 10 miles away). You can opt for a swim in the nearby pool or relax on the patio or sun deck. In-room telephones and laundry service are other amenities. Your host, a graphic designer, fine artist, and energy worker, invites you to share his large, homey living room with a fireplace, and enjoy a complimentary coffee, tea, or juice. If arriving from the airport, you can take an airport Stagecoach shuttle dropping you at the B&B's front door.

SEASON

open all year

ACCOMMODATIONS

two rooms with private baths;
two rooms with shared bath

NATURAL
Bed & Breakfast

The Free Man House

Jennifer and Jim Freeman
1773 Lakeshore Drive
Branson, Missouri 65616
Tel: (417) 334-6262
Fax: (417) 337-9541
$$ – $$$

ABOUT THE B&B

A world-famous resort town nestled in the beautiful Ozark mountains, Branson is home to a variety of music shows and to three of the finest fishing lakes in the country. It is also home to The Free Man House, situated in a park-like setting along Lake Taneycomo (renowned nationwide for some of the finest trout fishing anywhere). This B&B offers fishermen all the amenities you could want: Cast your line by the nearby dock or by boat then warm up in one of the hot tubs after your brisk morning on the lake. For the non-fishermen, you can enjoy a relaxing day in one of Free Man House's three distinctive suites or around the pool, or browse through the quaint shops in Branson. In the evening, you can treat your ears to one of the many music shows in town — just minutes away. Free Man House has a conference room and retreat center that can accommodate family reunions or small conferences. Lodging is extended to Lakeshore Resort, also part of the property.

SEASON

all year

ACCOMMODATIONS

three suites with private baths

Hearty Granola

"This recipe was given to my mother-in-law by the wife of one of the original Jordannaires singers (who later started the Foggy River Boy theater of Branson, Missouri)." — Jennifer Freeman

½ cup margarine or butter
1 cup brown sugar
2 tablespoons water
4½ cups large-flake rolled oats
1 cup sunflower seeds (unsalted)
1 cup chopped nuts (pecans, walnuts, almonds, or mixture of these)
1 cup whole wheat or graham flour
1 teaspoon ground cinnamon
1 cup raisins (optional)
1 cup flaked unsweetened coconut (optional)

Bananas and milk

Preheat the oven to 350°F. Heat the margarine, brown sugar, and water together in a 13 x 9" pan until the margarine melts. Stir in the oats, sunflower seeds, nuts, flour, and cinnamon and bake for 45 minutes, stirring every 10 minutes. After you remove the granola from the oven, add the raisins and flaked coconut, if wished. Serve with fresh bananas and milk. *Yield: 15 – 20 servings.*

Hot Carob Granola Drink

⅓ cup powdered non-fat milk
1 cup granola
1 tablespoon carob powder
¼ teaspoon vanilla or 1 teaspoon instant coffee
1 cup hot water
1 tablespoon honey or sugar (or to taste)
Whipped cream (optional)
Sprinkle of granola (optional)

In a blender, combine the powdered milk, granola, carob powder, and vanilla. Add the hot water and honey, and blend until liquefied. Pour into cups. Top with whipped cream and sprinkle with granola, if desired. *Yield: 2 servings.*

NATURAL
Bed & Breakfast

Natural
Bed & Breakfast

L. Marc Haberman
3150 East Presidio Road
Tucson, Arizona 85716
Tel: (520) 881-4582
Fax: (520) 326-1385
$$

ABOUT THE B&B

As much a private retreat as a B&B, the Natural B&B offers visitors natural, whole foods served in a non-toxic, non-allergenic environment, professional therapeutic massages, and health consultation services. Wake to a full vegetarian breakfast and spend your day horseback riding in the beautiful Tucson desert or visiting the Sonora Museum (only 10 miles away). You can opt for a swim in the nearby pool or relax on the patio or sun deck. In-room telephones and laundry service are other amenities. Your host, a graphic designer, fine artist, and energy worker, invites you to share his large, homey living room with a fireplace, and enjoy a complimentary coffee, tea, or juice. If arriving from the airport, you can take an airport Stagecoach shuttle dropping you at the B&B's front door.

SEASON

open all year

ACCOMMODATIONS

two rooms with private baths;
two rooms with shared bath

Red Brook Inn

Ruth Keyes
PO Box 237
Old Mystic, Connecticut 06372
Tel: (860) 572-0349
E-mail: Rkeyes1667@aol.com
$$$$

ABOUT THE B&B

Nestled on a hillside, the Red Brook Inn offers Colonial life at its best. Capturing the spirit and simple pleasures of early New England, two beautifully restored historic buildings offer stone walls, antique-filled rooms, and well-banked fires to keep toes from frosting on chilly nights. Ten guest rooms are decorated with period furnishings, stenciled walls, and canopy beds. Six of the guest rooms have fireplaces and two have whirlpool tubs. A hearty breakfast of home-cooked specialties is served each morning in the Keeping Room. In autumn and winter months, special packages include Colonial dinners cooked over an open hearth. The inn is within minutes of the Mystic Marinelife Aquarium, Old Mystic Village, Mystic Seaport Museum, shops, and two of the world's largest casinos.

SEASON

all year

ACCOMMODATIONS

10 rooms with private baths

Mulled Cider

1 gallon apple cider
1 apple, studded with whole cloves
1 orange, thinly sliced
1 cup orange juice
Dash of ground cinnamon
Cinnamon sticks (for serving)

Pour the cider into a kettle. Add the apple, orange, orange juice, and cinnamon. Simmer 5 – 10 minutes. Serve with a cinnamon stick.
Yield: About 16 (8-ounce) servings.

Orange-Banana Smoothie

"This is a great, healthy breakfast beverage that's high in potassium and vitamin C and whips up like a rich and frothy milkshake."
— Elizabeth Browne

1 cup orange juice
½ banana, sliced
Orange slice
Mint leaf

In a blender, whip the orange juice and banana until well mixed. Serve in a tall glass, garnished with an orange slice and a mint leaf. *Tip:* This drink tastes best when made to order. *Yield: 1 serving.*

The Parsonage Inn

Elizabeth and Ian Browne
202 Main Street
East Orleans, Massachusetts 02643
Tel: (508) 255-8217
Fax: (508) 255-8216
$$$

ABOUT THE B&B

Dating back to around 1770, The Parsonage Inn was a vicarage in the 1880s and is now a romantic inn. Despite having been remodeled over the years, the house still retains the feeling of historic old Cape Cod. Each of the eight guest rooms (with its own private bath) is uniquely decorated with country antiques, quilts, stenciling, and fresh flowers. A delicious breakfast of waffles, French toast, crêpes, scones, muffins, and fresh fruit is served in the dining room or on the brick patio (a popular gathering place for guests). The Parsonage Inn is conveniently located close to Cape Cod's main attractions — Nauset Beach, the National Seashore, and the many bike paths that crisscross the Cape — and is within walking distance of fine restaurants and antique stores. Both innkeepers were born in England; Elizabeth was raised in Kenya and is a pianist and piano teacher, while Ian is an accountant and former medical group executive.

SEASON

all year

ACCOMMODATIONS

eight rooms with private baths

Turtleback Farm Inn

Susan and William Fletcher
Route 1, Box 650
Eastsound (Orcas Island),
Washington 98245
Tel: (800) 376-4914 or (360) 376-4914
Fax: (360) 376-5329
$$ – $$$$

ABOUT THE B&B

Located on the loveliest of the San Juan Islands, Turtleback Farm Inn is noted for its detail-perfect restoration, elegantly comfortable rooms, glorious setting, and award-winning breakfasts. A short ferry ride from Anacortes, Washington, Orcas Island is a haven for anyone who enjoys spectacular scenery, varied outdoor activities, unique shopping, and superb food. As spring turns into summer, the warm days encourage you to enjoy nature and island life at their best: Flowers are in full bloom, birds flutter, and whales, seals, and porpoises lazily coast through the shimmering waters of the Sound. After a day of hiking, fishing, bicycling, kayaking, sailing, windsurfing, or just reading by the inn's pond, enjoy a relaxing soak in your private bath or a sherry on the deck overlooking the valley below. After a tasty dinner at one of the Island's many fine restaurants, snuggle down under one of the inn's custom-made woolen comforters and peacefully doze off — with visions of the delicious breakfast awaiting you in the morning.

SEASON

all year

ACCOMMODATIONS

11 rooms (including four suites)
with private baths

Spiced Cider with Apple Brandy

2 cinnamon sticks, broken
1 tablespoon allspice berries
3 cloves
4 cups apple cider or apple juice
6 ounces apple brandy (Calvados) or applejack
6 cinnamon sticks (for serving)

Tie the cinnamon, allspice, and cloves in a cheesecloth bag. Place in a 2-quart pot and add the cider. Heat slowly until hot but not boiling. Put 1 ounce brandy and 1 cinnamon stick in each of 6 mugs. Remove the cheesecloth bag from the cider, and pour the hot cider into the mugs; stir with the cinnamon sticks to blend. Serve immediately. *Yield: 6 servings.*

Strawberry Frappé

"This recipe is one of our guests' favorites. It's like having a milkshake for breakfast." — Leicha Welton

2 cups orange juice
1 cup whipping cream
2 cups frozen strawberries
4 ripe bananas

Put the orange juice, whipping cream, strawberries, and peeled bananas in a blender. Whip at high speed until smooth. Pour into tall, clear glasses and serve. *Yield: 8 servings.*

7 Gables Inn

Leicha and Paul Welton
PO Box 80488
Fairbanks, Alaska 99708
Tel: (907) 479-0751
Fax: (907) 479-2229
E-mail: gables7@alaska.net
www.alaska.net/~gables7
$$ – $$$

ABOUT THE B&B

This 10,000 square foot Tudor-style house is located within walking distance of the University of Alaska Fairbanks campus, which is probably why 7 Gables began as a fraternity house. Its convenient location (between the airport and train station) is further enhanced by being right in the middle of a number of major attractions in the area: Riverboat Discovery, Pump House Restaurant, Cripple Creek Resort, University Museum, and Alaskaland. You enter the B&B through a floral solarium into a foyer with antique stained glass and an indoor waterfall. Other features include cathedral ceilings, wine cellar, and wedding chapel. Some additional amenities include laundry facilities, Jacuzzis, in-room cable TV and phones, canoes, bikes, gourmet breakfasts, luggage or game storage, and library collection. Leicha enjoys cooking, music, hosting parties, and learning foreign languages, while Paul collects books and manages the inn's marketing and maintenance.

SEASON

all year

ACCOMMODATIONS

12 rooms with private baths

Down the Shore B&B

Annette and Al Bergins
201 Seventh Avenue
Belmar, New Jersey 07719
Tel: (732) 681-9023
Fax: (732) 681-7795
E-mail: lodgings@cris.com
$$

ABOUT THE B&B

Down the Shore B&B was built specifically to be used as a residence and as a bed and breakfast. There are three guest rooms with a shared guest parlor and a shaded 40-foot front porch. Down the Shore B&B is located one block from the beach and boardwalk. The house may be new but the proprietors are not new to innkeeping. Before moving to Belmar, they operated another bed and breakfast in their lakeside home in Denville, New Jersey. As you can see from this recipe, healthful food is the mainstay of the breakfasts here.

SEASON

all year

ACCOMMODATIONS

one room with private bath;
two rooms with shared bath

Walnut Granola

"We like to serve this granola as a topping for vanilla yogurt, fresh fruit, and various cereals." — Annette Bergins

4 cups large-flake rolled oats
1 cup chopped walnuts
1 cup water
¾ cup raisins
2 teaspoons ground cinnamon
1 teaspoon grated nutmeg
½ teaspoon salt
½ teaspoon orange extract
3 tablespoons maple syrup
¼ cup orange juice
2 tablespoons canola oil

Preheat the oven to 350°F. Combine the oats and walnuts; set aside. Boil the water, remove it from heat, and add the raisins; set aside. Combine the cinnamon, nutmeg, salt, orange extract, maple syrup, orange juice, and oil. Mix well and pour over the oat mixture. Spread the mixture on an ungreased baking pan or cookie sheet. Bake for 15 minutes, stir it around, then bake another 15 minutes. Allow the mixture to cool, then dry the raisins and add to the mixture. Store in airtight containers.
Yield: About 6 cups.

West Hill House Granola

4 cups large-flake rolled oats
1 cup wheat germ
1 cup shredded unsweetened coconut
¾ cup chopped walnuts
½ cup sesame seeds
¾ cup brown sugar
½ cup hot water
¼ cup honey
¼ cup vegetable oil
1 cup chopped dates
¾ cup golden raisins

Preheat the oven to 250°F. Mix the oats, wheat germ, coconut, walnuts, sesame seeds, and sugar together in a large bowl. Mix the water, honey, and oil together and pour over the oat mixture. Mix until moistened. Spread in large flat pans. Bake for 3 hours or until dry, stirring every ½ hour. Add the dates about ½ hour before done. Add the raisins after the baking mixture is done. Store in an airtight container to maintain freshness. Use as a cereal (serving 16 – 24) or as a topping for fruit, yogurt, or ice cream. *Yield: 8 cups.*

West Hill House

Dotty Kyle and Eric Brattstrom
RR #1, Box 292
Warren, Vermont 05674
Tel: (800) 898-1427 or (802) 496-7162
Fax: (802) 496-6443
$$ – $$$

ABOUT THE B&B

Up a quiet country lane on nine peaceful acres, this 1860s farmhouse boasts stunning mountain views, gardens, a pond and apple orchard, and is just one mile from Sugarbush Ski Resort and adjacent golf course and cross-country ski trails. Besides having an outdoor sports paradise at its doorstep, West Hill House is also near fine restaurants, quaint villages, covered bridges, shops, antique hunting, museums, theater, and concerts. After a busy day, guests enjoy the comfortable front porch or roaring fireplace, library of eclectic books and videos, Oriental rugs, art, antiques, and the interesting company of other guests. Bedrooms feature premium linens, down comforters, and good reading lights. There's also a common guest pantry with wet bar and refrigerator. Breakfast specialties include sticky buns, soufflés, baked apple pancakes, fresh fruit, and more. Dotty and Eric, veteran B&B vacationers themselves, work to create an atmosphere of warmth and hospitality in their lovely small inn. Dotty's the chef, artist, and decorator, while Eric's the creative builder, remodeler, and stained glass artisan.

SEASON

all year

ACCOMMODATIONS

six rooms with private baths

Appetizers & Side Dishes

Artichoke Balls

3 cups canned artichoke hearts, reserving slightly less than ¼ cup of
    the water
2 heaping tablespoons minced garlic
Slightly less than ¼ cup olive oil
1¼ cups Italian-style bread crumbs
½ cup grated Parmesan cheese

Chop the artichokes. Add the garlic, water, and olive oil and mix
well. Chill. Combine the bread crumbs and Parmesan cheese. Roll the
artichoke mixture into balls and coat with the bread crumb mixture.
Yield: 100 small balls.

Lafitte Guest House

Robert D. Guyton and
Bobby L'Hoste
1003 Bourbon Street
New Orleans, Louisiana 70116
Tel: (800) 331-7971 or (504) 581-2678
Fax: (504) 581-2677
www.Lafitteguesthouse.com
$$$ – $$$$

ABOUT THE B&B

Built in 1849, the ivy-covered
French-roofed Lafitte Guest
House was constructed as a
single-family dwelling for the then-
enormous price of $11,700. The home
has had numerous owners since and
has operated as a guest house or apart-
ments since 1952. In 1980, present
owner Robert Guyton undertook a
major restoration to restore the building
to its original grandeur. Fourteen guest
rooms are decorated with antiques,
crystal chandeliers, and many original
furnishings. All rooms have private
baths, some with fireplaces and balco-
nies. The parlor is pure Victorian with
red velvet drapes and settee. Breakfast is
served in the parlor, courtyard, or in
your room. Lafitte Guest House is
located in the Vieux Carré and, right
outside its door, guests will enjoy the
colorful sights and sounds of the French
Quarter.

SEASON

all year

ACCOMMODATIONS

14 rooms with private baths

George Schumaker
PO Box 491
105 Greenwoods Road East
Norfolk, Connecticut 06058
Tel: (860) 542-5439
$$$$

ABOUT THE B&B

*C*alled *"a Connecticut jewel" by* Country Inns Bed & Breakfast *magazine, Greenwoods Gate combines a touch of romance with a sense of the past. This Federal-era inn offers four distinctive and elegant suites to choose from, with niceties such as fresh-cut flowers, fluffy robes, and crisp-ironed linens. A generous gourmet breakfast is served in the formal dining room, after which guests can linger in the center hall library or the grand parlor, with its antiques, Oriental rugs, and original Federal fireplace. Greenwoods Gate is conveniently located in the picture-perfect village of Norfolk, one half mile east of the Village Green. Innkeeper George Schumaker, a veteran of the hospitality business, organizes a B&B internship program three times per year for people considering owning and operating an inn.*

SEASON

all year

ACCOMMODATIONS

four suites with private baths

Bacon Curls

½ pound bacon, thickly sliced

Preheat the oven to 450°F. Cut the bacon strips in ½. Roll into a circle and secure with a toothpick. Place on a broiler rack and bake 10 – 15 minutes or until crisp and cooked (there is no need to turn). Remove toothpicks and serve. *Yield: 4 servings.*

Baked Tomatoes

1½ tablespoons olive oil
3 large and firm tomatoes, cut in halves and with seeds removed
3 teaspoons Dijon mustard
½ cup Italian-style bread crumbs
1 tablespoon sugar
¼ cup grated Parmesan cheese
3 large mushrooms, chopped (optional)
6 teaspoons butter

Preheat the oven to 400°F. Cover the bottom of an ovenproof glass dish with the olive oil. Place the 6 tomato halves in the dish, cut side up. Cover each tomato with some mustard. Mix the bread crumbs, sugar, Parmesan cheese, and mushrooms (if wished), then sprinkle over each tomato, covering completely. Top each with 1 teaspoon of butter. Bake until fork-tender (approximately 20 – 25 minutes). Serve immediately. *Yield: 6 servings.*

Sleepy Hollow Farm Bed & Breakfast

Beverley Allison and
Dorsey Allison Comer
16280 Blue Ridge Turnpike
Gordonsville, Virginia 22942
Tel: (800) 215-4804 or (540) 832-5555
Fax: (540) 832-2515
$$ – $$$$

ABOUT THE B&B

A long the scenic and historic byway of Virginia Route 231, a red mailbox signals your arrival at Sleepy Hollow Farm. If you miss the mailbox, look for a green barn with a very red roof, a gazebo, a pond, and a brick house snoozing under trees in a sleepy hollow. Generations of farm families have lived here since the late 1700s, and today Sleepy Hollow Farm attracts a wide spectrum of guests, including many international sojourners. Memories to take home with you include the "Dolley Madison hospitality" of innkeepers Beverley Allison and Dorsey Allison Comer, the farm's pure spring water, and the commanding landscapes of surrounding horse, cattle, and sheep farms. And, unlike many B&Bs, this one is equipped to handle children!

SEASON

all year

ACCOMMODATIONS

four rooms (including one suite)
with private baths;
guest cottage with two suites
and private baths

Down to Earth Lifestyles Bed and Breakfast

Lola and Bill Coons
12500 North West Crooked Road
Parkville, Missouri 64152
Tel: (816) 891-1018
$$

ABOUT THE B&B

*L*ocated near downtown Kansas City, Down to Earth Lifestyles is a beautiful earth-integrated home situated on 86 acres of peaceful woods and rolling hills. Each quiet, cozy room features a private bath, telephone, radio, color TV, and skylights or picture windows. Spacious leisure areas include a guest lounge and patio where you can enjoy a cold beverage and complimentary popcorn, and an indoor, heated swimming pool where you can take a soothing dip. The "great room" is the perfect place to relax with music, games, books, and magazines, or just relax in front of the fire. Comfortable walking shoes are a must as nature and wildlife are abundant. Stroll through woods and over pastures among the cattle, horses, and geese. Fishermen will want to try their luck in the two stocked ponds. Breakfast is truly a mouthwatering experience, served where and when you'd like. Your hosts have a background in education, music, counseling, and agriculture, and invite you to commune with nature and enjoy their down-to-earth hospitality.

SEASON

all year

ACCOMMODATIONS

four rooms with private baths

Barbecued Green Beans

4 strips bacon
¼ cup chopped onion
½ cup ketchup
¼ cup brown sugar
1 tablespoon Worcestershire sauce
2 (10-ounce) cans French-style green beans, well drained

Preheat the oven to 350°F. Cook the bacon in a skillet until crisp. Using the bacon grease, cook the onions until they turn yellow. Add the ketchup, brown sugar, and Worcestershire sauce to the bacon grease and onions. Crumble the bacon slices into the sauce and simmer for 2 minutes. Place the green beans in a casserole dish; pour the sauce over top (do not stir). Bake for about 20 minutes. *Yield: 6 servings.*

Blueberry-Lemon Soup

2 cups blueberries (preferably Maine wild)
1 cup water
½ cup granulated sugar
1 lemon, thinly sliced
1 cinnamon stick
1 cup and 6 teaspoons plain low-fat yogurt
2 tablespoons freshly squeezed lemon juice
2 tablespoons confectioners' sugar
Ground cinnamon

Combine the berries, water, granulated sugar, lemon, and cinnamon stick in a saucepan. Bring to a boil over medium heat. Reduce the heat and simmer 15 minutes. Cool. Remove the cinnamon stick and process the berry mixture in a blender until quite smooth. Chill overnight. Next day, combine 1 cup yogurt, the lemon juice, and confectioners' sugar. Whisk into the blueberry mixture. Top with a swirl of yogurt and sprinkle with ground cinnamon. *Yield: 6 servings.*

Gundalow Inn

Cevia and George Rosol
6 Water Street
Kittery, Maine 03904
Tel/Fax: (207) 439-4040
$$ – $$$$

ABOUT THE B&B

Gundalow Inn is a brick Victorian on the Kittery town green and on the banks of the Piscataqua River, just across the bridge from Colonial Portsmouth. Six romantic guest rooms all have private baths, and many overlook the river. The friendly, hospitable innkeepers have furnished this non-smoking inn for your comfort and invite you to join them in the pleasures of another era. Situated halfway between Boston and Portland, the inn's a short drive away from beaches and outlet malls, and a pleasant walk from Portsmouth's harbor, museums, theaters, shops, and restaurants. Fireside breakfasts feature fresh juices, a fruit dish (such as baked apple with homemade granola), freshly baked scones, and an entrée served with meat or fish (perhaps honey-pecan pancakes and homemade sausage, or creamy scrambled eggs with George's own smoked salmon). Before opening Gundalow Inn in 1990, George was an electrical engineer and Cevia an editor. Their love of music and books is evident throughout the inn, which has been recommended by the New York Times.

SEASON

all year

ACCOMMODATIONS

six rooms with private baths

Grünberg Haus
Bed and Breakfast

Christopher Sellers and
Mark Frohman
RR #2, Box 1595RD,
Route 100 South
Waterbury, Vermont 05676-9621
Tel: (800) 800-7760 or (802) 244-7726
Fax: (802) 244-1283
E-mail: grunhaus@aol.com
$$ – $$$$

ABOUT THE B&B

This picture-postcard Austrian-style B&B is tucked away on a secluded hillside in the Green Mountains, perfectly situated for visits to Stowe, Montpelier, Waterbury, and Burlington. Individually decorated guest rooms open onto the carved wood balcony, which offers wonderful views. Help Mark feed the chickens, then enjoy a full breakfast — with selections such as maple-poached pears, apple and cheddar muffins, and ricotta-stuffed French toast — while Chris plays the grand piano. The giant stone fireplace and wood stove in the BYOB pub are favorite gathering places. Nearby activities include spectacular autumn leaf-picking, world-class downhill skiing, golf, boating, bicycling, gliding, canoeing, antique hunting, outlet shopping, and touring Ben & Jerry's ice cream factory. And you can enjoy the B&B's own Jacuzzi, sauna, tennis courts, and cross-country and hiking trails.

SEASON

all year

ACCOMMODATIONS

seven rooms (including one suite)
with private baths;
five rooms with shared baths;
two cabins with private baths

Broiled Grapefruit

"Guests claim they've never enjoyed grapefruit so much!"
— *Christopher Sellers*

2 grapefruit
4 tablespoons maple syrup
Ground cinnamon

Cut the grapefruit into halves. Remove all seeds and loosen the sections in each half. Top each half with 1 tablespoon of maple syrup and dust with cinnamon. Broil the grapefruit until the edges just turn brown. Serve warm. *Yield: 4 servings.*

Grünberg Haus Bed & Breakfast
Waterbury, Vermont

Butternut Squash Soup

2 pounds butternut squash, trimmed, seeded, and cleaned
4 cups water
1 tablespoon salt
½ cup diced celery
½ cup diced onion
½ cup diced green bell pepper
½ cup butter, melted
¼ cup white wine
1 teaspoon tarragon
½ teaspoon ground cinnamon
½ teaspoon grated nutmeg
¼ teaspoon ground cloves
4 cups chicken stock
¼ cup all-purpose flour
½ cup Vermont maple syrup
¼ cup dry sherry

Add the squash to a large pot with the water, add the salt, and cook until soft (approximately 40 minutes). Strain the squash, reserving 2 cups of the liquid and discarding the rest. In a large pot, sauté the diced vegetables in ¼ cup of the butter and the wine for 5 minutes. Add the herbs and spices. Add the chicken stock and 1 cup of the reserved liquid. Bring the mixture to a boil, then thicken it with a roux made by mixing the flour with the remaining ¼ cup of butter, melted. Purée the cooked squash in a blender or food processor with the remaining 1 cup of reserved liquid. Add to the pot and cook it on low heat for 5 minutes, stirring often. Add the syrup and sherry. Mix well and serve. *Yield: 12 – 16 servings.*

The Inn at The Brass Lantern

Andy Aldrich
717 Maple Street
Stowe, Vermont 05672
Tel: (800) 729-2980 or (802) 253-2229
Fax: (802) 253-7425
$$ – $$$$

ABOUT THE B&B

*T*he Inn at The Brass Lantern is located at the edge of the village of Stowe, Vermont. Stowe is a full-service, four-season resort town, and boasts many world-class restaurants and activities, a cultural center, unique cottage industries, craftspeople, and artists. Originally built as a farmhouse and carriage barn, The Brass Lantern was restored by Andy Aldrich, the current innkeeper, to retain its original Vermont character (for which he won an award). Today, the inn carries the traditional Vermont B&B theme throughout — from its decor of period antiques, handmade quilts, and locally crafted amenities to the food and beverages reflecting local and Vermont state products. In addition, guests are treated to a unique ambiance and casual, attentive service. The inn's setting provides panoramic views of Mount Mansfield and its valley from nearly every room.

SEASON

all year

ACCOMMODATIONS

nine rooms with private baths

Mr. and Mrs. Harry Carter Sharp
1114 First East Street
Vicksburg, Mississippi 39188
Tel: (601) 636-6968
Fax: (601) 661-0079
$$ – $$$$

ABOUT THE B&B

The Duff Green Mansion is located in Vicksburg's historic district. Built in 1856, it's considered one of the finest examples of Paladian architecture in the state of Mississippi. The mansion was built by Duff Green, a prosperous merchant, for his bride Mary Lake Green (whose parents gave the land as a wedding gift). Many parties were held here during the antebellum days but it was hastily converted to a hospital for both Confederate and Union soldiers during the siege of Vicksburg and the remainder of the Civil War. Mary Green gave birth to a son during the siege in one of the caves next to the mansion and appropriately named him Siege Green. The over 12,000-square-foot mansion has been restored and features seven guest rooms with private baths, luxurious antiques, room service, southern plantation breakfasts, cocktails, and a swimming pool.

SEASON

all year

ACCOMMODATIONS

seven rooms (including two suites) with private baths

Fruit Kabobs

"A slightly modern twist on an old southern favorite."
— *Stephen Kerr, chef of Duff Green Mansion*

8 (12" long) wooden skewers
16 strips bacon
1 pineapple, peeled and cored
2 Granny Smith apples
2 Rome apples
6-ounce can pineapple juice
⅓ cup brown sugar, firmly packed

Soak the wooden skewers in water and set aside. Cook the bacon until limp but not crisp; drain and set aside. Cut the pineapple in 1" pieces. Core the apples and cut into 1" pieces. Combine the pineapple, apple, and pineapple juice, tossing to coat the fruit. Thread the end of a piece of bacon on a skewer, alternate the pieces of Granny Smith apple, pineapple, and Rome apple (in that order), weaving the bacon around each. Add another slice of bacon to the skewer when needed. Repeat with the remaining skewers, bacon, and fruit. Sprinkle each kabob with the brown sugar. Broil the skewers 6" from the heat for 6 minutes, turning once or until the fruit begins to brown around the edges.
Yield: 8 kabobs.

Jeanne's Zucchini Fritters

"When I was growing up, my mother used to make wonderful squash pancakes. I don't recall ever seeing a recipe written down, so this is my version, developed for Gundalow Inn and using those wonderful ingredients found in today's market. I've named the recipe for my mother." — Cevia Rosol

3 pounds zucchini, grated
1 small onion, chopped
1 medium red bell pepper, chopped
3 extra-large eggs
1½ cups all-purpose flour
1 tablespoon baking powder
¾ teaspoon salt
¾ teaspoon Hungarian sweet paprika
Canola oil

Sour cream

Combine the zucchini, onion, red pepper, eggs, flour, baking powder, salt, and paprika well. Heat a griddle or large, heavy skillet and add the oil. Drop the batter by large spoonfuls and fry until crispy and brown on both sides. Serve hot with sour cream. *Yield: About 24 fritters.*

Gundalow Inn

Cevia and George Rosol
6 Water Street
Kittery, Maine 03904
Tel/Fax: (207) 439-4040
$$ – $$$$

ABOUT THE B&B

Gundalow Inn is a brick Victorian on the Kittery town green and on the banks of the Piscataqua River, just across the bridge from Colonial Portsmouth. Six romantic guest rooms all have private baths, and many overlook the river. The friendly, hospitable innkeepers have furnished this non-smoking inn for your comfort and invite you to join them in the pleasures of another era. Situated halfway between Boston and Portland, the inn's a short drive away from beaches and outlet malls, and a pleasant walk from Portsmouth's harbor, museums, theaters, shops, and restaurants. Fireside breakfasts feature fresh juices, a fruit dish (such as baked apple with homemade granola), freshly baked scones, and an entrée served with meat or fish (perhaps honey-pecan pancakes and homemade sausage, or creamy scrambled eggs with George's own smoked salmon). Before opening Gundalow Inn in 1990, George was an electrical engineer and Cevia an editor. Their love of music and books is evident throughout the inn, which has been recommended by the New York Times.

SEASON

all year

ACCOMMODATIONS

six rooms with private baths

Volden Farm Bed and Breakfast

JoAnne and Jim Wold
RR #2, Box 50
Luverne, North Dakota 58056
Tel: (701) 769-2275
$$ – $$$

ABOUT THE B&B

After living all over the world, JoAnne and Jim Wold settled "where we belong — on the wide open prairie of North Dakota." Here, they opened Volden Farm, a B&B with an old-world atmosphere, thanks to the Russian and Norwegian decor and collectibles, which reflect the hosts' heritage and interests. Part of the home was built in 1926, comprising the parlor, music room, library, and two guest bedrooms. A new addition was built in 1978 to include a fireplace and dining area overlooking miles of tranquil prairie land. Bedrooms are filled with family heirloom quilts and one-of-a-kind antiques. Also available is a separate small house called the Law Office — with a bath, limited kitchen facilities, and fabulous view — where Jim used to have his office. The Scandinavian breakfast takes advantage of fresh ingredients from the farm and garden. After breakfast, guests can wander through 300 acres of fields, woods, hills, coulees, and virgin prairie. JoAnne and Jim take pleasure in reading, gardening, singing, and raising animals.

SEASON

all year

ACCOMMODATIONS

two rooms with shared bath
in main house;
two rooms with shared bath
in private cottage

Norwegian Sweet Soup (Sot Suppe)

"This soup can be served warm or cold." — JoAnne Wold

2 cups pitted prunes
1 cup dark raisins
1 cup light raisins
½ cup currants
1 cup dried apricots
1 unpeeled orange, sliced
2 cinnamon sticks
1 teaspoon ground cloves
¼ teaspoon grated nutmeg
¼ cup brown sugar
¼ cup tapioca

Crème fraîche (see recipe below)

Place the prunes, raisins, currants, apricots, orange, cinnamon sticks, cloves, and nutmeg in a large pot and add water to cover. Simmer for 1 hour. Add the brown sugar and tapioca. Simmer, stirring a couple of times, for another 15 minutes. Let cool in the pot. Remove the cinnamon sticks. Serve immediately or refrigerate. Serve with a dollop of crème fraîche. *Tip:* You can add some orange or apple juice to the soup before serving, which will thin out the consistency. *Yield: 12 servings.*

Crème fraîche:
2 cups heavy cream
2 tablespoons buttermilk

Thoroughly mix the cream and buttermilk. Cover tightly with plastic wrap and let stand at room temperature until thickened, about 24 – 30 hours. *Tip:* Will keep up to 2 weeks refrigerated in a jar with a tight-fitting lid. *Yield: 2 cups.*

Oyster-Artichoke Soup

"A recipe from Nottoway's chef Johnny 'Jambalaya' Percle."
— Cindy Hidalgo

1 cup butter
½ cup chopped onion
½ cup chopped celery
2 cups chicken stock
1 cup quartered artichoke hearts
4 cups fresh oysters, chopped
4 cups heavy cream
2 cups half-and-half
Chopped green onion

In a large saucepan, melt the butter. Add the onion and celery and simmer for 5 minutes. Add the chicken stock and cook on low heat for 15 minutes. Add the artichokes and oysters and simmer for 10 minutes more. Add the cream and half-and-half. Heat thoroughly for 15 minutes on low heat. Serve garnished with some chopped green onion.
Yield: 12 servings.

Nottoway Plantation

Cindy Hidalgo
PO Box 160
White Castle, Louisiana 70788
Tel: (504) 545-2730
Fax: (504) 545-8632
$$$$

ABOUT THE B&B

Located half an hour from Baton Rouge and an hour-and-a-half from New Orleans, Nottoway is the largest surviving antebellum mansion in the South. Once the home of wealthy sugar planter John Randolph, Nottoway is a gem of Italianate and Greek Revival style — boasting 53,000 square feet — that has withstood the test of time. The intricate lacy plaster friezework, hand-painted Dresden porcelain doorknobs, hand-carved marble mantles, and 65-foot Grand Ballroom are all intact. Guests stay in the mansion itself, in the boy's wing, or in the overseer's cottage. B&B guests receive a complimentary tour of the mansion, a wake-up call of hot coffee, sweet potato-cinnamon muffins, and orange juice, and a full plantation breakfast in the Breakfast Room. A restaurant on the grounds features Cajun and Creole cuisine, presided over by Chef Johnny "Jambalaya" Percle whose cooking embodies the "good, straightforward, unpretentious cuisine" that he considers the soul of Louisiana food.

SEASON

all year

ACCOMMODATIONS

13 rooms (including three suites) with private baths

The Albert Stevens Inn & Cat's Garden

Diane and Curt Diviney-Rangen
127 Myrtle Avenue
Cape May, New Jersey 08204
Tel: (609) 884-4717
Fax: (609) 884-8320
E-mail: CRangen@
Beachcomber.com
www.capemaycats.com
$$$

ABOUT THE B&B

Built in 1898 by Dr. Albert G. Stevens, this Victorian Queen Anne classic features a unique floating staircase suspended from the third-floor turret. After enjoying a three-course Norwegian-style breakfast, you can wander off to the nearby shopping mall, swimming beaches, the lighthouse, bird observatory, and shops. Or, you may want to unwind in the Cat's Garden. Established in 1992 as a safe haven for the wild or forgotten cats that wander the shore, the garden is landscaped with hundreds of plants and herbs and a little pond, and enjoyed by cats and humans alike. Innkeepers Diane and Curt invite you to join them in rediscovering the soothing sights and sounds of the shore. Here, you'll find two hard-working individuals who escaped the corporate world for a life now dedicated to balancing man with nature.

SEASON

February to December

ACCOMMODATIONS

nine rooms (including two suites)
with private baths

Pumpkin Soup

"On cool mornings, this sweet harvest soup is a great start with a slice of pumpkin bread topped with cream cheese."
— Diane Diviney-Rangen

1 small onion, chopped
¼ cup butter
4 cups fresh pumpkin, cooked and mashed
4 cups chicken broth
1 cup brown sugar
⅔ cup half-and-half
¼ teaspoon paprika
Pinch of grated nutmeg
Vanilla yogurt
Croutons

Pumpkin bread (see recipe on page 107) topped with cream cheese

Cook the onion in butter for 3 minutes until softened but not brown. Add the pumpkin, broth, and brown sugar. Bring to a boil, then simmer for 25 minutes. In a blender or food processor, purée the mixture. Clean the pan, pour in the purée, and stir in the half-and-half — adding a little of the half-and-half at a time so as not to thin the soup too much. While warming the mixture, stir in the paprika. To serve, top each bowl with the nutmeg and a swirl of vanilla yogurt. Add 2 or 3 croutons for a little crunch! *Yield: 6 – 8 servings.*

Root Veggie Soup

1 large potato, peeled and cut into bite-sized chunks
1 large sweet potato, peeled and cut into bite-sized chunks
2 parsnips, peeled and cut into bite-sized chunks
2 carrots, peeled and cut into bite-sized chunks
1 rutabaga, peeled and cut into bite-sized chunks
1 large onion, cut into bite-sized chunks
4 cloves garlic, chopped
½ red bell pepper, sliced
1 tomato, sliced
Chopped parsley or cilantro (also known as coriander) to taste
2 tablespoons chicken stock granules

Place the potatoes, parsnips, carrots, rutabaga, onion, garlic, red pepper, tomato, parsley, and chicken stock granules in a large pot and add water to cover. Simmer for 1 hour. Serve immediately. *Tip:* May be thickened with 1 slice wheat bread, cubed. *Yield: 8 servings.*

Volden Farm
Bed and Breakfast

JoAnne and Jim Wold
RR #2, Box 50
Luverne, North Dakota 58056
Tel: (701) 769-2275
$$ – $$$

ABOUT THE B&B

After living all over the world, JoAnne and Jim Wold settled "where we belong — on the wide open prairie of North Dakota." Here, they opened Volden Farm, a B&B with an old-world atmosphere, thanks to the Russian and Norwegian decor and collectibles, which reflect the hosts' heritage and interests. Part of the home was built in 1926, comprising the parlor, music room, library, and two guest bedrooms. A new addition was built in 1978 to include a fireplace and dining area overlooking miles of tranquil prairie land. Bedrooms are filled with family heirloom quilts and one-of-a-kind antiques. Also available is a separate small house called the Law Office — with a bath, limited kitchen facilities, and fabulous view — where Jim used to have his office. The Scandinavian breakfast takes advantage of fresh ingredients from the farm and garden. After breakfast, guests can wander through 300 acres of fields, woods, hills, coulees, and virgin prairie. JoAnne and Jim take pleasure in reading, gardening, singing, and raising animals.

SEASON

all year

ACCOMMODATIONS

two rooms with shared bath
in main house;
two rooms with shared bath
in private cottage

The Signal House

Betsy and Vic Billingsley
234 North Front Street
Ripley, Ohio 45167
Tel/Fax: (937) 392-1640
$$

ABOUT THE B&B

Located just one hour east of Cincinnati, this stately and historic 1830s home on the Ohio River offers spectacular sunsets from three relaxing porches and elegant twin parlors, with river views from every room. Two Civil War officers lived in this house and legend has it that it was also part of the Underground Railroad. Steeped in a rich past, the village of Ripley includes 55 acres that are recorded in the National Register of Historic Places. Visit antique and specialty shops, restaurants, three museums (themed on the early pioneers and the Underground Railroad), covered bridges, and lots of friendly people. The beautiful Ohio River offers boating, fishing, and water and jet skiing, with pick-up service from local marinas provided by The Signal House. Your hosts Betsy and Vic enjoy their B&B guests, family, grandchildren, river sports, and life in general! Vic is a letter carrier for the US Postal Service and Betsy is a former dental assistant and business telephone trainer. A full homemade breakfast is served at guests' preferred time.

SEASON

all year

ACCOMMODATIONS

two rooms with shared bath

Scalloped Pineapple

"I serve this dish with ham and eggs and also as a side dish for a pork or roast beef dinner." — Betsy Billingsley

½ cup margarine
20-ounce can crushed pineapple
¾ cup sugar
1 tablespoon all-purpose flour
2 eggs, lightly beaten
5 slices bread, diced

Ham and eggs, or pork or roast beef dinner

Preheat the oven to 350°F. In a skillet, brown the margarine. Remove from the heat and cool. In a medium bowl, add the pineapple, sugar, and flour. Add the pineapple mixture to the margarine in the skillet. Stir in the eggs and mix. Place ½ the bread in the bottom of a 9" square pan. Cover with the pineapple mixture and top with the remaining bread. Bake for 35 minutes. *Tip:* Recipe can be doubled and baked in a 13 x 9" pan. *Yield: 4 – 6 servings.*

Shrimp Gazpacho

"Looks great in stemmed glasses!" — Pat O'Brien

1 quart clam-flavored tomato cocktail
½ cup peeled and chopped cucumber
⅓ cup thinly sliced green onion
1 teaspoon dried dill weed
¼ pound small shrimp, cooked
2 tablespoons olive oil
2 tablespoons red wine vinegar
1 tablespoon sugar
1 clove garlic, minced
3 ounces cream cheese, cut in ¼ – ½" cubes
1 medium avocado, peeled, pitted, and diced
2 – 3 dashes hot pepper sauce (such as Tabasco)
Sour cream
Minced fresh cilantro (also known as coriander)

In a deep bowl, combine the clam cocktail, cucumber, green onions, dill, shrimp, oil and vinegar, sugar, garlic, cream cheese, and avocado. Stir until well blended. Season with the hot pepper sauce. Cover and chill (up to 2 days). If storing longer than 6 – 8 hours, add the shrimp and cream cheese just before serving. Ladle into bowls and garnish with the sour cream and minced cilantro. *Yield: 4 – 5 servings.*

Blue Spruce Inn

Pat and Tom O'Brien
2815 Main Street
Soquel, California 95073
Tel: (800) 559-1137 or (408) 464-1137
Fax: (408) 475-0608
E-mail: pobrien@BlueSpruce.com
$$ – $$$$

ABOUT THE B&B

The Blue Spruce Inn welcomes you with the distinct Pacific breeze that freshens the Central Coast hillsides golden with poppies, tempers the heat of the summer sun, and warms the sands during afternoon strolls on winter beaches. The inn is four miles south of Santa Cruz and one mile from Capitola Beach at the northern curve of Monterey Bay. Gracious personal service is the hallmark of this 1875 B&B inn, where beds are graced with Amish quilts and walls hung with original local art that blends the flavor of yesteryear with the luxury of today. There are quiet gardens in which to enjoy the sunshine of Soquel Village, delightful antique shops at the corner of the street, and, a little farther, wineries, gift shops, and regional art displays. Bountiful breakfasts feature fresh fruit, homemade breads, and exceptional entrées. At the end of the day, the hot tub offers welcome respite and, when guests return to their rooms, pillows are fluffed and a special treat awaits.

SEASON

all year

ACCOMMODATIONS

five rooms with private baths

New Berne House Inn

Marcia Drum and Howard Bronson
709 Broad Street
New Bern, North Carolina 28560
Tel: (800) 842-7688 or (919) 636-2250
$$

ABOUT THE B&B

New Berne House Inn is centrally located in the Colonial town of New Bern and within comfortable walking distance of numerous historic sights, highlighted by Tryon Palace and its formal gardens, only one block away. Quaint shops, fine restaurants, and historic buildings are all in the neighborhood. New Berne House's seven guest rooms feature queen- and king-size beds, antiques and collectibles, private baths, and telephones and clock radios, along with other amenities to pamper guests. A full breakfast is served in the dining room from 8:00 to 9:00 am, but coffee is available as early as 6:30 am. Throughout the day, guests are invited to join the innkeepers in the library or parlor for light refreshments, television, and good conversation. Two weekends each month are reserved for a "juicy" who-done-it mystery package, which blends in nicely with the inn's two haunted rooms (where "odd occurrences" have been reported over the years!).

SEASON

all year

ACCOMMODATIONS

seven rooms with private baths

Spiced Bacon

1 cup brown sugar
1 teaspoon ground cinnamon
3 tablespoons water
1 pound bacon, cut into strips

Preheat the oven to 350°F. Mix the brown sugar, cinnamon, and water into a thick syrup. Half cook the bacon in a skillet until it is reduced in size but still not crisp. Remove and drain on a paper towel. Arrange the bacon in a single layer in an ovenproof dish. Brush with the cinnamon mixture. Put in the oven and cook to the desired crispness. Drain on a pastry rack set in a baking sheet. Serve immediately. *Yield: 4 – 6 servings.*

Strawberry Breakfast Soup

2 cups sliced strawberries, plus extra for garnish
1 cup orange juice
8 ounces plain yogurt
1 tablespoon sugar
½ teaspoon vanilla
¾ cup champagne or dry white wine or white grape juice
½ cup sour cream
Mint sprigs

Blend the 2 cups strawberries, orange juice, yogurt, sugar, and vanilla until smooth. Chill. Just before serving, stir in the champagne. Pour into soup bowls and garnish with a dollop of sour cream, sliced strawberries, and a mint sprig. *Yield: 8 (½ cup) servings.*

Greenwoods Gate Bed & Breakfast Inn

George Schumaker
PO Box 491
105 Greenwoods Road East
Norfolk, Connecticut 06058
Tel: (860) 542-5439
$$$$

ABOUT THE B&B

*C*alled *"a Connecticut jewel"* by Country Inns Bed & Breakfast *magazine, Greenwoods Gate combines a touch of romance with a sense of the past. This Federal-era inn offers four distinctive and elegant suites to choose from, with niceties such as fresh-cut flowers, fluffy robes, and crisp-ironed linens. A generous gourmet breakfast is served in the formal dining room, after which guests can linger in the center hall library or the grand parlor, with its antiques, Oriental rugs, and original Federal fireplace. Greenwoods Gate is conveniently located in the picture-perfect village of Norfolk, one half mile east of the Village Green. Innkeeper George Schumaker, a veteran of the hospitality business, organizes a B&B internship program three times per year for people considering owning and operating an inn.*

SEASON

all year

ACCOMMODATIONS

four suites with private baths

"An Elegant Victorian Mansion" Bed & Breakfast Inn

Lily and Doug Vieyra
1406 "C" Street
Eureka, California 95501
Tel: (707) 444-3144
Fax: (707) 442-5594
www.bnbcity.com/inns/20016
$$$ – $$$$

ABOUT THE B&B

Featured in many newspapers and magazines — not to mention on television and radio — this restored national historic landmark offers prestigious and luxurious accommodations. Spirited and eclectic innkeepers provide lavish hospitality in the splendor of a meticulously restored 1888 Victorian masterpiece, complete with original family antique furnishings. The inviting guest rooms offer both graceful refinement and modern-day comfort, individually decorated with Victorian elegance. Guests enjoy gourmet breakfasts and a heavenly night's sleep on top-quality mattresses, as well as secured parking and laundry service. Located in a quiet, historic residential neighborhood overlooking the city and Humboldt Bay, the non-smoking inn is near carriage rides, bay cruises, restaurants, and the theater, and is just minutes from giant redwood parks, coastal beaches, ocean charters, and horseback riding.

SEASON

all year

ACCOMMODATIONS

two rooms (including one suite)
with private baths;
two rooms with shared bath

Stuffed Mushrooms

"These tasty morsels can be prepared in advance, refrigerated for a few hours, and baked just before serving." — Lily Vieyra

24 large mushrooms (1½ to 2" in diameter), washed and dried
3 – 4 green onions (white and green part), chopped
2 sprigs parsley, chopped
4 – 6 tablespoons butter
4 – 6 tablespoons sherry (or to taste)
3 ounces cream cheese, at room temperature

Remove the mushroom stems and chop them. Sauté the chopped stems with the onions and parsley in ½ of the butter until lightly browned. Add 3 tablespoons or so of sherry. Continue cooking until most of the liquid has evaporated. Remove from the heat and add to the cream cheese. Mix well, then set aside. Lightly sauté the mushroom caps with the remaining butter, then add about 2 tablespoons of the sherry. Do not overcook. Remove the mushrooms from the pan. When they are cool enough to handle, fill the caps with a generous amount of the cream cheese filling and place in a lightly greased baking dish. When ready to serve, heat the mushroom caps in a 325°F oven 10 – 15 minutes. Serve hot with a glass of your favorite white wine. ***Yield: 6 servings.***

Vivian's Baked Pear Brie

(*Recipe from* Secrets from the Pantry Kitchen of Gull Cottage.)

2½ pounds Brie
1 cup sliced almonds, toasted
12 ounces pear preserves
Grated nutmeg

English water wafers or sliced French bread

Preheat the oven to 350°F. Cut off the white crust on top of the Brie. Spread the pear preserves on the Brie. Bake for 15 minutes. Sprinkle the toasted almonds on top and serve warm with English water wafers or sliced French bread. *Variations:* Instead of the pear preserves, use sliced apples, brown sugar and walnuts, or other types of fruit preserves. *Yield: 20 – 25 servings.*

Barry's
Gull Cottage

Barry's Gull Cottage Bed and Breakfast

Vivian and Bob Barry
116 Chesapeake Street
Dewey Beach, Delaware 19971
Tel/Fax: (302) 227-7000
$$$ – $$$$

ABOUT THE B&B

Named *"one of the best places to stay at the beach"* by The Washingtonian Magazine, *Gull Cottage is a contemporary Nantucket-style beach house nestled in a pine and cherry grove, one-and-a-half blocks from the ocean and across the street from Lake Comegys. The warm and cozy decor includes antiques, white wicker furniture, quilts, stained glass, skylights, and ceiling fans. A full country gourmet breakfast is served on the screened porch, followed by afternoon tea and evening cake and coffee. The area offers many things to do: early morning walks along the dunes, windsurfing, water-skiing, fishing, and factory outlet shopping, to name a few. Nearby dining ranges from French cuisine to fresh seafood, and, to end the evening, you can relax by candlelight in the cottage's hot tub. Innkeepers Vivian and Bob Barry are retired Central Intelligence Agency officers who enjoy cooking for and pampering their guests.*

SEASON

May to October

ACCOMMODATIONS

three rooms with private baths; two rooms with half baths

Muffins

Apple-Cheddar Muffins

"Apple muffins without cheese are like a kiss without a squeeze. Naturally, we use Vermont cheddar in these." — Christopher Sellers

¼ cup margarine
¾ cup sugar
½ teaspoon vanilla
1 egg, lightly beaten
1½ cups all-purpose flour
1 teaspoon baking powder
½ teaspoon baking soda
½ teaspoon ground cinnamon
¼ teaspoon salt
¼ teaspoon grated nutmeg
1½ cups peeled chopped apple
1 cup grated Vermont cheddar cheese
1 tablespoon half-and-half

Preheat the oven to 350°F. Cream the margarine and sugar. Add the vanilla and beaten egg. In a separate bowl, stir together the flour, baking powder, baking soda, cinnamon, salt, and nutmeg and add to the margarine mixture, stirring just to moisten. Add the apples, cheese, and half-and-half, stirring gently. Pour the batter into 12 lightly greased muffins cups. Bake 20 – 25 minutes or until a toothpick inserted in the center comes out clean. *Yield: 12 muffins.*

Grünberg Haus Bed & Breakfast
Waterbury, Vermont

Grünberg Haus Bed and Breakfast

Christopher Sellers and
Mark Frohman
RR #2, Box 1595RD,
Route 100 South
Waterbury, Vermont 05676-9621
Tel: (800) 800-7760 or (802) 244-7726
Fax: (802) 244-1283
E-mail: grunhaus@aol.com
$$ – $$$$

ABOUT THE B&B

This picture-postcard Austrian-style B&B is tucked away on a secluded hillside in the Green Mountains, perfectly situated for visits to Stowe, Montpelier, Waterbury, and Burlington. Individually decorated guest rooms open onto the carved wood balcony, which offers wonderful views. Help Mark feed the chickens, then enjoy a full breakfast — with selections such as maple-poached pears, apple and cheddar muffins, and ricotta-stuffed French toast — while Chris plays the grand piano. The giant stone fireplace and wood stove in the BYOB pub are favorite gathering places. Nearby activities include spectacular autumn leaf-picking, world-class downhill skiing, golf, boating, bicycling, gliding, canoeing, antique hunting, outlet shopping, and touring Ben & Jerry's ice cream factory. And you can enjoy the B&B's own Jacuzzi, sauna, tennis courts, and cross-country and hiking trails.

SEASON

all year

ACCOMMODATIONS

seven rooms (including one suite)
with private baths;
five rooms with shared baths;
two cabins with private baths

Bishopsgate Inn

Colin, Jane, Colin, Jr.,
and Lisa Kagel
7 Norwich Road
East Haddam, Connecticut 06423
Tel: (860) 873-1677
Fax: (860) 873-3898
$$$ – $$$$

ABOUT THE B&B

Built in 1818 by Horace Heyden, a merchant and shipbuilder, this Colonial home welcomes guests seeking gracious hospitality and well-appointed accommodation in a secluded setting. The inn offers six guest rooms, including four with open fireplaces and a suite with a sauna. Tastefully furnished, each floor of the inn has its own sitting area for conversation, reading, and other restful pursuits. Known for its excellent kitchen, Bishopsgate offers ample breakfasts and, if desired, specially arranged candlelight dinners. The Kagels maintain an up-to-date library of local offerings and can help you plan your visit to the area: everything from the Goodspeed Opera House's renowned musical productions, the Historical Society Museum, Gillette Castle and Devil's Hopyard state parks, and cruises and canoe trips on the Connecticut River. Historic Essex, with its beautiful harbor, wonderful old houses, and intriguing shops, is just a few minutes' drive away.

SEASON

all year

ACCOMMODATIONS

six rooms (including one suite)
with private baths

Applesauce Muffins

"If you're daring, try using 1 tablespoon fresh, finely grated gingerroot for these muffins instead of 1 teaspoon powdered ginger. It's delicious!" — The Kagel Family

2 cups all-purpose flour
⅓ cup brown sugar
1 teaspoon ground ginger
1 teaspoon baking soda
¼ teaspoon salt
1 teaspoon ground cinnamon
1 cup applesauce
½ cup vegetable oil
1 egg
½ cup molasses

Topping:
2 tablespoons brown sugar
2 tablespoons all-purpose flour
½ teaspoon ground cinnamon
1 tablespoon unsalted chopped walnuts
1 tablespoon margarine

Preheat the oven to 400°F. Line a 12-cup muffin pan with paper baking cups. In a bowl, combine the flour, sugar, ginger, baking soda, salt, and cinnamon. In another bowl, combine the applesauce, vegetable oil, egg, and molasses and blend thoroughly.

(continued on next page)

Add the dry ingredients to the applesauce mixture and stir only until moistened. Spoon the batter evenly into the muffin cups. To make the topping, combine the sugar, flour, cinnamon, walnuts, and margarine until they are thoroughly mixed, then sprinkle over the batter in the cups. Bake 20 – 21 minutes or until a toothpick inserted in the center comes out clean. Let the muffins cool in the pan for 5 minutes, then remove and serve. *Yield: 12 muffins.*

Middle Plantation Inn

Shirley and Dwight Mullican
9549 Liberty Road
Frederick, Maryland 21701-3246
Tel: (301) 898-7128
E-mail: BandB@MPInn.com
www.MPInn.com
$$$

ABOUT THE B&B

This charming stone and log home, nestled on 26 acres, offers guests a peaceful setting, which includes Addison's Run (a nearby brook) and a 10-acre woods. You'll wake each morning to the sound of birds (and an occasional rooster) and see nature in all its glory. Your hosts take great pleasure in sharing their antique furnishings. Each guest room offers a delightful 19th-century ambiance combined with the modern conveniences of private bath, air conditioning, and TV. A massive stone fireplace, stained glass windows, and skylights highlight the public Keeping Room (a Colonial term for gathering place). A breakfast of seasonal fruit, fresh baked bread, cheese, and cereal are served each morning. Visit 33 historic blocks of downtown Frederick, with its mix of specialty and antique shops, dining establishments, museum, and art galleries. Nearby is New Market — antique capitol of Maryland. The inn is located near Baltimore (Maryland), the Antietam Battlefield in Sharpesburg (Maryland), Washington (DC), Gettysburg (Pennsylvania), and Harpers Ferry (West Virginia).

SEASON

all year

ACCOMMODATIONS

four rooms with private baths

Bacon-Cheddar Muffins

Cornmeal
1¾ cups all-purpose flour
½ cup grated sharp cheddar cheese
¼ cup sugar
2 teaspoons baking powder
¼ teaspoon salt
¼ teaspoon ground red pepper (cayenne)
1 egg, lightly beaten
¾ cup milk
⅓ cup vegetable oil
6 strips bacon, crisply cooked, drained, and crumbled

Preheat the oven to 400°F. Grease 8 muffin cups and the top of the pan. Sprinkle lightly with the cornmeal. In a bowl, stir together the flour, cheese, sugar, baking powder, salt, and pepper. Make a well in the center. In a small bowl, combine the egg, milk, and oil. Add the egg mixture all at once to the flour mixture, stirring just until moistened (the batter should be lumpy). Fold in the crumbled bacon. Fill the prepared muffin cups even with the top. Bake 20 – 25 minutes or until golden and a toothpick inserted in the center comes out clean. Remove the muffins from the pan and serve warm. *Tip:* Put a few tablespoons of water in any unused muffin cups to protect the pan and keep the rest of the muffins moist. *Yield: 8 muffins.*

Banana Crumb Muffins

¾ cup sugar
1 egg, lightly beaten
3 large bananas, mashed
⅓ cup butter or margarine, melted
1½ cups all-purpose flour
1 teaspoon baking soda
1 teaspoon baking powder
½ teaspoon salt

Crumb topping:
¼ cup all-purpose flour
¼ cup brown sugar
¼ cup large-flake rolled oats
2 tablespoons butter or vegetable shortening

Preheat the oven to 375°F. Add the sugar and egg to the bananas, and mix. Add the melted butter and mix. Add the flour, baking soda, baking powder, and salt and stir until moistened. Fill 12 greased muffin cups ⅓ full. To make the crumb topping, blend the flour, brown sugar, oats, and butter with a fork until moist crumbs form. Top the muffins with the crumbs. Bake for 20 minutes or until slightly brown on top and a toothpick inserted in the center comes out clean. *Tips:* These muffins are just as good without the crumbs. They also freeze very well — just pop them in your microwave oven for 1 minute to reheat. **Yield: 12 regular muffins or 36 mini muffins.**

The Hen-Apple Bed and Breakfast

Flo and Harold Eckert
409 South Lingle Avenue
Palmyra, Pennsylvania 17078
Tel: (717) 838-8282
$$

ABOUT THE B&B

Built around 1825, the Hen-Apple is an intimate and fully restored bed and breakfast filled to the brim with everything country and old-fashioned. It offers a relaxed atmosphere with six air conditioned guest rooms (each with private bath), a porch filled with rockers, a screened porch for warm weather dining, a herb garden, lots of flowers, and a shady retreat in the orchard. The Hen-Apple's well-rounded breakfasts are something to remember — especially the cinnamon French toast. Tea is served in the afternoon. Just two miles from Hershey, Pennsylvania, Palmyra is an antique lover's dream. In addition, wineries, shopping outlets, Hershey attractions, the riverboat, and horse racing are nearby. Your hosts, Flo and Harold Eckert, love going to flea markets and auctions, and enjoy reading, gardening, and music. Flo is also a Christmas enthusiast so, come the merry season, the B&B sports a tree in just about every room and an impressive Santa collection.

SEASON

all year

ACCOMMODATIONS

six rooms with private baths

Glynn House Victorian Inn

Betsy and Karol Paterman
43 Highland Street, PO Box 719
Ashland, New Hampshire 03217
Tel: (800) 637-9599 or (603) 968-3775
E-mail: glynnhse@lr.net
www.nettx.com/glynnhouse.html
$$ – $$$

ABOUT THE B&B

*C*ome enjoy the gracious elegance of this beautifully restored 1890 Queen Anne home — from the cupola of the inn's tower and gingerbread wraparound veranda to the carved oak foyer and pocket doors. Each of the beautifully appointed bedrooms has its own distinctive mood, distinguished by unique interior design, period furniture, the fragrance of fresh flowers, and soft, fluffy robes. A memorable full breakfast is served in the dining room, consisting perhaps of eggs Benedict or eggs Neptune, Belgian waffles, thick French toast, ambrosia, juice, and the specialty of the house — strudel. After breakfast, take a walk or boat ride around famous Squam Lake (where the movie On Golden Pond was filmed) just a few minutes away, and enjoy all that the Lakes Region and White Mountains have to offer. Allow Betsy and Karol to provide hospitality with a warm smile and make you feel as though you're part of their family.

SEASON

all year

ACCOMMODATIONS

eight rooms with private baths

Banana-White Chocolate Muffins

1 egg
¼ cup vegetable oil
4 bananas, puréed
½ cup milk
2 cups all-purpose flour
¼ cup sugar
2 tablespoons baking powder
⅓ cup grated white chocolate
⅓ cup ground pecans

Preheat the oven to 400°F. In a bowl, blend the egg, oil, banana, and milk. In a separate bowl, mix together the flour, sugar, baking powder, white chocolate, and pecans. Make a well in the center of the dry ingredients, and pour in the egg mixture. Stir until moistened (do not overmix). Fill 16 greased muffin cups ¾ full. Bake 15 – 20 minutes or until tops are golden brown and a toothpick inserted in the center comes out clean.
Tip: Put a few tablespoons of water in any unused muffin cups to protect the pan and keep the rest of the muffins moist. *Yield: 16 muffins.*

Best Ever Chocolate Chip-Banana Muffins

3 large ripe bananas
¾ cup sugar
1 egg, lightly beaten
⅓ cup butter, melted
1½ cups all-purpose flour
1 teaspoon baking soda
1 teaspoon baking powder
½ teaspoon salt
6 ounces chocolate chips

Preheat the oven to 375°F. Mash the bananas, and add the sugar and egg. Add the melted butter, then add the flour, baking soda, baking powder, and salt. Stir in the chocolate chips. Pour the batter into a greased 12-cup muffin pan and bake for 20 minutes or until a toothpick inserted in the center comes out clean. *Yield: 12 muffins.*

The Signal House

Betsy and Vic Billingsley
234 North Front Street
Ripley, Ohio 45167
Tel/Fax: (937) 392-1640
$$

ABOUT THE B&B

Located just one hour east of Cincinnati, this stately and historic 1830s home on the Ohio River offers spectacular sunsets from three relaxing porches and elegant twin parlors, with river views from every room. Two Civil War officers lived in this house and legend has it that it was also part of the Underground Railroad. Steeped in a rich past, the village of Ripley includes 55 acres that are recorded in the National Register of Historic Places. Visit antique and specialty shops, restaurants, three museums (themed on the early pioneers and the Underground Railroad), covered bridges, and lots of friendly people. The beautiful Ohio River offers boating, fishing, and water and jet skiing, with pick-up service from local marinas provided by The Signal House. Your hosts Betsy and Vic enjoy their B&B guests, family, grandchildren, river sports, and life in general! Vic is a letter carrier for the US Postal Service and Betsy is a former dental assistant and business telephone trainer. A full homemade breakfast is served at guests' preferred time.

SEASON

all year

ACCOMMODATIONS

two rooms with shared bath

The Summer House

Marjorie and Kevin Huelsman
158 Main Street
Sandwich, Massachusetts 02563
Tel: (800) 241-3609 or (508) 888-4991
E-mail: sumhouse@capecod.net
$$ – $$$

ABOUT THE B&B

The Summer House is an elegant circa 1835 Greek Revival twice featured in Country Living magazine. It was owned by Hiram Dillaway, a prominent mold-maker and colorist at the Boston & Sandwich Glass Factory. Large, sunny bedchambers feature antiques, hand-stitched quilts, and working fireplaces. Stroll to dining, shops, museums, galleries, a pond and gristmill, and a boardwalk to the beach. Bountiful breakfasts change daily and include freshly ground coffee, tea, fruit juice, and fresh fruit served in stemware. Entrées of frittata, stuffed French toast, quiche, or omelets are accompanied by scones, puff pastry, muffins, or fruit cobblers. Dishes are enhanced with vegetables, berries, and herbs from the inn's garden. English-style afternoon tea is served at an umbrella table in the garden. Boston, Newport, Providence, Martha's Vineyard, and Nantucket make pleasant day trips.

SEASON

all year

ACCOMMODATIONS

five rooms with private baths

Carrot-Zucchini Muffins

1¾ cups all-purpose flour
2½ teaspoons baking powder
¾ teaspoon salt
3 tablespoons sugar
½ teaspoon ground cinnamon
1 cup coarsely grated carrot
1 cup coarsely grated zucchini
2 eggs
¼ cup canola oil
¼ cup orange juice
Sprinkle of ground cinnamon
Sprinkle of sugar

Preheat the oven to 400°F. In a large bowl, combine the flour, baking powder, salt, sugar, cinnamon, carrot, and zucchini. In a small bowl, combine the eggs, oil, and juice. Make a well in the center of the dry ingredients, pour in the liquid mixture, and combine until the dry ingredients are just moistened (don't overmix). Spoon into a 12-cup nonstick muffin pan and sprinkle the tops with a mixture of cinnamon and sugar. Bake 15 – 18 minutes or until the tops spring back when gently touched and a toothpick inserted in the center comes out clean. *Yield: 12 muffins.*

Chocolate Cheesecake Muffins

3 ounces cream cheese
2 tablespoons and ½ cup granulated sugar
1 cup all-purpose flour
3 tablespoons unsweetened cocoa powder
2 teaspoons baking powder
½ teaspoon salt
1 egg, lightly beaten
¾ cup milk
⅓ cup vegetable oil
Confectioners' sugar

Preheat the oven to 375°F. In a small bowl, beat the cream cheese and 2 tablespoons of the granulated sugar until light and fluffy; set aside. In a large bowl, stir together the flour, remaining ½ cup granulated sugar, cocoa powder, baking powder, and salt. Make a well in the center of the dry ingredients. Combine the egg, milk, and oil. Add all at once to the dry ingredients, stirring just until moistened (the batter should be lumpy). Spoon about 2 tablespoons of the batter into each greased muffin cup. Drop 1 teaspoon of the cream cheese mixture on top and cover with more chocolate batter. Bake for 20 minutes or until the tops spring back when gently touched. Dust with the confectioners' sugar when cool. *Yield: 12 muffins.*

The Hen-Apple Bed and Breakfast

Flo and Harold Eckert
409 South Lingle Avenue
Palmyra, Pennsylvania 17078
Tel: (717) 838-8282
$$

ABOUT THE B&B

Built around 1825, the Hen-Apple is an intimate and fully restored bed and breakfast filled to the brim with everything country and old-fashioned. It offers a relaxed atmosphere with six air conditioned guest rooms (each with private bath), a porch filled with rockers, a screened porch for warm weather dining, a herb garden, lots of flowers, and a shady retreat in the orchard. The Hen-Apple's well-rounded breakfasts are something to remember — especially the cinnamon French toast. Tea is served in the afternoon. Just two miles from Hershey, Pennsylvania, Palmyra is an antique lover's dream. In addition, wineries, shopping outlets, Hershey attractions, the riverboat, and horse racing are nearby. Your hosts, Flo and Harold Eckert, love going to flea markets and auctions, and enjoy reading, gardening, and music. Flo is also a Christmas enthusiast so, come the merry season, the B&B sports a tree in just about every room and an impressive Santa collection.

SEASON

all year

ACCOMMODATIONS

six rooms with private baths

Victoria Place

Edee Seymour
3459 Lawai Loa Lane
Koloa, Kauai, Hawaii 96756
(Mailing address: PO Box 930,
Lawai, HI 96765-0930)
Tel: (808) 332-9300
Fax: (808) 332-9465
www.hshawaii.com/KVP/Victoria
$$ – $$$

ABOUT THE B&B

Perched high in the lush hills of southern Kauai, overlooking thick jungle, whispering cane fields, and the beckoning Pacific, Victoria Place offers a private oasis. Three bedrooms in one wing of this spacious, skylit home open directly through glass doors onto a pool surrounded by flowering walls of hibiscus, gardenia, ginger, and bougainvillea. By day, guests can relax by the poolside or explore the island. By evening, they may retreat to the "lanai" (a long, second-story deck) and watch plumeria, coconut, banana, and avocado trees become silhouettes under the stars. Enjoy waking up each morning to the aroma of Hawaiian coffee, hot homemade bread and muffins, plus an assortment of fresh fruit adorned with gardenias and hibiscus, served at poolside. Victoria Place is nestled on a quiet cul-de-sac, about two minutes from Highway 50, Kauai's main route, which links all major towns and attractions.

SEASON

all year

ACCOMMODATIONS

three rooms with private baths;
one studio apartment
with private bath

Coconut Muffins

"This recipe was sent to me by a physician and his wife from Michigan who have stayed at Victoria Place twice already."
— *Edee Seymour*

1 egg
1¾ cups all-purpose flour
½ cup sugar
3 teaspoons baking powder
1 cup shredded unsweetened coconut
1 cup milk
¼ cup vegetable oil

Preheat the oven to 400°F. Beat the egg until well mixed. Stir in the flour, sugar, baking powder, coconut, milk, and oil and place this mixture evenly into greased muffin cups. Bake for 20 minutes or until a toothpick inserted in the center comes out clean. ***Yield: 12 muffins.***

Cranberry-Almond Muffins

(*Recipe from* The Best of High Meadows — A Selected Recipe Collection.)

1½ cups all-purpose flour
½ cup sugar
1 teaspoon baking powder
¼ teaspoon baking soda
¼ teaspoon salt
2 eggs
¼ cup butter, melted
½ cup sour cream
½ teaspoon almond extract
¾ cup sliced almonds
½ cup whole cranberry sauce

Preheat the oven to 375°F. Mix the flour, sugar, baking powder, baking soda, and salt in a large bowl. Break the eggs into another bowl and whisk in the butter, sour cream, and almond extract. When blended, stir in ½ cup of the almonds. Pour the egg mixture over the dry ingredients and fold in until the dry ingredients are moistened. Spoon 2 tablespoons of this batter into each greased muffin cup and top with a tablespoon of cranberry sauce. Sprinkle the remaining almonds over the batter. Bake 30 – 35 minutes or until the tops spring back when gently touched. Cool 15 minutes before serving. *Tip:* Put a few tablespoons of water in any unused muffin cups to protect the pan and keep the rest of the muffins moist. *Yield: 10 muffins.*

High Meadows Inn

Peter Sushka and Mary Jae Abbitt
High Meadows Lane, Route 4, Box 6
Scottsville, Virginia 24590
Tel: (800) 232-1832 or (804) 286-2218
Fax: (804) 286-2124
E-mail: peterhmi@aol.com
www.highmeadows.com
$$ – $$$$

ABOUT THE B&B

As Virginia's only inn that is on the National Register of Historic Homes and has a Renaissance farm vineyard, High Meadows offers a rare opportunity to experience 170 years of architectural history and 10 years of new viticultural growth. High Meadows is a grand house, where guests are welcomed with champagne and stay in rooms furnished with period antiques and art, each with private bath. The innkeepers' many special touches and attention to detail make your visit one to be remembered. Enjoy the simplicity of nature on the 50 surrounding acres of gardens, footpaths, forests, and ponds. Owner/chef Peter Sushka ensures that dining at High Meadows is just as pleasurable as lodging there. Start with a breakfast of fresh orange juice, a variety of homemade breads, muffins, and scones, fresh fruit, gourmet egg dishes, and coffee or tea. End your day with a multi-course dinner, offering distinctive northern European and Mediterranean dishes.

SEASON

all year

ACCOMMODATIONS

14 rooms (including four suites)
with private baths

Holmberg House Bed & Breakfast

Jo Meacham and Michael Cobb
766 DeBarr
Norman, Oklahoma 73069
Tel: (405) 321-6221
$$

ABOUT THE B&B

Holmberg House was built in 1914 by Professor Fredrik Holmberg — the first dean of the University of Oklahoma's fine arts program and the state's first symphony conductor. Since 1993, Holmberg House B&B has been a home away from home for visiting professors, scholars, parents, and alumni. Located across the street from the university, right next door to Campus Corner, this comfortable craftsman-style house is decorated with period antique furnishings and memorabilia. Guest rooms are reminiscent of the good old days — including an antique iron bed and claw foot tubs — yet are equipped with the conveniences of today. In the morning, guests enjoy a gourmet breakfast in the dining room, then gather for conversation on the front porch or in the parlor. Come dinnertime, guests can choose from no less than 15 restaurants that are within walking distance of the B&B's front door. If you are celebrating a birthday, anniversary, or special occasion during your stay at Holmberg House, Jo and Michael will gladly assist you with the arrangements — whether you need tickets for an event or flowers from the local florist.

SEASON

all year

ACCOMMODATIONS

four rooms with private baths

French Breakfast Puffs

⅓ cup vegetable shortening, softened
½ cup sugar
1 egg
1½ cups all-purpose flour
1½ teaspoons baking powder
½ teaspoon salt
¼ teaspoon grated nutmeg
½ cup milk

Topping:
6 teaspoons butter, melted
½ cup sugar mixed with 1 teaspoon ground cinnamon

Preheat the oven to 350°F. Mix together the shortening, sugar, and egg. Sift together the flour, baking powder, salt, and nutmeg. Stir the dry ingredients, alternating with the milk, into the shortening mixture. Fill greased muffin cups ⅔ full. Bake 20 – 25 minutes or until golden brown and a toothpick inserted in the center comes out clean. When the muffins are ready, remove them from the pan and immediately dip the muffin tops first into the butter and then into the sugar mixture.
Yield: 12 muffins.

Gingerbread Muffins

(Recipe from Breakfast at Nine, Tea at Four: Favorite Recipes from Cape May's Mainstay Inn.)

2 cups all-purpose flour
1½ teaspoons baking powder
½ teaspoon baking soda
1½ teaspoons ground ginger
1 teaspoon ground cinnamon
½ teaspoon grated nutmeg
¼ teaspoon ground cloves
¼ teaspoon salt
1 egg, beaten
¾ cup milk
¼ cup molasses
¼ cup maple syrup
2 tablespoons sugar
½ cup chopped dates
4 tablespoons butter, melted

Preheat the oven to 350°F. Grease 12 muffin cups. In a large bowl, stir the flour, baking powder, baking soda, spices, and salt until thoroughly mixed. To the beaten egg, add the milk, molasses, maple syrup, sugar, dates, and melted butter, mixing well. Pour this over the flour mixture and stir just until the dry ingredients are well mixed in. Scoop the batter into the prepared muffin cups. Bake for 20 minutes or until a toothpick inserted in the center comes out clean. *Yield: 12 muffins.*

The Mainstay Inn

Sue and Tom Carroll
635 Columbia Avenue
Cape May, New Jersey 08204
Tel: (609) 884-8690
$$$ – $$$$

ABOUT THE B&B

According to the Washington Post, *"The jewel of them all has got to be the Mainstay."* Built by a pair of wealthy gamblers in 1872, this elegant and exclusive clubhouse is now among the premier B&B inns in the country. The Mainstay now comprises three historic buildings on one of the most beautiful streets of the historic Cape May district. Guests enjoy 16 antique-filled rooms and suites (some with fireplaces and whirlpool baths), three parlors, spacious gardens, and rocker-filled verandas. Breakfast and afternoon tea are served daily. Beautiful beaches, historic attractions, biking, birding, golf, and tennis are all available in Cape May, a National Historic Landmark community.

SEASON

all year

ACCOMMODATIONS

16 rooms (including seven suites) with private baths

La Corsette Maison Inn

Kay Owen
629 1st Avenue East
Newton, Iowa 50208
Tel: (515) 792-6833
$$ – $$$$

ABOUT THE B&B

To spend the night at the Maison Inn is to be the personal house guest of Kay Owen, and to enjoy charming French bedchambers, down-filled pillows, and beckoning hearths. Kay lives in this opulent, mission-style mansion built in 1909 by early Iowa state senator August Bergman. Here amid the charm of the original mission oak woodwork, art nouveau stained glass windows, brass light fixtures, and even some of the original furnishings, Kay operates the highly acclaimed La Corsette restaurant, considered a unique dining experience by gourmets nationwide. The Maison Inn is a delightful extension of that experience. Choose from seven distinctive accommodations (some with double whirlpools and fireplaces), including the penthouse, where you'll be nudged awake in the morning by a rainbow of sunlight coming through the mass of beveled glass windows. In the morning, be prepared for a delectable breakfast served in the gracious tradition of La Corsette.

SEASON

all year

ACCOMMODATIONS

seven rooms (including two suites)
with private baths

Hazelnut Muffins

¾ cup vegetable shortening
2¼ cups all-purpose flour
1 cup granulated sugar
1 teaspoon baking powder
1 teaspoon salt
¾ teaspoon baking soda
¾ teaspoon ground cinnamon
¾ cup brown sugar
¾ cup milk
¼ cup hazelnut liqueur
3 eggs
¾ cup chopped walnuts

Preheat the oven to 350°F. Stir the shortening just to soften. Sift in the flour, granulated sugar, baking powder, salt, baking soda, and cinnamon. Add the brown sugar, milk, and liqueur; mix well until all the flour is dampened. Beat vigorously for 2 minutes. Add the eggs; beat 2 minutes more. Add the walnuts. Bake in a paper-lined 12-cup muffin pan 30 – 35 minutes or until a toothpick inserted in the center comes out clean. *Yield: 12 muffins.*

Healthy Cornbread Muffins

"This corn recipe reflects the combined influence of the south, the gold miners, and the American Indians on our county."
— *Melisande Hubbs*

1 cup cornmeal
1 cup all-purpose flour
4 teaspoons baking powder
1 tablespoon sugar
½ teaspoon salt
1½ cups milk
4 tablespoons vegetable oil
3 egg whites

Preheat the oven to 375°F. Mix the cornmeal, flour, baking powder, sugar, and salt well. Add the milk and oil, mixing well. Beat the egg whites until they stand in soft peaks. Fold them into the batter. Spoon this into a greased 12-cup muffin pan and bake for 20 minutes or until a toothpick inserted in the center comes out clean. ***Yield: 12 muffins.***

The Heirloom

Melisande Hubbs and Patricia Cross
214 Shakeley Lane
Ione, California 95640
Tel: (209) 274-4468
$$ – $$$

ABOUT THE B&B

Down a country lane to an expansive English romantic garden is a touch of the old south. The Heirloom is a brick, two-story southern antebellum home, circa 1863, located in the heart of California gold country. It was built by Virginians who came to California during the Gold Rush to be merchants in Ione, the supply center of the mining camps of Amador County. Sweet magnolias, wisteria, hammocks, croquet, verandas, cozy fireplaces, and heirloom antiques (including a historic piano) await you, not to mention a royal breakfast and gracious hospitality. Near the inn are over 20 wineries, Gold Rush historical points, museums, and nature walks, and opportunities for gourmet dining, gold panning, gliding, and hiking.

SEASON

all year

ACCOMMODATIONS

four rooms with private baths;
two rooms with shared bath

Angel Arbor
Bed & Breakfast Inn

Marguerite and Dean Swanson
848 Heights Boulevard
Houston, Texas 77007
Tel: (713) 868-4654
Fax: (713) 861-3189
E-mail: b-bhontx@wt.net
www.angelarbor.com
$$ – $$$

ABOUT THE B&B

A *few minutes from downtown Houston, this elegant 1920s Georgian-style brick residence graces historic Heights Boulevard with its gazebo-dotted esplanade and walking trail. The first floor boasts an antique-filled parlor, a cozy reading room, a gracious formal dining room, and a sunroom for game playing or casual dining. A wicker-furnished solarium overlooks the backyard garden with its manicured lawn, angel statue, and vine-laden arbor with a tranquil sitting area. Upstairs, three spacious bedrooms, each with an angel-inspired name, feature queen beds and private baths, two with whirlpool tubs for two. A separate outside suite provides seclusion and has its own sitting room and deck. A full delicious breakfast is served daily. Former owners of Durham House B&B, Marguerite and Dean Swanson bring their many years of innkeeping experience to Angel Arbor. The B&B also hosts parties and small meetings, and Marguerite's renowned murder mystery dinner parties.*

SEASON

all year

ACCOMMODATIONS

four rooms (including one suite)
with private baths

Lemon-Zucchini Muffins

2 cups all-purpose flour
¾ cup sugar
1 tablespoon baking powder
½ teaspoon salt
Grated zest of 1 lemon
½ teaspoon grated nutmeg
½ cup chopped pecans or walnuts
2 eggs
½ cup milk
⅓ cup vegetable oil
1 teaspoon lemon extract
1½ cups grated zucchini

Preheat the oven to 400°F. In a large bowl, mix the flour, sugar, baking powder, salt, lemon zest, and nutmeg. Stir in the nuts. In a small bowl, lightly beat the eggs. Beat in the milk, oil, and lemon extract. Add to the flour mixture and stir in the grated zucchini just until blended. Fill a greased 12-cup muffin pan with the mixture. Bake for 20 minutes or until a toothpick inserted in the center comes out clean. *Yield: 12 muffins.*

Light and Easy Orange Muffins

"Easy, quick, and great served hot right out of the oven!"
— Jo Meacham

2 cups Bisquick baking mix
¾ cup and a sprinkle of sugar
2 eggs
1¼ cups fresh orange juice
Slivered almonds

Preheat the oven to 425°F. Blend the baking mix, ¾ cup of the sugar, eggs, and orange juice. Pour the batter into greased muffin cups and sprinkle with the almonds and sugar. Bake 20 – 25 minutes or until a toothpick inserted in the center comes out clean. ***Yield: 12 muffins.***

Holmberg House Bed & Breakfast

Jo Meacham and Michael Cobb
766 DeBarr
Norman, Oklahoma 73069
Tel: (405) 321-6221
$$

ABOUT THE B&B

Holmberg House was built in 1914 by Professor Fredrik Holmberg — the first dean of the University of Oklahoma's fine arts program and the state's first symphony conductor. Since 1993, Holmberg House B&B has been a home away from home for visiting professors, scholars, parents, and alumni. Located across the street from the university, right next door to Campus Corner, this comfortable craftsman-style house is decorated with period antique furnishings and memorabilia. Guest rooms are reminiscent of the good old days — including an antique iron bed and claw foot tubs — yet are equipped with the conveniences of today. In the morning, guests enjoy a gourmet breakfast in the dining room, then gather for conversation on the front porch or in the parlor. Come dinnertime, guests can choose from no less than 15 restaurants that are within walking distance of the B&B's front door. If you are celebrating a birthday, anniversary, or special occasion during your stay at Holmberg House, Jo and Michael will gladly assist you with the arrangements — whether you need tickets for an event or flowers from the local florist.

SEASON

all year

ACCOMMODATIONS

four rooms with private baths

The Woods Family
715 North Street East
Talladega, Alabama 35160-2527
Tel: (205) 362-0662
$$

ABOUT THE B&B

Built in 1847, this antebellum home is listed on the National Register of Historic Places. The house was commissioned by Andrew Bowie, the first mayor of Talladega. Enjoy browsing through the antique stores in the area, visiting the International Motorsports Hall of Fame, or exploring the lovely DeSoto Caverns. A public golf course and tennis courts and beautiful Cheaha Mountain State Park are nearby. The hearty breakfast your hosts serve features homemade biscuits, bran muffins, and southern grits. Traveling businesspeople and vacationers alike will enjoy this retreat into the quiet elegance of a bygone era.

SEASON

all year

ACCOMMODATIONS

one room with
his and her private bath;
two rooms with shared bath

Low-fat Bran Muffins

2 cups Nabisco brand 100% Bran cereal
1 cup All-Bran cereal
1 cup boiling water
¾ cup applesauce
1 cup honey
3 eggs
2½ cups all-purpose flour
2½ teaspoons baking soda
½ teaspoon salt
2 cups buttermilk
1 cup raisins
1½ cups chopped pecans or walnuts

Combine the 2 cereals. Pour the boiling water over the cereal and allow to cool. Preheat the oven to 400°F. Add the applesauce and honey to the bran mixture, stirring slightly. Add the eggs, 1 at a time, beating lightly after each addition. Combine the flour, baking soda, and salt in a separate bowl and add, alternating with the buttermilk, to the bran mixture (mix well but do not beat). Add the raisins and nuts, stirring only until well mixed. Fill lightly greased muffin cups ½ full and bake for 20 minutes or until a toothpick inserted in the center comes out clean. *Tip:* The batter will keep for up to 5 weeks in an airtight container in the refrigerator. Simply scoop out batter as needed (do not stir). *Yield: 36 muffins.*

Mexican Muffins

1 cup cornmeal
2 cups all-purpose flour
2 teaspoons sugar
1½ teaspoons baking powder
½ teaspoon baking soda
Dash of salt
½ cup grated cheddar cheese
½ cup taco sauce
½ cup sour cream
1 egg, lightly beaten
3 tablespoons corn oil
3 – 4-ounce can chopped green chilies, drained

Preheat the oven to 400°F. Grease or paper-line 9 muffin cups. In a large bowl, combine the cornmeal, flour, sugar, baking powder, baking soda, and salt; stir in the cheese. In another bowl, stir together the taco sauce, sour cream, egg, oil, and chilies to combine. Make a well in the center of the dry ingredients; add the liquid mixture and stir to combine. Spoon the batter into the prepared muffin cups and bake 15 – 20 minutes or until a toothpick inserted in the center comes out clean. Cool 5 minutes before removing them from the pan. *Tips:* Put a few tablespoons of water in any unused muffin cups to protect the pan and keep the rest of the muffins moist. These muffins freeze well. *Yield: 9 muffins.*

Blue Spruce Inn

Pat and Tom O'Brien
2815 Main Street
Soquel, California 95073
Tel: (800) 559-1137 or (408) 464-1137
Fax: (408) 475-0608
E-mail: pobrien@BlueSpruce.com
$$ – $$$$

ABOUT THE B&B

The Blue Spruce Inn welcomes you with the distinct Pacific breeze that freshens the Central Coast hillsides golden with poppies, tempers the heat of the summer sun, and warms the sands during afternoon strolls on winter beaches. The inn is four miles south of Santa Cruz and one mile from Capitola Beach at the northern curve of Monterey Bay. Gracious personal service is the hallmark of this 1875 B&B inn, where beds are graced with Amish quilts and walls hung with original local art that blends the flavor of yesteryear with the luxury of today. There are quiet gardens in which to enjoy the sunshine of Soquel Village, delightful antique shops at the corner of the street, and, a little farther, wineries, gift shops, and regional art displays. Bountiful breakfasts feature fresh fruit, homemade breads, and exceptional entrées. At the end of the day, the hot tub offers welcome respite and, when guests return to their rooms, pillows are fluffed and a special treat awaits.

SEASON

all year

ACCOMMODATIONS

five rooms with private baths

Victoria Place

Edee Seymour
3459 Lawai Loa Lane
Koloa, Kauai, Hawaii 96756
(Mailing address: PO Box 930,
Lawai, HI 96765-0930)
Tel: (808) 332-9300
Fax: (808) 332-9465
www.hshawaii.com/KVP/Victoria
$$ – $$$

ABOUT THE B&B

Perched high in the lush hills of southern Kauai, overlooking thick jungle, whispering cane fields, and the beckoning Pacific, Victoria Place offers a private oasis. Three bedrooms in one wing of this spacious, skylit home open directly through glass doors onto a pool surrounded by flowering walls of hibiscus, gardenia, ginger, and bougainvillea. By day, guests can relax by the poolside or explore the island. By evening, they may retreat to the "lanai" (a long, second-story deck) and watch plumeria, coconut, banana, and avocado trees become silhouettes under the stars. Enjoy waking up each morning to the aroma of Hawaiian coffee, hot homemade bread and muffins, plus an assortment of fresh fruit adorned with gardenias and hibiscus, served at poolside. Victoria Place is nestled on a quiet cul-de-sac, about two minutes from Highway 50, Kauai's main route, which links all major towns and attractions.

SEASON

all year

ACCOMMODATIONS

three rooms with private baths;
one studio apartment
with private bath

Mini Fruit Muffins

"While watching me bake one day, one of my guests jotted down this recipe for me to try. I'm glad she did because my guests simply love it." — Edee Seymour

3 eggs, lightly beaten
¼ cup brown sugar
¾ cup chopped walnuts
¾ cup white raisins
¾ cup shredded unsweetened coconut
¾ cup dried apricots

Preheat the oven to 325°F. Mix together the eggs, sugar, walnuts, raisins, coconut, and apricots and pour the batter evenly into foil or paper-lined mini muffin pans. Bake for approximately 30 minutes or until a toothpick inserted in the center comes out clean. *Tips:* Flour is not used in this recipe. As a result, if mini muffin pans are not used, the muffins may fall apart. Put a few tablespoons of water in any unused muffin cups to protect the pan and keep the rest of the muffins moist. ***Yield: 24 – 32 mini muffins.***

Mixed-Berry Muffins with Pecan-Streusel Topping

Streusel topping:
½ cup dark brown sugar, firmly packed
¼ cup all-purpose flour
1½ teaspoons grated lemon zest
¾ cup chopped pecans, toasted and cooled completely
2 tablespoons butter, melted and cooled to room temperature

Batter:
1¾ cups all-purpose flour
½ cup dark brown sugar, firmly packed
¼ cup granulated sugar
2 teaspoons baking powder
1½ teaspoons grated lemon zest
1 teaspoon ground cinnamon
¼ teaspoon salt
½ cup milk
½ cup butter, melted and cooled
2 eggs, lightly beaten
¾ cup frozen blueberries
¾ cup frozen raspberries

(continued on next page)

The Voss Inn

Frankee and Bruce Muller
319 South Willson
Bozeman, Montana 59715
Tel: (406) 587-0982
Fax: (406) 585-2964
www.wtp.net/go/vossinn
$$$

ABOUT THE B&B

Built in 1883 by a prominent journalist and mining engineer named Mat Alderson, The Voss Inn is an elegant brick Victorian with a spacious front porch overlooking an English cottage perennial garden. The six guest rooms and guest parlor are furnished in Victorian antiques. Guests eat a full gourmet breakfast in their rooms or family-style in the guest parlor. The antique radiator bun warmer is a star attraction of the upstairs buffet area where guests help themselves to an elegant fruit plate, freshly baked muffins or cinnamon rolls, and their choice of an egg/meat dish served in individual ramekins or hot or cold cereal. Afternoon tea is served daily, featuring a variety of freshly baked desserts and tea sandwiches. Owners Frankee and Bruce Muller previously operated a photographic safari camp in the African country of Botswana. Their special interests include wildlife, fly fishing, skiing, golf, and, of course, gourmet cooking — all of which can be enjoyed to the utmost in Bozeman. The Voss Inn is located three blocks from historic downtown Bozeman and is within walking distance of shops and dining.

SEASON

all year

ACCOMMODATIONS

six rooms with private baths

To prepare the streusel: Mix the sugar, flour, and lemon zest in a bowl. Stir in the pecans and melted butter. Set aside (the streusel should be dry and crumbly).

To prepare the batter: Preheat the oven to 375°F. Grease a 12-cup muffin pan and line it with 2½" paper baking cups. Combine 1½ cups of the flour, the sugar, baking powder, lemon zest, cinnamon, and salt in a large bowl. Make a well in the center. Mix the milk, butter, and eggs together and pour into the well. Mix until smooth. Combine the frozen berries and remaining ¼ cup of flour and toss well. Fold the berries into the batter and spoon into the prepared muffin cups. Top each cup with 1 heaping tablespoon of the streusel. Bake 25 – 30 minutes or until a toothpick inserted in the center comes out clean. Cool 10 – 15 minutes in the pan on a rack. Remove the muffins from the pan and serve warm. *Yield: 12 muffins.*

Plantation Muffins

1 cup chopped pecans
2 cups all-purpose flour
1 teaspoon baking soda
1 teaspoon salt
3 ounces cream cheese, softened
1 cup sugar
2 teaspoons vanilla
1 egg, lightly beaten
½ cup sour cream
20-ounce can crushed pineapple, drained

Preheat the oven to 400°F. Grease well a 12-cup muffin pan and sprinkle it with the pecans; set aside. Sift together the flour, baking soda, and salt and set aside. In a separate bowl, beat the cream cheese, sugar, and vanilla, and then add the egg. Mix in the flour mixture alternately with the sour cream. Fold in the drained pineapple. Bake 20 – 25 minutes or until a toothpick inserted in the center comes out clean. *Yield: 12 muffins.*

Middle Plantation Inn

Shirley and Dwight Mullican
9549 Liberty Road
Frederick, Maryland 21701-3246
Tel: (301) 898-7128
E-mail: BandB@MPInn.com
www.MPInn.com
$$$

ABOUT THE B&B

*T**his charming stone and log home, nestled on 26 acres, offers guests a peaceful setting, which includes Addison's Run (a nearby brook) and a 10-acre woods. You'll wake each morning to the sound of birds (and an occasional rooster) and see nature in all its glory. Your hosts take great pleasure in sharing their antique furnishings. Each guest room offers a delightful 19th-century ambiance combined with the modern conveniences of private bath, air conditioning, and TV. A massive stone fireplace, stained glass windows, and skylights highlight the public Keeping Room (a Colonial term for gathering place). A breakfast of seasonal fruit, fresh baked bread, cheese, and cereal are served each morning. Visit 33 historic blocks of downtown Frederick, with its mix of specialty and antique shops, dining establishments, museum, and art galleries. Nearby is New Market — antique capitol of Maryland. The inn is located near Baltimore (Maryland), the Antietam Battlefield in Sharpesburg (Maryland), Washington (DC), Gettysburg (Pennsylvania), and Harpers Ferry (West Virginia).*

SEASON

all year

ACCOMMODATIONS

four rooms with private baths

Flo and Harold Eckert
409 South Lingle Avenue
Palmyra, Pennsylvania 17078
Tel: (717) 838-8282
$$

ABOUT THE B&B

Built around 1825, the Hen-Apple is an intimate and fully restored bed and breakfast filled to the brim with everything country and old-fashioned. It offers a relaxed atmosphere with six air conditioned guest rooms (each with private bath), a porch filled with rockers, a screened porch for warm weather dining, a herb garden, lots of flowers, and a shady retreat in the orchard. The Hen-Apple's well-rounded breakfasts are something to remember — especially the cinnamon French toast. Tea is served in the afternoon. Just two miles from Hershey, Pennsylvania, Palmyra is an antique lover's dream. In addition, wineries, shopping outlets, Hershey attractions, the riverboat, and horse racing are nearby. Your hosts, Flo and Harold Eckert, love going to flea markets and auctions, and enjoy reading, gardening, and music. Flo is also a Christmas enthusiast so, come the merry season, the B&B sports a tree in just about every room and an impressive Santa collection.

SEASON

all year

ACCOMMODATIONS

six rooms with private baths

Potluck Muffins

1 cup all-purpose flour
2 tablespoons baking powder
½ teaspoon salt
½ cup sugar
¼ cup butter or margarine, melted
1 egg, lightly beaten
½ cup milk
Potluck (anything you have in your cupboard, such as chocolate or peanut butter chips, creamy peanut butter, nuts, fruit, or shredded unsweetened coconut), to taste

Preheat the oven to 375°F. Stir together the flour, baking powder, salt, and sugar. Add the butter and egg to the milk. Add the liquid ingredients to the flour mixture. Stir only enough to moisten. Add the potluck ingredients. Bake 15 – 20 minutes or until a toothpick inserted in the center comes out clean. *Tips:* Also good without the potluck ingredients and served with homemade jam. Put a few tablespoons of water in any unused muffin cups to protect the pan and keep the rest of the muffins moist. *Yield: 8 muffins.*

Pumpkin-Chocolate Chip Muffins

3⅓ cups all-purpose flour
1½ cups sugar
2 tablespoons pumpkin pie spice
2 teaspoons baking soda
1 teaspoon baking powder
½ teaspoon salt
4 eggs, lightly beaten
2 cups plain canned pumpkin
1 cup butter, melted
1½ cups chocolate chips

Preheat the oven to 350°F. Thoroughly mix the flour, sugar, pie spice, baking soda, baking powder, and salt in a large bowl. In a smaller bowl, mix together the eggs, pumpkin, and butter and blend well. Stir in the chocolate chips. Pour this mixture into the dry ingredients and fold in with a spatula until the dry ingredients are just moistened. Spoon into 2 greased 6-cup muffin pans and bake for about 25 minutes or until a toothpick inserted in the center comes out clean. *Yield: 12 large muffins.*

The Melville House

Vince De Rico and David Horan
39 Clarke Street
Newport, Rhode Island 02840
Tel: (401) 847-0640
Fax: (401) 847-0956
E-mail: Innkeeper@ids.net
www.melvillehouse.com
$$$ – $$$$

ABOUT THE B&B

Built circa 1750 and on the National Register of Historic Places, The Melville House is located in the heart of Newport's historic Hill District on a quiet gas-lit street. One of the few inns in Newport dedicated to the Colonial style, it's just one block up from Thames Street with its Brick Market and the harborfront where many of the city's finest restaurants, luxurious sailboats, antique shops, and galleries can be found. The Melville House is also close to the Tennis Hall of Fame, lavish Vanderbilt, Astor, and Belmont family mansions, the Naval War College, and Newport's finest ocean beaches. The Melville House breakfast menu features homemade granola, muffins, breads, buttermilk biscuits, scones, Yankee cornbread, stuffed French toast, fresh fruit sourdough pancakes, and Rhode Island johnnycakes. An afternoon tea is served every day, featuring refreshments, homemade biscotti, and soup (on cold days), over which innkeepers Vince and David share their Newport experiences.

SEASON

all year

ACCOMMODATIONS

five rooms with private baths;
two rooms with shared bath;
winter fireplace suite

Hidden Pond
Bed & Breakfast

Priscilla and Larry Fuerst
PO Box 461
Fennville, Michigan 49408
Tel: (616) 561-2491
$$$

ABOUT THE B&B

Hidden Pond Bed & Breakfast is set on 28 acres of woods, perfect for bird-watching, hiking, cross-country skiing, or just relaxing in a rowboat on the pond. Guests can enjoy seven entry-level rooms, including bedrooms and baths, living room with fireplace, dining room, library, kitchen, and breakfast porch. Priscilla and Larry, who work for rival airlines, understand the importance of a soothing, calm, and slow-paced overnight stay. They enjoy pleasing guests and creating an atmosphere of quiet elegance. Unwind and take in the sun on the outdoor deck or patio. Turndown service, complimentary soft drinks, tea, hot chocolate, or an evening sherry are offered. Full hot breakfast is served in the sun-washed garden room at your leisure, and features fresh fruit, breads, muffins, and a hot entrée. This lovely retreat is near the beaches of Lake Michigan, the boutiques of Saugatuck, and the winery and cider mill in Fennville.

SEASON

all year

ACCOMMODATIONS

two rooms with private baths

Pumpkin Muffins

2 cups all-purpose flour
2 teaspoons baking powder
½ teaspoon baking soda
1 teaspoon ground cinnamon
½ teaspoon grated nutmeg
½ teaspoon ground allspice
½ teaspoon ground ginger
½ teaspoon salt
1 cup freshly cooked or canned pumpkin
¾ cup sugar
½ cup milk
2 eggs
2 tablespoons vegetable oil
2 tablespoons applesauce
¼ cup whole wheat flour

Preheat the oven to 400°F. Sift the flour, baking powder, baking soda, spices, and salt. Set aside. Combine the pumpkin, sugar, milk, eggs, oil, and applesauce and add to the dry ingredients. Beat until blended. Add the whole wheat flour until blended. Bake 20 – 25 minutes or until a toothpick inserted in the center comes out clean. *Tip:* Put a few tablespoons of water in any unused muffin cups to protect the pan and keep the rest of the muffins moist. *Yield: 8 – 10 muffins.*

Rhubarb Muffins

"This recipe comes from my friend, Ruth Roemer, who has a huge part of her garden devoted to rhubarb, which she shares with her friends. Often, we'll pack up a few of these muffins for our departing guests to munch on as they continue their travels." — Erma Rummel

½ cup buttermilk
½ cup vegetable oil
1 egg
2 teaspoons vanilla
1¼ cups brown sugar
2½ cups all-purpose flour
1 teaspoon salt
1 teaspoon baking soda
1 teaspoon baking powder
1½ cups diced rhubarb
½ cup chopped pecans

Topping:
1¼ teaspoons butter or margarine, melted
⅓ cup sugar
1 (generous) tablespoon all-purpose flour
1 teaspoon ground cinnamon

Preheat the oven to 400°F. Beat the buttermilk, oil, egg, vanilla, sugar, flour, salt, baking soda, and baking powder. Add the rhubarb and pecans. Mix well. Fill 24 greased (or paper-lined) muffin cups ⅔ full. To make the topping, mix together the butter, sugar, flour, and cinnamon and sprinkle this over the muffins. Bake 18 – 20 minutes or until a toothpick inserted in the center comes out clean. *Tip:* These muffins freeze well. *Yield: 24 muffins.*

Rummel's Tree Haven Bed & Breakfast

Erma and Carl Rummel
41 North Beck Street (M-25)
Sebewaing, Michigan 48759
Tel: (517) 883-2450
$$

ABOUT THE B&B

Located in the village of Sebewaing, Michigan, in the hollow of the thumb on Saginaw Bay, Rummel's Tree Haven was originally built as the farm home of Barbara and Frederick Beck in 1878. Today, Erma and Carl Rummel call it home and offer comfort and convenience to all travelers. The B&B is surrounded by many trees, which gives it an air of privacy — one tree even grows right through the porch roof! Saginaw Bay offers fine fishing, hunting, boating, bird-watching, or just relaxing. The Rummels love having company and will make you feel welcome.

SEASON

all year

ACCOMMODATIONS

two rooms with private baths

Brambly Hedge Cottage

Jacquelyn Smyers
HCR 31, Box 39
Jasper, Arkansas 72641
Tel: 1-800-BRAMBLY or
(501) 446-5849
$$

ABOUT THE B&B

"*Absolutely charming,*" *wrote
National Geographic
Traveler of this old Ozark
mountaintop farmhouse, four miles
south of Jasper, Arkansas. A Tennessee
guest commented, "The place is
uniquely beautiful, the food delicious,
and the view inspiring." Three guest
rooms with private baths reflect coun-
try French elegance in a homestead log
cabin. A full breakfast is served on the
deck overlooking Buffalo River Valley
or behind the screened porch in rocking
chairs. You're only minutes from
the "Grand Canyon of the Ozarks,"
challenging-to-easy hiking trails, and
canoeing on Buffalo National River. If
art is more your style, you'll find the
work of true artisans in the Jasper area.
For those who wish to sample a night
out on the town, Eureka Springs and
Branson (Missouri) are nearby. Small
group special-interest tours and relax-
ing massages can be arranged. Hostess
Jacquelyn Smyers includes her hand-
made tatted lace and samovar collection
in the decor. She's also a designer, com-
mercial artist, and author of* Come
For Tea *and the children's book* The
Cloud That Came Into The Cabin
*(inspired by the clouds on Sloan Moun-
tain where Brambly Hedge is located).*

SEASON

all year

ACCOMMODATIONS

three rooms with private baths

Six-Week Muffins

"People love these hot or cold. They freeze well, too."
— *Jacquelyn Smyers*

15 ounces Raisin Bran cereal
3 cups sugar
5 cups all-purpose flour
5 teaspoons baking soda
2 teaspoons salt
1 cup vegetable oil
4 eggs, lightly beaten
1 quart buttermilk

Mix the cereal, sugar, flour, baking soda, and salt in a large bowl. Add
the oil, eggs, and buttermilk and mix well. Store this in a covered con-
tainer in the refrigerator and use as needed — the batter will keep for up
to 6 weeks. To bake: Preheat the oven to 375 – 400°F. Fill greased muffin
cups ⅔ full and bake 15 – 20 minutes or until a toothpick inserted in the
center comes out clean. *Yield: 5 dozen muffins.*

Sour Cream-Peach Muffins

1½ cups brown sugar
⅔ cup vegetable oil
1 egg
1 teaspoon vanilla
1 cup sour cream
2¼ cups all-purpose flour
1 teaspoon baking soda
1 teaspoon salt
1½ cups chopped peaches (fresh or canned), drained, or fresh
    raspberries
½ cup chopped walnuts

Preheat the oven to 325°F. Mix the brown sugar, oil, egg, vanilla, and sour cream. Beat well. Combine the flour, baking soda, and salt in a bowl, and slowly stir it into the brown sugar mixture (do not beat or overmix). Fold in the peaches and walnuts. Spoon into 24 greased muffin cups. Bake for 25 minutes or until a toothpick inserted in the center comes out clean. *Yield: 24 muffins.*

Custer Mansion B&B

Carole and Mill Seaman
35 Centennial Drive
Custer, South Dakota 57730
Tel: (605) 673-3333
$$ – $$$

ABOUT THE B&B

This unusual 1891 Victorian Gothic home is on the National Register of Historic Places. *Antique light fixtures, ceiling fans, door transoms, stained glass windows, and gingerbread accents help preserve Custer Mansion's turn-of-the-century mood. Bedrooms, including one family suite and two honeymoon/anniversary suites, are individually decorated in country and Victorian flavor and are named for songs. Delicious home-cooked breakfasts are served in the spacious dining room, with an adjacent butler pantry used for serving juice, coffee, and tea. The one-acre yard offers plenty of room for outdoor relaxing and features a shaded patio near a natural rocky hillside. Custer Mansion is located near Mount Rushmore, Crazy Horse Memorial, Custer State Park, and many other attractions. Nearby activities include swimming, hiking, fishing, golfing, and hiking in the beautiful Black Hills. Mill, a retired school administrator, and Carole, mother of six and grandmother of 15, specialize in western hospitality and delicious food.*

SEASON

all year

ACCOMMODATIONS

five rooms (including three suites)
with private baths

Nottoway Plantation

Cindy Hidalgo
PO Box 160
White Castle, Louisiana 70788
Tel: (504) 545-2730
Fax: (504) 545-8632

$$$$

ABOUT THE B&B

Located half an hour from Baton Rouge and an hour-and-a-half from New Orleans, Nottoway is the largest surviving antebellum mansion in the South. Once the home of wealthy sugar planter John Randolph, Nottoway is a gem of Italianate and Greek Revival style — boasting 53,000 square feet — that has withstood the test of time. The intricate lacy plaster friezework, hand painted Dresden porcelain doorknobs, hand-carved marble mantles, and 65-foot Grand Ballroom are all intact. Guests stay in the mansion itself, in the boy's wing, or in the overseer's cottage. B&B guests receive a complimentary tour of the mansion, a wake-up call of hot coffee, sweet potato-cinnamon muffins, and orange juice, and a full plantation breakfast in the Breakfast Room. A restaurant on the grounds features Cajun and Creole cuisine, presided over by Chef Johnny "Jambalaya" Percle whose cooking embodies the "good, straightforward, unpretentious cuisine" that he considers the soul of Louisiana food.

SEASON

all year

ACCOMMODATIONS

13 rooms (including three suites) with private baths

Sweet Potato-Cinnamon Muffins

"These muffins whet guests' appetites before our full plantation breakfast." — Cindy Hidalgo

¾ cup cooked, mashed sweet potato
¼ cup butter, melted
⅔ cup milk
¼ teaspoon vanilla
1¼ cups all-purpose flour
4 teaspoons baking powder
2 tablespoons sugar
1 teaspoon salt
1 teaspoon ground cinnamon

Preheat the oven to 450°F. Beat the sweet potato together with the butter. Mix in the milk and vanilla. Add the flour, baking powder, sugar, and salt and stir to blend (don't overmix). Spoon the batter into 12 muffin cups lined with paper. Bake 15 minutes or until a toothpick inserted in the center comes out clean. *Yield: 12 muffins.*

Wild Raspberry Muffins

1¼ cups sugar
½ cup margarine
2 eggs
1 cup sour cream
1 teaspoon vanilla
2 cups all-purpose flour
1 teaspoon baking powder
½ teaspoon baking soda
¼ teaspoon salt
1 cup fresh or frozen (thawed and drained) wild raspberries

Topping:
2 tablespoons sugar
¼ teaspoon ground cinnamon
¼ teaspoon grated nutmeg

Preheat the oven to 375°F. Cream the sugar and margarine. Add the eggs, sour cream, and vanilla. Sift the flour, baking powder, baking soda, and salt. Add the dry ingredients to the liquid mixture and mix until just moist. Fold in the berries. Pour the batter in 2 greased muffin pans. To make the topping, mix the sugar, cinnamon, and nutmeg and sprinkle ¼ teaspoon on each muffin. Bake 25 – 30 minutes or until a toothpick inserted in the center comes out clean. *Yield: 24 muffins.*

Lindgren's Bed & Breakfast

Shirley Lindgren
County Road 35, PO Box 56
Lutsen, Minnesota 55612-0056
Tel: (218) 663-7450
$$ – $$$$

ABOUT THE B&B

Less than two hours from Duluth, Minnesota, and Thunder Bay, Ontario, this 1920s rustic log home with manicured grounds and walkable shoreline resides on Lake Superior in Superior National Forest. The living room features an 18-foot beamed ceiling, massive stone fireplace, and hunting trophies. Guest rooms are cozily designed in either knotty cedar, pine, or rustic paneling. Scenic points of interest include Split Rock Lighthouse, Gooseberry Falls, and Tettegouche State Park. Depending on the season, you can choose from hiking trails, skyrides, alpine slides, mountain biking, horseback riding, golf, tennis, fishing, snowmobiling, and cross-country and downhill skiing. Any number of fine restaurants are nearby, and you're within walking distance of Lutsen Resort, the oldest in the state. Your hosts are retired after 35 years of owning and operating a successful garden center, landscaping, nursery, and floral business in Minneapolis, and enjoy fishing, hunting and, most of all, people, which is why they opened their home as a bed and breakfast!

SEASON

all year

ACCOMMODATIONS

four rooms with private baths

Quick & Yeast Breads

Anadama Bread

3½ cups water
¾ cup molasses
½ cup margarine
1 cup cornmeal
2 packages active dry yeast (2 tablespoons)
1 tablespoon salt
About 10 cups all-purpose flour

In a medium pot, heat the water, molasses, and margarine to boiling. Stir in the cornmeal with a wire whisk and cook for 2 minutes, stirring constantly. Set aside and cool for about 45 minutes. In a large bowl, combine the yeast, salt, and 2 cups of the flour. Stir in the cooled cornmeal mixture and beat for several minutes. Add 1½ cups flour and beat for several more minutes. Add 5 cups of flour to form a soft dough. Knead for 5 – 10 minutes, adding more flour if needed. Shape into a ball and place in a greased bowl. Cover with a damp cloth and let rise. Punch down the center with your fist and let rest 15 minutes. Lightly grease 2 large bread pans; roll out the dough, divide in ½, and place it into the pans. Let rise for 45 minutes. Preheat the oven to 350°F and bake 30 – 35 minutes. Remove immediately from the pans and cool. *Yield: 2 loaves.*

The Inn at The Brass Lantern

Andy Aldrich
717 Maple Street
Stowe, Vermont 05672
Tel: (800) 729-2980 or (802) 253-2229
Fax: (802) 253-7425
$$ – $$$$

ABOUT THE B&B

The Inn at The Brass Lantern is located at the edge of the village of Stowe, Vermont. Stowe is a full-service, four-season resort town, and boasts many world-class restaurants and activities, a cultural center, unique cottage industries, craftspeople, and artists. Originally built as a farmhouse and carriage barn, The Brass Lantern was restored by Andy Aldrich, the current innkeeper, to retain its original Vermont character (for which he won an award). Today, the inn carries the traditional Vermont B&B theme throughout — from its decor of period antiques, handmade quilts, and locally crafted amenities to the food and beverages reflecting local and Vermont state products. In addition, guests are treated to a unique ambiance and casual, attentive service. The inn's setting provides panoramic views of Mount Mansfield and its valley from nearly every room.

SEASON

all year

ACCOMMODATIONS

nine rooms with private baths

Caledonia Farm — 1812

Phil Irwin
47 Dearing Road
Flint Hill, Virginia 22627
Tel: (800) BNB-1812 or
(540) 675-3693
Fax: (540) 675-3693
$$ – $$$$

ABOUT THE B&B

With Virginia's Blue Ridge Mountains as a backdrop, Caledonia Farm offers its guests a beautiful setting amid scenic pasturelands surrounded by stone fences. The farm's Federal-style house and companion summer kitchen were completed in 1812. Restoration was completed in 1965, with the original two-foot-thick stone walls and 32-foot-long beams remaining intact along with the original mantels, paneled windows, and wide pine floors. The winter kitchen's huge fireplace provides a delightful atmosphere during cool seasons while three porches offer a variety of views in the warmer months. Guest rooms are air conditioned, and have working fireplaces, individual heat control, and fine double beds. The B&B is called Caledonia (the mythological name for Scotland) to honor the original immigrants to this magnificent area.

SEASON

all year

ACCOMMODATIONS

two suites with private baths;
two rooms with shared bath

Apple-Nut Bread

2 cups all-purpose flour
¾ cup sugar
1 tablespoon baking powder
½ tablespoon baking soda
½ tablespoon ground cinnamon
1 egg
1 cup applesauce
2 tablespoons vegetable oil
1 cup chopped walnuts

Preheat the oven to 350°F. In a mixing bowl, combine the flour, sugar, baking powder, baking soda, and cinnamon. Add the egg, applesauce, and oil, and blend. Add the walnuts. Pour the batter into a greased 9 x 5" loaf pan (or a 12-cup muffin pan). Bake for 45 minutes. Cool and serve. *Yield: 1 loaf.*

A-to-Z Bread

3 cups all-purpose flour
1 teaspoon baking soda
1 teaspoon salt
3 teaspoons ground cinnamon
½ teaspoon baking powder
3 eggs
1 cup vegetable oil
2 cups sugar
2 cups A-to-Z mix (see below)
3 teaspoons vanilla
1 cup chopped walnuts or almonds

Preheat the oven to 325°F. Sift the flour, baking soda, salt, cinnamon, and baking powder; set aside. Beat the eggs in a large bowl. Add the oil and sugar and cream well. Add the A-to-Z mix and vanilla to the egg mixture. Add the dry ingredients and mix well. Stir in the nuts. Spoon into 2 well-greased loaf pans. Bake for 1 hour. *Yield: 2 loaves.*

A-to-Z mix — Use 1 or a combination of ingredients to equal 2 cups (except as indicated):

Grated apples, applesauce, chopped apricots, mashed bananas, grated carrots, pitted and chopped cherries, freshly ground coconut, pitted and chopped dates, ground eggplant, finely chopped figs, seedless grapes,

(continued on next page)

Manor House

Diane and Hank Tremblay
PO Box 447
Norfolk, Connecticut 06058
Tel/Fax: (860) 542-5690
$$$$

ABOUT THE B&B

Manor House is a historic 1898 mansion built for the leisure class of an earlier era. Today, it's designated as "Connecticut's most romantic hideaway" (The Discerning Traveler). *Relax in the living room beside the baronial fireplace, retreat to the sun porch to enjoy a book from the inn's library, or take a stroll around the grounds to enjoy the perennial gardens. The inn exudes Victorian elegance, with its Tiffany windows, architectural detail, and antique furnishings. Awake to the wonderful aromas of Manor House's full breakfast, including homemade bread or muffins and honey harvested from the inn's own hives, all served in the elegant dining room. If you have a more romantic breakfast in mind, innkeepers Diane and Hank Tremblay will pamper you with breakfast in bed. Manor House is close to Tanglewood, summer theater, vineyards, and a host of summer and winter activities, including hiking, biking, water sports, and alpine and cross-country skiing.*

SEASON

all year

ACCOMMODATIONS

eight rooms with private baths

honey (omit sugar in recipe above), ½ cup lemon juice, marmalade (omit 1 cup sugar in recipe above), mincemeat, chopped oranges, fresh or canned chopped peaches, ½ cup chopped peppermint leaves, chopped pears, drained crushed pineapple, 1 cup chopped pitted prunes, canned pumpkin, raisins, raspberries, chopped rhubarb, fresh or frozen (drained) strawberries, cooked tapioca, grated sweet potatoes, chopped tomatoes (add an extra ½ cup sugar), cooked and mashed yams, plain or flavored yogurt, grated zucchini.

Aunt Marie's Spoon Bread

2 cups milk
¾ cup white cornmeal or ½ cup yellow cornmeal
1 tablespoon butter
¼ teaspoon salt
1 tablespoon sugar
2 eggs, separated

Preheat the oven to 350°F. In a medium saucepan, scald the milk. Stir in the cornmeal, butter, salt, and sugar. Remove from the heat. Beat the egg yolks and add to the saucepan. Cool. Beat the egg whites until they stand in soft peaks, then fold them into the milk mixture until slightly thickened and paler yellow. Pour into a covered 1 quart baking dish and set in a pan of warm water. Bake for 1 hour. Just before serving, uncover the dish and brown the top until golden. Serve with butter as a side dish or breakfast entrée. *Yield: 1 loaf.*

The Heirloom

Melisande Hubbs and Patricia Cross
214 Shakeley Lane
Ione, California 95640
Tel: (209) 274-4468
$$ – $$$

ABOUT THE B&B

Down a country lane to an expansive English romantic garden is a touch of the old south. The Heirloom is a brick, two-story southern antebellum home, circa 1863, located in the heart of California gold country. It was built by Virginians who came to California during the Gold Rush to be merchants in Ione, the supply center of the mining camps of Amador County. Sweet magnolias, wisteria, hammocks, croquet, verandas, cozy fireplaces, and heirloom antiques (including a historic piano) await you, not to mention a royal breakfast and gracious hospitality. Near the inn are over 20 wineries, Gold Rush historical points, museums, and nature walks, and opportunities for gourmet dining, gold panning, gliding, and hiking.

SEASON

all year

ACCOMMODATIONS

four rooms with private baths;
two rooms with shared bath

The Ancient Pines B&B

Genevieve Simmens
2015 Parley Street
Nauvoo, Illinois 62354
Tel: (217) 453-2767

$

ABOUT THE B&B

Surrounded by 140-year-old evergreens, this turn-of-the-century home features exquisite exterior brick detailing, stained glass windows, and etched glass front door — all part of the original construction. Pressed tin ceilings, carved woodwork, an open staircase, claw-foot tubs, and lovingly decorated bedrooms grace the interior. You can relax on the front veranda and watch the workers at the nearby winery or find seclusion on the side porch. There are herb and flower gardens to wander in, a lawn for croquet, and a library for playing chess or music. When the day is done, you'll drift off in clean, comfortable beds, lulled to sleep by the whispering pines, then awake to the smell of baking bread. A heart-healthy menu can be provided upon request.

SEASON

all year

ACCOMMODATIONS

three rooms with shared baths

B&B Mini Loaves

2 packages active dry yeast (2 tablespoons)
2 cups lukewarm water
2 tablespoons sugar
1 tablespoon salt
¼ cup vegetable oil
½ cup potato flour
4 – 6 cups all-purpose flour

In a large bowl, dissolve the yeast in lukewarm water. Let it rest until foam rises to the top (about 5 minutes). Add the sugar, salt, oil, potato flour, and 2½ cups of the all-purpose flour. Beat until smooth. Add enough additional all-purpose flour, stirring, until the dough is ready to knead and not too sticky. Knead 10 minutes by hand. Put the dough in a warm place in a lightly greased bowl. Let it rise until doubled. Punch it down, then let it rest 10 minutes. Preheat the oven to 400°F. Shape the dough into 10 mini loaves and place them on lightly greased baking sheets. Let them rise and bake them 20 minutes on the bottom shelf of the oven. *Yield: 10 mini loaves.*

Beer Bread

3½ cups all-purpose flour
¼ cup sugar
1 teaspoon salt
1 teaspoon baking soda
1 teaspoon baking powder
12-ounce bottle warm (but not flat) beer
1 egg

Preheat the oven to 350°F. Mix the flour, sugar, salt, baking soda, and baking powder. Add the beer and egg and mix well. Pour into a greased standard loaf pan and bake approximately 50 minutes, or divide among 3 greased mini-sized loaf pans and bake approximately 35 minutes.
Yield: 1 loaf or 3 mini-sized loaves.

Hutton House

Loretta Murray and Dean Ahren
PO Box 88, Route 250/219
Huttonsville, West Virginia 26273
Tel: (304) 335-6701
$$

ABOUT THE B&B

Majestically situated above the tiny town of Huttons-ville, this meticulously restored turn-of-the-century Queen Anne Victorian commands a broad view of the Tygart River Valley and the Laurel Mountains. Hutton House, which is listed in the National Register of Historic Places, features original oak woodwork, ornate windows, a three-story turret, arched pocket doors, wraparound porch, and a winding staircase. Antiques abound, and each of the guest rooms is furnished in its own individual style. Breakfast is a time to get to know your hosts and the other guests, while enjoying a variety of pancake, French toast, and egg dishes along with fresh fruit, crème brûlée, sorbet, or even porridge. Guests can then relax on the porch, play games on the lawn, or take a leisurely hike on the trail behind the house. Nearby attractions include Cass Railroad, National Radio Observatory, underground caverns, and rock climbing.

SEASON

all year

ACCOMMODATIONS

six rooms with private baths

High Meadows Inn

Peter Sushka and Mary Jae Abbitt
High Meadows Lane, Route 4, Box 6
Scottsville, Virginia 24590
Tel: (800) 232-1832 or (804) 286-2218
Fax: (804) 286-2124
E-mail: peterhmi@aol.com
www.highmeadows.com
$$ – $$$$

ABOUT THE B&B

As Virginia's only inn that is on the National Register of Historic Homes and has a Renaissance farm vineyard, High Meadows offers a rare opportunity to experience 170 years of architectural history and 10 years of new viticultural growth. High Meadows is a grand house, where guests are welcomed with champagne and stay in rooms furnished with period antiques and art, each with private bath. The innkeepers' many special touches and attention to detail make your visit one to be remembered. Enjoy the simplicity of nature on the 50 surrounding acres of gardens, footpaths, forests, and ponds. Owner/chef Peter Sushka ensures that dining at High Meadows is just as pleasurable as lodging there. Start with a breakfast of fresh orange juice, a variety of homemade breads, muffins, and scones, fresh fruit, gourmet egg dishes, and coffee or tea. End your day with a multi-course dinner, offering distinctive northern European and Mediterranean dishes.

SEASON

all year

ACCOMMODATIONS

14 rooms (including four suites) with private baths

Blackberry-Orange Tea Bread

(Recipe from The Best of High Meadows — A Selected Recipe Collection.*)*

5 cups all-purpose flour
1 cup granulated sugar
1 cup brown sugar
2 tablespoons and 1 teaspoon baking powder
2 teaspoons salt
2 cups fresh blackberries
2 teaspoons grated orange zest
2 eggs
2½ cups milk
2 teaspoons vanilla
6 tablespoons vegetable oil

Preheat the oven to 350°F. Mix together the flour, sugar, baking powder, and salt. Add the blackberries, orange zest, eggs, milk, vanilla, and oil and mix gently. Pour into 2 greased loaf pans and bake for 1 hour.
Yield: 2 loaves.

Brass Lantern Banana-Nut Bread

"Served hot at breakfast." — *Andy Aldrich*

3 ripe bananas, mashed
2 eggs, lightly beaten
2 cups all-purpose flour
¾ cup sugar
½ teaspoon salt
1 teaspoon baking soda
½ cup chopped walnuts
Splash of your favorite brandy

Preheat the oven to 350°F. Grease and flour a 9 x 5" loaf pan. Mix the bananas, eggs, flour, sugar, salt, baking soda, walnuts, and brandy together in a bowl. Pour the batter into the pan and bake for 1 hour. Serve hot or cold. *Yield: 1 loaf.*

The Inn at The Brass Lantern

Andy Aldrich
717 Maple Street
Stowe, Vermont 05672
Tel: (800) 729-2980 or (802) 253-2229
Fax: (802) 253-7425
$$ – $$$$

ABOUT THE B & B

The Inn at The Brass Lantern is located at the edge of the village of Stowe, Vermont. Stowe is a full-service, four-season resort town, and boasts many world-class restaurants and activities, a cultural center, unique cottage industries, craftspeople, and artists. Originally built as a farmhouse and carriage barn, The Brass Lantern was restored by Andy Aldrich, the current innkeeper, to retain its original Vermont character (for which he won an award). Today, the inn carries the traditional Vermont B&B theme throughout — from its decor of period antiques, handmade quilts, and locally crafted amenities to the food and beverages reflecting local and Vermont state products. In addition, guests are treated to a unique ambiance and casual, attentive service. The inn's setting provides panoramic views of Mount Mansfield and its valley from nearly every room.

SEASON

all year

ACCOMMODATIONS

nine rooms with private baths

The Mainstay Inn

Sue and Tom Carroll
635 Columbia Avenue
Cape May, New Jersey 08204
Tel: (609) 884-8690
$$$ – $$$$

ABOUT THE B&B

According to the Washington Post, *"The jewel of them all has got to be the Mainstay."* Built by a pair of wealthy gamblers in 1872, this elegant and exclusive club-house is now among the premier B&B inns in the country. The Mainstay now comprises three historic buildings on one of the most beautiful streets of the historic Cape May district. Guests enjoy 16 antique-filled rooms and suites (some with fireplaces and whirlpool baths), three parlors, spacious gardens, and rocker-filled verandas. Breakfast and afternoon tea are served daily. Beautiful beaches, historic attractions, biking, birding, golf, and tennis are all available in Cape May, a National Historic Landmark community.

SEASON

all year

ACCOMMODATIONS

16 rooms (including seven suites) with private baths

Cheddar Cheese Date-Nut Bread

(Recipe from Breakfast at Nine, Tea at Four: Favorite Recipes from Cape May's Mainstay Inn.)

1 cup all-purpose flour
1 cup whole wheat flour
1 cup sugar
3 teaspoons baking powder
½ teaspoon salt
1 egg, lightly beaten
¼ cup vegetable oil
1 cup milk
1 cup grated sharp cheddar cheese
½ cup chopped dates
½ cup chopped walnuts

Preheat the oven to 350°F. Grease a 9 x 5" loaf pan. Mix the flour, sugar, baking powder, and salt. In a separate bowl, beat the egg, oil, and milk. Add to the flour mixture, stirring just until the dry ingredients are moistened. Fold in the cheese, dates, and walnuts. Turn into the prepared loaf pan and bake for 45 minutes. *Yield: 1 loaf.*

Cinnamon Crunch Walnut Bread

1½ cups coarsely chopped walnuts
1 tablespoon margarine, melted, and ¼ cup margarine
1 cup sugar
2 teaspoons ground cinnamon
3 cups all-purpose flour
1½ teaspoons salt
4½ teaspoons baking powder
1 egg
1¼ cups milk

Preheat the oven to 350°F. Toss the walnuts with the 1 tablespoon of melted margarine, then add ¼ cup of the sugar and the cinnamon, mixing until coated. Reserve ¼ cup for the topping and set the rest aside. Mix the flour, salt, baking powder, remaining ¾ cup of sugar, and ¼ cup margarine. Beat the egg lightly and add the milk. Stir this into the flour mixture. Add the bulk of the walnut mixture to the batter and mix. Spoon into 2 greased 9 x 5" loaf pans. Sprinkle with the reserved ¼ cup nut mixture and let stand 15 minutes. Bake for approximately 1 hour or until done. Let stand 10 minutes before turning out of the pans.
Yield: 2 loaves.

Ghent House Bed & Breakfast

Diane and Wayne Young
411 Main Street, PO Box 478
Ghent, Kentucky 41045
Tel: (502) 347-5807
$$ – $$$

ABOUT THE B&B

Halfway between Cincinnati and Louisville, Ghent House is a gracious reminder of the antebellum days of the old South. It was built in 1833 in the usual style of the day — a central hall with rooms on either side of the kitchen and a dining room in back. A beautiful fantail window and two English coach lights enhance the front entrance, while a rose garden and gazebo grace the rear of the home. There are crystal chandeliers, fireplaces, and Jacuzzis in the guest rooms. Ghent House has a spectacular view of the Ohio River, and one can almost imagine the time when steamboats regularly traveled up and down its waters. Awake mornings to the aroma of coffee and tea, then have your breakfast in either the formal dining room or the breakfast room overlooking the river. At Ghent House, you'll enjoy and appreciate the charming blend of yesteryear with modern convenience and relaxation.

SEASON

all year

ACCOMMODATIONS

three suites with private baths

Isaiah Hall B&B Inn

Marie Brophy
PO Box 1007, 152 Whig Street
Dennis, Massachusetts 02638
Tel: (800) 736-0160 or (508) 385-9928
Fax: (508) 385-5879
$$$

ABOUT THE B&B

Enjoy country ambiance and hospitality in the heart of Cape Cod. Located on a quiet historic street, this lovely 1857 farmhouse is a leisurely walk from the beach or village with its restaurants, shops, theater, and fine arts museum. Close by, enjoy bike trails, tennis, golf, and whale watching. The inn offers an ideal home base for day trips to other points of interest — from Provincetown to Plymouth — as well as to the Islands (including Nantucket and Martha's Vineyard). Or, you can choose to simply relax in the inn's beautiful gardens or parlor surrounded by antiques and Oriental rugs, or cozy up in the carriage house "great room" with its white wicker furniture and knotty pine walls. Guest rooms are decorated with charming country antiques with most having queen beds, a few having two beds or balconies, and one having a fireplace.

SEASON

April to October

ACCOMMODATIONS

10 rooms (including one suite) with private baths

Cranberry-Orange Nut Bread

"The inn is located in front of the oldest, cultivated cranberry bog in America. Isaiah Hall's brother Henry cultivated the first cranberries here in 1816, while Isaiah patented and produced the first cranberry barrels for transport." — Marie Brophy

¾ cup orange juice
1 egg, lightly beaten
2 tablespoons vegetable oil
2 cups all-purpose flour
¾ cup sugar
1½ teaspoons baking powder
½ teaspoon baking soda
1 teaspoon salt
1 cup chopped fresh or frozen cranberries
½ cup chopped walnuts

Preheat the oven to 350°F. Combine the orange juice, egg, and oil; set aside. Stir together the flour, sugar, baking powder, baking soda, and salt. Add the orange juice mixture and stir until moistened. Fold in the cranberries and walnuts. Turn into a lightly greased and floured 9 x 5" loaf pan. Bake 50 – 60 minutes. Cool 10 minutes, remove from the pan, and cool on a rack. *Tip: Freezes well. **Yield: 1 loaf.***

Cranberry-Pumpkin Bread

2 eggs, lightly beaten
1 cup sugar
½ cup canola oil
1 cup canned pumpkin
2¼ cups all-purpose flour
1 tablespoon pumpkin pie spice
1 teaspoon baking soda
½ teaspoon salt
1 cup chopped cranberries

Preheat the oven to 350°F. Combine the eggs, sugar, oil, and pumpkin, and mix well. Combine the flour, pie spice, baking soda, and salt in a large bowl, making a well in the center. Pour the pumpkin mixture into the well, and stir just until the dry ingredients are moistened. Stir in the cranberries. Spoon the batter into 2 greased and floured 9 x 5" loaf pans. Bake for about 1 hour. *Yield: 2 loaves.*

The Summer House

Marjorie and Kevin Huelsman
158 Main Street
Sandwich, Massachusetts 02563
Tel: (800) 241-3609 or (508) 888-4991
E-mail: sumhouse@capecod.net
$$ – $$$

ABOUT THE B&B

The Summer House is an elegant circa 1835 Greek Revival twice featured in Country Living magazine. It was owned by Hiram Dillaway, a prominent mold-maker and colorist at the Boston & Sandwich Glass Factory. Large, sunny bedchambers feature antiques, hand-stitched quilts, and working fireplaces. Stroll to dining, shops, museums, galleries, a pond and gristmill, and a boardwalk to the beach. Bountiful breakfasts change daily and include freshly ground coffee, tea, fruit juice, and fresh fruit served in stemware. Entrées of frittata, stuffed French toast, quiche, or omelets are accompanied by scones, puff pastry, muffins, or fruit cobblers. Dishes are enhanced with vegetables, berries, and herbs from the inn's garden. English-style afternoon tea is served at an umbrella table in the garden. Boston, Newport, Providence, Martha's Vineyard, and Nantucket make pleasant day trips.

SEASON

all year

ACCOMMODATIONS

five rooms with private baths

Middle Plantation Inn

Shirley and Dwight Mullican
9549 Liberty Road
Frederick, Maryland 21701-3246
Tel: (301) 898-7128
E-mail: BandB@MPInn.com
www.MPInn.com
$$$

ABOUT THE B&B

This charming stone and log home, nestled on 26 acres, offers guests a peaceful setting, which includes Addison's Run (a nearby brook) and a 10-acre woods. You'll wake each morning to the sound of birds (and an occasional rooster) and see nature in all its glory. Your hosts take great pleasure in sharing their antique furnishings. Each guest room offers a delightful 19th-century ambiance combined with the modern conveniences of private bath, air conditioning, and TV. A massive stone fireplace, stained glass windows, and skylights highlight the public Keeping Room (a Colonial term for gathering place). A breakfast of seasonal fruit, fresh baked bread, cheese, and cereal are served each morning. Visit 33 historic blocks of downtown Frederick, with its mix of specialty and antique shops, dining establishments, museum, and art galleries. Nearby is New Market — antique capitol of Maryland. The inn is located near Baltimore (Maryland), the Antietam Battlefield in Sharpesburg (Maryland), Washington (DC), Gettysburg (Pennsylvania), and Harpers Ferry (West Virginia).

SEASON

all year

ACCOMMODATIONS

four rooms with private baths

Easy Apple Bread

3 cups all-purpose flour
3 cups peeled sliced apples
4 eggs
2 cups sugar
1 cup vegetable oil
1 teaspoon salt
1 teaspoon vanilla
1 teaspoon baking soda

Preheat the oven to 300°F. Combine the flour, apples, eggs, sugar, oil, salt, vanilla, and baking soda and mix well with an electric mixer. Pour the batter into 2 greased and floured loaf pans. Bake for 1½ hours. *Tip:* This bread freezes well. ***Yield: 2 loaves.***

Honey Wheat Bread

(*Recipe from* The Campbell Ranch Inn Cookbook.)

"I serve these individual honey wheat loaves piping hot on bread boards for each guest. Even though I make them ahead and freeze them, they smell and taste like they're freshly baked."
— Mary Jane Campbell

1½ cups boiling water
1 cup large-flake rolled oats
¾ cup honey
3 tablespoons butter, softened, and some extra butter, melted, for
   brushing tops of bread
2 teaspoons salt
1 package active dry yeast (1 tablespoon)
2 cups lukewarm water
1 cup 7-grain cereal
3 cups whole wheat flour
4 cups all-purpose flour

Pour the boiling water over the oats and let stand 30 minutes. Add the honey, butter, and salt. Dissolve the yeast in the lukewarm water and let it rest 3 – 5 minutes before adding the oat mixture. Stir in the 7-grain cereal and whole wheat flour. Add the all-purpose flour to make a medium-soft dough. Turn onto a floured board, and knead 10 minutes until smooth and elastic. Place the dough in a greased bowl. Grease the top of the dough and cover with a towel. Let it rise until doubled in size. Knead again 4 – 5 minutes. Divide the dough into 6 equal portions.

(continued on next page)

Campbell Ranch Inn

Mary Jane and Jerry Campbell
1475 Canyon Road
Geyserville, California 95441
Tel: (800) 959-3878 or (707) 857-3476
Fax: (707) 857-3239
$$$$

ABOUT THE B&B

Whether swimming in the pool, relaxing in the hot tub spa, or playing tennis, you're always surrounded by the Campbell Ranch Inn's spectacular valley and mountain views and beautiful flower gardens. In warm weather, breakfast is served on the terrace where you overlook rolling hills and vineyards. Only 80 miles north of San Francisco, the inn has five spacious rooms with king-size beds, fresh flowers, and fruit. You may choose to read or visit by the living room fireplace. Play tennis, horseshoes, or ping-pong, hike the trails at Lake Sonoma, or use the available bikes to tour the neighboring wine country. The surrounding area has many wineries and excellent restaurants, but remember to save some room for Campbell Ranch's homemade pie and coffee served every evening.

SEASON

all year

ACCOMMODATIONS

four rooms with private baths;
one private cottage with
private bath

Shape into small loaves and place in 6 lightly greased 5 x 3 x 2" loaf pans. Place the pans on a large cookie sheet, cover with a towel, and let rise until doubled in size. Preheat the oven to 400°F. Bake the loaves for 5 minutes. Lower the heat to 350°F and bake 25 – 30 minutes longer (until the loaves sound hollow when tapped). Remove them from the pans onto wire cooling racks and brush the tops with butter. Serve warm or wrap in foil when completely cold and freeze (reheat in the oven to serve). *Yield: 6 small loaves.*

Irish Soda Bread

"An Irish specialty I learned during (of all things!) a Spanish course taught by Joyce McNamara. I brought it to The Quail's Nest and found it to be a hit. Thanks, Joyce!" — Nancy Diaz

2 cups whole wheat flour
2 cups all-purpose flour
1 tablespoon sugar
3 teaspoons baking powder
1 teaspoon baking soda
1 teaspoon salt
¼ teaspoon vegetable shortening
1½ cups buttermilk
1 egg

Preheat the oven to 350°F. Place the flour, sugar, baking powder, baking soda, and salt in a mixing bowl. Cut in the shortening. In a separate bowl, mix the buttermilk and egg together, then add to the dry ingredients. Mix just until blended (do not overmix). Knead just until smooth (do not overknead). Divide into 2 rounds. Make 2 (¼") cross-shaped cuts in the top of each loaf. Bake on a lightly greased cookie sheet for 40 minutes or until golden brown. **Yield: 2 loaves.**

The Quail's Nest Bed and Breakfast

Nancy and Gregory Diaz
PO Box 221, Main Street
Danby, Vermont 05739
Tel: (802) 293-5099
Fax: (802) 293-6300
E-mail: Quails_nest@ compuserve.com
$$

ABOUT THE B&B

A circa 1835 country inn, The Quail's Nest is located just off Route 7 in Danby, Vermont — a quiet and picturesque town reminiscent of the last century. The inn's six rooms are wrapped in the warmth of handmade quilts, and a delightful home-cooked breakfast will tempt you out of those quilts each morning! To the east of the inn is the magnificent Green Mountains National Forest, which boasts some of the finest swimming, hiking, fishing, hunting, and skiing in Vermont. Located 13 miles to the south, Manchester, Vermont, features factory outlet shopping, while crafts and antiques can be purchased right in the heart of Danby. A wide variety of restaurants to satisfy every palate are either a short drive or walk away.

SEASON

all year

ACCOMMODATIONS

four rooms with private baths; two rooms with shared bath

Grünberg Haus
Bed and Breakfast

Christopher Sellers and
Mark Frohman
RR #2, Box 1595RD,
Route 100 South
Waterbury, Vermont 05676-9621
Tel: (800) 800-7760 or (802) 244-7726
Fax: (802) 244-1283
E-mail: grunhaus@aol.com
$$ – $$$$

ABOUT THE B&B

This picture-postcard Austrian-style B&B is tucked away on a secluded hillside in the Green Mountains, perfectly situated for visits to Stowe, Montpelier, Waterbury, and Burlington. Individually decorated guest rooms open onto the carved wood balcony, which offers wonderful views. Help Mark feed the chickens, then enjoy a full breakfast — with selections such as maple-poached pears, apple and cheddar muffins, and ricotta-stuffed French toast — while Chris plays the grand piano. The giant stone fireplace and wood stove in the BYOB pub are favorite gathering places. Nearby activities include spectacular autumn leaf-picking, world-class downhill skiing, golf, boating, bicycling, gliding, canoeing, antique hunting, outlet shopping, and touring Ben & Jerry's ice cream factory. And you can enjoy the B&B's own Jacuzzi, sauna, tennis courts, and cross-country and hiking trails.

SEASON

all year

ACCOMMODATIONS

seven rooms (including one suite)
with private baths;
five rooms with shared baths;
two cabins with private baths

Lemon Bread

1½ cups all-purpose flour
1 cup sugar
1 teaspoon baking powder
½ teaspoon salt
2 eggs
½ cup milk
½ cup vegetable oil
Grated zest of 1 lemon

Lemon glaze:
Juice of 1 lemon
⅓ cup sugar

Preheat the oven to 350°F. Stir together the flour, sugar, baking powder, and salt. In a separate bowl, beat together the eggs, milk, oil, and lemon zest, and add to the flour mixture, stirring just until blended. Pour the batter into a greased loaf pan and bake for 45 minutes. While the bread is baking, prepare the lemon glaze by heating the lemon juice and sugar together, stirring until the sugar dissolves. When the bread finishes baking, use a long skewer to poke numerous holes all the way to the bottom of the loaf. Drizzle the hot glaze over the top so it slowly soaks into the bread. Cool in the pan for 15 minutes, then turn out onto a rack to cool. *Yield: 1 loaf.*

Grünberg Haus Bed & Breakfast
Waterbury, Vermont

Ono Banana-Nut Bread

"This bread is very 'ono' — the Hawaiian word for good!"
— Susan Kauai

½ cup granulated sugar
½ cup brown sugar
½ cup butter
2 eggs
2 cups all-purpose flour
½ teaspoon baking powder
½ teaspoon salt (optional)
3 tablespoons buttermilk
1 teaspoon baking soda
3 – 4 bananas, mashed
1 cup chopped macadamia nuts, or pecans, or walnuts
1 teaspoon vanilla

Preheat the oven to 350°F. Grease a 9 x 5 x 3" loaf pan (or bundt pan, or 24 muffin cups). Cream the sugar and butter. Blend in the eggs. Sift the flour, baking powder, and salt together and add to the batter. Combine the buttermilk and baking soda and stir into the batter. Add the mashed bananas, nuts, and vanilla. Pour into the prepared pan. Bake 45 minutes if using the loaf or bundt pan, or 30 minutes if using the muffin pans. *Yield: 1 loaf.*

Kula View
Bed and Breakfast

Susan Kauai
PO Box 322, 140 Holopuni Road
Kula, Hawaii 96790
Tel: (808) 878-6736
$$

ABOUT THE B&B

Singing birds, blossoming flowers, glorious sunrises and sunsets, and sweeping panoramic views of the ocean from every window make your stay in "upcountry" Maui pure magic. Nestled in Kula at the 2,000-foot level on the slopes of Haleakala (the dormant volcano), Kula View offers an upper-level suite featuring a private entrance, private deck overlooking the flower and herb garden, queen-size bed, reading area, wicker breakfast nook, and mini refrigerator. Awake to a morning meal of exotic island fruit and juice, home-baked breads and muffins, and a pot of freshly brewed Kona coffee or tea. Kula View is located in a rural setting just 20 minutes from the Kahului Airport, close to shopping centers, restaurants, points of interest, Haleakala National Park, and beaches. Your host Susan, who's an avid hiker, gardener, and cyclist, is descended from a Kamaaina (old-time) Hawaii family. She has lived on Maui for over 19 years and will guide you to those special parts of the island as only a native resident can.

SEASON

all year

ACCOMMODATIONS

one suite with private bath

Natural Bed & Breakfast

L. Marc Haberman
3150 East Presidio Road
Tucson, Arizona 85716
Tel: (520) 881-4582
Fax: (520) 326-1385
$$

ABOUT THE B&B

As much a private retreat as a B&B, the Natural B&B offers visitors natural, whole foods served in a non-toxic, non-allergenic environment, professional therapeutic massages, and health consultation services. Wake to a full vegetarian breakfast and spend your day horseback riding in the beautiful Tucson desert or visiting the Sonora Museum (only 10 miles away). You can opt for a swim in the nearby pool or relax on the patio or sun deck. In-room telephones and laundry service are other amenities. Your host, a graphic designer, fine artist, and energy worker, invites you to share his large, homey living room with a fireplace, and enjoy a complimentary coffee, tea, or juice. If arriving from the airport, you can take an airport Stagecoach shuttle, dropping you off at the B&B's front door.

SEASON

open all year

ACCOMMODATIONS

two rooms with private baths;
two rooms with shared bath

Orange-glazed Pear-Nut Bread

16-ounce can pear halves
¼ cup vegetable oil
1 egg, lightly beaten
1 tablespoon grated orange zest
1½ cups all-purpose flour
¾ cup sugar
1 tablespoon baking powder
1 teaspoon salt
¼ teaspoon ground allspice
1 cup whole wheat flour
1 cup chopped walnuts

Glaze:
2 – 3 tablespoons orange juice
1 cup confectioners' sugar

Preheat the oven to 350°F. Drain the pears, reserving the syrup. Reserve 1 pear half for the garnish. Purée the remaining pears. Add the reserved syrup to the puréed pears to measure 1 cup. Mix the puréed pears with the oil, egg, and orange zest. Sift together the all-purpose flour, sugar, baking powder, salt, and allspice. Stir in the whole wheat flour. Stir the pear mixture into the flour mixture. Blend in the nuts. Pour into a greased 9 x 5" loaf pan. Cut the reserved pear half into 6 slices. Place the slices on the batter. Bake 50 – 55 minutes. Blend the orange juice into the confectioners' sugar to make a thin glaze. Remove the warm bread from the pan and spoon the glaze over top. Store the bread overnight before slicing. *Yield: 1 loaf.*

NATURAL
Bed & Breakfast

Paradise Pear Bread

3 cups all-purpose flour
1 teaspoon baking soda
1 teaspoon baking powder
1 teaspoon salt
1 tablespoon ground cinnamon
1 cup chopped pecans
¾ cup vegetable oil
3 eggs, lightly beaten
2 cups sugar
2 cups extra-ripe pears, peeled and diced
1 tablespoon vanilla

Preheat the oven to 350°F. Combine the flour, baking soda, baking powder, salt, cinnamon, and pecans in a large bowl, then make a well in the center of the mixture. Combine the oil, eggs, sugar, pears, and vanilla. Add to the dry ingredients, stirring just until moistened. Spoon the mixture into 2 well-greased and floured 9 x 5 x 3" loaf pans. Bake for 30 minutes, then reduce the heat to 325°F and bake until a toothpick inserted in the center comes out clean. Cool 10 minutes before removing from pans. *Yield: 2 loaves.*

Angel Arbor Bed & Breakfast Inn

Marguerite and Dean Swanson
848 Heights Boulevard
Houston, Texas 77007
Tel: (713) 868-4654
Fax: (713) 861-3189
E-mail: b-bhontx@wt.net
www.angelarbor.com
$$ – $$$

ABOUT THE B&B

A few minutes from downtown Houston, this elegant 1920s Georgian-style brick residence graces historic Heights Boulevard with its gazebo-dotted esplanade and walking trail. The first floor boasts an antique-filled parlor, a cozy reading room, a gracious formal dining room, and a sunroom for game playing or casual dining. A wicker-furnished solarium overlooks the backyard garden with its manicured lawn, angel statue, and vine-laden arbor with a tranquil sitting area. Upstairs, three spacious bedrooms, each with an angel-inspired name, feature queen beds and private baths, two with whirlpool tubs for two. A separate outside suite provides seclusion and has its own sitting room and deck. A full delicious breakfast is served daily. Former owners of Durham House B&B, Marguerite and Dean Swanson bring their many years of innkeeping experience to Angel Arbor. The B&B also hosts parties and small meetings, and Marguerite's renowned murder mystery dinner parties.

SEASON

all year

ACCOMMODATIONS

four rooms (including one suite) with private baths

The Babbling Brook Inn

Dan Floyd
1025 Laurel Street
Santa Cruz, California 95060
Tel: (800) 866-1131 or (408) 427-2437
Fax: (408) 458-0989
E-mail: lodging@
babblingbrookinn.com
$$$ – $$$$

ABOUT THE B&B

Cascading waterfalls, a meandering creek, and a romantic gazebo grace an acre of gardens, pines, and redwoods surrounding this secluded inn. Built in 1909 on the foundation of an 1870 tannery, a 1790 grist mill, and a 2,000-year old Indian fishing village, the Babbling Brook features rooms in country French decor, all with private bath, telephone, and television, and most with cozy fireplace, private deck, and outside entrance. Included in your stay is a large, country breakfast and afternoon wine and cheese, where the inn's prize-winning cookies await you on the tea cart in front of a roaring fireplace. Two blocks off Highway 1, the Babbling Brook is within walking distance of the beach, wharf, boardwalk, shops, tennis, running paths, and historic homes. Three golf courses and 200 restaurants are within 15 minutes' drive.

SEASON

all year

ACCOMMODATIONS

12 rooms with private baths

Persimmon Bread

2 eggs
2 cups brown sugar
3 tablespoons butter
2 cups fresh persimmon pulp
2 cups chopped walnuts
1 cup raisins
1 cup chopped dates
1 tablespoon grated orange zest
4 cups all-purpose flour
4 teaspoons baking soda
3 teaspoons baking powder
2 teaspoons ground cinnamon
½ teaspoon ground cloves
½ teaspoon ground allspice
½ teaspoon grated nutmeg
1 cup buttermilk
2 teaspoons vanilla

Cream cheese

Preheat the oven to 325°F. In a large bowl, beat together the eggs, sugar, butter, and persimmon pulp. Stir in the walnuts, raisins, dates, and orange zest. Sift together the flour, baking soda, baking powder, and spices and add alternately with the buttermilk and vanilla. Turn the batter into 2 well-greased 9 x 5 x 3" loaf pans. Bake for 1 hour and 15 minutes or until a toothpick inserted in the center comes out clean. Cool and serve with cream cheese. *Yield: 2 loaves.*

Pilialoha Grain Bread

"I've been baking bread for over 25 years. When we opened our B&B, I created some healthy bread and muffin recipes and this one has proved to be the most popular." — Machiko Heyde

Pre-dough mixture:
1 cup milk, scalded and then cooled to lukewarm
⅓ cup honey
1 package active dry yeast (1 tablespoon)
1 cup lukewarm water
1¾ cups all-purpose flour

Dough mixture:
2½ teaspoons salt
¼ cup vegetable oil
1 cup mixed grain of your choice (Stone-buhr brand 4 Grain Cereal
   Mates recommended)
About 3 cups all-purpose flour

Macadamia-cranberry conserve (see recipe on page 374)

To prepare the pre-dough mixture: In a large bowl, mix the milk and honey. In a small bowl, dissolve the yeast in the lukewarm water; stir well. Let dissolve 3 – 5 minutes. Add to the milk and honey in the bowl. Add the flour. With a whisk or wooden spoon, whip for 100 strokes. Cover the bowl with a towel and let the dough rest 45 minutes to 1 hour.

(continued on next page)

Pilialoha
Bed & Breakfast
Cottage

Machiko and Bill Heyde
2512 Kaupakulua Road
Haiku, Maui, Hawaii 96708-6024
Tel: (808) 572-1440
Fax: (808) 572-4612
E-mail: heyde@mauigateway.com
www.mauigateway.com/~heyde
$$$

ABOUT THE B&B

Located in cool upcountry Maui, this quiet cottage sits on lush pasture land, surrounded by a rose and flower garden and overlooking a eucalyptus grove. Only 20 minutes from Kahului Airport and less than five minutes from Makawao town, Pilialoha is also close to Haleakala National Park, the quaint town of Hana, and other points of interest. This private cottage is furnished with a full kitchen (stocked with gourmet coffees and teas), cable TV and a VCR, phone, washer/dryer, picnic coolers, beach chairs, mats and towels, snorkel gear, as well as informative books and videos. It's most comfortable for two people but will accommodate up to five. Freshly baked bread or muffins, fruit, and juice are brought to the cottage daily. Your hosts Machiko (an artist) and Bill (a self-employed computer technician) live on the same property and are available to provide visitor information during your stay.

SEASON

all year

ACCOMMODATIONS

one fully furnished cottage
with private bath

To prepare the dough mixture: Add the salt, oil, grain, and 2½ cups of the flour to the dough in the bowl. Mix with a wooden spoon, then, by hand, gradually fold in until the dough holds together and begins to come cleanly off the sides of the bowl. Flour your hands and begin kneading on a lightly floured board or countertop until the dough feels springy (the consistency of your ear lobe). You may add more flour a little at a time, if necessary, and only enough to prevent the dough from sticking to your hands (it's better to be a little on the sticky side than too dry with too much flour).

In a clean and large oiled bowl, place the kneaded dough. Cover with a towel, and let the dough rest until it has doubled in size.

Punch down the dough, knead, then place it back in the bowl. Cover and let it rise again (it will take less time to double in size this time around).

Punch the dough down and knead again. Divide the dough into 4 equal portions and shape into buns (if the dough gets too sticky, flour your hands). Place 2 buns onto each of 2 lightly greased cookie sheets, allowing about 4" space between them. Let them rise until they are almost doubled in size. Preheat the oven to 375°F and bake for 35 minutes. Serve with macadamia-cranberry conserve. *Tips:* This bread is good sliced and toasted, or for sandwiches. Place it in a plastic bag as soon as it becomes cool. Store the portion you don't plan to use within the next 2 days in your freezer. *Yield: 4 large buns.*

Rhubarb Bread

"This bread can be served with a meal or, as I enjoy it, as a mid-morning coffee cake." — Andy Aldrich

1½ cups brown sugar
¾ cup vegetable oil
1 egg
2½ cups all-purpose flour
1 cup buttermilk (or add 1 tablespoon of vinegar to fresh milk)
1 teaspoon salt
1 teaspoon baking soda
1 teaspoon ground cinnamon
1 teaspoon vanilla
2½ cups chopped rhubarb
½ cup chopped walnuts or pecans (optional)
½ cup granulated sugar
1 tablespoon butter, melted

Preheat the oven to 325°F. In a medium bowl, mix the brown sugar, oil, and egg together, then add the flour, buttermilk, salt, baking soda, cinnamon, and vanilla. Fold in the rhubarb (and the nuts, if wished). Place in 2 greased 9 x 5" loaf pans. Combine the granulated sugar and butter and glaze over the top of the loaves. Bake for 1 hour. *Yield: 2 loaves.*

The Inn at
The Brass Lantern

Andy Aldrich
717 Maple Street
Stowe, Vermont 05672
Tel: (800) 729-2980 or (802) 253-2229
Fax: (802) 253-7425
$$ – $$$$

ABOUT THE B&B

The Inn at The Brass Lantern is located at the edge of the village of Stowe, Vermont. Stowe is a full-service, four-season resort town, and boasts many world-class restaurants and activities, a cultural center, unique cottage industries, craftspeople, and artists. Originally built as a farmhouse and carriage barn, The Brass Lantern was restored by Andy Aldrich, the current innkeeper, to retain its original Vermont character (for which he won an award). Today, the inn carries the traditional Vermont B&B theme throughout — from its decor of period antiques, handmade quilts, and locally crafted amenities to the food and beverages reflecting local and Vermont state products. In addition, guests are treated to a unique ambiance and casual, attentive service. The inn's setting provides panoramic views of Mount Mansfield and its valley from nearly every room.

SEASON

all year

ACCOMMODATIONS

nine rooms with private baths

Isaiah Hall B&B Inn

Marie Brophy
PO Box 1007, 152 Whig Street
Dennis, Massachusetts 02638
Tel: (800) 736-0160 or (508) 385-9928
Fax: (508) 385-5879
$$$

ABOUT THE B&B

*E*njoy country ambiance and hospitality in the heart of Cape Cod. Located on a quiet historic street, this lovely 1857 farmhouse is a leisurely walk from the beach or village with its restaurants, shops, theater, and fine arts museum. Close by, enjoy bike trails, tennis, golf, and whale watching. The inn offers an ideal home base for day trips to other points of interest — from Provincetown to Plymouth — as well as to the Islands (including Nantucket and Martha's Vineyard). Or, you can choose to simply relax in the inn's beautiful gardens or parlor surrounded by antiques and Oriental rugs, or cozy up in the carriage house "great room" with its white wicker furniture and knotty pine walls. Guest rooms are decorated with charming country antiques with most having queen beds, a few having two beds or balconies, and one having a fireplace.

SEASON

April to October

ACCOMMODATIONS

10 rooms (including one suite)
with private baths

Spicy Pumpkin Bread

"A great fall recipe when there's an abundance of pumpkin."
— *Marie Brophy*

1 cup brown sugar, firmly packed
⅓ cup vegetable shortening
2 eggs
1 cup canned pumpkin
¼ cup milk
2 cups all-purpose flour
2 teaspoons baking powder
¼ teaspoon baking soda
½ teaspoon salt
1 teaspoon ground cloves
½ cup chopped walnuts and/or ½ cup raisins

Preheat the oven to 350°F. Cream together the sugar and shortening. Beat in the eggs. Add the pumpkin and milk and mix together well. In a separate bowl, stir together the flour, baking powder, baking soda, salt, and cloves. Add this to the wet ingredients. Stir in the walnuts and/or raisins. Pour into a greased loaf pan. Bake 55 – 60 minutes. Cool 10 minutes, remove from the pan, and cool on a rack. *Tip:* This bread freezes well. *Yield: 1 loaf.*

Vince's Five-Day Sourdough Bread

The Melville House

Vince De Rico and David Horan
39 Clarke Street
Newport, Rhode Island 02840
Tel: (401) 847-0640
Fax: (401) 847-0956
E-mail: Innkeeper@ids.net
www.melvillehouse.com
$$$ – $$$$

"Having a sourdough starter is popular out west but not here in the east. So, after months of testing, I developed this five-day starter recipe for those easterners who wanted to try their hand at a sourdough bread but didn't want to tend a starter forever. The Melville House has a starter going all the time, which is fed every day or two to keep it active." — Vince De Rico

Starter:
3 cups lukewarm water
4 cups all-purpose flour
2 tablespoons honey
1 package active dry yeast (1 tablespoon)

Variations:

- For a better sour flavor, add 3 tablespoons each of any or all of the following: buttermilk, plain yogurt, or sour cream.

- Replace 2 cups of the all-purpose flour with rye or stone-ground wheat or a mixture of the two.

(continued on next page)

ABOUT THE B&B

Built circa 1750 and on the National Register of Historic Places, The Melville House is located in the heart of Newport's historic Hill District on a quiet gas-lit street. One of the few inns in Newport dedicated to the Colonial style, it's just one block up from Thames Street with its Brick Market and the harborfront where many of the city's finest restaurants, luxurious sailboats, antique shops, and galleries can be found. The Melville House is also close to the Tennis Hall of Fame, lavish Vanderbilt, Astor, and Belmont family mansions, the Naval War College, and Newport's finest ocean beaches. The Melville House breakfast menu features homemade granola, muffins, breads, buttermilk biscuits, scones, Yankee cornbread, stuffed French toast, fresh fruit sourdough pancakes, and Rhode Island johnnycakes. An afternoon tea is served every day, featuring refreshments, homemade biscotti, and soup (on cold days), over which innkeepers Vince and David share their Newport experiences.

SEASON

all year

ACCOMMODATIONS

five rooms with private baths; two rooms with shared bath; winter fireplace suite

Bread:
1 package active dry yeast (1 tablespoon)
½ cup lukewarm water
3 tablespoons non-fat powdered milk
4 tablespoons butter, melted
4 tablespoons sugar
3 teaspoons salt
5 – 7 cups all-purpose flour
Vegetable oil

To make the starter: In a large bowl, mix the water, flour, honey, and yeast together and leave uncovered in a warm place for 1 day, stirring down several times. Cover it with a towel for another 2 – 4 days, stirring down twice a day for the remaining time. *Note:* If you already have a good starter and don't want to wait 5 days, add 3½ cups starter (if it's thin) or 4 cups starter (if it's thick) to the bread recipe below.

To make the bread: Put all of the five-day starter in a large bowl. Add the yeast to the lukewarm water and let dissolve 3 – 5 minutes. Add this to the powdered milk, butter, sugar, salt, and 3 cups of the flour. Beat the mixture until smooth, then cover with a cloth and let stand until bubbly and doubled in size. Stir in enough flour to make a workable dough and turn out on a floured board. Knead for 10 minutes until smooth, adding additional flour if needed. Cut into 2 pieces and let rest while you lightly grease 2 large bread pans. Form the dough into loaves, place in the pans, and brush the tops with oil (this keeps the crust soft and chewy). Cover with a cloth and let rise until doubled in size.

Preheat the oven to 375°F and bake 45 – 55 minutes until golden brown. Remove from the pan and place on racks to cool. *Tip:* The bread's taste is enhanced when toasted. *Yield: 2 loaves.*

Wild Blueberry-Banana Bread

⅔ cup sugar
1½ cups all-purpose flour
¼ teaspoon salt
2 teaspoons baking powder
¾ cup quick-cooking rolled oats
⅓ cup vegetable oil
2 eggs, lightly beaten
2 large bananas, mashed
¾ cup fresh or frozen wild blueberries, or raspberries or strawberries

Preheat the oven to 350°F. Sift together the sugar, flour, salt, and baking powder in a mixing bowl. Stir in the oats. Add the oil, eggs, bananas, and blueberries, and stir just until ingredients are mixed and moist. Pour into a greased and floured 9 x 5" loaf pan. Bake 60 – 65 minutes. Cool in the pan 10 minutes, remove, and let cool on a wire rack. Wrap and store in the refrigerator for several hours before slicing. **Yield: 1 loaf.**

Lindgren's Bed & Breakfast

Shirley Lindgren
County Road 35, PO Box 56
Lutsen, Minnesota 55612-0056
Tel: (218) 663-7450
$$ – $$$$

ABOUT THE B&B

Less than two hours from Duluth, Minnesota, and Thunder Bay, Ontario, this 1920s rustic log home with manicured grounds and walkable shoreline resides on Lake Superior in Superior National Forest. The living room features an 18-foot beamed ceiling, massive stone fireplace, and hunting trophies. Guest rooms are cozily designed in either knotty cedar, pine, or rustic paneling. Scenic points of interest include Split Rock Lighthouse, Gooseberry Falls, and Tettegouche State Park. Depending on the season, you can choose from hiking trails, skyrides, alpine slides, mountain biking, horseback riding, golf, tennis, fishing, snowmobiling, and cross-country and downhill skiing. Any number of fine restaurants are nearby, and you're within walking distance of Lutsen Resort, the oldest in the state. Your hosts are retired after 35 years of owning and operating a successful garden center, landscaping, nursery, and floral business in Minneapolis, and enjoy fishing, hunting and, most of all, people, which is why they opened their home as a bed and breakfast!

SEASON

all year

ACCOMMODATIONS

four rooms with private baths

Campbell Ranch Inn

Mary Jane and Jerry Campbell
1475 Canyon Road
Geyserville, California 95441
Tel: (800) 959-3878 or (707) 857-3476
Fax: (707) 857-3239
$$$$

ABOUT THE B&B

Whether swimming in the pool, relaxing in the hot tub spa, or playing tennis, you're always surrounded by the Campbell Ranch Inn's spectacular valley and mountain views and beautiful flower gardens. In warm weather, breakfast is served on the terrace where you overlook rolling hills and vineyards. Only 80 miles north of San Francisco, the Inn has five spacious rooms with king-size beds, fresh flowers, and fruit. You may choose to read or visit by the living room fireplace. Play tennis, horseshoes, or ping-pong, hike the trails at Lake Sonoma, or use the available bikes to tour the neighboring wine country. The surrounding area has many wineries and excellent restaurants, but remember to save some room for Campbell Ranch's homemade pie and coffee served every evening.

SEASON

all year

ACCOMMODATIONS

four rooms with private baths;
one private cottage
with private bath

Zucchini Bread

(Recipe from The Campbell Ranch Inn Cookbook.)

3 extra-large eggs
1 cup vegetable oil
2 cups sugar
1 teaspoon salt
1 teaspoon baking soda
1 teaspoon baking powder
3 teaspoons ground cinnamon
1 tablespoon vanilla
2 cups all-purpose flour
1 cup whole wheat flour
3 cups grated zucchini

Preheat the oven to 350°F. Cream together the eggs, oil, and sugar. Add, in this order, the salt, baking soda, baking powder, cinnamon, vanilla, flour, and zucchini. Grease 2 large loaf pans (or 6 small loaf pans) and divide the dough evenly between them. Bake for 1 hour for large loaves or 35 – 40 minutes for small loaves. Be careful not to overbake! *Tip:* This bread freezes well. ***Yield: 2 large or 6 small loaves.***

Zucchini-Nut Loaf

1½ cups all-purpose flour
½ teaspoon baking soda
¼ teaspoon baking powder
1 teaspoon ground cinnamon
½ teaspoon grated nutmeg
½ teaspoon salt
1 cup grated unpeeled zucchini
1 cup sugar
1 egg
½ cup vegetable oil
¼ teaspoon grated lemon zest
½ cup chopped walnuts

Preheat the oven to 350°F. Mix together the flour, baking soda, baking powder, cinnamon, nutmeg, and salt; set aside. In a separate mixing bowl, beat together the sugar, zucchini, and egg. Mix the oil and lemon zest in well to this mixture. Stir the flour mixture into the zucchini mixture. Fold in the walnuts. Turn the batter into a greased loaf pan and bake 55 – 60 minutes. Cool in the pan for 10 minutes, then remove and cool on a rack. *Tip:* This bread freezes well. *Yield: 1 loaf.*

Isaiah Hall B&B Inn

Marie Brophy
PO Box 1007, 152 Whig Street
Dennis, Massachusetts 02638
Tel: (800) 736-0160 or (508) 385-9928
Fax: (508) 385-5879
$$$

ABOUT THE B&B

Enjoy country ambiance and hospitality in the heart of Cape Cod. Located on a quiet historic street, this lovely 1857 farmhouse is a leisurely walk from the beach or village with its restaurants, shops, theater, and fine arts museum. Close by, enjoy bike trails, tennis, golf, and whale watching. The inn offers an ideal home base for day trips to other points of interest — from Provincetown to Plymouth — as well as to the Islands (including Nantucket and Martha's Vineyard). Or, you can choose to simply relax in the inn's beautiful gardens or parlor surrounded by antiques and Oriental rugs, or cozy up in the carriage house "great room" with its white wicker furniture and knotty pine walls. Guest rooms are decorated with charming country antiques with most having queen beds, a few having two beds or balconies, and one having a fireplace.

SEASON

April to October

ACCOMMODATIONS

10 rooms (including one suite) with private baths

Cakes

Apple Annie Coffee Cake

2 cups all-purpose flour
½ cup sugar
2 teaspoons baking powder
½ teaspoon salt
¼ cup vegetable shortening
1 egg
½ cup milk
1 teaspoon vanilla
2 cups peeled and thinly sliced apple
½ cup brown sugar, firmly packed
½ teaspoon ground cinnamon
¼ teaspoon grated nutmeg
⅓ cup butter, melted

Preheat the oven to 400°F. Sift the flour, sugar, baking powder, and salt together, then cut in the shortening. Combine the egg, milk, and vanilla and beat lightly until well mixed. Add to the dry ingredients and mix only until moistened (batter will be stiff). Spread the batter into a well-greased 8" square pan. Arrange the sliced apples evenly over the top of the batter. Combine the cinnamon, nutmeg, and brown sugar. Sprinkle over the sliced apples. Drizzle the melted butter over the sugar and spices. Bake for 25 minutes. Serve warm. *Yield: About 6 servings.*

Angel Arbor
Bed & Breakfast Inn

Marguerite and Dean Swanson
848 Heights Boulevard
Houston, Texas 77007
Tel: (713) 868-4654
Fax: (713) 861-3189
E-mail: b-bhontx@wt.net
www.angelarbor.com
$$ – $$$

ABOUT THE B&B

A few minutes from downtown Houston, this elegant 1920s Georgian-style brick residence graces historic Heights Boulevard with its gazebo-dotted esplanade and walking trail. The first floor boasts an antique-filled parlor, a cozy reading room, a gracious formal dining room, and a sunroom for game playing or casual dining. A wicker-furnished solarium overlooks the backyard garden with its manicured lawn, angel statue, and vine-laden arbor with a tranquil sitting area. Upstairs, three spacious bedrooms, each with an angel-inspired name, feature queen beds and private baths, two with whirlpool tubs for two. A separate outside suite provides seclusion and has its own sitting room and deck. A full delicious breakfast is served daily. Former owners of Durham House B&B, Marguerite and Dean Swanson bring their many years of innkeeping experience to Angel Arbor. The B&B also hosts parties and small meetings, and Marguerite's renowned murder mystery dinner parties.

SEASON

all year

ACCOMMODATIONS

four rooms (including one suite)
with private baths

The Inn at
The Brass Lantern

Andy Aldrich
717 Maple Street
Stowe, Vermont 05672
Tel: (800) 729-2980 or (802) 253-2229
Fax: (802) 253-7425
$$ – $$$$

ABOUT THE B&B

The Inn at The Brass Lantern is located at the edge of the village of Stowe, Vermont. Stowe is a full-service, four-season resort town, and boasts many world-class restaurants and activities, a cultural center, unique cottage industries, craftspeople, and artists. Originally built as a farmhouse and carriage barn, The Brass Lantern was restored by Andy Aldrich, the current innkeeper, to retain its original Vermont character (for which he won an award). Today, the inn carries the traditional Vermont B&B theme throughout — from its decor of period antiques, handmade quilts, and locally crafted amenities to the food and beverages reflecting local and Vermont state products. In addition, guests are treated to a unique ambiance and casual, attentive service. The inn's setting provides panoramic views of Mount Mansfield and its valley from nearly every room.

SEASON

all year

ACCOMMODATIONS

nine rooms with private baths

Apple Crumb Cake

"A special favorite for the Brass Lantern's afternoon tea."
— Andy Aldrich

Crumb topping:
¼ cup sugar
3 tablespoons all-purpose flour
½ teaspoon ground cinnamon
2 tablespoons butter

Batter:
2 cups all-purpose flour
1¼ cups sugar
1 tablespoon baking powder
1¼ teaspoons ground cinnamon
1 teaspoon salt
½ teaspoon baking soda
½ teaspoon ground allspice
¼ teaspoon ground cloves
½ cup butter, melted
1¼ cups sour cream
2 eggs
1½ cups finely diced apple

Preheat the oven to 350°F. Butter a 9" tube pan. In a small bowl, mix together the crumb topping ingredients. In a large bowl, mix the batter ingredients. Spread the cake batter into the pan and sprinkle on the crumb topping. Bake for approximately 60 minutes, then let cool and serve. *Yield: 10 – 12 servings.*

Applesauce Cake

"Our family never liked fruitcake so at Christmas my mother baked an applesauce cake to which she added glazed fruit and nuts. This particular recipe, which was given to me by one of the inn's first guests, reminds me of my childhood Christmas traditions."
— *Pat O'Brien*

¾ cup raisins
⅓ cup cream sherry or apple juice
½ cup vegetable oil
1½ cups brown sugar
1 teaspoon salt
½ teaspoon ground cinnamon
½ teaspoon ground allspice
¼ teaspoon ground cloves
¼ teaspoon grated nutmeg
2 eggs
1½ cups applesauce
2½ cups all-purpose flour
¾ cup chopped walnuts (optional)
2 teaspoons baking soda

Preheat the oven to 350°F. Grease and flour a 12-cup bundt pan (or 9 x 5" loaf pan or 12-cup muffin pan). In a medium saucepan, combine the raisins and sherry and heat to boiling; set aside. In a mixing bowl, beat the oil, sugar, salt, spices, and eggs until smooth and creamy (scrape the bowl often). Blend in the applesauce, then the flour and walnuts. Stir the baking soda into the raisin mixture and add to the batter. Mix well, then pour into the bundt pan. Bake 45 minutes. **Yield: 12 – 16 servings.**

Blue Spruce Inn

Pat and Tom O'Brien
2815 Main Street
Soquel, California 95073
Tel: (800) 559-1137 or (408) 464-1137
Fax: (408) 475-0608
E-mail: pobrien@
BlueSpruce.com
$$ – $$$$

ABOUT THE B&B

The Blue Spruce Inn welcomes you with the distinct Pacific breeze that freshens the Central Coast hillsides golden with poppies, tempers the heat of the summer sun, and warms the sands during afternoon strolls on winter beaches. The inn is four miles south of Santa Cruz and one mile from Capitola Beach at the northern curve of Monterey Bay. Gracious personal service is the hallmark of this 1875 B&B inn, where beds are graced with Amish quilts and walls hung with original local art that blends the flavor of yesteryear with the luxury of today. There are quiet gardens in which to enjoy the sunshine of Soquel Village, delightful antique shops at the corner of the street, and, a little farther, wineries, gift shops, and regional art displays. Bountiful breakfasts feature fresh fruit, homemade breads, and exceptional entrées. At the end of the day, the hot tub offers welcome respite and, when guests return to their rooms, pillows are fluffed and a special treat awaits.

SEASON

all year

ACCOMMODATIONS

five rooms with private baths

Barry's Gull Cottage
Bed and Breakfast

Vivian and Bob Barry
116 Chesapeake Street
Dewey Beach, Delaware 19971
Tel/Fax: (302) 227-7000
$$$ – $$$$

ABOUT THE B&B

Named "one of the best places to stay at the beach" by The Washingtonian Magazine, *Gull Cottage* is a contemporary Nantucket-style beach house nestled in a pine and cherry grove, one-and-a-half blocks from the ocean and across the street from Lake Comegys. The warm and cozy decor includes antiques, white wicker furniture, quilts, stained glass, skylights, and ceiling fans. A full country gourmet breakfast is served on the screened porch, followed by afternoon tea and evening cake and coffee. The area offers many things to do: early morning walks along the dunes, windsurfing, water-skiing, fishing, and factory outlet shopping, to name a few. Nearby dining ranges from French cuisine to fresh seafood, and, to end the evening, you can relax by candlelight in the cottage's hot tub. Innkeepers Vivian and Bob Barry are retired Central Intelligence Agency officers who enjoy cooking for and pampering their guests.

SEASON

May to October

ACCOMMODATIONS

three rooms with private baths; two rooms with half baths

Aunt Doris's Dark Fruitcake

(*Recipe from* Secrets from the Pantry Kitchen of Gull Cottage.)

"This cake was a specialty of my Aunt Doris, who was always secretive about the recipe. It took me 40 years to finally convince her that I was worthy of having it!" — *Vivian Barry*

3 cups raisins
4 cups water
1 cup vegetable shortening
2 cups sugar
2 teaspoons ground cinnamon
2 teaspoons ground cloves
2 teaspoons ground allspice
1½ cups maraschino cherries
1 cup finely diced lemon zest
1 cup candied citron
1 cup chopped walnuts
4 eggs, lightly beaten
4 cups all-purpose flour
2 teaspoons baking soda
Pinch of salt

Boil the raisins in the water for 20 minutes. Strain the raisins and set aside 2 cups of the raisin water. Preheat the oven to 350°F. Mix the shortening and sugar. Add the raisins, cinnamon, cloves, allspice, cherries, lemon zest, citron, and walnuts, mixing well. Mix in the eggs. Combine the flour, baking soda, and salt. Add the raisin water to the batter, alternating with the dry ingredients and mixing well. Pour into a greased 12" cake pan or two 6" cake pans. Bake for 1 hour and 15 minutes or until a toothpick inserted in the center comes out clean. *Yield: 12 servings.*

Austrian Breakfast Cake

2 eggs
1 cup milk
1 teaspoon vanilla
2½ cups all-purpose flour
1½ cups sugar
¾ cup cold butter
½ cup finely chopped nuts

Preheat the oven to 375°F. Whisk together the eggs, milk, and vanilla. In a separate bowl, blend together the flour, sugar, butter, and nuts to make coarse meal. Reserve ½ of this dry mixture. Stir the egg mixture into the dry mixture, and pour into a greased 12" bundt pan. Sprinkle the remaining dry mixture over the batter. Bake 25 – 30 minutes. *Yield: 12 servings.*

Alpen Rose Bed & Breakfast

Robin and Rupert Sommerauer
PO Box 769, 244 Forest Trail
Winter Park, Colorado 80482
Tel: (970) 726-5039
Fax: (970) 726-0993
$$ – $$$

ABOUT THE B&B

*H*idden in the forest just minutes from downtown Winter Park, the Alpen Rose is a bed and breakfast with Austrian warmth and hospitality. Share Robin and Rupert's love of the mountains by taking in the breathtaking view from the common room, enhanced by aspens, wildflowers, and lofty pines. At Alpen Rose, you'll feel right at home whatever the season — enjoying the spare cozy slippers, lushly quilted beds with down pillows, and steaming outdoor hot tub. What's more, each of the five bedrooms is decorated with treasures brought over from Austria, including traditional featherbeds. A full breakfast featuring homemade yogurt, granola, fresh fruit, freshly baked coffee cake or bread, an egg dish, and a meat dish awaits guests each morning in the sunny common room. Rupert was born in Salzburg, Austria. Robin, an American, met him in Germany after a stint there with Outward Bound.

SEASON

all year

ACCOMMODATIONS

five rooms with private baths

Custer Mansion B&B

Carole and Mill Seaman
35 Centennial Drive
Custer, South Dakota 57730
Tel: (605) 673-3333
$$ – $$$

ABOUT THE B&B

This unusual 1891 Victorian Gothic home is on the National Register of Historic Places. Antique light fixtures, ceiling fans, door transoms, stained glass windows, and gingerbread accents help preserve Custer Mansion's turn-of-the-century mood. Bedrooms, including one family suite and two honeymoon/anniversary suites, are individually decorated in country and Victorian flavor and are named for songs. Delicious home cooked breakfasts are served in the spacious dining room, with an adjacent butler pantry used for serving juice, coffee, and tea. The one-acre yard offers plenty of room for outdoor relaxing and features a shaded patio near a natural rocky hillside. Custer Mansion is located near Mount Rushmore, Crazy Horse Memorial, Custer State Park, and many other attractions. Nearby activities include swimming, hiking, fishing, golfing, and hiking in the beautiful Black Hills. Mill, a retired school administrator, and Carole, mother of six and grandmother of 15, specialize in western hospitality and delicious food.

SEASON

all year

ACCOMMODATIONS

five rooms (including three suites) with private baths

Blueberry Buckle Cake

¾ cup sugar
¼ cup vegetable oil
1 egg
½ cup milk
2 cups all-purpose flour
2 teaspoons baking powder
½ teaspoon salt
2 cups well-drained blueberries (fresh, canned, or frozen)

Crumb topping:
½ cup sugar
⅓ cup all-purpose flour
½ teaspoon ground cinnamon
¼ cup butter, softened

Preheat the oven to 375°F. Cream the sugar, oil, and egg together. Add the milk and blend well. Sift the flour, baking powder, and salt together. Stir into the creamed mixture (do not beat). Carefully fold in the blueberries. Spread the batter in a greased 9" square pan. Mix the ingredients for the crumb topping and sprinkle over the batter. Bake 45 – 50 minutes if using fresh blueberries and approximately 30 – 35 minutes if using canned or frozen blueberries. *Yield: 9 servings.*

Blueberry-Oat Coffee Cake

1 cup blueberries
2 tablespoons and ½ cup sugar
⅓ cup margarine, at room temperature
1 egg
¾ cup all-purpose flour
1 teaspoon baking powder
⅓ cup large-flake rolled oats
½ teaspoon grated lemon zest
½ teaspoon ground cinnamon
½ cup plain low-fat yogurt

Preheat the oven to 350°F. Grease the bottom and sides of a 9" round layer pan. Line the bottom with parchment or waxed paper. In a small bowl, combine the blueberries and 2 tablespoons of sugar. Spoon the mixture into the pan. In a large bowl, cream the margarine with ½ cup sugar. Add the egg and beat until light and fluffy. Combine the flour, baking powder, oats, lemon zest, and cinnamon. Stir into the egg mixture, alternating with the yogurt. Spoon the batter over the berries. Bake 30 – 40 minutes. *Yield: 8 servings.*

Bed & Breakfast at Edie's

Edie Senalik
PO Box 351, 233 East Harpole
Williamsville, Illinois 62693
Tel: (217) 566-2538
$ – $$

ABOUT THE B&B

Step back in time to an era when life was more leisurely. Bed & Breakfast at Edie's is located in the peaceful and charming village of Williamsville, Illinois, just 10 minutes north of Springfield. The 1915 mission-style house is large and gracious. Edie serves a delicious and bountiful continental breakfast, with homemade bagels being her specialty. Sleep in queen-size beds with down pillows. Relax in the large living room, TV room, or enjoy the wide wraparound veranda or rear patio. The nearby state capitol offers plays, symphonies, Abraham Lincoln's home and tomb, and many other interesting attractions. Lincoln's New Salem village is just 20 minutes to the east.

SEASON

all year

ACCOMMODATIONS

four rooms with shared baths

1874 Stonehouse on Mulberry Hill

Carrie and Dan Riggs
RR #1, Box 67A
Cottonwood Falls, Kansas 66845
Tel: (316) 273-8481
E-mail: shmh1874@aol.com
$$

ABOUT THE B&B

If these stone walls could talk! This historic farmhouse was built of quarried stone in 1874 and today has been restored and modernized as a B&B. Three upstairs bedrooms have distinctive furnishings, while the downstairs fireplace room and parlor offer inviting places for conversation or reading. Breakfast is served in the cozy fireplace room aglow with the morning sun. Fresh coffee and pastries and a full country breakfast are served. 1874 Stonehouse has over 120 acres to explore, including over 10 acres of woods, a fishing pond, old stone fences, and a river valley. The area is a haven for birders, cyclists, hikers, naturalists, antique hunters, historians, and photographers — or anyone escaping the city for a quiet and romantic break in the beautiful Flint Hills of Kansas.

SEASON

all year

ACCOMMODATIONS

three rooms with private baths

Blueberry-Sour Cream Somersault Coffee Cake

"This cake makes a wonderful centerpiece when garnished with fresh fruit." — Carrie Riggs

Topping:
¾ cup sugar
2 tablespoons ground cinnamon
1 cup finely chopped pecans

18¼-ounce package yellow cake mix
4 eggs, well beaten
1 cup sour cream
¼ cup vegetable oil
3¼-ounce package instant vanilla pudding
¾ cup water
1 teaspoon vanilla
1 cup fresh blueberries
Fresh fruit, sliced (optional)

Preheat the oven to 350°F. Grease a large bundt pan. Mix the sugar, cinnamon, and pecans together and set aside. Combine the cake mix, eggs, sour cream, oil, pudding mix, water, and vanilla and mix well. Cover the bottom and sides of the pan with ½ of the topping mixture then pour ½ of the batter into the pan, sprinkle with the blueberries, then cover with the remaining batter. Bake for 1 hour. Set on a rack and let cool completely. Invert onto a plate, garnish with fresh fruit slices if desired, and serve. *Tip:* This is a very moist cake and can be made ahead and left in the pan for up to 2 days before serving "fresh from the oven." *Yield: 12 servings.*

Bourbon Street Fudge Cake

(Recipe from The Best of High Meadows — A Selected Recipe Collection.*)*

"This is the best chocolate cake ever! It tastes delicious with cream cheese frosting or with fresh raspberries or strawberries."
— *Peter Sushka*

Dusting of unsweetened cocoa
1¾ cups water
2 teaspoons instant coffee
¼ cup bourbon
5 ounces unsweetened chocolate
1 cup butter
2 cups sugar
2 cups all-purpose flour
1 teaspoon baking soda
2 eggs
1 teaspoon vanilla

Grease a bundt pan and dust it with the unsweetened cocoa (this will work better than flour). Preheat the oven to 275°F (no higher!). Simmer the water, coffee, and bourbon together for 3 minutes. Add the chocolate and butter and stir gently over medium heat until melted and smooth. Remove from the heat, stir in the sugar until blended, and cool 3 minutes. Transfer the chocolate to a large bowl of an electric mixer. In another bowl, stir together the flour and baking soda. At medium speed, add the flour ½ cup at a time to the chocolate batter, then mix another minute. Add the eggs 1 at a time, then add the vanilla (the batter will be thin). Pour it into the bundt pan and bake for 1 hour and 20 minutes or until done. Cool it on a rack 20 minutes. *Tip:* This cake is best if not refrigerated. *Yield: 12 – 14 servings.*

High Meadows Inn

Peter Sushka and Mary Jae Abbitt
High Meadows Lane, Route 4, Box 6
Scottsville, Virginia 24590
Tel: (800) 232-1832 or (804) 286-2218
Fax: (804) 286-2124
E-mail: peterhmi@aol.com
www.highmeadows.com
$$ – $$$$

ABOUT THE B&B

As Virginia's only inn that is on the National Register of Historic Homes and has a Renaissance farm vineyard, High Meadows offers a rare opportunity to experience 170 years of architectural history and 10 years of new viticultural growth. High Meadows is a grand house, where guests are welcomed with champagne and stay in rooms furnished with period antiques and art, each with private bath. The innkeepers' many special touches and attention to detail make your visit one to be remembered. Enjoy the simplicity of nature on the 50 surrounding acres of gardens, footpaths, forests, and ponds. Owner/chef Peter Sushka ensures that dining at High Meadows is just as pleasurable as lodging there. Start with a breakfast of fresh orange juice, a variety of homemade breads, muffins, and scones, fresh fruit, gourmet egg dishes, and coffee or tea. End your day with a multi-course dinner, offering distinctive northern European and Mediterranean dishes.

SEASON

all year

ACCOMMODATIONS

14 rooms (including four suites)
with private baths

Bed & Breakfast at Sills Inn

Tony Sills and Glenn Blind
270 Montgomery Avenue
Versailles, Kentucky 40383
Tel (800) 526-9801 or (606) 873-4478
Fax: (606) 873-7099
E-mail: SillsInn@aol.com
$$ – $$$$

ABOUT THE B&B

G uests are treated to true southern hospitality as soon as they step into this restored 1911, three-story Victorian inn in downtown Versailles — the center of bluegrass horse country and just seven minutes west of Lexington Airport/ Keeneland Racetrack and 10 minutes from the Lexington area. Each of the 12 accommodations is distinctively decorated and has its own private bath, including nine suites with double Jacuzzis. A full gourmet breakfast is served on the sun porch, complete with china, crystal, and linen. Guests are also treated to freshly baked chocolate-chip cookies, refreshments, and popcorn any time they're in need of a snack. The pampering continues as guests choose from the inn's restaurant menu book, have dinner reservations made for them, and are given a map highlighting their way to the restaurant.

SEASON

all year

ACCOMMODATIONS

12 rooms (including nine suites) with private baths

Brown Sugar Pound Cake

1 cup butter (no substitutes)
1 cup brown sugar
2 cups granulated sugar
6 eggs
1 heaping cup sour cream
2 teaspoons almond extract
¼ teaspoon baking soda
3 cups all-purpose flour
2 cups chopped pecans

Preheat the oven to 300°F. Melt the butter; cream with the sugar. Add the eggs, sour cream, and almond extract. Add the baking soda and flour. Add the pecans. Spray 18 mini bundt pans well with nonstick cooking spray. Pour in the batter and bake 30 – 35 minutes. *Yield: 18 mini bundt cakes.*

Carrot Spice Cake

1⅓ cups butter
1¾ cups sugar
4 eggs
2 cups all-purpose flour
2 teaspoons baking soda
1 teaspoon ground cinnamon
½ teaspoon ground allspice
¼ teaspoon grated nutmeg
¼ teaspoon ground cloves
3 cups grated carrot
1¼ cups chopped walnuts and ¼ cup whole walnuts (for decoration)
¼ cup golden raisins

Cream cheese frosting:
¼ cup butter, softened
6 ounces cream cheese, softened
2¾ cups confectioners' sugar
2 teaspoons lemon juice

Preheat the oven to 325°F. Grease and flour 2 cake pans (9 or 10"). Cream the butter and sugar until light and fluffy, then add the eggs 1 at a time. Sift the flour, baking soda, and spices together, add to the butter mixture, and blend well. Stir in the carrots, chopped walnuts, and raisins. Spread into the pans and bake 45 – 55 minutes, then cool before taking out of pans. To make the frosting, cream the butter and cream cheese together, then add the sugar and lemon juice. Beat until smooth. Frost the cakes when cool, stack one on top of the other, and decorate the layer cake with the whole walnuts. *Yield: 12 – 16 servings.*

The Inn at The Brass Lantern

Andy Aldrich
717 Maple Street
Stowe, Vermont 05672
Tel: (800) 729-2980 or (802) 253-2229
Fax: (802) 253-7425
$$ – $$$$

ABOUT THE B&B

The Inn at The Brass Lantern is located at the edge of the village of Stowe, Vermont. Stowe is a full-service, four-season resort town, and boasts many world-class restaurants and activities, a cultural center, unique cottage industries, craftspeople, and artists. Originally built as a farmhouse and carriage barn, The Brass Lantern was restored by Andy Aldrich, the current innkeeper, to retain its original Vermont character (for which he won an award). Today, the inn carries the traditional Vermont B&B theme throughout — from its decor of period antiques, handmade quilts, and locally crafted amenities to the food and beverages reflecting local and Vermont state products. In addition, guests are treated to a unique ambiance and casual, attentive service. The inn's setting provides panoramic views of Mount Mansfield and its valley from nearly every room.

SEASON

all year

ACCOMMODATIONS

nine rooms with private baths

Middle Plantation Inn

Shirley and Dwight Mullican
9549 Liberty Road
Frederick, Maryland 21701-3246
Tel: (301) 898-7128
E-mail: BandB@MPInn.com
www.MPInn.com
$$$

ABOUT THE B&B

This charming stone and log home, nestled on 26 acres, offers guests a peaceful setting, which includes Addison's Run (a nearby brook) and a 10-acre woods. You'll wake each morning to the sound of birds (and an occasional rooster) and see nature in all its glory. Your hosts take great pleasure in sharing their antique furnishings. Each guest room offers a delightful 19th-century ambiance combined with the modern conveniences of private bath, air conditioning, and TV. A massive stone fireplace, stained glass windows, and skylights highlight the public Keeping Room (a Colonial term for gathering place). A breakfast of seasonal fruit, fresh baked bread, cheese, and cereal are served each morning. Visit 33 historic blocks of downtown Frederick, with its mix of specialty and antique shops, dining establishments, museum, and art galleries. Nearby is New Market — antique capitol of Maryland. The inn is located near Baltimore (Maryland), the Antietam Battlefield in Sharpesburg (Maryland), Washington (DC), Gettysburg (Pennsylvania), and Harpers Ferry (West Virginia).

SEASON

all year

ACCOMMODATIONS

four rooms with private baths

Cherry Coffee Cake

18¼-ounce package yellow cake mix
1 cup all-purpose flour
1 package active dry yeast (1 tablespoon)
⅔ cup lukewarm water
2 eggs
21-ounce can cherry pie filling, or any other pie filling
⅓ cup butter or margarine

Glaze:
1 cup sifted confectioners' sugar
1 tablespoon light corn syrup
1 tablespoon water

Preheat the oven to 350°F. Combine 1½ cups of the cake mix, the flour, and yeast in a bowl; add the lukewarm water, stirring until smooth. Stir in the eggs. Spoon the batter into a greased 13 x 9 x 2" pan. Spoon the pie filling evenly over the batter; set aside. Cut the butter into the remaining cake mix with a pastry blender or fork until the mixture is crumbled. Sprinkle it over the pie filling. Bake 25 – 30 minutes. While the cake is cooling in the pan on a wire rack, prepare the glaze by combining the confectioners' sugar, corn syrup, and water. Drizzle the glaze over the cake and cut it into squares. *Yield: 15 – 18 servings.*

Cinnamon Coffee Cake

Batter:
½ cup margarine
2 eggs, lightly beaten
2 cups all-purpose flour
1 teaspoon baking powder
1 teaspoon baking soda
1 teaspoon vanilla
¾ cup sugar
1 cup buttermilk
Dash of salt

Topping:
1 tablespoon ground cinnamon
¾ cup brown sugar
3 tablespoons margarine, melted
1 cup chopped nuts of your choice

Glaze:
1 cup sugar
2 teaspoons vanilla
½ cup milk
½ cup butter

Preheat the oven to 340°F. Mix all batter ingredients together. Pour ½ the batter into a greased 13 x 9" baking pan. Mix all topping ingredients and sprinkle the batter in the pan with ½ of the topping. Add the rest of the batter to the pan, followed by the remaining topping. Bake for 45 minutes. While the cake is still warm, prepare the glaze by boiling all the ingredients together (do not beat) for 1 minute. Pour the hot glaze over the cake. *Yield: 12 servings.*

Down to Earth Lifestyles Bed and Breakfast

Lola and Bill Coons
12500 North West Crooked Road
Parkville, Missouri 64152
Tel: (816) 891-1018
$$

ABOUT THE B&B

Located near downtown Kansas City, Down to Earth Lifestyles is a beautiful earth-integrated home situated on 86 acres of peaceful woods and rolling hills. Each quiet, cozy room features private baths, telephones, radios, color TV, and skylights or picture windows. Spacious leisure areas include a guest lounge and patio where you can enjoy a cold beverage and complimentary popcorn, and an indoor, heated swimming pool where you can take a soothing dip. The "great room" is the perfect place to relax with music, games, books, and magazines, or just relax in front of the fire. Comfortable walking shoes are a must as nature and wildlife are abundant. Stroll through woods and over pastures among the cattle, horses, and geese. Fishermen will want to try their luck in the two stocked ponds. Breakfast is truly a mouthwatering experience, served where and when you'd like. Your hosts have a background in education, music, counseling, and agriculture, and invite you to commune with nature and enjoy their down-to-earth hospitality.

SEASON

all year

ACCOMMODATIONS

four rooms with private baths

Singleton House

Barbara Gavron
11 Singleton
Eureka Springs, Arkansas 72632
Tel: (800) 833-3394 or (501) 253-9111
$$ – $$$

ABOUT THE B&B

Singleton House is an old-fashioned place with a touch of magic. Sheltering a hidden enchanted garden on a hillside in Eureka Spring's historic district, this 1890s Victorian home is whimsically decorated with an eclectic collection of cherished antiques and unexpected treasures. Light and airy guest rooms are furnished with romantic touches and homey comforts. In addition, a honeymoon cottage with a Jacuzzi for two is located in a separate wooded area. Enjoy a full breakfast served on the balcony overlooking the fantasy wildflower garden, winding stone paths, and a lily-filled goldfish pond. Browse through the small nature library and identify the feathered inhabitants of some 50 birdhouses scattered over the grounds. A short stroll down a scenic wooded footpath leads to shops and cafes. For would-be B&Bers, your host offers an apprenticeship program with hands-on training for anyone wanting to try on the innkeeper's hat before taking the plunge!

SEASON

all year

ACCOMMODATIONS

five rooms (including one suite)
with private baths;
one honeymoon cottage with
private bath

Couscous Cake with Apricot Glaze

"This recipe is excellent for people watching their sugar intake."
— *Barbara Gavron*

Batter:
5 cups apple juice
Pinch of sea salt
Grated zest and juice of 1 lemon
5 – 8 tablespoons agar-agar flakes*
2 cups couscous (uncooked)
1 cup dried apricots, soaked until soft

Apricot glaze:
3 cups apple juice
3 tablespoons kudzu powder or arrowroot**
Pinch of sea salt
1 – 2 tablespoons rice syrup* or barley malt (optional, for extra sweetness)**
2 cups dried apricots, soaked until soft
1 cup slivered almonds, toasted

*Agar-agar is an unflavored, gelatinous product made from seaweed that's high in protein. You can find it in health food stores.

**Kudzu powder is a thickening agent made from a fast-growing green, popular in Japan and China. You can find it in Asian markets and health food stores.

***Rice syrup is made from brown rice and is used as a natural sweetener instead of sugar. You can find it in health food stores.

(continued on next page)

Bring the apple juice and salt to a boil in a saucepan. Add the lemon zest and juice. Add the agar-agar and cook until the flakes dissolve. Add the couscous, lower the heat, and stir until almost thick. Remove this mixture from the stove and stir in the apricots. Oil a mold and pour the mixture into it (you may also use a cake pan). If using a mold, allow the cake to cool, unmold it, then spoon the glaze over the cake.

To make the glaze, bring 2½ cups of the apple juice to a simmer. Add the kudzu to the ½ cup remaining cold apple juice and dissolve, then add to the simmering apple juice and stir until thickened. Add a pinch of salt and the rice syrup, if desired. Stir in the apricots, pour this glaze over the couscous cake, and scatter almonds over the glaze. *Yield: 8 – 10 servings.*

The Shaw House Bed and Breakfast

Mary and Joe Shaw
613 Cypress Court
Georgetown, South Carolina 29440
Tel: (803) 546-9663
$$

ABOUT THE B&B

The Shaw House Bed and Breakfast is a spacious two-story home in a serene, natural setting. From the glass-walled den, enjoy bird-watching and a beautiful view overlooking miles of marshland formed by four rivers, which converge and flow into the Intercoastal Waterway. Outlined by tall white columns, the wide front porch extends the width of the home and features old-fashioned rockers — ready and waiting for guests who are welcomed as family. All rooms are air conditioned, with private baths and a smattering of antiques. Enjoy a full southern breakfast come morning and bed turn-backs and chocolate come bedtime.

SEASON

all year

ACCOMMODATIONS

three rooms with private baths

Delicious Apple Cake

1½ cups vegetable oil
3 eggs
2¼ cups sugar
2 teaspoons vanilla
3 cups all-purpose flour
1 teaspoon baking soda
1 teaspoon salt
1½ cups chopped pecans
3 cups peeled sliced apple

Glaze:
1 cup light brown sugar
¼ cup half-and-half
½ cup butter

Preheat the oven to 300°F. Mix the oil, eggs, sugar, and vanilla together. In a separate bowl, sift together the flour, baking soda, and salt. Combine the 2 mixtures and blend well. Fold in the pecans and apple slices. Pour the batter into a greased tube pan and bake for 1 hour and 45 minutes. To make the glaze, combine the sugar, half-and-half, and butter in a saucepan and bring to a boil. Boil for 3 minutes. Pour it over the hot cake and let the cake set in the pan for 2 hours before serving. *Yield: 20 generous servings.*

Graham-Streusel Coffee Cake

"Our guests often seem embarrassed to have eaten a whole basket of this coffee cake." — Christopher Sellers

Streusel:
1½ cups graham cracker crumbs
¾ cup chopped walnuts
¾ cup brown sugar, firmly packed
1½ teaspoons ground cinnamon
⅔ cup butter, melted

Batter:
18¼-ounce package yellow cake mix
1 cup water
¼ cup vegetable oil
3 eggs

Maple icing:
1 cup confectioners' sugar
Maple syrup

Preheat the oven to 350°F. For the streusel, combine the graham cracker crumbs, walnuts, brown sugar, and cinnamon. Stir in the melted butter. Set aside. Combine the cake mix, water, vegetable oil, and eggs. Beat on low speed until moistened, then on high speed for 2 minutes. Pour ½ the batter into a greased 13 x 9" pan. Bake for 7 minutes, then top with the remaining batter and ½ the streusel topping. Bake 7 minutes longer, then top with the remaining streusel topping. Continue baking 35 – 40 minutes. Cool. For the maple icing, combine the confectioners' sugar with enough maple syrup to make a mixture that is of drizzling consistency. Drizzle this over the cool cake. *Yield: 12 – 14 servings.*

Grünberg Haus Bed & Breakfast
Waterbury, Vermont

Grünberg Haus Bed and Breakfast

Christopher Sellers and
Mark Frohman
RR #2, Box 1595RD,
Route 100 South
Waterbury, Vermont 05676-9621
Tel: (800) 800-7760 or (802) 244-7726
Fax: (802) 244-1283
E-mail: grunhaus@aol.com
$$ – $$$$

ABOUT THE B&B

This picture-postcard Austrian-style B&B is tucked away on a secluded hillside in the Green Mountains, perfectly situated for visits to Stowe, Montpelier, Waterbury, and Burlington. Individually decorated guest rooms open onto the carved wood balcony, which offers wonderful views. Help Mark feed the chickens, then enjoy a full breakfast — with selections such as maple-poached pears, apple and cheddar muffins, and ricotta-stuffed French toast — while Chris plays the grand piano. The giant stone fireplace and wood stove in the BYOB pub are favorite gathering places. Nearby activities include spectacular autumn leaf-picking, world-class downhill skiing, golf, boating, bicycling, gliding, canoeing, antique hunting, outlet shopping, and touring Ben & Jerry's ice cream factory. And you can enjoy the B&B's own Jacuzzi, sauna, tennis courts, and cross-country and hiking trails.

SEASON

all year

ACCOMMODATIONS

seven rooms (including one suite)
with private baths;
five rooms with shared baths;
two cabins with private baths

Garth Woodside Mansion

Diane and Irv Feinberg
RR #3, Box 578
Hannibal, Missouri 63401
Tel: (573) 221-2789
E-mail: Garth@nemonet.com
www.hanmo.com/garth
$$ – $$$

ABOUT THE B&B

*E**xperience affordable elegance in this 1871 Victorian country estate on 39 acres of meadows and woodlands. On the National Register of Historic Places, Garth Woodside Mansion has remained unchanged outside, and graceful arched doors, handsomely decorated rooms featuring original furnishings spanning over 150 years, and magnificent three-story spiral "Flying Staircase" await you inside. You'll enjoy marble fireplaces, canopy beds, your own nightshirt to wear during your stay, an exceptional full breakfast, an afternoon beverage, and more. All rooms are air conditioned and have a private bath. The location is ideal for seeing Mark Twain Country.*

SEASON

all year

ACCOMMODATIONS

eight rooms with private baths

Ladyfinger Cake

(*Recipe from* Breakfast Inn Bed, Easy and Elegant Recipes from Garth Woodside Mansion.)

8 ounces cream cheese
1 cup sugar
1 teaspoon vanilla
2 cups heavy cream
3 packages unfilled ladyfingers (about 30)
21-ounce can pie filling (cherry, blueberry, or strawberry)

Mix the cream cheese, sugar, and vanilla. In a separate bowl, beat the cream until stiff. Add it to the cheese mixture. Line the bottom and sides of a 9" springform pan with the ladyfingers, putting the brown side of the ladyfingers toward the pan. Layer the cheese mixture and the remaining ladyfingers, ending with the cheese mixture. Refrigerate the cake overnight. Release the springform pan and top with the pie filling of your choice. Keep the cake refrigerated until you're ready to serve.
Yield: 10 – 12 servings.

Lemon-Walnut Breakfast Cake

"My all-time favorite!" — Lily Vieyra

⅓ cup butter
¾ cup sugar
2 eggs
1⅛ cups all-purpose flour
⅛ teaspoon baking soda
⅛ teaspoon salt
⅜ cup buttermilk (or ⅜ cup regular milk with 1 teaspoon lemon juice)
Grated zest of ½ lemon
Scant ½ cup chopped walnuts

Glaze:
Juice of ½ lemon
⅜ cup sugar

Preheat the oven to 350°F. Cream the butter with the sugar, and add the eggs 1 at a time, mixing well between additions. Combine the flour, baking soda, and salt and add to the butter mixture. Add the buttermilk and mix well. Add the lemon zest and walnuts, and mix well. Place in a 9 x 5" greased loaf pan. Bake 30 – 35 minutes. Prepare the glaze by combining the lemon juice and sugar to make a spreadable mixture, adding more lemon juice if needed. Spread the glaze over the top of the cake while it's still warm. Cool the cake completely and serve. *Tip:* This cake can be stored 2 – 3 days in the refrigerator. *Yield: 8 servings.*

"An Elegant Victorian Mansion" Bed & Breakfast Inn

Lily and Doug Vieyra
1406 "C" Street
Eureka, California 95501
Tel: (707) 444-3144
Fax: (707) 442-5594
$$$ – $$$$

ABOUT THE B&B

Featured in many newspapers and magazines — not to mention on television and radio — this restored national historic landmark offers prestigious and luxurious accommodations. Spirited and eclectic innkeepers provide lavish hospitality in the splendor of a meticulously restored 1888 Victorian masterpiece, complete with original family antique furnishings. The inviting guest rooms offer both graceful refinement and modern-day comfort, individually decorated with Victorian elegance. Guests enjoy gourmet breakfasts and a heavenly night's sleep on top-quality mattresses, as well as secured parking and laundry service. Located in a quiet, historic residential neighborhood overlooking the city and Humboldt Bay, the non-smoking inn is near carriage rides, bay cruises, restaurants, and the theater, and is just minutes from giant redwood parks, coastal beaches, ocean charters, and horseback riding.

SEASON

all year

ACCOMMODATIONS

two rooms (including one suite) with private baths; two rooms with shared bath

The Rosewood Mansion Inn

Lynn and David Hausner
54 North Hood Street
Peru, Indiana 46970
Tel: (765) 472-7051
Fax: (765) 472-5575
E-mail: rosewood@netusa1.net
$$

ABOUT THE B&B

Built by Elbert Shirk in 1872, *The Rosewood Mansion Inn is a lovely Victorian home situated near downtown Peru, Indiana. The mansion has 19 rooms, including 11 bedrooms, each with private bath. As a welcome change from impersonal hotel or motel accommodations, the inn offers the warmth and friendliness of home, coupled with the privacy and elegance of a fine hotel — a combination that makes for a truly unique experience. Enjoy the warmth of the oak-paneled library, the splendor of the three-story staircase with stained glass windows, the elegance of the Victorian parlor, and the comfort and charm of your room. Consider Rosewood Mansion for your next romantic getaway, anniversary, party, business meeting, or corporate retreat. Nearby points of interest include Mississinewa Reservoir (featuring boating, fishing, hiking, picnicking, and water-skiing), Miami County Museum, International Circus Hall of Fame, Cole Porter's home and burial site, tennis, golf, and antique shops.*

SEASON

all year

ACCOMMODATIONS

11 rooms with private baths

Oatmeal Coffee Cake

1¼ cups boiling water
1 cup large-flake rolled oats
½ cup butter
1 cup granulated sugar
1 cup brown sugar
1½ cups all-purpose flour
1 teaspoon ground cinnamon
1 teaspoon baking powder
1 teaspoon baking soda
½ teaspoon salt
½ cup chopped walnuts
1 teaspoon vanilla
2 eggs

Topping:
6 tablespoons butter
¼ cup evaporated milk
½ cup sugar
¼ cup chopped walnuts
½ cup shredded unsweetened coconut
½ teaspoon vanilla

Preheat the oven to 350°F. Mix the boiling water, oats, and butter together, and let it stand until the butter melts. Combine the sugar, flour, cinnamon, baking powder, baking soda, salt, and walnuts. Add to the oat mixture along with the vanilla and eggs. Mix well. Pour this into a greased 13 x 9" pan. Bake for 35 minutes. To prepare the topping, melt the butter, then stir in the milk, sugar, walnuts, coconut, and vanilla and pour over the hot cake. *Yield: 12 – 15 servings.*

Quick Coffee Cake

¼ cup and 1 tablespoon butter
½ cup granulated sugar
½ cup brown sugar
2 eggs, well beaten
1½ cups and 1 tablespoon all-purpose flour
½ teaspoon salt
2 teaspoons baking powder
1 cup milk
½ cup chopped nuts (such as walnuts)
1 teaspoon ground cinnamon

Preheat the oven to 350°F. Cream ¼ cup of the butter with the sugar. Add the eggs. Mix 1½ cups of the flour with the salt and baking powder in a bowl. Add the flour mixture, alternating with the milk, to the butter mixture. Pour ½ of the batter in a buttered 8 x 8" pan. Combine the nuts, cinnamon, and the remaining 1 tablespoon of butter and flour. Put ½ of this nut mixture on top of the batter in the pan. Cover it with the remaining batter. Sprinkle it with the remaining nut mixture. Bake 30 – 35 minutes. *Yield: 6 servings.*

Dreams of Yesteryear Bed and Breakfast

Bonnie and Bill Maher
1100 Brawley Street
Stevens Point, Wisconsin 54481
Tel: (715) 341-4525
Fax: (715) 344-3047
$$ – $$$$

ABOUT THE B&B

This elegant, turn-of-the-century Victorian Queen Anne was home to three generations of the Jensen family before being purchased in 1987 and restored by current owners Bonnie and Bill Maher. An article Bonnie wrote about the restoration was featured in the Winter 1991 issue of Victorian Homes magazine. In 1990, after giving many tours, the Mahers opened their home as the Dreams of Yesteryear Bed and Breakfast. Listed on the National Register of Historic Places, Dreams of Yesteryear is located three blocks from historic downtown Stevens Point, two blocks from the Wisconsin River and Green Circle jogging, hiking, biking trails, a half mile from the University of Wisconsin, and near wonderful restaurants, theaters, and antique shops. Your visit includes a gourmet breakfast, warm hospitality, and wonderful memories.

SEASON

all year

ACCOMMODATIONS

two suites with private baths;
two rooms with shared bath

Campbell Ranch Inn

Mary Jane and Jerry Campbell
1475 Canyon Road
Geyserville, California 95441
Tel: (800) 959-3878 or (707) 857-3476
Fax: (707) 857-3239
$$$$

ABOUT THE B&B

Whether swimming in the pool, relaxing in the hot tub spa, or playing tennis, you're always surrounded by the Campbell Ranch Inn's spectacular valley and mountain views and beautiful flower gardens. In warm weather, breakfast is served on the terrace where you overlook rolling hills and vineyards. Only 80 miles north of San Francisco, the inn has five spacious rooms with king-size beds, fresh flowers, and fruit. You may choose to read or visit by the living room fireplace, play tennis, horseshoes, or ping-pong, hike the trails at Lake Sonoma, or use the available bikes to tour the neighboring wine country. The surrounding area has many wineries and excellent restaurants, but remember to save some room for Campbell Ranch's homemade pie and coffee served every evening.

SEASON

all year

ACCOMMODATIONS

four rooms with private baths;
one private cottage
with private bath

Raspberry-Cream Cheese Coffee Cake

Batter:
2½ cups all-purpose flour
¾ cup sugar
¾ cup butter
½ teaspoon baking powder
½ teaspoon baking soda
¼ teaspoon salt
¾ cup sour cream
1 egg
1 teaspoon almond extract

Filling:
8 ounces cream cheese
¼ cup sugar
1 egg
½ cup raspberry jam

Topping:
½ cup sliced almonds

(continued on next page)

Preheat the oven to 350°F. In a large bowl, combine the flour and sugar; cut in the butter using a pastry blender until the mixture resembles coarse crumbs. Reserve 1 cup of the crumbs for the topping. To the remaining crumb mixture, add the baking powder, baking soda, salt, sour cream, egg, and almond extract. Blend well. Spread the batter over the bottom and 2" up the sides of a greased and floured 9" springform pan. The batter should be ¼" thick on the sides.

For the filling: In a small bowl, combine the cream cheese, sugar, and egg and blend well. Pour it over the batter in the pan. Spoon the jam evenly over the cheese filling. In a small bowl, combine the reserved crumbs and the almonds and sprinkle over the top of the cake. Bake 55 – 60 minutes or until the cream cheese is set and the crust is a deep golden brown. Cool 15 minutes, remove the sides, and cool completely. *Tip:* Best served at room temperature. *Yield: 8 servings.*

New Berne House Inn

Marcia Drum and Howard Bronson
709 Broad Street
New Bern, North Carolina 28560
Tel: (800) 842-7688 or (919) 636-2250
$$

ABOUT THE B&B

New Berne House Inn is *centrally located in the Colonial town of New Bern and within comfortable walking distance of numerous historic sights, highlighted by Tryon Palace and its formal gardens, only one block away. Quaint shops, fine restaurants, and historic buildings are all in the neighborhood. New Berne House's seven guest rooms feature queen- and king-size beds, antiques and collectibles, private baths, and telephones and clock radios, along with other amenities to pamper guests. A full breakfast is served in the dining room from 8:00 to 9:00 am, but coffee is available as early as 6:30 am. Throughout the day, guests are invited to join the innkeepers in the library or parlor for light refreshments, television, and good conversation. Two weekends each month are reserved for a "juicy" who-done-it mystery package, which blends in nicely with the inn's two haunted rooms (where "odd occurrences" have been reported over the years!).*

SEASON

all year

ACCOMMODATIONS

seven rooms with private baths

Ricotta Cake

18¼-ounce package white or yellow cake mix
2 pounds ricotta cheese
4 eggs
1 cup granulated sugar
1 teaspoon vanilla
1 teaspoon lemon juice
Confectioners' sugar
Whipped cream and berries, or ground cinnamon and sugar

Preheat the oven to 350°F. Prepare the white cake mix according to the package directions and pour it into a well-greased 13 x 9" pan. Mix the cheese, eggs, granulated sugar, vanilla, and lemon juice together. Pour this over the white cake. Bake 50 – 60 minutes, until brown on top. Sprinkle with confectioners' sugar and top with the whipped cream and berries if serving as a dessert, or with cinnamon and sugar as a breakfast pastry. *Tip:* This cake freezes well. *Yield: About 24 servings.*

Skillet Almond Coffee Cake

"Easy and flavorful, this cake is loved by our guests."
— *Rita and John Kovacevich*

¾ cup butter
1¾ cups sugar
2 eggs
1½ cups all-purpose flour
Pinch of salt
1 teaspoon almond extract
½ cup slivered almonds

Preheat the oven to 350°F. Melt the butter and add to 1½ cups of the sugar. Beat in the eggs 1 at a time. Add the flour, salt, and almond extract, mixing well. Line a 10" cast-iron skillet with aluminum foil extending up over the sides. Pour the batter into the lined skillet. Sprinkle the almonds and remaining ¼ cup sugar over the batter. Bake 30 – 40 minutes. Allow the cake to cool, then remove from the skillet by lifting out the foil. Slice the cake and serve warm. *Yield: 12 servings.*

Hoyt House Bed and Breakfast

Rita and John Kovacevich
804 Atlantic Avenue
Amelia Island, Florida 32034
Tel: (800) 432-2085 or (904) 277-4300
Fax: (904) 277-9626
E-mail: hoythouse@
b&b.net-magic.net
www.hoythouse.com
$$$ – $$$$

ABOUT THE B&B

*S*troll up the brick path, enter through the double Yankee doors, and pass into the elegance and charm of a home from a bygone era. Built in 1905 using only the finest materials and craftsmen, Hoyt House is an example of Queen Anne-style architecture that demonstrates an attention to detail and quality that is rare. Guest chambers, some with fireplaces, are each unique in style, blending antique furnishings, current reproductions, custom-designed window treatments, and inspiring colors. Breakfast begins with a beautiful table setting, fresh flowers, china, European-sized silverware, and fine table linens, and includes juice, fresh fruit, coffee, tea, homemade baked specialties, plus a gourmet breakfast entrée. Located in the heart of the downtown historic district, Hoyt House is steps away from shops, fine antique emporiums, the Museum of History, and many excellent restaurants. Amelia Island is home to golf, tennis, sportfishing, horseback riding, historic Fort Clinch, and miles of endless beach.

SEASON

all year

ACCOMMODATIONS

nine rooms with private baths

1874 Stonehouse on Mulberry Hill

Carrie and Dan Riggs
RR #1, Box 67A
Cottonwood Falls, Kansas 66845
Tel: (316) 273-8481
E-mail: shmh1874@aol.com
$$

ABOUT THE B&B

*I*f these stone walls could talk! This historic farmhouse was built of quarried stone in 1874 and today has been restored and modernized as a B&B. Three upstairs bedrooms have distinctive furnishings, while the downstairs fireplace room and parlor offer inviting places for conversation or reading. Breakfast is served in the cozy fireplace room aglow with the morning sun. Fresh coffee and pastries and a full country breakfast are served. 1874 Stonehouse has over 120 acres to explore, including over 10 acres of woods, a fishing pond, old stone fences, and a river valley. The area is a haven for birders, cyclists, hikers, naturalists, antique hunters, historians, and photographers — or anyone escaping the city for a quiet and romantic break in the beautiful Flint Hills of Kansas.

SEASON

all year

ACCOMMODATIONS

three rooms with private baths

Sun-Sational Cheesecake

Crust:
1 cup graham cracker crumbs
3 tablespoons sugar
3 tablespoons butter, melted

Filling:
24 ounces cream cheese, softened
1 cup sugar
3 tablespoons all-purpose flour
2 tablespoons lemon juice
1 tablespoon grated lemon zest
½ teaspoon vanilla
3 whole eggs
1 egg white (reserve egg yolk for glaze)

Finishing:
Fresh lemon slices
¾ cup sugar
2 tablespoons cornstarch
½ cup water
¼ cup lemon juice
1 egg yolk, lightly beaten
Mint leaves

To make the crust: Preheat the oven to 325°F. Combine the crumbs, sugar, and butter. Press into the bottom of a 9" springform pan. Bake 10 minutes and let cool.

(continued on next page)

To make the filling: Preheat the oven to 450°F. Combine the cream cheese, sugar, flour, lemon juice, lemon zest, and vanilla, mixing only until combined. Add the whole eggs, 1 at a time, mixing well after each. Beat in the egg white. Pour the mixture over the crust. Place the cheesecake in the oven on the center rack. Place a pan of water on the rack beneath the center rack to add moisture and prevent the cake from cracking. Bake 10 minutes, then reduce the oven to 250°F and bake 30 minutes more (until the cake's center is no longer moist looking.) Cool the cake completely on a wire rack before decorating and glazing it.

To finish: Remove the cake from the pan. Place the lemon slices in a decorative fashion on the cooled cake. In a saucepan, combine the sugar and cornstarch until well mixed. Add the water and lemon juice and mix well. Cook over low heat, stirring constantly, until clear and thickened. Add a small amount of beaten egg yolk at a time until all is added and cook a few minutes more. Let cool slightly, then spoon over the lemon slices on the cake.

Chill the cake until firm, then decorate with fresh mint leaves before serving. *Yield: 12 servings.*

Other Baked Goods & Desserts

Almond Custard

1 envelope unflavored gelatin (1 tablespoon)
¼ cup and 2 tablespoons water
1¼ cups vanilla low-fat yogurt
½ cup sugar
1 egg or ½ cup egg substitute
½ teaspoon almond extract
Chopped nuts, kiwi slices, or berries

Sprinkle the gelatin over the water in a saucepan. Let stand 1 minute. Cook over low heat until the gelatin dissolves. Combine the yogurt, sugar, egg, and almond extract in a blender and mix until smooth. Gradually add the gelatin mixture and blend well. Pour into 4 custard cups and chill to set. Top with nuts, kiwi, or berries. **Yield: 4 servings.**

Lara House Bed & Breakfast

Bobbye and Doug Boger
640 NW Congress
Bend, Oregon 97701
Tel: (800) 766-4064 or (541) 388-4064
Fax: (541) 388-4064
$$$

ABOUT THE B & B

Apioneer Bend merchant, A.M. Lara built this house in 1910. In 1983, the Lara House Bed & Breakfast was established as Bend's first B&B. With over 5,000 square feet, Lara House is three stories tall and features six distinctive, large bedrooms with private baths and seating areas. On the main floor, there is a spacious living room with a large brick fireplace to curl up in front of on cold winter nights. Off the living room is a bright sunroom — where a homemade breakfast is served — with large windows that look out over the scenic grounds that surround the house. Lara House is directly across from Drake Park and Mirror Pond. Two blocks away, historic Bend awaits with its several fine restaurants and quaint gift shops.

SEASON

all year

ACCOMMODATIONS

six rooms with private baths

Angel Arbor
Bed & Breakfast Inn

Marguerite and Dean Swanson
848 Heights Boulevard
Houston, Texas 77007
Tel: (713) 868-4654
Fax: (713) 861-3189
E-mail: b-bhontx@wt.net
www.angelarbor.com
$$ – $$$

ABOUT THE B&B

A few minutes from downtown Houston, this elegant 1920s Georgian-style brick residence graces historic Heights Boulevard with its gazebo-dotted esplanade and walking trail. The first floor boasts an antique-filled parlor, a cozy reading room, a gracious formal dining room, and a sunroom for game playing or casual dining. A wicker-furnished solarium overlooks the backyard garden with its manicured lawn, angel statue, and vine-laden arbor with a tranquil sitting area. Upstairs, three spacious bedrooms, each with an angel-inspired name, feature queen beds and private baths, two with whirlpool tubs for two. A separate outside suite provides seclusion and has its own sitting room and deck. A full delicious breakfast is served daily. Former owners of Durham House B&B, Marguerite and Dean Swanson bring their many years of innkeeping experience to Angel Arbor. The B&B also hosts parties and small meetings, and Marguerite's renowned murder mystery dinner parties.

SEASON

all year

ACCOMMODATIONS

four rooms (including one suite) with private baths

Amorous Pears

29-ounce can pear halves
Ground cinnamon
1½ cups light ricotta cheese
3 tablespoons sugar
¼ teaspoon grated nutmeg
3 tablespoons orange liqueur
½ cup sliced almonds, toasted

Preheat the oven to 325°F. Empty the pears and juice into a shallow baking dish and arrange the pears cut side up. Sprinkle each pear half with the cinnamon. Bake for 20 minutes. Meanwhile, in a small bowl, combine the ricotta cheese, sugar, nutmeg, and liqueur. Whip with a fork until smooth. Refrigerate. When the pears are warmed, remove each with a slotted spoon and place a pear half in each of 8 stemmed sherbet or small champagne glasses. Spoon the chilled cheese mixture evenly over the tops of the pears. Top each with toasted almond slices.
Yield: 8 servings.

Apple Brownies

"This recipe was given to me by a dear friend, Terry Farr, and is served for our afternoon tea. It's great in the fall and winter when fresh apples abound." — Andy Aldrich

¾ cup butter
1½ cups sugar
2 cups all-purpose flour
2 eggs
1 teaspoon baking powder
1 teaspoon baking soda
1 teaspoon salt
1 teaspoon ground cinnamon
2 cups peeled and chopped apple

Preheat the oven to 350°F. Mix the butter, sugar, flour, eggs, baking powder, baking soda, salt, cinnamon, and apples together and place in a 13 x 9" greased pan. Bake for 35 minutes. Cut into squares.
Yield: 30 brownies.

The Inn at The Brass Lantern

Andy Aldrich
717 Maple Street
Stowe, Vermont 05672
Tel: (800) 729-2980 or (802) 253-2229
Fax: (802) 253-7425
$$ – $$$$

ABOUT THE B&B

The Inn at The Brass Lantern is located at the edge of the village of Stowe, Vermont. Stowe is a full-service, four-season resort town, and boasts many world-class restaurants and activities, a cultural center, unique cottage industries, craftspeople, and artists. Originally built as a farmhouse and carriage barn, The Brass Lantern was restored by Andy Aldrich, the current innkeeper, to retain its original Vermont character (for which he won an award). Today, the inn carries the traditional Vermont B&B theme throughout — from its decor of period antiques, handmade quilts, and locally crafted amenities to the food and beverages reflecting local and Vermont state products. In addition, guests are treated to a unique ambiance and casual, attentive service. The inn's setting provides panoramic views of Mount Mansfield and its valley from nearly every room.

SEASON

all year

ACCOMMODATIONS

nine rooms with private baths

Brambly Hedge Cottage

Jacquelyn Smyers
HCR 31, Box 39
Jasper, Arkansas 72641
Tel: 1-800-BRAMBLY or
(501) 446-5849
$$

ABOUT THE B&B

"*Absolutely charming*," *wrote National Geographic Traveler of this old Ozark mountaintop farmhouse, four miles south of Jasper, Arkansas. A Tennessee guest commented, "The place is uniquely beautiful, the food delicious, and the view inspiring." Three guest rooms with private baths reflect country French elegance in a homestead log cabin. A full breakfast is served on the deck overlooking Buffalo River Valley or behind the screened porch in rocking chairs. You're only minutes from the "Grand Canyon of the Ozarks," challenging-to-easy hiking trails, and canoeing on Buffalo National River. If art is more your style, you'll find the work of true artisans in the Jasper area. For those who wish to sample a night out on the town, Eureka Springs and Branson (Missouri) are nearby. Small group special-interest tours and relaxing massages can be arranged. Hostess Jacquelyn Smyers includes her handmade tatted lace and samovar collection in the decor. She's also a designer, commercial artist, and author of* Come For Tea *and the children's book* The Cloud That Came Into The Cabin *(inspired by the clouds on Sloan Mountain where Brambly Hedge is located).*

SEASON

all year

ACCOMMODATIONS

three rooms with private baths

Applesauce Sundae

"This little dish is easy, looks special, and is good for your guests."
— *Jacquelyn Smyers*

⅔ cup applesauce
Ground cinnamon
2 heaped tablespoons raisins
2 heaped tablespoons walnuts (large broken pieces)
2 tablespoons plain non-fat unsweetened yogurt

Divide the applesauce into 2 small bowls. Sprinkle generously with the cinnamon, followed by the raisins and walnuts. Top with 1 tablespoon of yogurt in the center of each dish. *Yield: 2 servings.*

Apricot, White Chocolate, and Walnut Scones

3 cups all-purpose flour
½ cup sugar
2½ teaspoons baking powder
½ teaspoon baking soda
¾ cup cold butter, cut into small chunks
¾ cup chopped dried apricots
1 cup buttermilk
¾ cup white chocolate chips
¼ cup chopped walnuts (optional)
2 tablespoons heavy cream or half-and-half

Preheat the oven to 425°F. In the bowl of a food processor, mix the flour, sugar, baking powder, and baking soda. Add the butter and combine, pulsing until the mixture resembles coarse meal. Transfer to a large bowl, add the apricots, buttermilk, white chocolate chips, and walnuts (if wished) and mix with a fork until just combined. Turn the dough onto a floured surface and knead 8 – 10 times. Shape into a 10" circle about ¾" thick. Cut into 10 – 12 wedges or interesting shapes using a round fluted or heart-shaped cookie cutter. Place the scones on a greased baking sheet. Brush the tops with the heavy cream and bake 15 – 20 minutes. *Yield: 10 – 12 scones.*

King-Keith House Bed & Breakfast

Jan and Windell Keith
889 Edgewood Avenue NE
Atlanta, Georgia 30307
Tel: (800) 728-3879 or (404) 688-7330
Fax: (404) 584-0730
E-mail: KingKeith@travelbase.com
$$ – $$$

ABOUT THE B&B

*S*outhern hospitality is alive and well at the King-Keith House. Located in a National Register of Historic Places neighborhood, which includes the home of the founder of Coca-Cola, this Queen Anne B&B is one of the most photographed houses in Atlanta. Built in 1890 by the local hardware magnate, George E. King, it boasts 12-foot ceilings, carved fireplaces, and elegant public spaces, one of which showcases a baby grand piano. Guest rooms are furnished with period antiques and elegant accessories and have access to a private upstairs porch. A gourmet breakfast is served around a large oak table and may include orange French toast, blueberry multi-grain pancakes, homemade breads and coffee cakes, and fruit. The architect owner and his wife enjoy old home restoration, antique hunting, decorating, gardening, and cooking. King-Keith House is within walking distance of the Little Five Pointe commercial district, and is close to Atlanta's most popular in-town shopping, restaurant, and theater areas.

SEASON

all year

ACCOMMODATIONS

four rooms (including one suite) with private baths; two rooms with shared bath

"An Elegant Victorian Mansion" Bed & Breakfast Inn

Lily and Doug Vieyra
1406 "C" Street
Eureka, California 95501
Tel: (707) 444-3144
Fax: (707) 442-5594
www/bnbcity.com/inns/20016
$$$ – $$$$

ABOUT THE B&B

Featured in many newspapers and magazines — not to mention on television and radio — this restored national historic landmark offers prestigious and luxurious accommodations. Spirited and eclectic innkeepers provide lavish hospitality in the splendor of a meticulously restored 1888 Victorian masterpiece, complete with original family antique furnishings. The inviting guest rooms offer both graceful refinement and modern-day comfort, individually decorated with Victorian elegance. Guests enjoy gourmet breakfasts and a heavenly night's sleep on top-quality mattresses, as well as secured parking and laundry service. Located in a quiet, historic residential neighborhood overlooking the city and Humboldt Bay, the non-smoking inn is near carriage rides, bay cruises, restaurants, and the theater, and is just minutes from giant redwood parks, coastal beaches, ocean charters, and horseback riding.

SEASON

all year

ACCOMMODATIONS

two rooms (including one suite) with private baths; two rooms with shared bath

Austrian Apple Strudel

"I like to prepare the strudel in advance and freeze until baking time. It's a favorite at the inn's breakfast table, and is also wonderful in the afternoon with tea or coffee." — Lily Vieyra

1 sheet puff pastry (Pepperidge Farm brand recommended)
1 large green apple (such as Granny Smith)
3 tablespoons butter
½ cup golden raisins
8 – 10 dried apricot halves, cut in quarters
¼ cup water
¼ cup light brown sugar (or to taste)
½ teaspoon ground cinnamon (or to taste)
¼ teaspoon grated nutmeg (or to taste)
1 egg yolk, lightly beaten with 1 tablespoon water

Thaw the puff pastry if frozen. Cut and core the apple and chop into small ½" chunks. Over medium heat, melt the butter in a large skillet. Add the apple, raisins, and apricots. Mix well and sauté a few minutes. Add the water, sugar, cinnamon, and nutmeg. Cover and simmer for about 10 minutes, until the apple is tender but not overcooked. Add additional sugar or spices to taste. If the mixture appears too dry, add a little water or, if too moist, cook a few minutes without the cover. Remove from the skillet and cool.

(continued on next page)

Place the puff pastry on a flat surface and distribute the apple mixture down the middle ⅓ of the sheet. Make 2½" long cuts diagonally along both sides of the exposed pastry at 1½" intervals. Fold the strips over the apples, alternating from left to right. Press the dough together where the ends overlap and seal the top and bottom edge of the dough with a fork. At this point, refrigerate for 30 minutes or wrap and freeze. At the time of baking, brush with the egg wash and place the strudel on a cookie sheet covered with parchment paper (to prevent the bottom burning). Preheat the oven to 400°F and bake for 25 minutes or until the pastry is light golden brown and puffed. *Yield: 1 strudel, serving 4 – 6.*

Captain Ezra Nye House

Elaine and Harry Dickson
152 Main Street
Sandwich, Massachusetts 02563
Tel: (800) 388-2278 or (508) 888-6142
Fax: (508) 833-2897
E-mail: captnye@aol.com
$$$

ABOUT THE B&B

A sense of history and romance fills this 1829 Federal home, built by the distinguished sea captain, Ezra Nye. Located in the heart of historical Sandwich Village, Captain Ezra Nye House is within walking distance of Sandwich Glass and Doll museums, Thornton Burgess Museum, Shawme Lake, fine dining, and antique shops. Heritage Plantation, the marina, an auction house, as well as Cape Cod Bay and Canal are nearby. Activities also include whale watching or a day at the beach. The inn was chosen one of the top 50 inns in America, one of the five best on the Cape, and was Cape Cod Life *magazine's readers' choice as best bed and breakfast on the upper Cape. It has been featured in* Glamour, Toronto Life, *and* Innsider *magazines. A full breakfast is served each morning, and specialties include walnut goat cheese soufflé, peach kuchen, or baked French toast. Harry's interests include golfing and collecting Chinese export porcelain, while Elaine is an avid cyclist and enjoys yoga.*

SEASON

all year

ACCOMMODATIONS

six rooms (including one suite)
with private baths

Baked Apples New England

6 baking apples (Cortland or McIntosh)
6 heaping teaspoons sugar mixed with 1 teaspoon ground cinnamon
6 heaping teaspoons butter
2 tablespoons water
Raisins and dark rum (optional)

Preheat the oven to 350°F. Core the apples and make a slit through the skin with a knife all the way around, about ⅓ of the way from the top (this keeps the apples from exploding). Place the apples in a glass pie plate. Spoon a heaping teaspoon of sugar-cinnamon mixture into the center of each apple, followed by a dab of butter. Pour the water into the pie plate. Bake 1 hour, basting after 30 minutes. *Tip:* For a little different flavor, add raisins to the apple centers or a tablespoon of dark rum to the water. *Yield: 6 servings.*

Captain Ezra Nye House
Sandwich, MA

Banana Bread Pudding

4 day-old rolls (medium- or large-sized)
1¼ cups milk, half-and-half, or heavy cream
3 eggs
½ cup dark brown sugar
½ teaspoon vanilla
2 teaspoons dark rum or rum extract
2 bananas, sliced
Cream cheese
Margarine (preferably in a squirt container)

Fresh blueberries and blueberry syrup

Preheat the oven to 350°F. Grease 4 individual (6-ounce) casserole dishes. Cut the rolls lengthwise. Put the bottom half of the roll in each casserole (should cover about ¾ of the bottom of the dish). Mix together the milk, eggs, sugar, vanilla, and rum. Soak the top halves of the rolls in this mixture for several minutes. Put ¼ of the banana slices in each dish. Dot with small pieces of cream cheese. Cover each casserole with the top half of a roll. Squirt or dot some margarine on top. Bake for 30 minutes. Let set for about 5 minutes, then serve with fresh blueberries and blueberry syrup. *Tips:* This dish can be assembled the night before it is to be baked. The bananas will not turn brown if the casseroles are tightly covered with plastic wrap and refrigerated overnight. *Yield: 4 servings.*

Holmberg House Bed & Breakfast

Jo Meacham and Michael Cobb
766 DeBarr
Norman, Oklahoma 73069
Tel: (405) 321-6221
$$

ABOUT THE B&B

Holmberg House was built in 1914 by Professor Fredrik Holmberg — the first dean of the University of Oklahoma's fine arts program and the state's first symphony conductor. Since 1993, Holmberg House B&B has been a home away from home for visiting professors, scholars, parents, and alumni. Located across the street from the university, right next door to Campus Corner, this comfortable craftsman-style house is decorated with period antique furnishings and memorabilia. Guest rooms are reminiscent of the good old days — including an antique iron bed and claw foot tubs — yet are equipped with the conveniences of today. In the morning, guests enjoy a gourmet breakfast in the dining room, then gather for conversation on the front porch or in the parlor. Come dinnertime, guests can choose from no less than 15 restaurants that are within walking distance of the B&B's front door. If you are celebrating a birthday, anniversary, or special occasion during your stay at Holmberg House, Jo and Michael will gladly assist you with the arrangements — whether you need tickets for an event or flowers from the local florist.

SEASON

all year

ACCOMMODATIONS

four rooms with private baths

The Oval Door

Judith McLane and Dianne Feist
988 Lawrence Street
Eugene, Oregon 97401
Tel: (800) 882-3160 or (541) 683-3160
Fax: (541) 485-5339
$$ – $$$

ABOUT THE B&B

This early 20th-century farmhouse-style home with a two-sided wraparound porch is actually newly built, yet its vintage 1920s design fits into the neighborhood so well that people are surprised to learn it was built circa 1990! Each of the four spacious guest rooms features a private bath. In addition, guests can enjoy the Tub Room — a whirlpool bath for two, with bubbles, candles, and music. Newly decorated and inviting, the common living room has a fireplace and the library offers comfortable chairs for watching TV, using the VCR, or browsing through the travel books. Located just three blocks from the city's center, it's an easy walk to the Hult Center for the Performing Arts, many of Eugene's fine restaurants and shops, and a short drive to the University of Oregon. Guests enjoy a full breakfast served in the dining room. Extra touches include terry robes, Perrier, and candies.

SEASON

all year

ACCOMMODATIONS

four rooms with private baths

Betty's Apricot Kugel

1 pound dried apricots
½ cup apricot preserves
½ cup butter
12 ounces wide egg noodles
¼ cup sugar
2 cups sour cream
5 eggs

Preheat the oven to 375°F. Simmer the apricots in enough water to cover until they're soft. Drain any remaining water. Mix in the preserves; set aside. Cut the butter into 8 pieces and place in a large bowl. Cook the noodles in boiling water until just al dente. Add the drained noodles to the butter and stir until the butter has melted. Add the sugar and sour cream; let cool. Beat the eggs and add to the mixture. Place in a buttered 13 x 9" glass dish. Spread the apricot mixture on top. Bake for 1 hour. *Yield: 8 servings.*

Biscuit Mold

"A favorite at Hidden Pond since the beginning!" — Larry Fuerst

7 tablespoons butter
½ cup brown sugar
1 tablespoon maple syrup
¾ – 1 cup pecan halves or pieces
1 package refrigerated buttermilk biscuits (Pillsbury brand recommended)

Preheat the oven to 375°F. Melt the butter with the sugar and syrup on the bottom of a 5-cup mold. Sprinkle the nuts on the melted mixture. Stand biscuits up in the mold. Bake 25 – 30 minutes. **Yield: 4 servings.**

Hidden Pond Bed & Breakfast

Priscilla and Larry Fuerst
PO Box 461
Fennville, Michigan 49408
Tel: (616) 561-2491
$$$

ABOUT THE B&B

Hidden Pond Bed & Breakfast is set on 28 acres of woods, perfect for bird-watching, hiking, cross-country skiing, or just relaxing in a rowboat on the pond. Guests can enjoy seven entry-level rooms, including bedrooms and baths, living room with fireplace, dining room, library, kitchen, and breakfast porch. Priscilla and Larry, who work for rival airlines, understand the importance of a soothing, calm, and slow-paced overnight stay. They enjoy pleasing guests and creating an atmosphere of quiet elegance. Unwind and take in the sun on the outdoor deck or patio. Turndown service, complimentary soft drinks, tea, hot chocolate, or an evening sherry are offered. Full hot breakfast is served in the sun-washed garden room at your leisure, and features fresh fruit, breads, muffins, and a hot entrée. This lovely retreat is near the beaches of Lake Michigan, the boutiques of Saugatuck, and the winery and cider mill in Fennville.

SEASON

all year

ACCOMMODATIONS

two rooms with private baths

Brambly Hedge Cottage

Jacquelyn Smyers
HCR 31, Box 39
Jasper, Arkansas 72641
Tel: 1-800-BRAMBLY or
(501) 446-5849
$$

ABOUT THE B&B

"**A**bsolutely charming," wrote National Geographic Traveler *of this old Ozark mountaintop farmhouse, four miles south of Jasper, Arkansas. A Tennessee guest commented, "The place is uniquely beautiful, the food delicious, and the view inspiring." Three guest rooms with private baths reflect country French elegance in a homestead log cabin. A full breakfast is served on the deck overlooking Buffalo River Valley or behind the screened porch in rocking chairs. You're only minutes from the "Grand Canyon of the Ozarks," challenging-to-easy hiking trails, and canoeing on Buffalo National River. If art is more your style, you'll find the work of true artisans in the Jasper area. For those who wish to sample a night out on the town, Eureka Springs and Branson (Missouri) are nearby. Small group special-interest tours and relaxing massages can be arranged. Hostess Jacquelyn Smyers includes her hand-made tatted lace and samovar collection in the decor. She's also a designer, commercial artist, and author of* Come For Tea *and the children's book* The Cloud That Came Into The Cabin *(inspired by the clouds on Sloan Mountain where Brambly Hedge is located).*

SEASON

all year

ACCOMMODATIONS

three rooms with private baths

Brambly Hedge Fruit Mix

"A nice change from the usual citrus fruit makes this simple mixture taste quite special." — Jacquelyn Smyers

1 cup purple seedless grapes
1 cup canned pineapple chunks, drained
1 cup thickly sliced and halved banana
¼ cup Grand Marnier liqueur

Mix the grapes, pineapple, banana, and liqueur together, and serve in small, pretty bowls. ***Yield: 4 servings.***

Breakfast Bread Pudding

"We serve tea sandwiches on very thin white and whole wheat bread and remove and freeze the crusts, which we then use to make our breakfast bread pudding." — Marcia Drum

4 eggs
2 cups half-and-half
1 teaspoon vanilla
1 teaspoon ground cinnamon
⅛ teaspoon ground ginger
⅛ teaspoon grated nutmeg
⅛ teaspoon ground cloves
4 cups cubed white or whole wheat bread

Berries and cream or syrup

Preheat the oven to 350°F. Beat the eggs and half-and-half until well blended. Add the vanilla and spices. Pour over the bread and let stand 20 minutes. Pour this mixture into a lightly oiled 9 x 5 x 2" loaf pan. Bake 40 – 45 minutes or until a knife blade inserted in the center comes out clean. Spoon into cereal bowls and serve with berries and cream as bread pudding or slice and serve with syrup as French toast. **Tip:** Egg substitute and skimmed milk turns this into a dieter's delight. **Yield: 8 servings.**

New Berne House Inn

Marcia Drum and Howard Bronson
709 Broad Street
New Bern, North Carolina 28560
Tel: (800) 842-7688 or (919) 636-2250
$$

ABOUT THE B&B

New Berne House Inn is centrally located in the Colonial town of New Bern and within comfortable walking distance of numerous historic sights, highlighted by Tryon Palace and its formal gardens, only one block away. Quaint shops, fine restaurants, and historic buildings are all in the neighborhood. New Berne House's seven guest rooms feature queen- and king-size beds, antiques and collectibles, private baths, and telephones and clock radios, along with other amenities to pamper guests. A full breakfast is served in the dining room from 8:00 to 9:00 am, but coffee is available as early as 6:30 am. Throughout the day, guests are invited to join the innkeepers in the library or parlor for light refreshments, television, and good conversation. Two weekends each month are reserved for a "juicy" who-done-it mystery package, which blends in nicely with the inn's two haunted rooms (where "odd occurrences" have been reported over the years!).

SEASON

all year

ACCOMMODATIONS

seven rooms with private baths

Kula View
Bed and Breakfast

Susan Kauai
PO Box 322, 140 Holopuni Road
Kula, Hawaii 96790
Tel: (808) 878-6736
$$

ABOUT THE B&B

Singing birds, blossoming flowers, glorious sunrises and sunsets, and sweeping panoramic views of the ocean from every window make your stay in "upcountry" Maui pure magic. Nestled in Kula at the 2,000-foot level on the slopes of Haleakala (the dormant volcano), Kula View offers an upper-level suite featuring a private entrance, private deck overlooking the flower and herb garden, queen-size bed, reading area, wicker breakfast nook, and mini refrigerator. Awake to a morning meal of exotic island fruit and juice, home-baked breads and muffins, and a pot of freshly brewed Kona coffee or tea. Kula View is located in a rural setting just 20 minutes from the Kahului Airport, close to shopping centers, restaurants, points of interest, Haleakala National Park, and beaches. Your host Susan, who's an avid hiker, gardener, and cyclist, is descended from a Kamaaina (old-time) Hawaii family. She has lived on Maui for over 19 years and will guide you to those special parts of the island as only a native resident can.

SEASON

all year

ACCOMMODATIONS

one suite with private bath

Buttermilk Scone for Two

1 cup all-purpose flour
1½ tablespoons sugar
1 teaspoon baking powder
⅛ teaspoon baking soda
¼ cup cold butter or margarine, cut into small pieces
3 tablespoons currants
¼ teaspoon grated orange zest
¼ – ⅓ cup buttermilk (depending on how well dough holds together)
⅛ teaspoon ground cinnamon mixed with ½ teaspoon sugar

Preheat the oven to 375°F. In a bowl, combine the flour, sugar, baking powder, and baking soda. Add the butter; rub with your fingers to form fine crumbs. Stir in the currants and orange zest. Make a well in the center and pour in the buttermilk. Stir with a fork until the dough holds together. Pat the dough into a ball; knead lightly on a lightly floured board for 5 – 6 turns. Shape the dough into a smooth ball and place in a greased 8 or 9" cake or pie pan. Sprinkle with the cinnamon sugar mixture. Bake for 10 minutes then, with a sharp knife, quickly cut a cross ½" deep across the top of the scone. Bake approximately 20 minutes more until golden brown. Serve warm. *Yield: 2 servings.*

Cantaloupe Mousse

2 envelopes unflavored gelatin (2 tablespoons)
¼ cup cold water
½ medium cantaloupe, seeded, peeled, and puréed
2 cups heavy cream
2 cups sugar
4 egg whites at room temperature

Sprinkle the gelatin over cold water to soften. Stir it over a double boiler with the bottom pan full of hot water to dissolve. Cool and add to the puréed melon. Beat the cream until soft peaks form, then gradually add 1 cup of the sugar. Beat the egg whites until fluffy, then gradually add the remaining cup of sugar. Fold cream and egg mixtures together and fold them into the melon mixture. Chill 1 hour then serve.
Yield: 8 generous servings.

Buttonwood Inn

Liz Oehser
50 Admiral Road
Franklin, North Carolina 28734
Tel: (704) 369-8985
$$

ABOUT THE B&B

*T*his small mountain bed and breakfast with a cozy home atmosphere awaits your visit. *Sleep in chenille- or quilt-covered antique beds surrounded by country furnishings, collectibles, and crafts. Two rooms on the first floor each have a double and twin bed, while the two rooms on the second floor each have a double bed. Breakfast delights include artichoke quiche, sausage apple ring filled with puffy scrambled egg, Dutch babies with raspberry sauce, stuffed French toast, blintz soufflé, muffins, and cinnamon scones with homemade lemon butter. After breakfast, enjoy gem mining, hiking, horseback riding, water rafting, golf, or tennis. Stay long enough to tour the Biltmore Estate in nearby Asheville, drive through the Smokey Mountain Parkway to Cherokee Indian Reservation, or "shop 'till you drop" in Gatlinburg. Hospitality, comfort, and delightful breakfasts are this inn's priorities.*

SEASON

April to December 15

ACCOMMODATIONS

four rooms with private baths

Shadwick House
Bed & Breakfast

Ann Epperson
411 South Main Street
Somerset, Kentucky 42501
Tel: (606) 678-4675
$$

ABOUT THE B&B

Standing in the foothills of the Cumberland Mountains, Shadwick House has been known for its southern hospitality for over 70 years. Built in 1920 by Nellie Stringer Shadwick (the great-grandmother of the present owners), the house has been carefully restored to its original stature by Nellie's descendants. The first floor has been converted into a gift shop featuring authentic Kentucky antiques and crafts. There are four upstairs guest rooms, tastefully furnished in antiques. In the days of the roaring twenties and the great depression, Shadwick House served as a boarding house for railroad workers and traveling salesmen. It's rumored that John Dillinger once stayed here while casing the Farmers Bank in town. Nearby are great attractions such as the Big South Fork National Park, Renfro Valley, Cumberland Falls State Park, General Burnside Island State Park, Tombstone Junction, Lake Cumberland, Natural Arch State Park, and Daniel Boone National Forest.

SEASON

all year

ACCOMMODATIONS

four rooms with shared baths

Caramel Rolls

2 cups biscuit mix
½ cup milk
2 tablespoons margarine and ¼ cup margarine, melted
1 teaspoon ground cinnamon
½ cup brown sugar, firmly packed
½ cup chopped pecans

Preheat the oven to 350°F. Combine the biscuit mix and milk, stirring with a fork until blended. Turn the dough onto a lightly floured surface. Knead 4 – 5 times. Roll into a 15 x 9" rectangle, and spread with the 2 tablespoons of margarine. Combine the cinnamon and ¼ cup of the brown sugar. Sprinkle over the dough. Starting with the long side, roll the dough up jelly roll fashion, and pinch the seam to seal (do not seal ends). Cut into 12 slices. Combine the remaining ¼ cup brown sugar, ¼ cup of melted margarine, and pecans and divide equally on the bottom of 12 well-greased muffin cups. Place the slices, cut side down, in the pans. Bake 20 – 22 minutes or until lightly browned. Remove immediately from the pans. *Yield: 12 rolls.*

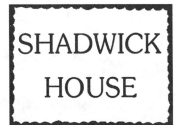

SHADWICK

HOUSE

Carrington's Gwenske Rolls

(Recipe from What's Cooking at Carrington's Bluff.*)*

⅔ cup finely chopped pecans
⅓ cup brown sugar
⅓ cup confectioners' sugar
1 teaspoon ground cinnamon
¼ cup butter, melted
2 loaves frozen bread dough, thawed

Topping:
1 cup confectioners' sugar
1 tablespoon butter, melted
2 – 3 tablespoons milk

Preheat the oven to 375°F. In a small bowl, combine the pecans, sugar, cinnamon, and butter. Roll out 1 loaf of dough into a rectangle. Spread with ½ the nut mixture. Roll the dough starting with the long side. Cut into 1" slices and place into 2 greased round pans. Repeat with the second loaf. Bake for 15 minutes or until golden brown. To make the topping, combine the confectioners' sugar, butter, and milk and drizzle over the warm rolls. *Yield: 12 – 15 rolls.*

Carrington's Bluff B&B

Lisa and Edward Mugford
1900 David Street
Austin, Texas 78705
Tel: (800) 871-8908 or (512) 479-0638
Fax: (512) 476-4769
$$$

ABOUT THE B&B

The setting is Shoal Creek Bluff and an 1877 Texas farmhouse nestled in the arms of a 500-year-old oak tree. Today, Carrington's Bluff B&B offers Texas hospitality to make your stay delightful. Upon arrival, you'll find yourself surrounded by rooms filled with English and American antiques, handmade quilts, and the sweet smell of potpourri. The 35-foot front porch beckons you to sit among the plants and flowers and enjoy the gentle breezes with your morning coffee or afternoon tea. The smell of fresh-brewed gourmet coffee invites you to a breakfast that begins with fresh fruit and homemade granola served on fine English china. Homemade muffins or breads and a house specialty ensure you won't go away hungry. Carrington's Bluff is near the University of Texas and the State Capital grounds, just minutes from parks, hiking and biking trails, shopping, and wonderful restaurants.

SEASON

all year

ACCOMMODATIONS

eight rooms with private baths

Durbin Street Inn B&B

Sherry and Don Frigon
843 South Durbin Street
Casper, Wyoming 82601
Tel: (307) 577-5774
Fax: (307) 266-5441
E-mail: Dfrigon@trib.com
$$

ABOUT THE B&B

*B*uilt in 1917, Durbin Street Inn *is a large two-story American foursquare located in Casper's historic district. The inn prides itself on good food and a friendly atmosphere. Choose from four large non-smoking guest rooms with shared baths. Each room has queen-size or double beds, robes, and one has a fireplace. Or, you can choose the non-smoking guest room with private bath, small sitting room, and refrigerator. Awake to a full country breakfast where scrambled eggs, bacon, sausage, hash browns, fruit juice, homemade jams, and such specialties as honey-wheat pancakes, biscuits and gravy, scones, brunch omelet torte, spicy sausage and potatoes, and roast beef hash are served family-style. After breakfast, gather in the common room by the fireplace, or enjoy the deck, patio, and flower and vegetable gardens. Nearby are walking, hiking, cycling trails, river rafting and canoeing, golfing, swimming, fishing, skiing, shopping, covered wagon and horseback trips along the Oregon Trail, museums, historic sites, Fort Casper, Independence Rock, Devil's Gate, and Hell's Half Acre.*

SEASON

all year

ACCOMMODATIONS

four rooms with shared baths;
one room with private bath

Cheddar-Dill Scones

2½ cups all-purpose flour
1 cup grated sharp cheddar cheese
¼ cup chopped fresh parsley
1 tablespoon baking powder
2 teaspoons dried dill weed
½ teaspoon salt
¾ cup butter or margarine
2 eggs, lightly beaten
½ cup milk

Preheat the oven to 400°F. In a medium bowl, combine the flour, cheese, parsley, baking powder, dill weed, and salt. Cut in the butter until crumbly. Stir in the eggs and milk until just moistened. Turn the dough onto a lightly floured surface and knead until smooth. Divide the dough in ½, and roll each into an 8" circle, then cut into 8 pie-shaped wedges. Place 1" apart on cookie sheets. Bake 15 – 20 minutes or until lightly browned. *Tip:* The dough can be made ahead, cut, and frozen for later use. To bake, place the frozen dough on a cookie sheet sprayed with cooking spray. Bake at 375°F for 15 minutes, then at 400°F 5 – 10 minutes.
Yield: 16 scones.

Cheese-Baked Apples

"I wait for cool fall mornings to serve these. The aroma literally plucks my guests from their warm beds." — Diane Damato

6 large Cortland apples
8 ounces cream cheese, softened
1 egg
½ cup sugar
1 teaspoon vanilla
Sprinkle of ground cinnamon

Preheat the oven to 350°F. Peel away 1" of the skin around the top of each apple. Remove the core (being careful not to pierce the rest of the skin) and remove some of the pulp, leaving a shell about ¾" thick. Combine the cream cheese, egg, sugar, and vanilla. Beat until smooth and creamy. Put ⅓ cup of the filling in each apple and place the apples into greased ramekins. Place the ramekins in a baking pan and add about ½" of water to the pan. Sprinkle the tops of the apples with a little cinnamon. Bake 30 – 45 minutes. Check for consistent softness around the apples. Serve immediately. *Yield: 6 servings.*

Ferry Point House Bed & Breakfast on Lake Winnisquam

Diane and Joe Damato
100 Lower Bay Road
Sanbornton, New Hampshire 03269
Tel: (603) 524-0087
Fax: (603) 524-0959
$$ – $$$

ABOUT THE B&B

This gracious, 175-year-old country Victorian is located on picturesque Lake Winnisquam, in a spot commanding a panoramic view of lake and mountains. The gazebo on the point complements the sandy beach and allows for quiet moments by the water. A 60-foot veranda and all of the rooms are blessed with breathtaking views. Return to the warm, friendly feeling of New England's past with antique furniture, collectibles, and fresh flowers in your room. The lake and surrounding area offer an endless variety of activities, including swimming, fishing, and boating at the inn. Horseback riding, golf, tennis, dinner cruises, scenic train and plane rides, antique shopping, and fine restaurants are all close by. Each morning, you'll be treated to a very special gourmet breakfast with delights such as stuffed French toast, cheese-baked apples, poached pears, and select home-baked breads and muffins.

SEASON

May to November 1

ACCOMMODATIONS

six rooms with private baths

Calmar Guesthouse Bed & Breakfast

Lucille B. Kruse
103 West North Street
Calmar, Iowa 52132
Tel: (319) 562-3851
$$

ABOUT THE B&B

O*pen since 1986, the Calmar Guesthouse is a beautiful, remodeled Victorian home with warm hospitality, good food, and quiet elegance. The house features stained glass windows, refinished wood, handmade quilts, crafts, antiques, and queen-size beds. Breakfast is served in the formal dining room, with candles and music. Nearby activities include a bike trail, golf, tennis, outdoor swimming, canoeing, trout fishing, and more. Local places of interest include Billy Brothers world famous carved-wood clocks, the Norwegian Museum, the Laura Ingalls Museum, the World's Smallest Church, the Little Brown Church in the Vale (the inspiration for the song), the two-mile underground Niagara Cave, Spook Cave, and many beautiful parks.*

SEASON

all year

ACCOMMODATIONS

five rooms with shared baths

Cherry Bars

"My guests rave about these bars, served warm and fresh for breakfast." — Lucille Kruse

1½ cups sugar
1 cup butter
4 eggs
1 teaspoon vanilla
1½ teaspoons baking powder
3 cups all-purpose flour
1 teaspoon salt
20-ounce can cherry pie filling

Frosting:
6 tablespoons sugar
4 tablespoons margarine
4 tablespoons milk
½ teaspoon vanilla

Preheat the oven to 325°F. Cream the sugar and butter. Add the eggs 1 at a time and beat well. Add the vanilla, baking powder, flour, and salt. Spread ½ of the batter into a greased 17 x 11" pan. Spread the cherry pie filling on top of the batter. Drop the balance of the batter by the teaspoon on top of the cherries. Bake 35 – 40 minutes. While the bars are cooling, prepare the frosting. Combine the sugar, margarine, milk, and vanilla and boil for 2 minutes. Cool slightly, then drizzle on the cake. Cut into bars. **Yield: 15 bars.**

Chocolate Bread Pudding

"I bake this as a special Valentine's Day treat in a heart-shaped baking pan." — Andrea Mellon

6 cups ½" egg bread cubes (crusts removed), lightly packed
2½ cups half-and-half
8 ounces semisweet chocolate, chopped
4 egg yolks
¼ cup sugar
1 teaspoon vanilla
Salt to taste

½ cup whipped cream mixed with 1 tablespoon sugar

Divide the bread cubes evenly among 8 (¾ cup) lightly buttered custard cups. Bring the half-and-half to a simmer in a heavy medium-sized saucepan over medium heat. Remove the saucepan from the heat. Add the chocolate and stir until melted and smooth. Add the egg yolks, sugar, vanilla, and salt and whisk until well blended. Pour the chocolate custard over the bread cubes in the custard cups, dividing evenly. Press down on the bread cubes with the back of a spoon to saturate the bread completely. Let stand at room temperature for 25 minutes.

Preheat the oven to 325°F. Cover the custard cups loosely with foil. Bake about 30 minutes or until the puddings are set and a knife inserted in the center comes out with some moist chocolate custard. Serve warm with the sweetened whipped cream. *Yield: 8 servings.*

The Mellon Patch Inn

Andrea and Arthur Mellon
3601 North A-1-A,
North Hutchinson Island
Fort Pierce, Florida 34949
Tel: (800) 656-7824 or (561) 461-5231
Fax: (561) 464-6463
www.sunet.net/mlnptch
$$ – $$$

ABOUT THE B&B

North Hutchinson Island is a barrier island on the Atlantic Ocean with a beach that, *according to a University of Maryland study, is one of the most beautiful stretches of sand in the United States. In this idyllic setting you'll find The Mellon Patch Inn, a newly constructed Florida-style home designed specifically as a B&B. Each room is individually decorated with hand-painted walls and furniture done by a local artist. Choose from the exotic Tropical Paradise Room, the charm of the Patchwork Quilt Room, the tranquility of the Seaside Serenity Room, or the warmth of the Santa Fe Sunset Room. All rooms have air conditioning, television, private bath, and a water view. The Mellon Patch serves a full gourmet breakfast. Along with tennis, beach activities, sportfishing, and boating, guests have use of the inn's canoe to explore Florida's waterways. The Mellon Patch Inn is a quarter mile from the Jack Island Nature Preserve and the Pepper Park fishing docks.*

SEASON

all year

ACCOMMODATIONS

four rooms with private baths

Beaver Creek House

Shirley and Donald Day
20432 Beaver Creek Road
Hagerstown, Maryland 21740
Tel: (301) 797-4764
$$$

ABOUT THE B&B

Comfort, relaxation, and hospitality await you at this turn-of-the-century country Victorian home, located in the historic area of Beaver Creek, Maryland. Step back to a quiet, gentler time and enjoy the family antiques and memorabilia that fill the inn. Choose from five centrally air conditioned guest rooms, and enjoy a country breakfast served on the spacious wraparound screen porch or in the elegantly appointed dining room. Sit in the courtyard by the fountain, stroll through the country garden, or linger by the fish pond and gaze at the mountain. Nearby are the national historic parks of Antietam, Harpers Ferry, the C&O Canal, and the Appalachian Trail. Guests may also hike, bike, golf, ski, shop at the many local antique shops, and dine at excellent restaurants in Hagerstown.

SEASON

all year

ACCOMMODATIONS

five rooms with private baths

Cranberry-Liquered Apples

6 medium apples
3 teaspoons butter
6 tablespoons cranberry liqueur
12 teaspoons sugar
1½ teaspoons ground cinnamon
¾ teaspoon grated nutmeg
Ground ginger
¾ cup water with 1 drop of red food coloring

Preheat the oven to 350°F. Core and peel each apple and place in a baking dish. Put ½ teaspoon butter in the cavity of each apple. Evenly coat the apples with liqueur. Sprinkle 1 teaspoon sugar over each apple and put 1 teaspoon sugar in each apple cavity. Dust each apple with cinnamon and nutmeg. Add a dash of ginger to each. Add the water to the dish. Bake covered for 45 minutes or until tender, basting every 10 minutes. *Tip:* Be careful not to overcook the apples as they may fall apart. *Yield: 6 servings.*

Cranberry-Orange Rolls

2 loaves frozen bread dough
½ cup butter, softened
⅔ pound light brown sugar
12-ounce jar Ocean Spray brand Fruit Sauce

Thaw the bread dough, covered, for several hours at room temperature. Roll each into a rectangle. Spread each rectangle with the butter, sugar, and the fruit sauce. Roll the rectangles lengthwise and slice at 1" intervals. Place in a flat layer in a large iron skillet or casserole dish. Let rise until doubled in size or store (covered) overnight in the refrigerator (remove 45 minutes before baking). Bake in a preheated 350°F oven for approximately 30 minutes or until thoroughly browned. Serve warm. *Yield: 8 servings.*

Bedford's Covered Bridge Inn

Martha and Greg Lau
RD 2, Box 196
Schellsburg, Pennsylvania 15559
Tel: (814) 733-4093
$$ – $$$

ABOUT THE B&B

*S*ituated near Exit 11 of I-76 (the Pennsylvania Turnpike), Bedford's Covered Bridge Inn borders 4,000-acre Shawnee State Park, a lovely trout stream, and the Colvin covered bridge. From this idyllic location, guests can pursue hiking, biking, fishing, cross-country skiing, birding, and antique hunting right from the inn's door. Nearby swimming and boating on Shawnee Lake, visits to Old Bedford Village and Bedford's historic district, driving tours, downhill skiing at Blue Knob Resort, and tours of Bedford's 14 covered bridges round out the list of local activities. Inside the inn, the Lau's attention to detail creates an atmosphere that is comfortable and inviting. The historic farmhouse (circa 1823) boasts six guest rooms with private baths, traditional and country decor, and memorable breakfasts. "There's no doubt what everyone's favorite activity is," say Martha and Greg, "Sitting on the inn's wraparound porch and wishing they could live in Bedford County, too!"*

SEASON

all year

ACCOMMODATIONS

six rooms with private baths;
one cottage for couples or families

High Meadows Inn

Peter Sushka and Mary Jae Abbitt
High Meadows Lane, Route 4, Box 6
Scottsville, Virginia 24590
Tel: (800) 232-1832 or (804) 286-2218
Fax: (804) 286-2124
E-mail: peterhmi@aol.com
www.highmeadows.com
$$ – $$$$

ABOUT THE B&B

As Virginia's only inn that is on the National Register of Historic Homes and has a Renaissance farm vineyard, High Meadows offers a rare opportunity to experience 170 years of architectural history and 10 years of new viticultural growth. High Meadows is a grand house, where guests are welcomed with champagne and stay in rooms furnished with period antiques and art, each with private bath. The innkeepers' many special touches and attention to detail make your visit one to be remembered. Enjoy the simplicity of nature on the 50 surrounding acres of gardens, footpaths, forests, and ponds. Owner/ chef Peter Sushka ensures that dining at High Meadows is just as pleasurable as lodging there. Start with a breakfast of fresh orange juice, a variety of home-made breads, muffins, and scones, fresh fruit, gourmet egg dishes, and coffee or tea. End your day with a multi-course dinner, offering distinctive northern European and Mediterranean dishes.

SEASON

all year

ACCOMMODATIONS

14 rooms (including four suites) with private baths

Creamy Breakfast Ambrosia

(Recipe from The Best of High Meadows — A Selected Recipe Collection.)

2 cups peeled and sliced peach (or pear or apple)
2 bananas, sliced
10 – 12 strawberries, sliced
2 oranges, peeled and sliced
1 tablespoon lemon juice
1 cup shredded unsweetened coconut
1 cup miniature marshmallows
1 cup vanilla or lemon yogurt
1 tablespoon sugar (optional)

In a large bowl, combine the fruit and lemon juice. Toss lightly. Stir in the coconut, marshmallows, yogurt, and sugar. Chill ½ – 1 hour and serve in stemmed, clear sherbet glasses. *Yield: 8 servings.*

Crispies

"This easy, quick, and different breakfast 'bread' was taught to us by our Mexican exchange student, Ricardo, and has been a favorite in our house for many years." — *Muffy Vhay*

1 white or whole wheat flour tortilla
Vegetable oil
½ cup sugar
1 teaspoon ground cinnamon

Cut the tortilla into 4 quarters. Heat ½" of oil in a heavy frying pan until smoking hot (which ensures the tortilla won't absorb the oil). Fry the tortilla quarters (not overlapping) until crisp and puffed. Turn and brown the other side. Make sure the tortilla is totally crisped (about 1 minute). Drain on a paper towel. While still warm, shake the tortilla quarters in a paper bag filled with the sugar and cinnamon. Remove the tortilla quarters from the bag and keep warm in the oven until serving time (for up to 1 hour). Adapt the basic recipe for amount of servings needed. *Yield: 1 serving.*

Deer Run Ranch
Bed and Breakfast

Muffy and David Vhay
5440 Eastlake Boulevard
Washoe Valley, Carson City,
Nevada 89704
Tel: (702) 882-3643
$$$

ABOUT THE B&B

Relax and unwind on 200 of the most beautiful acres in western Nevada. This working alfalfa ranch is located just eight miles north of Carson City and 22 miles south of Reno, Nevada. Watch the deer in the fields, enjoy the smell of western sage, and listen for the night cry of coyotes. This architect-designed western ranch house, shaded by tall cottonwood trees, overlooks a pond, Washoe Valley, and the Sierra Nevada Mountains to the west. Two comfortable guest rooms have queen-size beds, private baths, window seats, spectacular views, and lots of privacy. Both guest rooms share the sitting room with wood-burning stove, dining area, guest refrigerator, TV/VCR, and other amenities. The owners' pottery studio and woodshop are also on the premises. Full ranch breakfasts include house specialties and fresh fruit and vegetables from the garden. Recreation at the ranch includes swimming, horseshoes, hiking, biking, and ice skating on the pond in winter. Deer Run is conveniently located near golf, skiing, casinos and show theaters, and many excellent restaurants.

SEASON

all year

ACCOMMODATIONS

two rooms with private baths

Dreams of Yesteryear Bed and Breakfast

Bonnie and Bill Maher
1100 Brawley Street
Stevens Point, Wisconsin 54481
Tel: (715) 341-4525
Fax: (715) 344-3047
$$ – $$$$

ABOUT THE B&B

This elegant, turn-of-the-century Victorian Queen Anne was home to three generations of the Jensen family before being purchased in 1987 and restored by current owners Bonnie and Bill Maher. An article Bonnie wrote about the restoration was featured in the Winter 1991 issue of Victorian Homes magazine. In 1990, after giving many tours, the Mahers opened their home as the Dreams of Yesteryear Bed and Breakfast. Listed on the National Register of Historic Places, Dreams of Yesteryear is located three blocks from historic downtown Stevens Point, two blocks from the Wisconsin River and Green Circle jogging, hiking, biking trails, a half mile from the University of Wisconsin, and near wonderful restaurants, theaters, and antique shops. Your visit includes a gourmet breakfast, warm hospitality, and wonderful memories.

SEASON

all year

ACCOMMODATIONS

two suites with private baths;
two rooms with shared bath

Danish Apple Bars

"This recipe conjures up memories of my childhood when we'd tag along with our parents to Aunt Catherine's card parties. After cards, a lunch including these Danish apple bars was served. I recall being bored waiting for the card games to end but the apple bars were worth waiting for." — Bonnie Maher

3 cups all-purpose flour
1 teaspoon salt
1 cup vegetable shortening
7 tablespoons milk
1 egg yolk, lightly beaten
1 cup crushed corn flakes
8 large apples, peeled, cored, and sliced (about 8 cups)
1 cup granulated sugar
1 teaspoon ground cinnamon
1 egg white, stiffly beaten
1 cup sifted confectioners' sugar
3 tablespoons water
1 teaspoon vanilla

Preheat the oven to 375°F. Sift together the flour and salt; cut in the shortening until crumbly. Combine the milk and egg yolk, stirring into the crumb mixture until evenly moistened. Divide the dough almost in ½. Roll out the larger half and place on a greased 15½ x 10½ x 1" jelly roll pan. Press the dough up onto the sides of the pan. Sprinkle with the corn flakes. Arrange the apple slices over the corn flakes. Combine the granulated sugar and cinnamon, and sprinkle over the apples. Roll out the other half of the dough to fit the top. Make vents in the top. Moisten the edges of the dough with water to seal. Spread the egg white over the crust. Bake for 1 hour or until golden. Slice into bars. Combine the confectioners' sugar, water, and vanilla and drizzle it over the bars while they're still warm, and serve. *Yield: 48 bars.*

Date-filled Cookies

Filling:
2 cups dates
1 cup water or orange juice
½ cup brown sugar
1 teaspoon grated orange zest
¼ teaspoon grated nutmeg
¾ cup chopped pecans

Dough:
1½ cups butter or margarine
2¼ cups light brown sugar
3 eggs
2¼ cups quick-cooking rolled oats
1½ teaspoons vanilla
4¾ cups all-purpose flour
1½ teaspoons cream of tartar
1½ teaspoons baking soda
¾ teaspoon salt

To make the filling: Place the dates and water in a saucepan and simmer for 5 minutes. Add the sugar and stir. Pour the mixture into a food processor or blender and pulse until the dates are slightly chopped. Pour into a bowl and mix in the zest, nutmeg, and pecans. Set aside.

To make the dough: Cream the butter and sugar. Add the eggs and beat until light. Add the remaining ingredients and mix until the dry ingredients are just moistened. Cover and refrigerate the dough for several hours. Roll out to ¼" thick and cut out the cookies with a cookie cutter. Preheat the oven to 375°F. Spread the date mixture over ½ the cookies and cover with the remaining cookies (you don't need to press the cookie edges together). Bake on ungreased cookie sheets 8 – 10 minutes or until the tops are tan colored. *Yield: About 10 dozen cookies.*

Volden Farm
Bed and Breakfast

JoAnne and Jim Wold
RR #2, Box 50
Luverne, North Dakota 58056
Tel: (701) 769-2275
$$ – $$$

ABOUT THE B&B

*A*fter living all over the world, JoAnne and Jim Wold settled "where we belong — on the wide open prairie of North Dakota." Here, they opened Volden Farm, a B&B with an old-world atmosphere, thanks to the Russian and Norwegian decor and collectibles, which reflect the hosts' heritage and interests. Part of the home was built in 1926, comprising the parlor, music room, library, and two guest bedrooms. A new addition was built in 1978 to include a fireplace and dining area overlooking miles of tranquil prairie land. Bedrooms are filled with family heirloom quilts and one-of-a-kind antiques. Also available is a separate small house called the Law Office — with a bath, limited kitchen facilities, and fabulous view — where Jim used to have his office. The Scandinavian breakfast takes advantage of fresh ingredients from the farm and garden. After breakfast, guests can wander through 300 acres of fields, woods, hills, coulees, and virgin prairie. JoAnne and Jim take pleasure in reading, gardening, singing, and raising animals.

SEASON

all year

ACCOMMODATIONS

two rooms with shared bath
in main house;
two rooms with shared bath
in private cottage

Idlewyld
Bed & Breakfast

Joan and Dan Barris
350 Walnut Street
Lakeside, Ohio 43440
(Mailing address:
13458 Parkway Drive
Lakewood, Ohio 44107)
Tel: (419) 798-4198
$ – $$

ABOUT THE B&B

Idlewyld has a homey atmosphere where guests can relax and enjoy the tranquil beauty and timeless charm of 19th century Lakeside, on the shores of Lake Erie. The century-old home has both an upper porch and a lower wraparound porch furnished with Amish hickory rockers. There are 15 rooms at Idlewyld, each distinctively decorated in a country style. Hosts Joan and Dan Barris take special pride in offering delicious and nutritious breakfast fare. Dan's specialty is popping corn on Saturday nights in the vintage popcorn popper on the front porch. Joan's special interest is nutrition, and Idlewyld is the site of an annual wellness/spa weekend held in late summer.

SEASON

May to October

ACCOMMODATIONS

five rooms with private baths;
10 rooms with shared baths

Date-Nut Pudding

"This recipe goes a long way back to my days at a girls' boarding school in Ohio. We all looked forward to enjoying this pudding at Thanksgiving and Christmas. Although it's called a 'pudding,' this delicious treat is very thick and chewy. On rainy days at Idlewyld, I often have impromptu tea parties for our house-bound guests and this might be one of my selections." — Joan Barris

4 eggs
2 cups sugar
2 tablespoons butter, melted
2 tablespoons hot water
2 cups finely chopped dates
1 cup chopped nuts (such as walnuts)
2 cups all-purpose flour
1 tablespoon baking powder
1 teaspoon salt

Whipped cream

Preheat the oven to 350°F. Beat the eggs well. Mix in the sugar gradually. Add the butter, hot water, dates, nuts, flour, baking powder, and salt and mix well. Bake in a greased 13 x 9" pan 35 – 40 minutes until a toothpick inserted in the center comes out clean. Serve warm with a dollop of whipped cream. *Yield: 18 – 24 servings.*

Double Chocolate Chunk Cookies

"A favorite for afternoon tea, the Holden House's bottomless chocolate chip cookie jar is always a hit with our bed and breakfast guests."
— *Sallie Clark*

¾ cup brown sugar
¾ cup butter or margarine
2 eggs
1 teaspoon vanilla
2½ cups all-purpose flour
1 teaspoon baking soda
6 ounces milk chocolate chunks
5 ounces white chocolate chips
¼ cup chopped walnuts

Preheat the oven to 375°F. Soften the brown sugar and butter in a microwave oven for 1 minute on high. Add the eggs and vanilla. Mix well. Add the flour and baking soda to the brown sugar mixture. When well mixed, add the chocolate chunks, white chocolate chips, and walnuts. Place well-rounded teaspoonfuls on an ungreased cookie sheet. Bake 10 – 12 minutes or until slightly brown on top. *Yield: About 24 cookies.*

Holden House — 1902 Bed & Breakfast Inn

Sallie and Welling Clark
1102 West Pikes Peak Avenue
Colorado Springs, Colorado 80904
Tel: (719) 471-3980
Fax: (719) 471-4740
E-mail: HoldenHouse@
worldnet.att.net
www.bbonline.com/co/holden/
$$$

ABOUT THE B&B

*E*xperience the romance of the past with the comforts of today at Holden House — 1902 *Bed & Breakfast Inn. This storybook Victorian and carriage house filled with antiques and family heirlooms is located in a residential area near the historic district and central to the Pikes Peak region. Enjoy the front parlor, living room with a fireplace and wingback chairs, or the wide veranda with mountain views. Immaculate suites boast queen-size beds, down pillows, private baths, tubs for two, and fireplaces. Enjoy complimentary refreshments, homemade cookies, and friendly resident cats Mingtoy and Muffin.*

SEASON

all year

ACCOMMODATIONS

five suites with private baths

Roses and Lace Inn

Faye and Wayne Payne
20 Rose Lane
Ashville, Alabama 35953
Tel: (205) 594-4366
$ – $$

ABOUT THE B&B

Built in 1890, this spacious three-story bed and breakfast is located in the center of quaint Ashville, Alabama. Listed on the National Register of Historic Places, the house is resplendent with Victorian elegance. Features such as wraparound porches, balconies, stained glass windows, carved mantles, winding stairs, and period furniture make Roses and Lace an excellent example of the area's craftsmanship and architectural integrity. Come and relax, walk to town and shop for antiques, or shop at the famed Boaz outlet city, just 30 minutes away.

SEASON

all year

ACCOMMODATIONS

three rooms with private baths;
two rooms with shared bath

Fresh Fruit Popovers

Fruit sauce:
1½ cups sour cream
2 tablespoons granulated sugar
2 tablespoons brown sugar
1 tablespoon rum
1 teaspoon orange or lemon zest
½ teaspoon ground cinnamon
¼ teaspoon grated nutmeg

Popovers:
6 tablespoons vegetable oil
2 eggs
1 cup milk
1 cup all-purpose flour
½ teaspoon salt
Orange segments, banana slices, and any other fresh fruit in season (e.g., peaches, strawberries, kiwis, and grapes)

Make the fruit sauce the night before by stirring together the sour cream, sugar, rum, orange zest, cinnamon, and nutmeg. Chill overnight.

To make the popovers: Preheat the oven to 425°F. Place 1 tablespoon oil in each of 6 custard cups. Place the cups on a cookie sheet and heat in the oven for 5 minutes. Meanwhile, beat the eggs well. Stir in the milk. Sift the flour and salt together, then add to the egg mixture. Stir just enough to get the lumps out. Pour into the sizzling hot custard cups. Cook 25 minutes, then cool to room temperature.

To assemble: Invert each custard cup to drop the popover out on a plate. Break the popover apart, tearing down the sides but leaving it in 1 piece. Spoon the fruit sauce over the popover and onto the plate. Pile with the fruit and serve. Repeat with the other popovers. *Yield: 6 servings.*

Fruit Cobbler

1½ cups orange juice
¼ cup sugar (if fruit is sweet, use less; for rhubarb or tart fruit,
    use more)
1 tablespoon cornstarch
4 cups fruit of your choice, cut into bite-sized pieces
1 cup all-purpose flour
2 tablespoons sugar
½ tablespoon salt
¼ cup canola oil (or butter or margarine, melted)
½ cup non-fat buttermilk
1 tablespoon sugar with dash of ground cinnamon mixed in

Ice cream

Preheat the oven to 375°F. In a heavy saucepan, stir the orange juice,
sugar, and cornstarch together until blended. Heat until bubbly. Add
the fruit and simmer until just cooked (this can be done the night before,
if wished). Remove from the heat and set aside. Spray a flat baking dish
with nonstick cooking spray, and pour the fruit mixture into it. In a mixing bowl, combine the flour, sugar, and salt. Whisk until blended. Add
the oil and fold in with a rubber spatula until the mixture looks crumbly.
Add the buttermilk and stir in just until you have a light fluffy dough.
Spoon dollops of the dough on the fruit, leaving some fruit showing
through. Sprinkle with the cinnamon sugar. Bake on the low rack of your
oven for about 8 minutes or until the fruit begins to bubble (do not overbake). If the dough has not turned a bit golden on top, set on the high
rack and brown the top for about 30 seconds. Serve warm with ice cream
on top. *Yield: 4 servings.*

The Summer House

Marjorie and Kevin Huelsman
158 Main Street
Sandwich, Massachusetts 02563
Tel: (800) 241-3609 or (508) 888-4991
E-mail: sumhouse@capecod.net
$$ – $$$

ABOUT THE B&B

The Summer House is an elegant
circa 1835 Greek Revival twice
featured in Country Living
magazine. It was owned by Hiram
Dillaway, a prominent mold-maker and
colorist at the Boston & Sandwich
Glass Factory. Large, sunny bedchambers feature antiques, hand-stitched
quilts, and working fireplaces. Stroll to
dining, shops, museums, galleries, a
pond and gristmill, and a boardwalk to
the beach. Bountiful breakfasts change
daily and include freshly ground coffee,
tea, fruit juice, and fresh fruit served in
stemware. Entrées of frittata, stuffed
French toast, quiche, or omelets are
accompanied by scones, puff pastry,
muffins, or fruit cobblers. Dishes are
enhanced with vegetables, berries, and
herbs from the inn's garden. English-
style afternoon tea is served at an
umbrella table in the garden. Boston,
Newport, Providence, Martha's Vineyard, and Nantucket make pleasant
day trips.

SEASON

all year

ACCOMMODATIONS

five rooms with private baths

Inn at Blush Hill

Pamela Gosselin
RR #1, Box 1266
Waterbury, Vermont 05676
Tel: (802) 244-7529
Fax: (802) 244-7314
E-mail: INNATBH@aol.com
$$ – $$$

ABOUT THE B&B

O*nce a stagecoach stop on the route between Montpelier and Stowe, this circa-1790 Cape Cod inn has become a haven for modern-day travelers seeking country comfort and hospitality. Cozy guest rooms are filled with country antiques and coordinated fabrics and wallpapers. One guest room has a fireplace, another has a queen canopy with Battenburg lace and a panoramic view of the mountains. On a chilly day, curl up with a book in front of one of the inn's roaring fireplaces. During summer, there's a large covered porch that beckons you to sit awhile and enjoy the magnificent view. The inn serves many native Vermont products, from fresh apple cider to Ben and Jerry's ice cream and Vermont maple syrup. The inn is adjacent to Ben and Jerry's Ice Cream Factory (the most popular tourist attraction in Vermont), within minutes of Cold Hollow Cider Mill, Green Mountain Chocolate Factory, and Cabot Creamery, and is just a 10-minute drive from the village of Stowe.*

SEASON

all year

ACCOMMODATIONS

five rooms with private baths

Glazed Bananas

2 teaspoons butter
2 tablespoons brown sugar
¼ teaspoon ground cinnamon
½ orange, peeled and diced
2 bananas, peeled and sliced into 1" rounds
Orange juice, if needed
Whipped cream
Fresh mint leaves

Melt the butter, brown sugar, and cinnamon in a sauté pan over low heat. Add the orange and stir until well melted and syrupy. Add the bananas and stir fry them over medium-high heat, just until hot. (If the syrup is too thick, add a little orange juice.) Be careful not to overcook as the bananas will become mushy. Serve in a stemmed glass and top with whipped cream and a mint leaf. *Tip:* Recipe is easily expandable for larger numbers. *Yield: 2 servings.*

Glazed Raisin Scones

2 cups all-purpose flour
¼ cup and 2 tablespoons sugar
2½ teaspoons baking powder
½ teaspoon salt
½ cup butter or margarine, softened
¾ cup raisins
2 eggs
¼ – ⅓ cup milk

Butter and fruit preserves

Preheat the oven to 400°F. In a large bowl, mix the flour, ¼ cup sugar, baking powder, and salt. Cut in the butter until the mixture resembles coarse crumbs. Mix in the raisins. In a small bowl, mix 1 whole egg and 1 egg yolk; reserve the remaining white in another bowl. Mix the eggs into the flour mixture. Mix in enough of the milk to make a dough that holds together. Turn onto a lightly floured surface and knead 5 – 6 times. Halve the dough. Pat each half into a circle ½" thick. Cut each into 8 triangles. Place spaced apart on a lightly greased baking sheet. With a fork, beat the reserved egg white until just bubbly and brush on the scones. Sprinkle them generously with the 2 tablespoons remaining sugar. Bake 14 – 18 minutes until golden brown. Serve warm with butter and fruit preserves. *Yield: 16 scones.*

Buttonwood Inn

Liz Oehser
50 Admiral Road
Franklin, North Carolina 28734
Tel: (704) 369-8985
$$

ABOUT THE B&B

This small mountain bed and breakfast with a cozy home atmosphere awaits your visit. Sleep in chenille- or quilt-covered antique beds surrounded by country furnishings, collectibles, and crafts. Two rooms on the first floor each have a double and twin bed, while the two rooms on the second floor each have a double bed. Breakfast delights include artichoke quiche, sausage apple ring filled with puffy scrambled egg, Dutch babies with raspberry sauce, stuffed French toast, blintz soufflé, muffins, and cinnamon scones with homemade lemon butter. After breakfast, enjoy gem mining, hiking, horseback riding, water rafting, golf, or tennis. Stay long enough to tour the Biltmore Estate in nearby Asheville, drive through the Smokey Mountain Parkway to Cherokee Indian Reservation, or "shop till you drop" in Gatlinburg. Hospitality, comfort, and delightful breakfasts are this inn's priorities.

SEASON

April to December 15

ACCOMMODATIONS

four rooms with private baths

Barry's Gull Cottage
Bed and Breakfast

Vivian and Bob Barry
116 Chesapeake Street
Dewey Beach, Delaware 19971
Tel/Fax: (302) 227-7000
$$$ – $$$$

ABOUT THE B&B

Named "one of the best places to stay at the beach" by The Washingtonian Magazine, *Gull Cottage* is a contemporary Nantucket-style beach house nestled in a pine and cherry grove, one-and-a-half blocks from the ocean and across the street from Lake Comegys. The warm and cozy decor includes antiques, white wicker furniture, quilts, stained glass, skylights, and ceiling fans. A full country gourmet breakfast is served on the screened porch, followed by afternoon tea and evening cake and coffee. The area offers many things to do: early morning walks along the dunes, windsurfing, water-skiing, fishing, and factory outlet shopping, to name a few. Nearby dining ranges from French cuisine to fresh seafood, and, to end the evening, you can relax by candlelight in the cottage's hot tub. Innkeepers Vivian and Bob Barry are retired Central Intelligence Agency officers who enjoy cooking for and pampering their guests.

SEASON

May to October

ACCOMMODATIONS

three rooms with private baths;
two rooms with half baths

Grandma Rull's Honey Balls

(Recipe from Secrets from the Pantry Kitchen of Gull Cottage.*)*

"My grandma was Italian through and through. There was always plenty of food on her table — including these honey balls — and you could not leave her home without taking something with you!"
— Vivian Barry

4 egg yolks
½ teaspoon salt
¼ cup confectioners' sugar
1 teaspoon vanilla
1 cup all-purpose flour
1 egg white
Canola oil
Honey

Beat the egg yolks and salt together for 10 minutes or until slightly thickened and paler yellow. Add the confectioner's sugar and vanilla and beat until well blended. Fold in the flour. Transfer the dough to a well-floured board and knead until blended. Cut the dough in ½ and roll each ½ into a log. Cut off pieces from the log and form into balls the size of walnuts. Drop into hot canola oil and fry until golden brown. Transfer to a paper towel to drain and cool. Serve in a bowl and cover with honey. ***Yield: About 36 honey balls.***

Barry's Gull Cottage

Indian Pudding (Vermont-Style)

½ cup coarsely ground cornmeal
½ cup maple syrup
4 cups scalding hot milk
2 tablespoons butter, melted
1½ teaspoons ground cinnamon
1 teaspoon ground ginger
½ teaspoon ground allspice
½ teaspoon salt
3 eggs, lightly beaten

Apple topping:
3 – 4 tart apples (such as Granny Smith)
4 tablespoons butter
¼ cup sugar
1 teaspoon ground cinnamon
½ teaspoon grated nutmeg

Heavy cream

To make the pudding: Preheat the oven to 350°F. Combine the cornmeal and maple syrup in the top of a double boiler. Stir in the hot milk. Put 2" of simmering water in the bottom of the double boiler, put the upper part with the cornmeal mixture over it and cook, stirring constantly, for about 20 minutes (until thick and smooth). Remove from the heat, take the top part off the bottom part of the double boiler, and stir the butter, spices, and salt into the cornmeal mixture. Add the eggs and beat well.

(continued on next page)

West Hill House

Dotty Kyle and Eric Brattstrom
RR #1, Box 292
Warren, Vermont 05674
Tel: (800) 898-1427 or (802) 496-7162
Fax: (802) 496-6443
$$ – $$$

ABOUT THE B&B

Up a quiet country lane on nine peaceful acres, this 1860s farmhouse boasts stunning mountain views, gardens, a pond and apple orchard, and is just one mile from Sugarbush Ski Resort and adjacent golf course and cross-country ski trails. Besides having an outdoor sports paradise at its doorstep, West Hill House is also near fine restaurants, quaint villages, covered bridges, shops, antique hunting, museums, theater, and concerts. After a busy day, guests enjoy the comfortable front porch or roaring fireplace, library of eclectic books and videos, Oriental rugs, art, antiques, and the interesting company of other guests. Bedrooms feature premium linens, down comforters, and good reading lights. There's also a common guest pantry with wet bar and refrigerator. Breakfast specialties include sticky buns, soufflés, baked apple pancakes, fresh fruit, and more. Dotty and Eric, veteran B&B vacationers themselves, work to create an atmosphere of warmth and hospitality in their lovely small inn. Dotty's the chef, artist, and decorator, while Eric's the creative builder, remodeler, and stained glass artisan.

SEASON

all year

ACCOMMODATIONS

six rooms with private baths

Pour the mixture into a generously buttered 1½-quart baking dish. Put the baking dish into a larger pan, and pour about 1" of boiling water into the larger pan. Bake for approximately 1½ hours or until the pudding is set, stirring every 30 minutes.

To make the apple topping: Thinly slice the apples. Melt the butter in a saucepan (do not let it brown) and place the apples inside. Mix the sugar, cinnamon, and nutmeg together and sprinkle over the apples in the pan. Continue cooking over medium-low heat until the apples are soft but not mushy, constantly stirring so they do not stick or brown (about 5 – 8 minutes).

Serve the pudding warm with apple topping and heavy cream poured over top. *Yield: 6 servings.*

Isle of Jersey Orange Cups

"This is an elegant finale to a wonderful breakfast. I first tasted this recipe at a bed and breakfast on the Isle of Jersey and have since modified it to enchant guests at our own breakfast table."
— *Carol Doelling*

6 medium oranges
½ cup sugar
2 tablespoons cornstarch
¼ cup amaretto liqueur
6 maraschino cherries, ½ cup whipped cream, or vanilla ice cream

Cut the top quarter off each orange. Scoop out the pulp and juice into a saucepan. Cut the top edge of each orange in a zigzag pattern. Discard any seeds or thick membrane, then set the orange shells aside. Over medium heat, stir together the orange juice and pulp, the sugar, and cornstarch until the mixture just starts to boil. Add the amaretto liqueur and continue to cook while constantly stirring until the mixture starts to thicken. Remove this mixture from the heat and pour the mixture into each orange shell. Chill in the refrigerator for at least 1 hour before serving. Top each orange with a maraschino cherry, whipped cream, or vanilla ice cream and serve. *Yield: 6 servings.*

Doelling Haus

Carol and David Doelling
4817 Towne South
St. Louis, Missouri 63128
Tel: (314) 894-6796
$$

ABOUT THE B&B

Rediscover old-world hospitality at Doelling Haus, where you'll delight in beautiful rooms reminiscent of a European country home decorated with German antiques and collectibles, handed down from the hosts' families and gathered during their travels. Hearty full breakfasts include German and Austrian delicacies, and homemade truffles await beside your bed. Many points of interest are nearby, including the famous Arch monument, Grant's Farm, the historic settlement of Kimmswick, recreational areas, shopping malls, and fine restaurants. Carol will direct you to wonderful shops for antique hunting and David, who owns a sports memorabilia store, will gladly show off his old baseball card collection. Come experience "Gemutlichkeit" (a sense of well-being) at Doelling Haus.

SEASON

all year

ACCOMMODATIONS

one room with private bath;
one room with shared bath

The Old Miners' Lodge

Susan Wynne, Liza Simpson,
and Lillian Hauze
PO Box 2639, 615 Woodside Avenue
Park City, Utah 84060
Tel: (801) 645-8068
Fax: (801) 645-7420
$$ – $$$$

ABOUT THE B&B

Located in the national historic district of the colorful resort of Park City, Utah, The Old Miners' Lodge was established in 1889 as a boarding house for local miners seeking their fortune in Park City's ore-rich mountains. Today, the spirited warmth and hospitality of Park City's illustrious past remains in this building, which has been lovingly restored to its original splendor. Named for historic Park City personalities, the lodge's rooms and suites are complete with period antiques and country furnishings, down pillows, and comforters. To start the day, guests are greeted in the cozy dining room with a hearty breakfast, fresh coffee and tea, and fruit nectars. A revitalizing, year-round, outdoor hot tub relaxes and rejuvenates guests after an active day of skiing, golfing, or sightseeing in Park City. The large living room has a fireplace and is a gathering place in the evening, with complimentary refreshments. And of course, knowledgeable innkeepers are always on hand to provide casual conversation on everything from Park City history to assistance with evening dinner and entertainment plans.

SEASON

all year

ACCOMMODATIONS

12 rooms (including three suites)
with private baths

Lemon-Yogurt Scones

1¼ cups all-purpose flour
½ cup whole wheat flour
¼ cup granulated sugar
1 teaspoon baking powder
½ teaspoon baking soda
¼ cup butter or margarine
½ cup low- or non-fat lemon yogurt
⅓ cup well-mashed banana
½ cup finely diced candied lemon peel
1 tablespoon turbinado sugar*

*Raw sugar that has been steam-cleaned, turbinado sugar is blond-colored and has a delicate molasses flavor.

Preheat the oven to 350°F. Combine the flour, granulated sugar, baking powder, and baking soda. Cut in the butter. Mix in the yogurt, banana, and lemon peel. Turn the dough out on a floured surface and shape with floured hands into an 8" circle (higher in the center). Cut the dough into 8 wedges and sprinkle with the turbinado sugar. Place ½" apart on an ungreased baking sheet and bake for 25 minutes or until lightly golden. *Yield: 8 scones.*

Maple-poached Pears

"A warm maple-scented pear served in a pool of creamy yogurt on a crystal plate often sends guests for their cameras before their forks!"
— *Christopher Sellers*

6 large pears
2 quarts boiling water
¾ cup Vermont maple syrup
12 ounces French vanilla yogurt
Grated nutmeg
12 mint sprigs

Peel, half, and core the pears. Combine the boiling water and syrup, and poach the pears in this mixture for 20 minutes. Drain the pears. To serve, create a pool of vanilla yogurt on a glass plate. Position each warm pear half, cut side down, on the pool of yogurt. Dust with the nutmeg. Garnish with a mint sprig in place of the pear stem. ***Yield: 12 servings.***

Grünberg Haus Bed & Breakfast
Waterbury, Vermont

Grünberg Haus Bed and Breakfast

Christopher Sellers and
Mark Frohman
RR #2, Box 1595RD,
Route 100 South
Waterbury, Vermont 05676-9621
Tel: (800) 800-7760 or (802) 244-7726
Fax: (802) 244-1283
E-mail: grunhaus@aol.com
$$ – $$$$

ABOUT THE B&B

This picture-postcard Austrian-style B&B is tucked away on a secluded hillside in the Green Mountains, perfectly situated for visits to Stowe, Montpelier, Waterbury, and Burlington. Individually decorated guest rooms open onto the carved wood balcony, which offers wonderful views. Help Mark feed the chickens, then enjoy a full breakfast — with selections such as maple-poached pears, apple and cheddar muffins, and ricotta-stuffed French toast — while Chris plays the grand piano. The giant stone fireplace and wood stove in the BYOB pub are favorite gathering places. Nearby activities include spectacular autumn leaf-picking, world-class downhill skiing, golf, boating, bicycling, gliding, canoeing, antique hunting, outlet shopping, and touring Ben & Jerry's ice cream factory. And you can enjoy the B&B's own Jacuzzi, sauna, tennis courts, and cross-country and hiking trails.

SEASON

all year

ACCOMMODATIONS

seven rooms (including one suite)
with private baths;
five rooms with shared baths;
two cabins with private baths

The Marlborough

Al Hammond
320 Woods Hole Road
Woods Hole, Massachusetts 02543
Tel: (508) 548-6218
Fax: (508) 457-7519
$$$

ABOUT THE B&B

*T*he Marlborough is a romantic Cape Cod cottage complete with picket fence, trellis, and garden set up on a hill among the trees. Rooms have private baths and are individually decorated with quilts, coordinated scented linens, and collectibles. Gather for conversation, read, or watch television in the large comfortable parlor. Full gourmet breakfast, including wonderfully brewed coffee and tea, is served outside by the kidney-shaped pool or inside by the fireplace, depending on the season. Informal afternoon tea is served in season, while high tea is served on Sundays in the off-season. Excellent restaurants are nearby, as is Woods Hole Oceanographic Institute, beaches, shopping, bike paths, and ferries to Martha's Vineyard. The Marlborough is a great starting point for day trips to locations all over Cape Cod and the islands, Plymouth, Boston, and Providence. Innkeeper Al Hammond enjoys helping guests get the most out of their visit. A long-time veteran of the foodservice industry, Al enjoys cooking and learning about Cape Cod history.

SEASON

all year

ACCOMMODATIONS

five rooms with private baths

Marlborough Baked Apples

6 large baking apples (Cortland, Winesap, Rome, or Golden Delicious)
2 cups granola
½ cup chopped dates or raisins
½ cup chopped walnuts
½ teaspoon ground cinnamon
¼ teaspoon grated nutmeg
3 tablespoons lemon juice
½ cup honey
9 tablespoons butter
1 cup fruit juice (such as apple or nectarine)
Whipped cream
Grated nutmeg
6 fresh mint sprigs

Preheat the oven to 350°F. Scoop out the apple cores, making a big hole to hold as much filling as possible. Combine ½ cup of the granola and the dates, walnuts, cinnamon, nutmeg, and lemon juice with 4 tablespoons of the honey to make the filling. Spoon the filling into the cored apples and place in a shallow baking pan. Combine the remaining honey with the butter and fruit juice and heat to boiling. Pour over the apples. Cover the pan with foil and bake for about 10 minutes. Remove the cover and baste the apples with the apple juices. Continue baking until the apples are tender when pricked with a fork (about 20 minutes more). Put the apples in individual serving bowls and top each with ¼ cup granola, some of the leftover apple juices from baking, and a dollop of whipped cream. Sprinkle with a little nutmeg and garnish with a sprig of fresh mint. Serve warm. *Yield: 6 servings.*

Mary's Irish Raisin Scones

"This recipe was given to us by guest Mary Early. When she checked in, I thought she was right off the plane from Ireland — she had such a strong Irish accent. But she's actually lived in The Bronx for over 30 years! I made Mary's recipe on the day she checked out and her scones have been a hit ever since." — David Horan

4 cups all-purpose flour
¾ cup and a sprinkle of sugar
3 heaping teaspoons baking powder
¼ teaspoon baking soda
1 teaspoon salt
¼ cup butter
1 cup raisins
1 egg
2 tablespoons sour cream
2 cups buttermilk
Melted butter

(continued on next page)

The Melville House

Vince De Rico and David Horan
39 Clarke Street
Newport, Rhode Island 02840
Tel: (401) 847-0640
Fax: (401) 847-0956
E-mail: Innkeeper@ids.net
www.melvillehouse.com
$$$ – $$$$

ABOUT THE B&B

Built circa 1750 and on the National Register of Historic Places, The Melville House is located in the heart of Newport's historic Hill District on a quiet gas-lit street. One of the few inns in Newport dedicated to the Colonial style, it's just one block up from Thames Street with its Brick Market and the harborfront where many of the city's finest restaurants, luxurious sailboats, antique shops, and galleries can be found. The Melville House is also close to the Tennis Hall of Fame, lavish Vanderbilt, Astor, and Belmont family mansions, the Naval War College, and Newport's finest ocean beaches. The Melville House breakfast menu features homemade granola, muffins, breads, buttermilk biscuits, scones, Yankee cornbread, stuffed French toast, fresh fruit sourdough pancakes, and Rhode Island johnnycakes. An afternoon tea is served every day, featuring refreshments, homemade biscotti, and soup (on cold days), over which innkeepers Vince and David share their Newport experiences.

SEASON

all year

ACCOMMODATIONS

five rooms with private baths;
two rooms with shared bath;
winter fireplace suite

Preheat the oven to 425°F. Mix the flour, ¾ cup of the sugar, baking powder, baking soda, and salt together. Cut the butter into small pieces. With a pastry cutter, cut the butter into the flour mixture until well blended. Add the raisins to the flour mixture and mix well with your fingers. In a small bowl, beat together the egg, sour cream, and buttermilk. Pour this egg mixture slowly into the flour mixture, stirring constantly with a fork (you might not need all the egg mixture). Continue to stir with a fork just until it all comes together. Roll the dough out onto a floured surface, knead for about 2 minutes, then form into a ball. Divide the dough in ½ and form each half into a flat disk. Cut each disk with a pastry cutter into 6 triangles and place on an ungreased baking sheet. Bake for about 20 minutes or until golden brown and firm. Brush with butter and sprinkle with sugar. *Yield: 12 scones.*

Mary's Little Angels

"I like to use a heart-shaped cutter on these biscuits, which have a beautiful color and are really delicious." — Mary Shaw

2 packages active dry yeast (2 tablespoons)
¼ cup lukewarm water
5 cups self-rising flour
1 teaspoon baking soda
2 tablespoons sugar
1 cup vegetable shortening (Crisco brand recommended)
2 cups vegetable juice (V8 brand recommended)

Add the yeast to the lukewarm water, and let dissolve 3 – 5 minutes. Mix the flour, baking soda, and sugar. Add the shortening and mix. Add in the yeast and vegetable juice and mix well. Roll onto a floured board and cut out the biscuits with a cookie cutter. Start baking in a cold oven at 450°F until lightly browned (approximately 10 – 12 minutes).
Yield: 18 – 20 biscuits.

The Shaw House Bed and Breakfast

Mary and Joe Shaw
613 Cypress Court
Georgetown, South Carolina 29440
Tel: (803) 546-9663
$$

ABOUT THE B&B

The Shaw House Bed and Breakfast is a spacious two-story home in a serene, natural setting. From the glass-walled den, enjoy bird-watching and a beautiful view overlooking miles of marshland formed by four rivers, which converge and flow into the Intercoastal Waterway. Outlined by tall white columns, the wide front porch extends the width of the home and features old-fashioned rockers — ready and waiting for guests who are welcomed as family. All rooms are air conditioned, with private baths and a smattering of antiques. Enjoy a full southern breakfast come morning and bed turn-backs and chocolate come bedtime.

SEASON

all year

ACCOMMODATIONS

three rooms with private baths

The Babbling Brook Inn

Dan Floyd
1025 Laurel Street
Santa Cruz, California 95060
Tel: (800) 866-1131 or (408) 427-2437
Fax: (408) 458-0989
E-mail: lodging@
babblingbrookinn.com
$$$ – $$$$

ABOUT THE B&B

Cascading waterfalls, a meandering creek, and a romantic gazebo grace an acre of gardens, pines, and redwoods surrounding this secluded inn. Built in 1909 on the foundation of an 1870 tannery, a 1790 grist mill, and a 2,000-year old Indian fishing village, the Babbling Brook features rooms in country French decor, all with private bath, telephone, and television, and most with cozy fireplace, private deck, and outside entrance. Included in your stay is a large, country breakfast and afternoon wine and cheese, where the inn's prize-winning cookies await you on the tea cart in front of a roaring fireplace. Two blocks off Highway 1, the Babbling Brook is within walking distance of the beach, wharf, boardwalk, shops, tennis, running paths, and historic homes. Three golf courses and 200 restaurants are within 15 minutes' drive.

SEASON

all year

ACCOMMODATIONS

12 rooms with private baths

Mrs. King's Cookies

"This prize-winning cookie recipe was handed down to me by the former owner of the inn." — Dan Floyd

2 cups butter
2 cups brown sugar
2 cups granulated sugar
4 eggs
2 teaspoons vanilla
4 cups all-purpose flour
2 teaspoons baking powder
2 teaspoons baking soda
2 teaspoons salt
2 cups white chocolate chips
2 cups milk chocolate chips
3 cups raisins
3 cups chopped walnuts
2 cups large-flake rolled oats
3 cups orange-almond granola, or add grated orange zest (to taste) to plain granola

Preheat the oven to 375°F. Cream the butter and sugar. Add the eggs and vanilla. Sift the flour, baking powder, baking soda, and salt, and add to the creamed mixture, beating well. Stir in the chocolate chips, raisins, walnuts, oats, and granola. When well mixed, shape the dough into balls the size of golf balls and bake on an ungreased cookie sheet 8 – 10 minutes or until barely golden. *Tips:* Cookies are best when slightly undercooked and served warm from the oven. Dough keeps well when refrigerated — simply bake as needed. *Yield: 9 dozen cookies.*

Noodle Kagel

Bottom layer:
4 eggs
½ cup sugar
½ cup butter, softened
1 teaspoon vanilla

Middle layer:
1 pound medium egg noodles, cooked

Top layer:
1 pound creamed cottage cheese
4 eggs
2 cups sour cream
½ cup milk
Juice of 1 lemon
½ cup sugar
Ground cinnamon to taste

Preheat the oven to 350°F. Spray a 13 x 9" baking dish with nonstick cooking spray. Combine the eggs, sugar, butter, and vanilla. Pour into the baking dish. Cover with the noodles. Combine the cottage cheese, eggs, sour cream, milk, lemon juice, sugar, and cinnamon and pour over the noodles. Bake for 90 minutes or until the top is golden in color. Slice and serve immediately. *Yield: 10 servings.*

The Old Powder House Inn

Eunice and Al Howes
38 Cordova Street
St. Augustine, Florida 32084
Tel: (800) 447-4149
Fax: (904) 825-0143
E-mail: ahowes@aug.com
www.oldcity.com/powderhouse
$$$

ABOUT THE B&B

The Old Powder House Inn stands on the ground where, in the late 18th century, a powder house once stood, used by Spanish soldiers at nearby fort Castillo de San Marcos. Today, it's a charming turn-of-the-century Victorian inn. Lace curtains and hardwood floors adorn antique-filled rooms. Leave your cares behind as you relax on the veranda or sit by the fountain in the courtyard. The inn is located in the historic district steps away from quaint shops and landmarks of the nation's oldest city. Choose from one of eight distinctive rooms, each with private bath. The romantic Queen Anne's Lace, for example, features a queen-size pedestal bed with lace canopy, while Memories features its own Jacuzzi tub. Enjoy a gourmet breakfast in the formal dining room, where stuffed pears, granola, chocolate-chip muffins, and soufflés may be part of the morning menu. Join other guests and innkeepers Eunice and Al Howes for afternoon tea or evening wine with hors d'oeuvres.

SEASON

all year

ACCOMMODATIONS

eight rooms (including two suites) with private baths

The Albert Stevens Inn & Cat's Garden

Diane and Curt Diviney-Rangen
127 Myrtle Avenue
Cape May, New Jersey 08204
Tel: (609) 884-4717
Fax: (609) 884-8320
E-mail: CRangen@
Beachcomber.com
www.capemaycats.com
$$$

ABOUT THE B&B

Built in 1898 by Dr. Albert G. Stevens, this Victorian Queen Anne classic features a unique floating staircase suspended from the third-floor turret. After enjoying a three-course Norwegian-style breakfast, you can wander off to the nearby shopping mall, swimming beaches, the lighthouse, bird observatory, and shops. Or, you may want to unwind in the Cat's Garden. Established in 1992 as a safe haven for the wild or forgotten cats that wander the shore, the garden is landscaped with hundreds of plants and herbs and a little pond, and enjoyed by cats and humans alike. Innkeepers Diane and Curt invite you to join them in rediscovering the soothing sights and sounds of the shore. Here, you'll find two hard-working individuals who escaped the corporate world for a life now dedicated to balancing man with nature.

SEASON

February to December

ACCOMMODATIONS

nine rooms (including two suites)
with private baths

Norwegian Fruit Pizza

Crust:
¾ cup butter
½ cup confectioners' sugar
1½ cups all-purpose flour

Cream filling:
8 ounces cream cheese, softened
½ cup sugar
½ teaspoon vanilla
3 fruit of your choice (such as peaches, bananas, kiwis, strawberries, or blueberries)

Glaze:
1 cup fruit juice (such as apple)
2 tablespoons cornstarch
1 tablespoon lemon juice
½ cup sugar
2 tablespoons kirsch or brandy

Preheat the oven to 350°F. Mix the butter, sugar, and flour together until crumb-like. Pat it into a pizza pan and bake 11 – 13 minutes or until a light golden brown.

To make the cream filling: Blend the cream, sugar, and vanilla together. Spread it over the cooled crust. Top with the fruit.

To make the glaze: Heat together the fruit juice, cornstarch, lemon juice, sugar, and liqueur in a saucepan. Cook, stirring constantly, until clear and thick. Spread the glaze on top of the pizza after it's been sliced.
Yield: 10 – 12 servings.

Oatmeal-Carrot Cookies

"The wonderful aroma of these cookies gets anyone's stay at Dreams of Yesteryear off to a wonderful start. You can make a batch of these and then freeze unbaked cookies on a baking sheet. When guests are about to arrive, just pop a dozen or so in the oven for the best potpourri smell around." — Bonnie Maher

¾ cup margarine
1¾ cups all-purpose flour
¾ cup brown sugar
½ cup granulated sugar
1 egg
1 teaspoon baking powder
¼ teaspoon baking soda
½ teaspoon ground cinnamon
¼ teaspoon ground cloves
1 teaspoon vanilla
2 cups large-flake rolled oats
1 cup finely grated carrots
½ cup raisins (optional)

Preheat the oven to 370°F. Mix the margarine, flour, sugar, egg, baking powder, baking soda, cinnamon, cloves, vanilla, oats, carrots, and raisins together and drop by teaspoonfuls 2" apart on a lightly greased cookie sheet. Bake 10 – 12 minutes. ***Yield: 4 dozen cookies.***

Dreams of Yesteryear Bed and Breakfast

Bonnie and Bill Maher
1100 Brawley Street
Stevens Point, Wisconsin 54481
Tel: (715) 341-4525
Fax: (715) 344-3047
$$ – $$$$

ABOUT THE B&B

This elegant, turn-of-the-century Victorian Queen Anne was home to three generations of the Jensen family before being purchased in 1987 and restored by current owners Bonnie and Bill Maher. An article Bonnie wrote about the restoration was featured in the Winter 1991 issue of Victorian Homes *magazine*. In 1990, after giving many tours, the Mahers opened their home as the Dreams of Yesteryear Bed and Breakfast. Listed on the National Register of Historic Places, Dreams of Yesteryear is located three blocks from historic downtown Stevens Point, two blocks from the Wisconsin River and Green Circle jogging, hiking, biking trails, a half mile from the University of Wisconsin, and near wonderful restaurants, theaters, and antique shops. Your visit includes a gourmet breakfast, warm hospitality, and wonderful memories.

SEASON

all year

ACCOMMODATIONS

two suites with private baths;
two rooms with shared bath

Rockinghorse Bed & Breakfast

Sharleen and Jerry Bergum
RR #1, Box 133
Whitewood, South Dakota 57793
Tel: (605) 269-2625
$$

ABOUT THE B&B

A cedar clapboard-sided house built in 1914 to accommodate local timber teams, *Rockinghorse* was moved to its present location by Sharleen and Jerry, who have lovingly restored the interior. Handsome wood floors, columns, and trims, along with antiques, country charm decor, and the original stairway grace the home. Rockinghorse is situated in the rustic Black Hills, where you can watch deer graze nearby and wild turkeys strut across the valley. Listen to the sounds of coyotes in the evening while a rooster's crow awakens you in the morning. You can also pet a bunny, ride the horse-drawn wagon, or have wood/fiber artist Sharleen help you master the spinning wheel. A gift shop is also on the premises. The B&B is near historic Deadwood, the world renowned Passion Play, the scenic Spearfish Canyon route, and a one-hour drive from Mount Rushmore. Full breakfast includes fresh fruit (in season), homemade breads, blueberry pancakes, and special egg-cheese dishes.

SEASON

all year

ACCOMMODATIONS

three rooms with private baths

Overnight Cinnamon Rolls

"My grandma used to bake cinnamon rolls like this when I was a child. I've added the convenience of a blender and now use whole wheat grain — nonetheless they're just as good as ever."
— *Sharleen Bergum*

Dough:
4 cups whole wheat flour
5½ cups all-purpose flour
3 cups lukewarm water
1 package active dry yeast (1 tablespoon)
2 teaspoons salt
1 cup sugar
2 eggs
½ cup margarine

Frosting:
1 cup whipping cream
2 cups brown sugar
1 cup margarine

(continued on next page)

Filling:
Margarine
Brown sugar
Ground cinnamon
Raisins (optional)

Around 3:00 pm, make the dough. Combine the whole wheat and all-purpose flour in a large bowl and set aside. In a blender, blend the water, yeast, salt, sugar, eggs, and margarine. Pour the blender ingredients into the flour mixture and mix well. Cover and set the dough aside for several hours.

Around 10:00 pm, make the frosting. Mix together the whipping cream, brown sugar, and margarine. Place this mixture in 2 (13 x 11" or equivalent) baking pans. Roll the dough out into a rectangle.

To make the filling, spread the margarine over the dough, then sprinkle it with brown sugar, cinnamon, and raisins. Roll the dough into a tube and cut into ¼" slices. Place the slices cut side down into the prepared baking pans. Cover with a towel and place in a draft-free area. Let rise until morning. Preheat the oven to 350°F and bake for 25 minutes. Serve warm. *Yield: About 40 rolls.*

Chalet Kilauea —
The Inn at Volcano

Lisha and Brian Crawford
Box 998, Wright Road
Volcano, Hawaii 96785
Tel: (808) 967-7786
Fax: (808) 967-8660
E-mail: Reservations@
Volcano-Hawaii.com
$$$$

ABOUT THE B&B

Explore treasures from around the world at Chalet Kilauea, a lush Hawaiian haven nestled in Volcano Village. Owners Lisha and Brian Crawford are international travelers who know the art of hospitality. At the inn, choose from superior rooms inspired by Oriental, African, or European themes, or the Treehouse Suite, with most featuring marble Jacuzzis. Tempt your appetite with a candlelit, two-course gourmet breakfast featuring local and international cuisine. Luxuriate in the Jacuzzi, relax by the fireplace, peruse the library, or wander in the garden. The spacious vacation homes are particularly suited for families, larger parties, and those seeking complete privacy. All offer a full kitchen and include afternoon tea and use of the Jacuzzi. Near the inn, you'll find Hawaii Volcanoes National Park, Black Sand Beach, and the city of Hilo with all its splendors. Opportunities abound for lava viewing, hiking, biking, golfing, swimming, bird watching, exploring, and just plain unwinding!

SEASON

all year

ACCOMMODATIONS

six rooms with private baths;
six vacation homes

Papaya with Triple Cream

⅓ cup vanilla yogurt
⅓ cup sour cream
⅓ cup whipped cream
Passion fruit syrup to taste
½ papaya
Sliced kiwi and strawberries
Mint leaf
Sprinkle of freshly grated nutmeg

Whip the yogurt, sour cream, and whipped cream together. Add syrup to taste. Fill the papaya half with the cream mixture. Garnish with the sliced kiwi and strawberries, and a mint leaf. Sprinkle with freshly grated nutmeg. *Yield: 1 serving.*

Peach Cobbler

"This is a very old family recipe for the best peach cobbler I've ever tasted. I use it as a breakfast dish because of the low sugar content — I let the natural sweetness of the peaches do the job (which my calorie-conscious guests appreciate!). The batter alone makes a great shortcake." — Joan Barris

2 eggs
½ cup and ⅔ cup sugar
6 tablespoons butter or margarine, melted
⅔ cup milk
2 cups all-purpose flour
4 teaspoons baking powder
½ teaspoon salt
12 large or 16 medium peaches, peeled, pitted, and sliced
1 teaspoon ground cinnamon

Milk, heavy or whipped cream, or ice cream

Preheat the oven to 375°F. In a large mixing bowl, beat the eggs until light. Add the ½ cup sugar, melted butter, and milk. Sift the flour, baking powder, and salt into the egg mixture. Mix thoroughly. Butter a 13 x 9" baking pan and fill with the peaches. Mix the ⅔ cup sugar and cinnamon together and sprinkle over the peaches. Pour the batter over the peaches. Bake 35 – 40 minutes. Serve warm with milk, heavy or whipped cream, or ice cream. *Yield: 15 – 18 servings.*

Idlewyld Bed & Breakfast

Joan and Dan Barris
350 Walnut Street
Lakeside, Ohio 43440
(Mailing address:
13458 Parkway Drive
Lakewood, Ohio 44107)
Tel: (419) 798-4198
$ – $$

ABOUT THE B&B

Idlewyld has a homey atmosphere where guests can relax and enjoy the tranquil beauty and timeless charm of 19th-century Lakeside, on the shores of Lake Erie. The century-old home has both an upper porch and a lower wraparound porch furnished with Amish hickory rockers. There are 15 rooms at Idlewyld, each distinctively decorated in a country style. Hosts Joan and Dan Barris take special pride in offering delicious and nutritious breakfast fare. Dan's specialty is popping corn on Saturday nights in the vintage popcorn popper on the front porch. Joan's special interest is nutrition, and Idlewyld is the site of an annual wellness/spa weekend held in late summer.

SEASON

May to October

ACCOMMODATIONS

five rooms with private baths;
10 rooms with shared baths

Ashling Cottage

Goodi and Jack Stewart
106 Sussex Avenue
Spring Lake, New Jersey 07762
Tel: (888) ASHLING
Fax: (732) 974-0831
E-mail: Ashling@lonekeep.com
$$$ – $$$$

ABOUT THE B&B

For generations, rambling Victorian homes have fronted the spring-fed lakes from which Spring Lake, New Jersey, gets its name. Tree-lined walkways surround the lakes, and wooden foot bridges connect grassy areas of park. Sun, sand, surf, and serenity in equal measure — Spring Lake offers all this and Ashling Cottage, too. Since 1877, the visiting gentry have enjoyed sumptuous breakfasts on the porches of this lovely and intimate seaside inn, overlooking both ocean and lake. Today, the tradition continues with casual hospitality and personal attention offered for your vacationing pleasure. While leisure activities abound (such as golf, tennis, biking, horseback riding, and sightseeing in nearby New York and Philadelphia), the most delightful feature of this inn and this town is the guilt-free ability to do absolutely nothing!

SEASON

May to October

ACCOMMODATIONS

eight rooms with private baths;
two rooms with shared bath

Peaches with Honey-Lime Whip

"This recipe came from the owners of a nearby 'pick your own' orchard where we pick our peaches and prepare them while they're still warm from the ripening sun." — Goodi Stewart

4 tablespoons honey
2 teaspoons grated lime zest
3 tablespoons lime juice
¼ teaspoon ground mace or nutmeg
9 – 10 medium peaches, peeled and sliced

Combine the honey, lime zest, lime juice, and mace in a small bowl, mixing well with a wire whisk. Pour it over the peaches, tossing gently.
Yield: 9 – 12 servings.

Peach Melba

1 tablespoon raspberry jam
1 tablespoon currant or apple jelly
½ cup frozen raspberries
1 peach, peeled and halved
Vanilla ice cream
Mint leaves

Melt the jam and jelly in a small saucepan over low heat. Add the frozen raspberries and stir. Simmer over low heat until warmed through. Arrange 1 peach half in a stemmed fruit glass. Top each with a melon ball-sized scoop of vanilla ice cream. Top with the warmed fruit sauce and garnish with a mint leaf. *Tip:* Recipe is easily expandable for larger numbers. *Yield: 2 servings.*

Inn at Blush Hill

Pamela Gosselin
RR #1, Box 1266
Waterbury, Vermont 05676
Tel: (802) 244-7529
Fax: (802) 244-7314
E-mail: INNATBH@aol.com
$$ – $$$

ABOUT THE B&B

*O*nce a stagecoach stop on the route between Montpelier and Stowe, this circa-1790 Cape Cod inn has become a haven for modern-day travelers seeking country comfort and hospitality. Cozy guest rooms are filled with country antiques and coordinated fabrics and wallpapers. One guest room has a fireplace, another has a queen canopy with Battenburg lace and a panoramic view of the mountains. On a chilly day, curl up with a book in front of one of the inn's roaring fireplaces. During summer, there's a large covered porch that beckons you to sit awhile and enjoy the magnificent view. The inn serves many native Vermont products, from fresh apple cider to Ben and Jerry's ice cream and Vermont maple syrup. The inn is adjacent to Ben and Jerry's Ice Cream Factory (the most popular tourist attraction in Vermont), within minutes of Cold Hollow Cider Mill, Green Mountain Chocolate Factory, and Cabot Creamery, and is just a 10-minute drive from the village of Stowe.

SEASON

all year

ACCOMMODATIONS

five rooms with private baths

The Duff Green Mansion

Mr. and Mrs. Harry Carter Sharp
1114 First East Street
Vicksburg, Mississippi 39188
Tel: (601) 636-6968
Fax: (601) 661-0079
$$ – $$$$

ABOUT THE B&B

The Duff Green Mansion is located in Vicksburg's historic district. Built in 1856, it's considered one of the finest examples of Paladian architecture in the state of Mississippi. The mansion was built by Duff Green, a prosperous merchant, for his bride Mary Lake Green (whose parents gave the land as a wedding gift). Many parties were held here during the antebellum days but it was hastily converted to a hospital for both Confederate and Union soldiers during the siege of Vicksburg and the remainder of the Civil War. Mary Green gave birth to a son during the siege in one of the caves next to the mansion and appropriately named him Siege Green. The over 12,000-square-foot mansion has been restored and features seven guest rooms with private baths, luxurious antiques, room service, southern plantation breakfasts, cocktails, and a swimming pool.

SEASON

all year

ACCOMMODATIONS

seven rooms (including two suites)
with private baths

Pecan Crescents

"One of Duff Green's favorite pecan recipes."
— Stephen Kerr, chef of Duff Green Mansion

8 tablespoons butter
¾ cup brown sugar
½ cup chopped pecans
¼ cup water
2 packages refrigerated crescent roll dough
¼ cup granulated sugar
2 teaspoons ground cinnamon

Preheat the oven to 375°F. Melt 5 tablespoons of the butter in a 13 x 9 x 2" pan. Sprinkle the brown sugar over the butter. Add the chopped pecans. Sprinkle with the water. Separate the crescent roll dough into rectangles. Mix together the remaining 3 tablespoons of butter with the granulated sugar and cinnamon. Spread on the dough. Roll up each rectangle. Using a thread or a very sharp knife, slice into 5 pieces. Place the crescents in the pan and bake for 20 minutes. Flip out of the pan onto wax paper. Let cool and serve. *Yield: 20 rolls.*

Pumpkin Casserole

15½-ounce can pumpkin
14-ounce can condensed milk
¼ cup butter, melted
½ cup sugar
4 eggs
2 teaspoons ground cinnamon

Preheat the oven to 325°F. Mix the pumpkin, milk, butter, sugar, eggs, and cinnamon well in a medium bowl and pour into a 2-quart baking dish. Bake for 45 minutes or until set. *Yield: 6 – 8 servings.*

Shadwick House Bed & Breakfast

Ann Epperson
411 South Main Street
Somerset, Kentucky 42501
Tel: (606) 678-4675
$$

ABOUT THE B&B

*S*tanding in the foothills of the Cumberland Mountains, Shadwick House has been known for its southern hospitality for over 70 years. Built in 1920 by Nellie Stringer Shadwick (the great-grandmother of the present owners), the house has been carefully restored to its original stature by Nellie's descendants. The first floor has been converted into a gift shop featuring authentic Kentucky antiques and crafts. There are four upstairs guest rooms, tastefully furnished in antiques. In the days of the roaring twenties and the great depression, Shadwick House served as a boarding house for railroad workers and traveling salesmen. It's rumored that John Dillinger once stayed here while casing the Farmers Bank in town. Nearby are great attractions such as the Big South Fork National Park, Renfro Valley, Cumberland Falls State Park, General Burnside Island State Park, Tombstone Junction, Lake Cumberland, Natural Arch State Park, and Daniel Boone National Forest.

SEASON

all year

ACCOMMODATIONS

four rooms with shared baths

West Hill House

Dotty Kyle and Eric Brattstrom
RR #1, Box 292
Warren, Vermont 05674
Tel: (800) 898-1427 or (802) 496-7162
Fax: (802) 496-6443
$$ – $$$

ABOUT THE B&B

Up a quiet country lane on nine peaceful acres, this 1860s farmhouse boasts stunning mountain views, gardens, a pond and apple orchard, and is just one mile from Sugarbush Ski Resort and adjacent golf course and cross-country ski trails. Besides having an outdoor sports paradise at its doorstep, West Hill House is also near fine restaurants, quaint villages, covered bridges, shops, antique hunting, museums, theater, and concerts. After a busy day, guests enjoy the comfortable front porch or roaring fireplace, library of eclectic books and videos, Oriental rugs, art, antiques, and the interesting company of other guests. Bedrooms feature premium linens, down comforters, and good reading lights. There's also a common guest pantry with wet bar and refrigerator. Breakfast specialties include sticky buns, soufflés, baked apple pancakes, fresh fruit, and more. Dotty and Eric, veteran B&B vacationers themselves, work to create an atmosphere of warmth and hospitality in their lovely small inn. Dotty's the chef, artist, and decorator, while Eric's the creative builder, remodeler, and stained glass artisan.

SEASON

all year

ACCOMMODATIONS

six rooms with private baths

Ranger Cookies

"I was first offered these cookies by my friend, Vilma Smith, whose mother made them often. When I was 12 years old, I asked her for the recipe and have been making them ever since (and I'm a grandma several times over!)." — Dotty Kyle

½ cup butter
½ cup granulated sugar
½ cup light brown sugar
1 egg
½ teaspoon vanilla
1 cup all-purpose flour
¼ teaspoon baking powder
½ teaspoon baking soda
¼ teaspoon salt
1 cup large-flake rolled oats
½ cup shredded unsweetened coconut

Preheat the oven to 350°F. Cream the butter and sugar together until fluffy. Add the egg and vanilla, beating well. Add the flour, baking powder, baking soda, salt, oats, and coconut together and mix well. Drop the batter by rounded tablespoonfuls onto an ungreased baking sheet. Cook 10 – 12 minutes. The cookies should be slightly soft and light brown on the bottom. Allow them to cool for 1 minute before removing from the sheet. *Yield: 24 cookies.*

Spiced Broiled Peaches

8 peach halves
Sprinkle of ground cinnamon
8 tablespoons brown sugar
Maple syrup

Arrange the peach halves, cut side up, in a shallow baking pan. Sprinkle each with the cinnamon. Press 1 tablespoon brown sugar into the cavity. Pour a little syrup onto each half. Broil on the top shelf of the oven until the brown sugar melts. *Yield: 8 servings.*

Bedford's Covered Bridge Inn

Martha and Greg Lau
RD 2, Box 196
Schellsburg, Pennsylvania 15559
Tel: (814) 733-4093
$$ – $$$

ABOUT THE B&B

*S*ituated near Exit 11 of I-76 (the Pennsylvania Turnpike), Bedford's Covered Bridge Inn borders 4,000-acre Shawnee State Park, a lovely trout stream, and the Colvin covered bridge. From this idyllic location, guests can pursue hiking, biking, fishing, cross-country skiing, birding, and antique hunting right from the inn's door. Nearby swimming and boating on Shawnee Lake, visits to Old Bedford Village and Bedford's historic district, driving tours, downhill skiing at Blue Knob Resort, and tours of Bedford's 14 covered bridges round out the list of local activities. Inside the inn, the Lau's attention to detail creates an atmosphere that is comfortable and inviting. The historic farmhouse (circa 1823) boasts six guest rooms with private baths, traditional and country decor, and memorable breakfasts. "There's no doubt what everyone's favorite activity is," say Greg and Martha, "Sitting on the inn's wraparound porch and wishing they could live in Bedford County, too!"

SEASON

all year

ACCOMMODATIONS

six rooms with private baths;
one cottage for couples
or families

Golden Maple Inn

Jo and Dick Wall
Wolcott Village, Vermont
05680-0035
Tel: (800) 639-5234 or (802) 888-6614
Fax: (802) 888-6614
E-mail: GoldnMaple@aol.com
$$

ABOUT THE B&B

Originally the home of prominent mill owner H.B. Bundy, this historic 1865 B&B is nestled alongside northern Vermont's Lamoille River — famous for excellent trout fishing and quiet canoeing. Guests can read or doze in the library, put together puzzles in the parlor, or listen to the gurgle of the river from the comfort of an Adirondack chair. Jo and Dick's delightful candlelit breakfasts include fresh-ground coffees, teas, juice, fresh fruit in season, homemade granolas, and a scrumptious daily specialty entrée, all prepared in their country kitchen from only the finest local ingredients. To complete the day, teas and sweets are served to guests each evening in the library and parlor. Country walks, trout fishing, canoeing, biking, and back-country skiing are all available right from the inn. Golden Maple is located near the historic Fisher Covered Railroad Bridge, Bread & Puppet Museum, Cabot Creamery, Ben & Jerry's Ice Cream Factory, and the shops of Stowe Village.

SEASON

all year

ACCOMMODATIONS

four rooms (including two suites)
with private baths

Spicy Lemon Scones

"A delightful breakfast treat best served with an egg entrée."
— Dick Wall

2½ cups all-purpose flour
1 tablespoon baking powder
1 teaspoon ground cinnamon
¼ teaspoon ground allspice
¼ teaspoon ground cloves
½ teaspoon salt
8 tablespoons cold butter, cut into small pieces
½ cup currants or dark raisins
¼ cup sugar
2 tablespoons candied lemon peel, finely diced
⅔ cup milk

Icing:
⅓ cup confectioners' sugar
1½ teaspoons milk

Preheat the oven to 375°F. Thoroughly stir the flour, baking powder, spices, and salt into a bowl. With your fingers, rub pieces of the butter into the flour mixture until fine granules are formed. Add the currants, sugar, and lemon peel. Add the milk and stir to form a soft dough. Lightly flour a board and turn out the dough, kneading it lightly about 10 times. Separate the dough into 8 or 10 balls and place on an ungreased cookie sheet. Bake 12 – 15 minutes or until golden brown. Cool on a wire rack. To make the icing, mix the confectioners' sugar and milk until smooth. Drizzle the icing over each scone and serve.
Yield: 8 – 10 scones.

Stuffed Orange Cups

"These orange cups have lots of eye appeal and are very refreshing on a warm summer morning." — Diane Damato

6 large navel oranges
½ cup chopped dates
½ cup shredded unsweetened coconut
½ cup chopped pecans or walnuts
Mint leaves

Cut off the tops of the oranges. Remove the orange segments with a paring knife and cut them into bite-size pieces, discarding the membranes. Catch any juices over a bowl. In the same bowl, mix the orange pieces, dates, coconut, and nuts together. Put the mixture in the hollowed out orange shells (you may need to cut a thin slice from the bottom of the oranges to prevent tipping). Serve on glass plates with fresh mint leaves. *Tip:* Do not prepare ahead of time — these are best served immediately after preparing. *Yield: 6 servings.*

Ferry Point House Bed & Breakfast on Lake Winnisquam

Diane and Joe Damato
100 Lower Bay Road
Sanbornton, New Hampshire 03269
Tel: (603) 524-0087
Fax: (603) 524-0959
$$ – $$$

ABOUT THE B&B

This gracious, 175-year-old country Victorian is located on picturesque Lake Winnisquam, in a spot commanding a panoramic view of lake and mountains. The gazebo on the point complements the sandy beach and allows for quiet moments by the water. A 60-foot veranda and all of the rooms are blessed with breathtaking views. Return to the warm, friendly feeling of New England's past with antique furniture, collectibles, and fresh flowers in your room. The lake and surrounding area offer an endless variety of activities, including swimming, fishing, and boating at the inn. Horseback riding, golf, tennis, dinner cruises, scenic train and plane rides, antique shopping, and fine restaurants are all close by. Each morning, you'll be treated to a very special gourmet breakfast with delights such as stuffed French toast, cheese-baked apples, poached pears, and select home-baked breads and muffins.

SEASON

May to November 1

ACCOMMODATIONS

six rooms with private baths

Bishopsgate Inn

Colin, Jane, Colin, Jr.,
and Lisa Kagel
7 Norwich Road
East Haddam, Connecticut 06423
Tel: (860) 873-1677
Fax: (860) 873-3898
$$$ – $$$$

ABOUT THE B&B

Built in 1818 by Horace Heyden, a merchant and shipbuilder, this Colonial home welcomes guests seeking gracious hospitality and well-appointed accommodation in a secluded setting. The inn offers six guest rooms, including four with open fireplaces and a suite with a sauna. Tastefully furnished, each floor of the inn has its own sitting area for conversation, reading, and other restful pursuits. Known for its excellent kitchen, Bishopsgate offers ample breakfasts and, if desired, specially arranged candlelight dinners. The Kagels maintain an up-to-date library of local offerings and can help you plan your visit to the area: everything from the Goodspeed Opera House's renowned musical productions, the Historical Society Museum, Gillette Castle and Devil's Hopyard state parks, and cruises and canoe trips on the Connecticut River. Historic Essex, with its beautiful harbor, wonderful old houses, and intriguing shops, is just a few minutes' drive away.

SEASON

all year

ACCOMMODATIONS

six rooms (including one suite)
with private baths

Summer Fruit Tarts

"We choose the fruit for our summer tarts based on varied color and texture." — The Kagel Family

Frozen pastry for 1 double-crust 9" pie
6 cups fresh fruit (such as strawberries, blueberries, blackberries, bananas)
2 cups prepared strawberry glaze
All-purpose flour
¾ cup fresh whipped cream
Mint leaves
Edible flowers (such as violets or nasturtiums)

Let the frozen pie crust thaw to room temperature (about 30 minutes).

In a large bowl, carefully mix the fruit and glaze until all the fruit is evenly coated (be careful not to bruise the fruit). Chill.

Preheat the oven to 450°F. Separate the pie crusts (top and bottom) and lightly sprinkle one side of each with flour. Cut 5 round or scalloped circles (about 4" in diameter) out of each crust using a cookie cutter.

Using an ungreased 12-cup muffin pan, place the pie crust circles over the cups (flour side down). *Tip:* Place a few tablespoons of water in any unused muffin cups to protect the pan and keep the rest of the tarts moist. Pleat the pie crust evenly so that it fits the cup snugly and neatly. Using a fork, prick the crust sufficiently to prevent air bubbles from lifting the crust. Bake 10 – 11 minutes or until the cups are a honey golden brown (watch this step closely when making this recipe for the first time!). Cool the tarts to room temperature and carefully remove them from the pan.

Fill each pie crust with the fruit filling and top with a dollop of whipped cream. Place on a dessert plate and garnish with mint leaves or edible flowers. *Yield: 10 tarts.*

Sweet Cheese Rolls

(*Recipe from* Breakfast Inn Bed, Easy and Elegant Recipes from Garth Woodside Mansion.)

¾ cup sugar
¼ cup chopped pecans
1 tablespoon grated orange zest
6 ounces cream cheese, softened
2 (10-ounce) packages refrigerated flaky biscuits
½ cup margarine, melted

Preheat the oven to 350°F. Combine the sugar, pecans, and zest and set aside. Cut the cream cheese into 20 equal pieces. Separate each biscuit into 2 layers, and place 1 piece of cream cheese between the layers. Seal the edges. Dip each filled biscuit in the melted margarine, then in the sugar mixture. Place on a cookie sheet and bake 15 – 20 minutes or until lightly browned. *Yield: 20 rolls.*

Garth Woodside Mansion

Diane and Irv Feinberg
RR #3, Box 578
Hannibal, Missouri 63401
Tel: (573) 221-2789
E-mail: Garth@nemonet.com
www.hanmo.com/garth
$$ – $$$

ABOUT THE B&B

Experience affordable elegance in this 1871 Victorian country estate on 39 acres of meadows and woodlands. On the National Register of Historic Places, Garth Woodside Mansion has remained unchanged outside, and graceful arched doors, handsomely decorated rooms featuring original furnishings spanning over 150 years, and magnificent three-story spiral "Flying Staircase" await you inside. You'll enjoy marble fireplaces, canopy beds, your own nightshirt to wear during your stay, an exceptional full breakfast, an afternoon beverage, and more. All rooms are air conditioned and have a private bath. The location is ideal for seeing Mark Twain Country.

SEASON

all year

ACCOMMODATIONS

eight rooms with private baths

Pickett's Harbor
Bed and Breakfast

Sara and Cooke Goffigon
28288 Nottingham Ridge Lane
Cape Charles, Virginia 23310
Tel: (757) 331-2212
E-mail: pickharb@aol.com
$$ – $$$

ABOUT THE B&B

Chesapeake Bay on Virginia's historic Eastern Shore is home to seagulls, pelicans, sandpipers — and Pickett's Harbor Bed and Breakfast. Enjoy acres of private beach on the southernmost tip of the Delmarva Peninsula. Your hosts Sara and Cooke are descended from the original settlers of the area and, in 1976, built this traditional home by the seashore, complete with high ceilings, fireplaces, antiques, and wooden floorboards made from 200-year-old barns along the James River. Every morning, awake to Sara's full country breakfast where, on any given day, you can sample a fruit cup, juice, paper-thin cured ham, and homemade three-fruit and fig jams (which Sara now sells). Set off on a quiet country lane and surrounded by sea grasses and a pine forest, Pickett's Harbor is marvelously isolated yet close to most attractions on the Eastern Shore, as well as to Norfolk, Hampton, and Virginia Beach.

SEASON

all year

ACCOMMODATIONS

three rooms with private baths; three rooms with shared baths

Sweet Potato Biscuits

2 cups warm mashed sweet potatoes
¾ cup sugar
½ cup vegetable shortening
2 cups all-purpose flour
7 teaspoons baking powder
1 teaspoon salt

Virginia ham and/or fig preserves

Preheat the oven to 350°F. Mix the sweet potatoes, sugar, and shortening together. Sift the flour, baking powder, and salt and add to the potato mixture. Roll out and cut the biscuits. Bake about 20 minutes. Serve with Virginia ham and/or fig preserves. *Yield: 12 biscuits.*

Swiss Scones

"A welcome change from the usual muffins, these scones have a very delicate taste and are wonderful with scrambled eggs or simply with a bowl of fresh fruit." — Lily Vieyra

1½ cups all-purpose flour
¼ cup sugar
¼ teaspoon baking soda
1¼ teaspoons baking powder
¼ teaspoon salt
⅓ cup cold butter, cut in small pieces
½ cup golden raisins, dates, or chocolate chips
Grated zest of 1 small orange
½ cup buttermilk (or ½ cup milk with 1 tablespoon lemon juice)
Enough cream or milk to brush top of scones
2 tablespoons sugar mixed with ¼ teaspoon ground cinnamon

Scrambled eggs or fresh fruit

Preheat the oven to 425°F. Place the flour, sugar, baking soda, baking powder, and salt in a medium bowl and mix well. Cut the butter into the flour mixture with a pastry cutter, until it resembles course meal. Add the raisins and orange zest. Add the buttermilk and mix with a fork until the dough leaves the sides of the bowl. Place the dough on a floured board and pat into a circle or rectangle ½" thick. Cut in 2" circles or hearts with a cookie cutter and place on a lightly greased cookie sheet (parchment paper also works). Space about 1½" apart. Brush the tops with the cream and sprinkle with the sugar-cinnamon mixture (avoid getting sugar on the cookie sheet as it will burn). Bake 12 – 14 minutes, until the tops are lightly browned. Serve fresh from the oven or let cool and place in an airtight container. Scones can be stored 1 – 2 days. **Yield: 12 scones.**

"An Elegant Victorian Mansion" Bed & Breakfast Inn

Lily and Doug Vieyra
1406 "C" Street
Eureka, California 95501
Tel: (707) 442-5594
Fax: (707) 442-5594
$$$ – $$$$

ABOUT THE B&B

Featured in many newspapers and magazines — not to mention on television and radio — this restored national historic landmark offers prestigious and luxurious accommodations. Spirited and eclectic innkeepers provide lavish hospitality in the splendor of a meticulously restored 1888 Victorian masterpiece, complete with original family antique furnishings. The inviting guest rooms offer both graceful refinement and modern-day comfort, individually decorated with Victorian elegance. Guests enjoy gourmet breakfasts and a heavenly night's sleep on top-quality mattresses, as well as secured parking and laundry service. Located in a quiet, historic residential neighborhood overlooking the city and Humboldt Bay, the non-smoking inn is near carriage rides, bay cruises, restaurants, and the theater, and is just minutes from giant redwood parks, coastal beaches, ocean charters, and horseback riding.

SEASON

all year

ACCOMMODATIONS

two rooms (including one suite)
with private baths;
two rooms with shared bath

Martin Oaks
Bed & Breakfast

Marie and Frank Gery
PO Box 207, 107 First Street
Dundas, Minnesota 55019
Tel: (507) 645-4644
$$

ABOUT THE B&B

*I*n 1869, the Archibald Brothers had this home built as a wedding present for their sister, Sarah Etta Archibald. Now listed on the National Register of Historic Places, Martin Oaks, the Archibald-Martin House, and the Carriage House occupy half a city block. Located in historic Dundas Village, Martin Oaks transports guests to an era where elegant women and fine gentlemen enjoyed good conversation and classical music, and savored elegant foods served on fine china. Two charming bedrooms filled with antiques offer the opportunity for a memorable, quiet evening. Recently featured in Minnesota Monthly Magazine, Martin Oaks is less than five minutes away from Northfield, Carleton, and St. Olaf colleges, and is near superb shopping and bookstore browsing, fine antique hunting on and off Division Street, golfing, hiking, and cross-country skiing. Minneapolis, St. Paul, and the Mall of America are within a 40-minute drive.

SEASON

April 1 to December 31

ACCOMMODATIONS

two rooms with shared baths

Tiny Tasty Tipsy Buns

Dough (prepared in bulk):
2 packages active dry yeast (2 tablespoons)
4 tablespoons sugar
¼ cup lukewarm water
½ teaspoon salt
¾ cup sour cream
Grated zest of 1 lemon
2 egg yolks
1 cup butter, melted
1 teaspoon vanilla
2 cups whole wheat flour
2 cups all-purpose flour

Bun filling:
½ cup currants
1 tablespoon brandy flavoring diluted with 2 tablespoons water
¾ cup brown sugar
2 tablespoons ground cinnamon
⅓ of the dough (see above)

(continued on next page)

Pan filling:
3 tablespoons butter
3 tablespoons honey
3 tablespoons brown sugar
⅓ cup pecan pieces

To make the dough: Stir together the yeast, sugar, water, and salt, and set aside 3 – 5 minutes to let the yeast bubble. Combine the sour cream, lemon zest, egg yolks, melted butter, and vanilla in a mixing bowl; mix well. Stir in the yeast mixture, then add the whole wheat flour and 1½ cups of the all-purpose flour. Knead this dough on a floured bread board, adding the rest of the flour as needed, until the dough is smooth and elastic (about 10 minutes). Turn the dough into a greased bowl, cover, and refrigerate at least 4 hours. Divide the dough into thirds, keeping ⅓ out to make buns and refrigerating the rest for up to 5 days. *Note:* Don't let the buns rise before baking or they won't be tiny.

To make the bun filling: Put the currants in a microwave-safe container with the diluted brandy, and heat in the microwave for 30 seconds. Mix the brown sugar and cinnamon. Roll the dough into a ⅛" thick rectangle on a floured board. Sprinkle the brown sugar mixture over the dough, then sprinkle on the currants. Roll up the dough tightly, and cut into 1" slices.

To make the pan filling: Preheat the oven to 350°F. Melt the butter and mix in the honey. Pour the butter mixture into a 10 x 8" or 9 x 9" glass baking dish. Sprinkle first with the brown sugar, then with the pecans. Place the roll slices on top of the pecans and brown sugar. Bake 20 – 25 minutes (keeping an eye on them for the last few minutes). After taking the dish out of the oven, immediately invert it on a serving plate. Let cool before serving. *Yield: About 18 buns.*

Garth Woodside Mansion

Diane and Irv Feinberg
RR #3, Box 578
Hannibal, Missouri 63401
Tel: (573) 221-2789
E-mail: Garth@nemonet.com
www.hanmo.com/garth
$$ – $$$

ABOUT THE B&B

Experience affordable elegance in this 1871 Victorian country estate on 39 acres of meadows and woodlands. On the National Register of Historic Places, Garth Woodside Mansion has remained unchanged outside, and graceful arched doors, handsomely decorated rooms featuring original furnishings spanning over 150 years, and magnificent three-story spiral "Flying Staircase" await you inside. You'll enjoy marble fireplaces, canopy beds, your own nightshirt to wear during your stay, an exceptional full breakfast, an afternoon beverage, and more. All rooms are air conditioned and have a private bath. The location is ideal for seeing Mark Twain Country.

SEASON

all year

ACCOMMODATIONS

eight rooms with private baths

Victorian Cookies

3 ounces cream cheese
½ cup butter or margarine
½ teaspoon grated lemon zest
1 cup all-purpose flour
2 tablespoons sugar
About ½ cup apricot or strawberry preserves

Preheat the oven to 375°F. Cream together the cream cheese and butter until smooth and light. Beat in the lemon zest. Combine the flour and sugar. Stir in ½ of the flour mixture to the creamed mixture, blending well. Stir in the remaining flour. Roll the dough onto a lightly floured board to ⅛" thickness (any thicker and cookies tend to unfold when baking). Cut into 2" rounds. Spoon ¼ – ½ teaspoon of the preserves in the center of each round. Form into a triangle by folding in the 3 edges. Pinch the edges together gently and bake 12 – 14 minutes. Cool the cookies for a few minutes. Remove to a rack to complete cooling. Store in an airtight container. *Yield: 36 – 48 cookies.*

Vieux Carré Bread Pudding with Brandy Sauce

6 eggs, separated
2 cups sugar
1 tablespoon vanilla
1 large loaf day old French bread, dried and cubed
1½ cups raisins
2 (16-ounce) cans fruit cocktail with syrup
½ teaspoon baking soda
12-ounce can evaporated milk
2 cups whole or skim milk
Brandy sauce (see recipe below)

Preheat the oven to 350°F. To the egg yolks, add the sugar and beat with an electric mixer. Add the vanilla, bread, raisins, and fruit cocktail and mix well. To the egg whites, add the baking soda and milk and beat with the mixer until soft peaks form. Add to the bread mixture. Place in an ungreased, 3- or 4-quart casserole. Place the casserole in a pan of water and bake 45 minutes to 1 hour. *Yield: 10 – 12 servings.*

(continued on next page)

Lafitte Guest House
Robert D. Guyton and
Bobby L'Hoste
1003 Bourbon Street
New Orleans, Louisiana 70116
Tel: (800) 331-7971 or (504) 581-2678
Fax: (504) 581-2677
www.Lafitteguesthouse.com
$$$ – $$$$

ABOUT THE B&B

Built in 1849, the ivy-covered French-roofed Lafitte Guest House was constructed as a single-family dwelling for the then-enormous price of $11,700. The home has had numerous owners since and has operated as a guest house or apartments since 1952. In 1980, present owner Robert Guyton undertook a major restoration to restore the building to its original grandeur. Fourteen guest rooms are decorated with antiques, crystal chandeliers, and many original furnishings. All rooms have private baths, some with fireplaces and balconies. The parlor is pure Victorian with red velvet drapes and settee. Breakfast is served in the parlor, courtyard, or in your room. Lafitte Guest House is located in the Vieux Carré and, right outside its door, guests will enjoy the colorful sights and sounds of the French Quarter.

SEASON

all year

ACCOMMODATIONS

14 rooms with private baths

Brandy sauce:
½ cup butter
2 cups sugar
3 cups milk
3 tablespoons all-purpose flour
1 cup brandy, rum, or bourbon

In a saucepan, melt the butter. Mix in the sugar, then the 2 cups of the milk. Mix the flour and remaining 1 cup of milk, then add to the butter mixture. Add the brandy and cook 2 more minutes or until the sauce thickens. Serve over the bread pudding.

Wheat and Peanut Butter Cookies

2½ cups whole grain white wheat flour (may substitute whole wheat
    flour)
1½ teaspoons baking soda
2 cups white or regular wheat bran*
1 cup butter or margarine
2 cups brown sugar, firmly packed
1 cup peanut butter
2 eggs
1 teaspoon vanilla

*Available in health food stores or substitute with regular bran (not bran breakfast
cereal).

Preheat the oven to 375°F. In a medium bowl, stir together the flour,
baking soda, and 1 cup of the bran. In a large bowl, beat the butter with
an electric mixer on medium speed until softened. Add the brown sugar,
peanut butter, eggs, and vanilla, beating well. Add the flour mixture,
beating on low speed until combined. Shape into 1" balls and roll in the
remaining bran. Place 2" apart on an ungreased cookie sheet and flatten
with the bottom of a glass. Bake 8 – 10 minutes or until lightly browned
on the bottom. *Yield: 5 dozen cookies.*

Thistle Hill
Bed & Breakfast

Mary and Dave Hendricks
Route 1, Box 93
Wakeeney, Kansas 67672-9736
Tel: (785) 743-2644
$$

ABOUT THE B&B

Described as "an oasis on the
prairie" by its guests, Thistle
Hill Bed & Breakfast is a
convenient, secluded cedar farm home
located halfway between Kansas City
and Denver, Colorado. Thistle Hill is
surrounded by native prairie, 60 acres
of wildflower-prairie restoration, and
cottage-style flower and herb gardens.
Accommodations range from the
spacious Oak Room with a rustic queen-
sized bed crafted of antique hedge fence
posts, the Sunflower Room with a hand-
made Kansas sunflower quilt, and the
Prairie Room honoring family members
who were pioneers of the area. After
being awakened by the rooster's crow,
feast on a hearty country breakfast of
fragrant homemade muffins or hot
cakes made from freshly ground Kansas
wheat, along with an egg dish, fresh
fruit and juice, and gourmet coffee or
herbal tea. Thistle Hill is located close
to Castle Rock, Cedar Bluff Reservoir,
the Cottonwood Ranch, and Sternberg
Museum.

SEASON

all year

ACCOMMODATIONS

three rooms with private baths

French Toast, Pancakes, & Waffles

Aebleskiver (Danish Ball Pancakes)

4 eggs, separated
2 tablespoons sugar
½ teaspoon salt
2 tablespoons vegetable oil
2 cups buttermilk
1 teaspoon baking soda
1 teaspoon baking powder
2 cups all-purpose flour
Vegetable oil or lard

Flavored butters, syrup, jam, and brown or granulated sugar

Beat the egg whites until they stand in soft peaks; set aside. Beat into the egg yolks the sugar, salt, oil, buttermilk, baking soda, baking powder, and flour until the batter is very smooth. Fold in the egg whites. Heat a well-seasoned monk's pan (see tip below) with ⅛ teaspoon oil in each of the 7 holes. Fill each hole with batter. When browned on one side (almost right away), turn with a knitting needle and keep turning until the needle comes out clean after piercing through the cake. Serve with flavored butters, syrup, jam, and brown or granulated sugar. *Tip:* You can purchase a cast-iron monk's pan at Scandinavian gift shops or at small town hardware stores in Danish communities. *Yield: About 48 ball pancakes, serving 6.*

Lindgren's Bed & Breakfast

Shirley Lindgren
County Road 35, PO Box 56
Lutsen, Minnesota 55612-0056
Tel: (218) 663-7450
$$ – $$$$

ABOUT THE B&B

Less than two hours from Duluth, Minnesota, and Thunder Bay, Ontario, this 1920s rustic log home with manicured grounds and walkable shoreline resides on Lake Superior in Superior National Forest. The living room features an 18-foot beamed ceiling, massive stone fireplace, and hunting trophies. Guest rooms are cozily designed in either knotty cedar, pine, or rustic paneling. Scenic points of interest include Split Rock Lighthouse, Gooseberry Falls, and Tettegouche State Park. Depending on the season, you can choose from hiking trails, skyrides, alpine slides, mountain biking, horseback riding, golf, tennis, fishing, snowmobiling, and cross-country and downhill skiing. Any number of fine restaurants are nearby, and you're within walking distance of Lutsen Resort, the oldest in the state. Your hosts are retired after 35 years of owning and operating a successful garden center, landscaping, nursery, and floral business in Minneapolis, and enjoy fishing, hunting and, most of all, people, which is why they opened their home as a bed and breakfast!

SEASON

all year

ACCOMMODATIONS

four rooms with private baths

Diane and Wayne Young
411 Main Street, PO Box 478
Ghent, Kentucky 41045
Tel: (502) 347-5807
$$ – $$$

ABOUT THE B&B

*H*alfway between Cincinnati and Louisville, Ghent House is a gracious reminder of the antebellum days of the old South. It was built in 1833 in the usual style of the day — a central hall with rooms on either side of the kitchen and a dining room in back. A beautiful fantail window and two English coach lights enhance the front entrance, while a rose garden and gazebo grace the rear of the home. There are crystal chandeliers, fireplaces, and Jacuzzis in the guest rooms. Ghent House has a spectacular view of the Ohio River, and one can almost imagine the time when steamboats regularly traveled up and down its waters. Awake mornings to the aroma of coffee and tea, then have your breakfast in either the formal dining room or the breakfast room overlooking the river. At Ghent House, you'll enjoy and appreciate the charming blend of yesteryear with modern convenience and relaxation.

SEASON

all year

ACCOMMODATIONS

three suites with private baths

Amish Cinnamon-Raisin French Toast

2 eggs
½ cup milk
1 teaspoon vanilla
12 – 14 slices cinnamon raisin bread
2 teaspoons ground cinnamon

Jam, jelly, confectioners' sugar, or syrup

Combine the eggs, milk, and vanilla, and beat. Dip the bread slices into the egg mixture. Place in a lightly greased skillet over medium heat. Sprinkle with the cinnamon, brown lightly, and flip over. Sprinkle with more cinnamon, and brown lightly. Serve with jam, jelly, confectioners' sugar, or syrup. *Yield: 6 – 8 servings.*

Annie's Breakfast Pancake Cookies

"For the teenagers in the crowd, add chocolate chips to the recipe instead of fruit to knock their socks off!" — Anne Stuart

5 cups skim milk
8 eggs, lightly beaten
½ cup light vegetable oil
12 ounces golden raisins
4 tablespoons brown sugar
5½ cups large-flake rolled oats
2 heaping cups whole wheat flour
2 tablespoons baking powder
1 teaspoon salt
4 large bananas, sliced, or 1 quart fresh blueberries (or fruit of your choice)
1½ cups chopped pecans, cashews, walnuts, or almonds
Maple syrup
Sour cream
Cinnamon sugar

In a large bowl, mix the milk, eggs, oil, raisins, sugar, and oats. Let this mixture soak for 10 minutes before proceeding. Add the flour, baking powder, and salt, mixing well. Add the fruit and fold in carefully. Add the nuts.

(continued on next page)

Annie's Bed and Breakfast

Anne and Larry Stuart
2117 Sheridan Drive
Madison, Wisconsin 53704
Tel/Fax: (608) 244-2224
$$$ – $$$$

ABOUT THE B&B

Opened April 1985 as Madison's first bed and breakfast inn, Annie's is a rustic cedar shake and stucco house in a quiet neighborhood overlooking the beautiful valley of Warner Park, a block away from Lake Mendota's eastern shore. Tall green spruces, shaggy birch trees, and extensive gardens surround the house, gazebo, and lily pond to frame views of meadows, water, and woods. Luxury, getaway accommodations include two comfortable two-bedroom suites filled with antiques and little surprises and a sumptuous whirlpool for two in a room by itself, surrounded by mirrors, lush plants, and music. Awake to Annie's famous homemade full country breakfast, then visit museums, art galleries, theaters, shopping malls, State Street, the University of Wisconsin campus, Olbrich Botanical Gardens, the Farmer's Market, and more. Warner Park nature trails, bicycle-jogging path, tennis courts, swimming beach, and boat docks are just outside the back door. Innkeepers Anne (an artist) and Larry (a financial planner) enjoy nature, art, architecture, literature, music, and people.

SEASON

all year

ACCOMMODATIONS

two suites with private baths

Oil an electric grill and set at no more than 300°F (pancake cookies need to cook slowly so they don't burn). Using a ¼ cup scoop, spread the batter on your grill, watching carefully. Turn once. The cookie will be nice and thick, and no more than 4" in diameter. Serve 2 to a plate, and top with maple syrup and a spoonful of sour cream sweetened with cinnamon sugar. *Tip:* These pancake cookies freeze very well and are easy to serve at a later date. Just spread them lightly with soft butter as you would a piece of toast and heat them on high in your microwave oven until hot — when the butter begins to melt, they are ready. *Yield: 14 dozen cookies.*

Apricot-Pecan French Toast

(Recipe from What's Cooking at Carrington's Bluff.*)*

½ cup finely chopped dried apricots
¼ cup orange juice
8 ounces cream cheese
¼ cup coarsely chopped pecans
16 slices sourdough bread
2 cups milk
1 cup half-and-half
6 eggs
6 tablespoons sugar
4 teaspoons grated orange zest
1 teaspoon vanilla
1 teaspoon salt
½ cup butter (or as needed)

Apricot syrup:
18 ounces apricot preserves
¾ cup orange juice

(continued on next page)

Carrington's Bluff B&B

Lisa and Edward Mugford
1900 David Street
Austin, Texas 78705
Tel: (800) 871-8908 or (512) 479-0638
Fax: (512) 476-4769
$$$

ABOUT THE B&B

The setting is Shoal Creek Bluff and an 1877 Texas farmhouse nestled in the arms of a 500-year-old oak tree. Today, Carrington's Bluff B&B offers Texas hospitality to make your stay delightful. Upon arrival, you'll find yourself surrounded by rooms filled with English and American antiques, handmade quilts, and the sweet smell of potpourri. The 35-foot front porch beckons you to sit among the plants and flowers and enjoy the gentle breezes with your morning coffee or afternoon tea. The smell of fresh-brewed gourmet coffee invites you to a breakfast that begins with fresh fruit and homemade granola served on fine English china. Homemade muffins or breads and a house specialty ensure you won't go away hungry. Carrington's Bluff is near the University of Texas and the State Capital grounds, just minutes from parks, hiking and biking trails, shopping, and wonderful restaurants.

SEASON

all year

ACCOMMODATIONS

eight rooms with private baths

In a saucepan, combine the apricots and orange juice and bring to a boil. Simmer for 10 minutes or until the apricots are tender, then cool to room temperature. In a small bowl, combine the cream cheese and pecans with the apricot mixture. Spread this over 8 slices of bread and cover with the remaining slices, forming 8 sandwiches. In a large bowl, combine the milk, half-and half, eggs, sugar, orange zest, vanilla, and salt and mix until blended. Dip the sandwiches into the egg mixture to completely coat. In a skillet, melt 2 tablespoons of the butter. Add the sandwiches, turning once, and cook until golden brown, adding more butter to the skillet as necessary. To make the apricot syrup: In a heavy saucepan, combine the preserves and orange juice. Bring to a boil, stirring occasionally. Serve the apricot syrup hot with the French toast. *Yield: 8 servings.*

Baked French Toast

4 slices Texas toast (1" thick white bread)
6 eggs
1½ cups milk
1 cup light cream
1 teaspoon vanilla
¼ teaspoon ground cinnamon
¼ teaspoon grated nutmeg
¼ cup butter or margarine, softened
½ cup brown sugar, firmly packed
1 tablespoon light corn syrup

Warm maple syrup

Butter a 9" square baking pan. Overlap the bread slices to completely fill the pan. In a medium bowl, combine the eggs, milk, cream, vanilla, cinnamon, and nutmeg, mixing well. Pour over the bread slices, then cover and refrigerate overnight. The next day, remove from the refrigerator ¾ hour before baking. Preheat the oven to 350°F. In a small bowl, combine the butter, brown sugar, and corn syrup, mixing well. Spread this mixture evenly over the bread. Bake 45 – 60 minutes or until puffed and golden. Cut into squares and serve with warm maple syrup. *Yield: 6 – 8 servings.*

The Inn On Golden Pond

Bonnie and Bill Webb
PO Box 680, Route 3
Holderness, New Hampshire 03245
Tel: (603) 968-7269
Fax: (603) 968-9226
E-mail: innongp@lr.net
$$$

ABOUT THE B&B

*I*n 1984, Bonnie and Bill Webb left their desk jobs in southern California to establish The Inn On Golden Pond, an 1879 Colonial home located near Squam Lake, setting for the classic film On Golden Pond. Ideal in all seasons, this central area of New Hampshire offers hiking, bicycling, golfing, water activities, skiing, and skating. The inn is known for its refreshingly friendly yet professional atmosphere. Rooms are individually decorated in traditional country style, featuring hardwood floors, braided rugs, country curtains, and bedspreads. There are seven spacious guest rooms and one extra-large suite, all with private baths. Morning is a treat as Bonnie makes all the breads, muffins, coffee cakes, and her special rhubarb jam. A full breakfast is offered each day featuring regional favorites such as baked French toast and apple pancakes.

SEASON

all year

ACCOMMODATIONS

eight rooms (including one suite) with private baths

Alexander Hamilton House

Barbara Notarius and Brenda Barta
49 Van Wyck Street
Croton-on-Hudson, New York
10520
Tel: (914) 271-6737
Fax: (914) 271-3927
E-mail: ALEXHMLTNHS@ aol.com
www.AlexanderHamiltonHouse.com
$$$ – $$$$

ABOUT THE B&B

The Alexander Hamilton House (circa 1889) is a sprawling Victorian home situated on a cliff overlooking the Hudson River. Grounds include a mini orchard and in-ground pool. The home has many period antiques and collections and offers a queen-bedded suite with a fireplace in the living room; a double-bedded suite with fireplace and a small sitting room; and a bridal chamber with king-size bed, Jacuzzi, entertainment center, pink marble fireplace, and skylights. A one-bedroom apartment is also available with a double bed, living room/kitchen, private bath, and separate entrance. Nearby attractions include West Point, the Sleepy Hollow Restorations, Lyndhurst Mansion, Boscobel (a fabulous Federal-period restoration), the Rockefeller mansion, hiking, biking, sailing, and New York City (under an hour away by train or car).

SEASON

all year

ACCOMMODATIONS

seven rooms (including three suites) with private baths

Banana and Walnut-stuffed French Toast

Cream cheese, softened
16 slices cinnamon raisin bread
4 large bananas, sliced
Chopped walnuts
Ground cinnamon
4 eggs
½ cup milk
½ teaspoon vanilla
Butter

Warm maple syrup

Spread the cream cheese on all the slices of bread. Place the sliced bananas on ½ of the bread slices and sprinkle with the walnuts and cinnamon. Cover with the remaining slices to form a sandwich. Combine the eggs, milk, and vanilla. Dip the sandwiches into the egg mixture. Melt butter in a skillet and sauté the sandwiches on both sides until lightly browned. Serve with warm maple syrup. *Yield: 4 servings*.

Belgian Waffles

2 cups all-purpose flour
2 teaspoons baking powder
2 tablespoons confectioners' sugar
1 tablespoon vegetable oil
2 cups milk
3 eggs, separated
2 teaspoons vanilla
Pinch of salt
Fruit of your choice
Whipped cream

Combine the flour, baking powder, confectioners' sugar, oil, milk, egg yolks, vanilla, and salt. Beat the egg whites until they stand in soft peaks and fold into the batter (do not overmix). Using a 4-ounce ladle, pour ⅛ of the mixture into a hot waffle iron and bake for about 2 minutes. Repeat with the remaining batter. Top with the fruit and whipped cream and serve hot. *Yield: 8 waffles.*

Glynn House Victorian Inn

Betsy and Karol Paterman
43 Highland Street, PO Box 719
Ashland, New Hampshire 03217
Tel: (800) 637-9599 or (603) 968-3775
E-mail: glynnhse@lr.net
www.nettx.com/glynnhouse.html
$$ – $$$

ABOUT THE B&B

*C*ome enjoy the gracious elegance of this beautifully restored 1890 Queen Anne home — from the cupola of the inn's tower and gingerbread wraparound veranda to the carved oak foyer and pocket doors. Each of the beautifully appointed bedrooms has its own distinctive mood, distinguished by unique interior design, period furniture, the fragrance of fresh flowers, and soft, fluffy robes. A memorable full breakfast is served in the dining room, consisting perhaps of eggs Benedict or eggs Neptune, Belgian waffles, thick French toast, ambrosia, juice, and the specialty of the house — strudel. After breakfast, take a walk or boat ride around famous Squam Lake (where the movie On Golden Pond was filmed) just a few minutes away, and enjoy all that the Lakes Region and White Mountains have to offer. Allow Betsy and Karol to provide hospitality with a warm smile and make you feel as though you're part of their family.

SEASON

all year

ACCOMMODATIONS

eight rooms with private baths

Blue Harbor House, A Village Inn

Jody Schmoll and Dennis Hayden
67 Elm Street
Camden, Maine 04843-1904
Tel: (800) 248-3196 or (207) 236-3196
Fax: (207) 236-6523
E-mail: balidog@midcoast.com
www.blueharborhouse.com
$$$ – $$$$

ABOUT THE B&B

A classic village inn on the Maine Coast, the Blue Harbor House welcomes guests to relax in a restored 1810 Cape where yesterday's charms blend perfectly with today's comforts. The beautiful town of Camden, renowned for its spectacular setting where the mountains meet the sea, is just outside the door. The inn's bright and inviting guest rooms surround you with country antiques and hand-fashioned quilts — several even have canopy beds and whirlpool tubs. Breakfasts feature such specialties as lobster quiche, cheese soufflé, and blueberry pancakes with blueberry butter. As for dinner, guests can arrange to have a romantic candle-lit affair or an old-fashioned down-east lobster feed.

SEASON

all year

ACCOMMODATIONS

eight rooms with private baths;
two carriage-house suites
with private baths

Blueberry-Buttermilk Pancakes with Blueberry Butter

¾ teaspoon baking soda
1½ cups buttermilk
1½ cups all-purpose flour
¾ cup whole wheat flour
¾ cup large-flake rolled oats (optional)
¾ teaspoon baking powder
1 teaspoon salt (optional)
1½ teaspoons sugar
6 eggs, separated
4½ tablespoons butter, melted
1½ cups milk
½ cup blueberries

Blueberry butter:
½ cup butter, softened
⅓ cup confectioners' sugar
1 teaspoon vanilla
10 ounces ripe blueberries
¼ cup shredded unsweetened coconut

(continued on next page)

Dissolve the baking soda in the buttermilk. Sift the flour, oats, baking powder, salt, and sugar together. Discard ¼ of the separated egg yolk, and beat the remaining ¾ with the melted butter into the dry ingredients. Add the buttermilk and milk, stirring to blend. Beat the egg whites until they stand in soft peaks and fold in. Drop by spoonfuls onto a hot griddle, add 6 – 10 blueberries, flipping the pancakes once when they're evenly browned.

To make the butter: In a food processor, mix the butter, sugar, and vanilla into a thick paste. Add the berries (saving a few for the garnish) and coconut. Smother the blueberry butter over the pancakes and garnish with a few berries. *Yield: 8 servings.*

The Blue Door

Anna Belle and Bob Schock
13707 Durango Drive
Del Mar, California 92014
Tel: (619) 755-3819
$$

ABOUT THE B&B

Enjoy New England charm in a quiet southern California setting overlooking Torrey Pines State Reserve. A garden-level two-room suite, with wicker accessories, king-size or twin beds, and adjoining private bath, is yours. The sitting room with couch, desk, chairs, and color TV opens onto your private patio. Breakfast is served in the spacious country kitchen-dining room warmed by a fire on chilly days. Anna Belle prides herself on creative breakfast menus featuring home-baked goods. Breakfast specialties include blueberry-banana muffins, Swedish oatmeal pancakes, and Blue Door orange French toast. Bob is a retired Navy Commander now designing and building custom furniture. Your hosts will gladly direct you to the nearby racetrack, beach, zoo, or University of California at San Diego campus.

SEASON

all year

ACCOMMODATIONS

two-room suite with private bath

Blue Door French Toast

"This is the specialty of the house. The distinctive orange sauce is made from navel oranges picked right off our tree."
— *Anna Belle Schock*

4 eggs
1 cup milk or half-and-half
¾ cup orange juice
8 slices French bread, cut diagonally 1½" thick
2 bananas, peeled and quartered

Orange sauce (see recipe below)

Blend the eggs, milk, and orange juice in a blender. Arrange the bread slices in a shallow tray and pour the egg mixture over them. Cover and refrigerate overnight. In the morning, let warm to room temperature. Fry on a lightly buttered griddle until golden brown on both sides and heated through. Garnish the plate with banana quarters. Serve with warm orange sauce. *Yield: 4 servings.*

Orange sauce:
5 teaspoons cornstarch
¼ cup sugar
¾ cup orange juice
4 – 5 navel oranges, peeled and sectioned
Grated zest of 1 orange

In a small saucepan or microwave-safe bowl, mix the cornstarch and sugar. Add the orange juice and stir until smooth. Cook over medium heat (or in the microwave oven on high), stirring often until thick and clear. Add the orange sections and zest and mix well.

Buttermilk-Pecan Pancakes

2 cups all-purpose flour
1 teaspoon baking soda
1 teaspoon salt
2 tablespoons sugar
½ cup coarsely chopped pecans
2 eggs, well beaten
2 cups buttermilk
2 tablespoons vegetable shortening, melted

Butter and warm maple syrup or honey

Sift the flour, baking soda, salt, sugar, and pecans together in a bowl. Combine the eggs and buttermilk to the melted shortening. Add to the dry ingredients, stirring until the flour is barely moistened (do not over-stir). Drop the batter on a hot, lightly greased griddle. Turn when golden brown. Serve with butter and warm maple syrup or honey. *Yield: About 16 pancakes.*

Beaver Creek House

Shirley and Donald Day
20432 Beaver Creek Road
Hagerstown, Maryland 21740
Tel: (301) 797-4764
$$$

ABOUT THE B&B

Comfort, relaxation, and hospitality await you at this turn-of-the-century country Victorian home, located in the historic area of Beaver Creek, Maryland. Step back to a quiet, gentler time and enjoy the family antiques and memorabilia that fill the inn. Choose from five centrally air conditioned guest rooms, and enjoy a country breakfast served on the spacious wraparound screen porch or in the elegantly appointed dining room. Sit in the courtyard by the fountain, stroll through the country garden, or linger by the fish pond and gaze at the mountain. Nearby are the national historic parks of Antietam, Harpers Ferry, the C&O Canal, and the Appalachian Trail. Guests may also hike, bike, golf, ski, shop at the many local antique shops, and dine at excellent restaurants in Hagerstown.

SEASON

all year

ACCOMMODATIONS

five rooms with private baths

The Hen-Apple
Bed and Breakfast

Flo and Harold Eckert
409 South Lingle Avenue
Palmyra, Pennsylvania 17078
Tel: (717) 838-8282
$$

ABOUT THE B&B

Built around 1825, the Hen-Apple is an intimate and fully restored bed and breakfast filled to the brim with everything country and old-fashioned. It offers a relaxed atmosphere with six air conditioned guest rooms (each with private bath), a porch filled with rockers, a screened porch for warm weather dining, a herb garden, lots of flowers, and a shady retreat in the orchard. The Hen-Apple's well-rounded breakfasts are something to remember — especially the cinnamon French toast. Tea is served in the afternoon. Just two miles from Hershey, Pennsylvania, Palmyra is an antique lover's dream. In addition, wineries, shopping outlets, Hershey attractions, the riverboat, and horse racing are nearby. Your hosts, Flo and Harold Eckert, love going to flea markets and auctions, and enjoy reading, gardening, and music. Flo is also a Christmas enthusiast so, come the merry season, the B&B sports a tree in just about every room and an impressive Santa collection.

SEASON

all year

ACCOMMODATIONS

six rooms with private baths

Buttermilk-Pecan Waffles

2 cups all-purpose flour
1 tablespoon baking powder
1 teaspoon baking soda
½ teaspoon salt
4 eggs
2 cups buttermilk
½ cup butter or margarine, melted
3 tablespoons chopped pecans

Combine the flour, baking powder, baking soda, and salt; set aside. Beat the eggs until light. Add the buttermilk to the eggs and mix well. Add the dry ingredients to the egg mixture and beat until smooth. Stir in the melted butter. Pour about ¾ cup of the batter onto a greased preheated waffle iron. Sprinkle with a few pecans. Cook until done. Repeat with the rest. Serve warm. *Yield: 7 waffles.*

Caboose Babies

2 eggs
½ cup milk
½ cup all-purpose flour
½ teaspoon almond extract
1 teaspoon grated lemon zest
4 tablespoons butter, melted
Sliced bananas dipped in fresh orange juice
⅛ teaspoon freshly grated nutmeg
¼ cup whipped topping

Preheat the oven to 475°F. Beat the eggs; add the milk, flour, almond extract, and lemon zest. Pour the hot, melted butter into a pie pan, pour the batter into the pan, then place in the oven. Cook 12 minutes or until the pancake is puffed. Serve immediately with sliced bananas dipped in fresh orange juice, and top with freshly grated nutmeg and whipped topping. *Yield: 2 servings.*

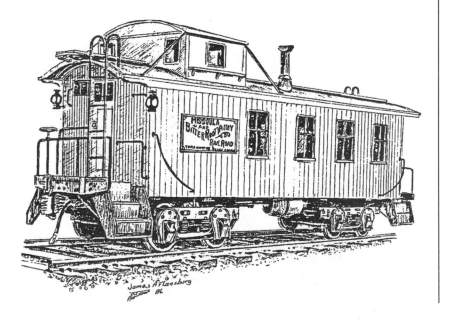

The Country Caboose

Lisa Thompson
852 Willoughby Lane
Stevensville, Montana 59870
Tel: (406) 777-3145
$$

ABOUT THE B&B

The Country Caboose is indeed that — an authentic caboose dating back to 1923, made of wood and painted red, of course. It is set on real rails in the middle of the countryside. The caboose sleeps two and offers a spectacular view of the Bitterroot Mountains right from your pillow. The Caboose breakfast menu features such goodies as huckleberry pancakes, strawberry waffles, French toast with fruit, and quiche. Local activities include touring St. Mary's Mission and the Marcus Daly Mansion, hiking mountain trails, fishing, and hunting.

SEASON

summer

ACCOMMODATIONS

room and private bath
in a 1923 wooden caboose

The Summer House

Marjorie and Kevin Huelsman
158 Main Street
Sandwich, Massachusetts 02563
Tel: (800) 241-3609 or (508) 888-4991
E-mail: sumhouse@capecod.net
$$ – $$$

ABOUT THE B&B

The Summer House is an *elegant circa 1835 Greek Revival twice featured in* Country Living *magazine. It was owned by Hiram Dillaway, a prominent mold-maker and colorist at the Boston & Sandwich Glass Factory. Large, sunny bedchambers feature antiques, hand-stitched quilts, and working fireplaces. Stroll to dining, shops, museums, galleries, a pond and gristmill, and a boardwalk to the beach. Bountiful breakfasts change daily and include freshly ground coffee, tea, fruit juice, and fresh fruit served in stemware. Entrées of frittata, stuffed French toast, quiche, or omelets are accompanied by scones, puff pastry, muffins, or fruit cobblers. Dishes are enhanced with vegetables, berries, and herbs from the inn's garden. English-style afternoon tea is served at an umbrella table in the garden. Boston, Newport, Providence, Martha's Vineyard, and Nantucket make pleasant day trips.*

SEASON

all year

ACCOMMODATIONS

five rooms with private baths

Cheese and Currant Pancakes

½ cup all-purpose flour
1 tablespoon sugar
1 teaspoon baking powder
¼ teaspoon ground cinnamon
2 eggs
½ cup creamed cottage cheese
2 tablespoons milk
1 tablespoon canola oil
1 teaspoon vanilla
2 tablespoons currants

Butter or margarine, and maple syrup

Combine the flour, sugar, baking powder, and cinnamon. In a separate bowl, beat together the eggs, cottage cheese, milk, oil, and vanilla. Add to the dry ingredients, stirring until blended but still slightly lumpy. Stir in the currants. For each pancake, pour 1 rounded tablespoon of batter onto a hot, lightly greased griddle. Cook until golden, turning to cook the other side when the pancake has a bubbly surface. Serve with butter or margarine, and maple syrup. *Yield: 12 pancakes.*

Chocolate French Toast with Raspberry Sauce

4 frozen petite croissants (Sara Lee brand recommended)

Filling:
4 ounces semisweet chocolate or sweet German chocolate, grated
½ cup cream cheese, whipped

Batter:
2 eggs
½ cup half-and-half
2 heaping tablespoons confectioners' sugar
¼ teaspoon vanilla
¼ teaspoon ground cinnamon
3 – 4 tablespoons butter

Raspberry sauce (see recipe below)
3 – 4 tablespoons butter (plus some extra, if needed)
Fresh raspberries
Mint sprigs

Thaw the croissants. To make the filling, mix the chocolate and cream cheese together to make a paste. On the inside edge of the croissant, cut a pocket from end to end (being careful not to cut all the way through). Squeeze gently to open the croissant and fill it with 1 heaping tablespoon of the filling.

(continued on next page)

Greenwoods Gate Bed & Breakfast Inn

George Schumaker
PO Box 491
105 Greenwoods Road East
Norfolk, Connecticut 06058
Tel: (860) 542-5439
$$$$

ABOUT THE B&B

Called "a Connecticut jewel" by Country Inns Bed & Breakfast *magazine, Greenwoods Gate combines a touch of romance with a sense of the past. This Federal-era inn offers four distinctive and elegant suites to choose from, with niceties such as fresh-cut flowers, fluffy robes, and crisp-ironed linens. A generous gourmet breakfast is served in the formal dining room, after which guests can linger in the center hall library or the grand parlor, with its antiques, Oriental rugs, and original Federal fireplace. Greenwoods Gate is conveniently located in the picture-perfect village of Norfolk, one half mile east of the Village Green. Innkeeper George Schumaker, a veteran of the hospitality business, organizes a B&B internship program three times per year for people considering owning and operating an inn.*

SEASON

all year

ACCOMMODATIONS

four suites with private baths

To make the batter, whisk the eggs, half-and-half, sugar, vanilla, and cinnamon together. Pour into a baking dish large enough to hold the filled croissants. Soak the croissants in the batter for about 15 minutes. Heat the butter in a skillet and cook the croissants evenly on both sides (add more butter as needed). Carefully stand each croissant on the end that isn't open to complete the cooking. Place on a plate and serve with warm raspberry sauce. Garnish with raspberries and a mint sprig. *Yield: 4 servings.*

Raspberry sauce:
10 ounces frozen raspberries, thawed
4 tablespoons red currant jelly
1 tablespoon orange juice

Combine the raspberries, jelly, and orange juice in a saucepan over moderate heat. Stir until the jelly is melted and the mixture is hot. Pour through a strainer, rubbing the pulp against the strainer to extract all the juice. Discard the seeds. Serve over the cooked chocolate French toast. *Yield: 1 cup.*

Cinnamon-Apple Puff Pancakes

1 very large tart apple (such as Granny Smith), peeled, cored, and
sliced very thin
3 tablespoons butter
3 eggs
½ cup all-purpose flour
½ cup milk
1 teaspoon granulated sugar
Dash of salt
2 tablespoons cinnamon sugar
Juice of 1 lemon

Preheat the oven to 475°F. Liberally grease a 9" fluted quiche dish. Sauté
the apple in 1 tablespoon of the butter until slightly tender. Spread the
apple slices evenly in the quiche dish. Mix together the eggs, flour, milk,
granulated sugar, and salt until blended well, and pour over the apple
slices. Bake for 10 minutes. Remove from the oven, dot with the remaining 2 tablespoons butter, and sprinkle with the cinnamon sugar. Return
to the oven for 5 minutes. Bring to the table puffed, and sprinkle the
lemon juice over the puff. *Yield: 4 servings.*

Sycamore Hill House & Gardens

Kerri and Stephen Wagner
110 Menefee Mountain Lane
Washington, Virginia 22747
Tel: (540) 675-3046
$$$ – $$$$

ABOUT THE B&B

Perched atop Menefee Mountain (elevation 1,043 feet) and situ-
ated on several hundred acres of pristine land, this large contemporary
stone home has a round, glass-walled living room and 65-foot veranda to
enhance the panoramic mountain vistas offered from every direction. The house
has light hardwood floors and Oriental rugs throughout, not to mention
Kerri's exotic plants and Stephen's original art. You may choose from three
elegant and tasteful rooms, each with private bath, queen-size bed, mountain
views, sitting/reading area, ceiling fan, and central heat and air conditioning.
A full sumptuous breakfast is served daily, and there are home-baked treats
in your room and mints by your bedside. A certified National Wildlife
habitat, Sycamore's gardens are the per-
fect spot for a stroll — perhaps you'll see a white-tailed deer or wild turkey.
Some of the finest dining in the east is just moments away. Also nearby is
Skyline Drive, Luray Caverns, Old Rag Mountain, vineyards, antique and
craft shops, golf, tennis, hot-air balloon-ing, canoeing, horseback riding, and
berry picking.

SEASON

all year

ACCOMMODATIONS

three rooms (including one suite)
with private baths

The Mainstay Inn

Sue and Tom Carroll
635 Columbia Avenue
Cape May, New Jersey 08204
Tel: (609) 884-8690
$$$ – $$$$

ABOUT THE B&B

According to the Washington Post, *"The jewel of them all has got to be the Mainstay."* *Built by a pair of wealthy gamblers in 1872, this elegant and exclusive clubhouse is now among the premier B&B inns in the country. The Mainstay now comprises three historic buildings on one of the most beautiful streets of the historic Cape May district. Guests enjoy 16 antique-filled rooms and suites (some with fireplaces and whirlpool baths), three parlors, spacious gardens, and rocker-filled verandas. Breakfast and afternoon tea are served daily. Beautiful beaches, historic attractions, biking, birding, golf, and tennis are all available in Cape May, a National Historic Landmark community.*

SEASON

all year

ACCOMMODATIONS

16 rooms (including seven suites) with private baths

Cornucopia's Croissants à l'Orange

6 croissants
9 ounces orange marmalade
3 ounces orange juice
5 eggs
1 cup heavy cream
1 teaspoon almond extract
Strawberries
Mandarin orange sections

Cut the croissants in ½ lengthwise and place the bottom halves in a buttered 12 x 9" ovenproof dish. Thin the marmalade with the orange juice and spoon it over each bottom half, saving a little to be used as a glaze. Replace the croissant tops. Beat the eggs, cream, and almond extract. Pour over the top of the croissants. Spoon some of the thinned marmalade over the top. Soak overnight. Remove from the refrigerator ¾ hour before baking. Bake in a preheated 350°F oven for about 25 minutes. Serve hot, and garnish with strawberries and mandarin orange sections. *Yield: 6 servings.*

Corn Waffles

5 cups all-purpose flour
⅓ cup baking powder
2½ teaspoons salt
3¾ cups cornmeal
⅓ cup sugar
10 egg whites
10 egg yolks
1½ quarts buttermilk
2½ cups applesauce
10 tablespoons butter, melted
2½ cups canned corn kernels, drained (optional)

Honey and maple syrup

In a large bowl, combine the flour, baking powder, salt, and cornmeal. Beat the sugar into the egg whites until soft peaks form; set aside. Beat the egg yolks until slightly thickened and paler yellow. Beat in the buttermilk, applesauce, and butter. Add to the dry ingredients and mix just until blended. Stir in ⅓ of the egg white mixture, then gently fold in the remainder. Gently fold in the corn. Bake the waffles on a large, hot waffle iron according to the manufacturer's directions. Serve with honey and maple syrup. *Tip:* These waffles freeze well and reheat best in the toaster oven. *Yield: 10 – 12 large waffles.*

The Old Miners' Lodge

Susan Wynne, Liza Simpson,
and Lillian Hauze
PO Box 2639, 615 Woodside Avenue
Park City, Utah 84060
Tel: (801) 645-8068
Fax: (801) 645-7420
$$ – $$$$

ABOUT THE B&B

Located in the national historic district of the colorful resort of Park City, Utah, The Old Miners' Lodge was established in 1889 as a boarding house for local miners seeking their fortune in Park City's ore-rich mountains. Today, the spirited warmth and hospitality of Park City's illustrious past remains in this building, which has been lovingly restored to its original splendor. Named for historic Park City personalities, the lodge's rooms and suites are complete with period antiques and country furnishings, down pillows, and comforters. To start the day, guests are greeted in the cozy dining room with a hearty breakfast, fresh coffee and tea, and fruit nectars. A revitalizing, year-round, outdoor hot tub relaxes and rejuvenates guests after an active day of skiing, golfing, or sightseeing in Park City. The large living room has a fireplace and is a gathering place in the evening, with complimentary refreshments. And of course, knowledgeable innkeepers are always on hand to provide casual conversation on everything from Park City history to assistance with evening dinner and entertainment plans.

SEASON

all year

ACCOMMODATIONS

12 rooms (including three suites)
with private baths

Bed & Breakfast at Edie's

Edie Senalik
PO Box 351, 233 East Harpole
Williamsville, Illinois 62693
Tel: (217) 566-2538
$ – $$

ABOUT THE B&B

Step back in time to an era when life was more leisurely. Bed & Breakfast at Edie's is located in the peaceful and charming village of Williamsville, Illinois, just 10 minutes north of Springfield. The 1915 mission-style house is large and gracious. Edie serves a delicious and bountiful continental breakfast, with homemade bagels being her specialty. Sleep in queen-size beds with down pillows. Relax in the large living room, TV room, or enjoy the wide wraparound veranda or rear patio. The nearby state capitol offers plays, symphonies, Abraham Lincoln's home and tomb and many other interesting attractions. Lincoln's New Salem village is just 20 minutes to the east.

SEASON

all year

ACCOMMODATIONS

four rooms with shared baths

Country Cottage Crêpes

"My Polish mother-in-law served these as a dessert, but my B&B guests love them as a very special and unusual breakfast treat."
— *Edie Senalik*

½ cup butter
1 pound cottage cheese
¼ cup raisins
½ cup sugar
2 eggs

Crêpe batter:
1 egg
1 tablespoon sugar
1 cup all-purpose flour
¾ cup water
Pinch of salt

Preheat the oven to 350°F. Melt the butter in a 13 x 9" baking dish and set aside. Mix the cottage cheese, raisins, sugar, and eggs and set aside. To make the crêpe batter, mix the egg, sugar, flour, water, and salt until smooth (if the batter is too thick, more water may be added). Fry a small amount of batter in a crêpe pan (or small skillet) in a small amount of butter. Turn when the top of the crêpe seems to dry. Place the cooked crêpe in the baking dish, fill with some of the cottage cheese filling, and fold the edges into the middle. When all the crêpes have been fried and filled, bake for 20 minutes. *Yield: 4 – 5 crêpes.*

Crème Caramel-Apple French Toast

2 cups light brown sugar
1 cup butter
4 tablespoons corn syrup
2 teaspoons vanilla
8 large Granny Smith apples, peeled, cored, and sliced
1 loaf French bread, sliced 1" thick
6 eggs
1 cup milk
½ cup heavy cream
1 teaspoon ground cinnamon
Whipped cream

In a saucepan, combine the sugar, butter, corn syrup, and 1 teaspoon of the vanilla. Melt and stir until smooth and caramelized. Spread ½ of the caramel in the bottom of a 13 x 9" nonstick baking pan (refrigerate the other ½ for the topping). Overlap the sliced apples on top of the caramel. Lay the sliced French bread on top of the apples. In a large bowl, blend the eggs, milk, cream, cinnamon, and remaining 1 teaspoon vanilla. Pour the mixture over the bread. Cover and refrigerate overnight. Remove from the refrigerator ¾ hour before baking. Bake uncovered in a preheated 350°F oven for approximately 35 – 45 minutes or until golden brown. Cut into 6 – 8 pieces and invert to serve. Drizzle the remaining caramel (heat if desired) over the bread and top each piece with a dollop of whipped cream. *Yield: 6 – 8 servings.*

Harbour Woods

Christine and Joe Titka
PO Box 1214
Southwest Harbor, Maine
04679-1214
Tel: (207) 244-5388
Fax: (207) 244-7156
E-mail: harbourwoods@acadia.net
$$ – $$$

ABOUT THE B&B

Christine and Joe welcome you to their gracious 1800s Maine farmhouse across the street from the Great Harbor Marina. Harbour Woods offers an intimate social setting accented by family keepsakes, antiques, flowers, and softly glowing oil lamps. What's more, the warm tones and subtle designs of the wall coverings create an atmosphere of casual elegance. Each morning, a candlelight breakfast becomes a dining experience of the finest kind. Listen to soft music and enjoy a variety of coffees, teas, juices, in-season fruit, home-baked breads, muffins, and entrées of the day, which are imaginatively prepared and presented. A cookie jar and tea for the munchies and a refrigerator stocked with complimentary soft drinks are always available. Guest rooms are distinctively decorated and feature queen-size beds, crackling fireplaces, evening mints and candy, telephones, and private baths with luxurious towels and a selection of rich soaps. And, of course, you may privately reserve the B&B's indoor spa, which awaits to refresh and relax you after a full day of activities in Acadia National Park.

SEASON

all year

ACCOMMODATIONS

three rooms with private baths

The Free Man House

Jennifer and Jim Freeman
1773 Lakeshore Drive
Branson, Missouri 65616
Tel: (417) 334-6262
Fax: (417) 337-9541
$$ – $$$

ABOUT THE B&B

A world-famous resort town nestled in the beautiful Ozark mountains, Branson is home to a variety of music shows and to three of the finest fishing lakes in the country. It is also home to The Free Man House, situated in a park-like setting along Lake Taneycomo (renowned nationwide for some of the finest trout fishing anywhere). This B&B offers fishermen all the amenities you could want: Cast your line by the nearby dock or by boat then warm up in one of the hot tubs after your brisk morning on the lake. For the non-fishermen, you can enjoy a relaxing day in one of Free Man House's three distinctive suites or around the pool, or browse through the quaint shops in Branson. In the evening, you can treat your ears to one of the many music shows in town — just minutes away. Free Man House has a conference room and retreat center that can accommodate family reunions or small conferences. Lodging is extended to Lakeshore Resort, also part of the property.

SEASON

all year

ACCOMMODATIONS

three suites with private baths

Dutch Babies

"Serve these puffed delights with a dab of strawberry, raspberry, or blueberry jam — and listen to the oohs and aahs."
— Jennifer Freeman

3 eggs
½ cup all-purpose flour
½ cup milk
2 tablespoons butter, melted
¼ teaspoon salt (or to taste)
Fruit jam of your choice

Preheat the oven to 400°F. With a whisk, lightly beat the eggs. Add the flour in 4 parts, whipping the mixture smooth each time. Add the milk in 2 parts, then add the melted butter and salt. Pour the mixture into 2 well-greased or buttered 9" pie pans (glass only). Bake for 10 minutes and reduce the oven to 350°F 5 – 10 minutes more, until the pancakes are puffed. Top each with a dollop of your favorite fruit jam and serve immediately. *Yield: 2 servings.*

Elegant Autumn French Toast

1 small apple, peeled, cored, and sliced
2 tablespoons cream cheese
2 slices cinnamon raisin or cinnamon apple bread
1 egg, lightly beaten
2 tablespoons milk
1 teaspoon sugar
¼ teaspoon salt
1 tablespoon butter, melted

Cooked bacon, sausage, or ham

Microwave the apple for 1 minute. Spread the cream cheese on each slice of bread. Top 1 slice with the baked apple and cover with the second bread slice to form a sandwich. In a shallow bowl, combine the egg, milk, sugar, and salt. Dip the sandwich in the French toast mixture and fry it in the melted butter until golden. Serve with cooked bacon, sausage, or ham. *Yield: 1 serving.*

Mulberry Bed and Breakfast

Frances A. Murphy
257 High Street
Wareham, Massachusetts 02571
Tel: (508) 295-0684
Fax: (508) 291-2909
$$

ABOUT THE B&B

Built in 1847 as a residence by blacksmith Aaron Sampson, Mulberry Bed and Breakfast was purchased in 1924 by the paternal grandfather of Mulberry's current owner, who turned it into a general store. In 1987, Frances (a retired elementary school teacher) transformed it into Mulberry Bed and Breakfast, which offers guests a Colonial Victorian atmosphere with antique furnishings throughout. Three guest rooms with two shared baths, a music room, two fireplaces, and a cozy kitchen enhance guests' visits. A hearty New England breakfast includes homemade jams, jellies, and breads along with French toast and other specialties. On pleasant mornings, breakfast may be served on the spacious deck in view of the impressive mulberry tree. Fran has lived in the area all her life and can direct guests to places of interest. She enjoys bicycling, gardening, cross-country skiing, and furniture restoration. She and Smoky and Tinsel (her cats) welcome your visit.

SEASON

all year

ACCOMMODATIONS

three rooms with shared baths

Rummel's Tree Haven Bed & Breakfast

Erma and Carl Rummel
41 North Beck Street (M-25)
Sebewaing, Michigan 48759
Tel: (517) 883-2450
$$

ABOUT THE B&B

Located in the village of Sebewaing, Michigan, in the hollow of the thumb on Saginaw Bay, Rummel's Tree Haven was originally built as the farm home of Barbara and Frederick Beck in 1878. Today, Erma and Carl Rummel call it home and offer comfort and convenience to all travelers. The B&B is surrounded by many trees, which gives it an air of privacy — one tree even grows right through the porch roof! Saginaw Bay offers fine fishing, hunting, boating, bird-watching, or just relaxing. The Rummels love having company and will make you feel welcome.

SEASON

all year

ACCOMMODATIONS

two rooms with private baths

Erma's Special French Toast

3 ounces cream cheese, softened
1½ tablespoons lemon curd
6 slices white bread
3 tablespoons chopped pecans
3 eggs
2 tablespoons milk
Sprinkle of confectioners' sugar
6 orange slices

Maple syrup

Mix the softened cream cheese and lemon curd together. Spread evenly on the bread slices. Sprinkle 3 of the bread slices with the chopped nuts. Press the other 3 slices on top and press firmly. Cut these sandwiches on the diagonal. Beat the eggs lightly with a fork. Add the milk and continue beating. Dip the sandwiches 1 at a time into the egg mixture, then let drain a little, and fry as you would regular French toast. Just before serving, sift a little confectioners' sugar on top. Garnish with the orange slices, and serve with syrup. *Tip:* Sandwiches can be made the night before. Simply wrap them in waxed paper and keep in the refrigerator. Remove from the refrigerator ¾ hour before you're ready to dip them in the egg mixture and fry. *Yield: 2 servings.*

Featherweight Whole Wheat Pancakes

"At Thistle Hill, fresh wheat berries are gathered each harvest from the fields of waving golden grain and are ground at the farm shortly before use. Needless to say, these pancakes are a favorite of our guests!" — Mary Hendricks

2 cups whole wheat flour
1 teaspoon baking soda
3 tablespoons sugar
½ teaspoon salt
2 eggs, well beaten
¼ cup white vinegar
1¾ cups milk
¼ cup vegetable oil

Sift the flour, baking soda, sugar, and salt together. Combine the eggs, vinegar, milk, and oil and mix well. Add the dry ingredients to the egg mixture and stir just until smooth. Pour the batter from the tip of a large spoon onto a hot, greased large frying pan or griddle. When bubbles appear on top and the underside is brown, turn to brown the other side. *Yield: About 22 pancakes.*

Thistle Hill Bed & Breakfast

Mary and Dave Hendricks
Route 1, Box 93
Wakeeney, Kansas 67672-9736
Tel: (785) 743-2644
$$

ABOUT THE B&B

Described as *"an oasis on the prairie"* by its guests, Thistle Hill Bed & Breakfast is a convenient, secluded cedar farm home located halfway between Kansas City and Denver, Colorado. Thistle Hill is surrounded by native prairie, 60 acres of wildflower-prairie restoration, and cottage-style flower and herb gardens. Accommodations range from the spacious Oak Room with a rustic queen-sized bed crafted of antique hedge fence posts, the Sunflower Room with a hand-made Kansas sunflower quilt, and the Prairie Room honoring family members who were pioneers of the area. After being awakened by the rooster's crow, feast on a hearty country breakfast of fragrant homemade muffins or hot cakes made from freshly ground Kansas wheat, along with an egg dish, fresh fruit and juice, and gourmet coffee or herbal tea. Thistle Hill is located close to Castle Rock, Cedar Bluff Reservoir, the Cottonwood Ranch, and Sternberg Museum.

SEASON

all year

ACCOMMODATIONS

three rooms with private baths

The Country Caboose

Lisa Thompson
852 Willoughby Lane
Stevensville, Montana 59870
Tel: (406) 777-3145
$$

ABOUT THE B&B

The Country Caboose is indeed that — an authentic caboose dating back to 1923, made of wood and painted red, of course. It is set on real rails in the middle of the countryside. The caboose sleeps two and offers a spectacular view of the Bitterroot Mountains right from your pillow. The Caboose breakfast menu features such goodies as huckleberry pancakes, strawberry waffles, French toast with fruit, and quiche. Local activities include touring St. Mary's Mission and the Marcus Daly Mansion, hiking mountain trails, fishing, and hunting.

SEASON

summer

ACCOMMODATIONS

room and private bath
in a 1923 wooden caboose

French Toast with Orange and Pecans

4 eggs
⅔ cup orange juice
⅓ cup milk
¼ cup sugar
¼ teaspoon grated nutmeg
¼ teaspoon vanilla
½ loaf French bread, sliced
⅓ cup butter, melted
2 tablespoons grated orange zest
½ cup pecan halves

Maple syrup or fresh fruit

Beat together the eggs, orange juice, milk, sugar, nutmeg, and vanilla. Place the bread slices in a single layer in a large dish. Pour the egg mixture over the bread. Cover and refrigerate overnight. In the morning, remove the dish from the refrigerator about ¾ hour before baking. Preheat the oven to 400°F, pour the melted butter into a baking pan, then place the bread in the pan. Sprinkle with the orange zest and pecans. Bake 20 – 25 minutes. Serve with maple syrup or fresh fruit. *Yield: 4 servings.*

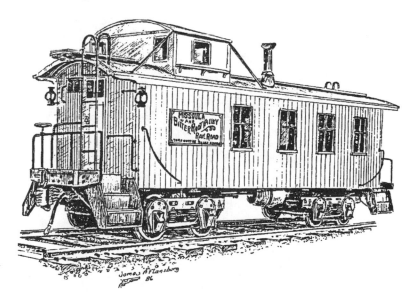

Fruit-stuffed French Toast with Strawberry-Nut Sauce

6 ounces cream cheese, softened
12 slices raisin bread
6 teaspoons strawberry jam
3 eggs
¼ cup milk
1 teaspoon vanilla
2 teaspoons sugar

Strawberry-nut sauce (see recipe below)

Spread the cream cheese on 6 slices of raisin bread. Spread jam on the remaining 6 slices of raisin bread. Put the bread slices together (cream cheese side to jam side) and set aside. Mix the eggs, milk, vanilla, and sugar. Dip the sandwiches in the egg mixture, then fry on both sides. Cut diagonally and spoon the sauce over the wedges before serving. *Yield: 6 servings.*

(continued on next page)

Bridgeford House

Denise and Michael McDonald
263 Spring Street
Eureka Springs, Arkansas 72632
Tel: (501) 253-7853
Fax: (501) 253-5497
E-mail: EurekaBnB@aol.com
$$ – $$$

ABOUT THE B&B

*I*n the heart of Eureka Springs's historic district, Bridgeford House is an 1884 Queen Anne/Eastlake-style Victorian delight. Outside, you'll find shady porches that invite you to pull up a wicker chair and enjoy the panorama of horse-drawn carriages and Victorian homes that is uniquely Spring Street. Yet Bridgeford House is far enough away from downtown that it affords you the luxury of a peaceful and quiet stay. Select from four distinct accommodations: a two-room suite or three large, comfortable bedrooms. From your private entrance, you'll step into rooms tastefully filled with antique furnishings. Your comfortable bedroom and large modern bathroom offer a variety of distinctive touches that let you know you are indeed a special guest — things like fresh hot coffee in your room, color TV, and air conditioning. The large gourmet breakfast is just the right send-off for a pleasant day in one of America's most charming and unusual cities. Denise and Michael are full-time innkeepers and can devote their full attention to all of your needs.

SEASON

all year

ACCOMMODATIONS

four rooms (including one suite) with private baths

Strawberry-nut sauce:
2 teaspoons cornstarch
⅔ cup cold water
1 cup strawberry jam
2 teaspoons lemon juice
¼ cup chopped walnuts

Mix the cornstarch and water and set aside. Heat the jam to a boil and add the cornstarch mixture. Stir constantly and bring to a boil, then simmer 3 minutes. Add the lemon juice, then the chopped walnuts. Spoon over the French toast wedges.

German Puff Pancakes with Spiced Apples

1 cup milk
1 cup all-purpose flour
6 eggs
2 teaspoons vanilla
8 pats butter or margarine

Spiced apples:
5 medium apples (any variety)
½ cup water
4 tablespoons butter or margarine
½ teaspoon ground cinnamon
½ teaspoon grated nutmeg
½ teaspoon ground ginger
½ cup brown sugar
½ cup mincemeat

Whipped cream
Freshly grated nutmeg
8 apple wedges

(continued on next page)

Holden House — 1902 Bed & Breakfast Inn

Sallie and Welling Clark
1102 West Pikes Peak Avenue
Colorado Springs, Colorado 80904
Tel: (719) 471-3980
Fax: (719) 471-4740
E-mail: HoldenHouse@
worldnet.att.net
www.bbonline.com/co/holden/
$$$

ABOUT THE B&B

Experience the romance of the past with the comforts of today at Holden House — 1902 Bed & Breakfast Inn. This storybook Victorian and carriage house filled with antiques and family heirlooms is located in a residential area near the historic district and central to the Pikes Peak region. Enjoy the front parlor, living room with a fireplace and wingback chairs, or the wide veranda with mountain views. Immaculate suites boast queen-size beds, down pillows, private baths, tubs for two, and fireplaces. Enjoy complimentary refreshments, homemade cookies, and friendly resident cats Mingtoy and Muffin.

SEASON

all year

ACCOMMODATIONS

five suites with private baths

Whip the milk, flour, eggs, and vanilla. Set aside. Place a pat of butter in each of 8 (12-ounce) individual soufflé/serving bowls. Preheat the bowls in a 400°F oven 10 – 15 minutes or until the butter is popping hot.

In the meantime, make the spiced apples. Cut the apples into chunks and place in a frying pan with the water and butter. Cook for 15 minutes or until the apples are moderately soft. Add a bit more water if the apples become too dry while cooking. When cooked, add the cinnamon, nutmeg, ginger, brown sugar, and mincemeat to the apples. Continue cooking another 5 – 10 minutes or until well mixed and hot.

When the butter in the dishes in the oven is popping hot, add an even measurement of pancake batter to each dish — being careful that the hot butter doesn't spatter. Turn up the oven to 425°F for 10 minutes then back down to 400°F for another 5 minutes or until the pancakes are puffed up and slightly brown on the edges. Remove from the oven, and place an even measure of spiced apple in the center of each pancake. Top with a dollop of whipped cream and sprinkle with freshly grated nutmeg. Place a wedge of apple on top as garnish and serve on a cloth doily on a plate (**this is necessary** as pancakes are extremely hot and may crack plates if doilies aren't used!). *Yield: 8 pancakes.*

Hawaiian French Toast

4 eggs
1 teaspoon vanilla
1 tablespoon maple syrup
1 tablespoon sour cream
1 tablespoon granulated sugar
8-ounce can crushed pineapple, drained
¼ cup milk
8 slices day-old bread, crusts trimmed if desired
6 tablespoons butter or margarine
Confectioners' sugar
Shredded unsweetened coconut

In a blender, whirl the eggs, vanilla, syrup, sour cream, granulated sugar, pineapple, and milk until smooth. Cut the bread slices diagonally in ½ and arrange in a large shallow dish. Pour the egg mixture over the bread and let it soak in, then turn to coat the other side. In a large frying pan over medium heat, melt about 2 tablespoons butter. Place a few pieces of soaked bread in the pan and cook until browned on the bottom. Turn and brown the other side. Use the remaining butter as needed. Remove to a warm platter and keep warm in a 200°F oven until all the bread has been cooked. Dust with the confectioners' sugar and sprinkle with the shredded coconut. *Yield: 4 servings.*

Papaya Paradise

Jeanette and Bob Martz
395 Auwinala Road
Kailua, Oahu, Hawaii 96734
Tel/Fax: (808) 261-0316
www.bnbweb.com/Papaya.html
$$

ABOUT THE B&B

If you're looking for privacy, quiet, and miles of beautiful, uncrowded white sandy beach, look no further than Papaya Paradise. Located 20 miles from Honolulu airport on the windward side of Oahu in Kailua, Papaya Paradise is removed from the hectic activity of Waikiki yet near all major attractions and Waikiki nightlife. Tropical rattan and wicker guest rooms have a private entrance, private bath, two comfortable beds and lounge chairs, ceiling fan, air conditioning, telephone, and cable TV, and open onto a large swimming pool and Jacuzzi surrounded by tropical plants, trees, and flowers. Breakfast is served on the lanai overlooking the pool and Jacuzzi. For your convenience, your hosts furnish beach towels, hats, chairs, coolers, boogie boards, a refrigerator and micro-wave oven, and a small library with relaxing reading chairs.

SEASON

all year

ACCOMMODATIONS

two rooms with private baths

The Georges

Marie and Carolyn George
57759 874th Road
Dixon, Nebraska 68732-9728
Tel: (402) 584-2625
E-mail: DixonMom@aol.com
$

ABOUT THE B&B

Look past the large grove of trees and you'll discover The Georges, a large remodeled, air conditioned farmhouse designed to comfortably accommodate the travel needs of a large family. Your stay includes a hearty breakfast featuring homemade jellies and jams, while other meals can be arranged. Bunking at The Georges offers you the opportunity to see a modern farming operation firsthand, including the planting and harvesting of corn, soybeans, and alfalfa. You'll also hear the chickens clucking and make the acquaintance of several farm cats. During the warm season, you can hike, bird-watch, relax with a book in a quiet spot, or visit county fairs and local festivals. In the fall, pheasant hunting season is in its prime and, depending on the winter snowfall, you can choose from sledding, hiking, cross-country skiing, or ice skating on farm ponds.

SEASON

all year

ACCOMMODATIONS

five rooms with shared baths

Lefse (Potato Pancakes)

"A traditional Norwegian potato pancake recipe from a Norwegian neighbor." — Marie George

3 cups mashed potatoes (not instant)
½ cup margarine or butter, melted
1 teaspoon salt (if mashed potatoes not already salted)
1 tablespoon granulated sugar
½ teaspoon baking powder
About 1½ cups all-purpose flour
Confectioners' sugar (optional)

Butter, ground cinnamon, and sugar
Jelly or jam
Maple syrup
Fresh fruit (such as strawberries, raspberries, or blueberries)

Combine the potatoes, margarine, salt, granulated sugar, and baking powder. Add enough flour so the dough doesn't stick to your hands. Form the dough into balls about the size of a walnut, and roll thin. Fry in an ungreased skillet over medium heat until set and lightly brown on the underside, then flip and brown lightly on the other side. Sprinkle with confectioners' sugar, if you wish. Serve with your choice of butter, ground cinnamon, and sugar; jelly or jam; maple syrup; or fresh fruit. You can roll the pancakes with any of these or serve them flat. *Tips:* Make these ahead and reheat in a skillet or microwave. An electric pancake griddle is ideal for frying 4 – 6 pancakes at a time.
Yield: 4 – 8 servings.

Lemon-Ricotta Pancakes

"One travel writer wrote that she still dreams about these pancakes."
— *Christopher Sellers*

¾ cup all-purpose flour
½ teaspoon grated nutmeg
1 cup ricotta cheese
1 tablespoon granulated sugar
1 teaspoon baking powder
2 eggs
⅔ cup milk
Juice and grated zest of 1 lemon
Confectioners' sugar

Vermont maple syrup

In a large bowl, combine the flour, nutmeg, cheese, granulated sugar, baking powder, eggs, milk, and lemon juice and zest. Pour ⅓ cup of the batter onto a hot greased griddle. Spread the batter into a 5" circle. Cook until golden, turning once. Arrange on a platter and dust with confectioners' sugar. Serve with Vermont maple syrup. *Yield: 10 – 12 pancakes.*

Grünberg Haus Bed & Breakfast
Waterbury, Vermont

Grünberg Haus Bed and Breakfast

Christopher Sellers and
Mark Frohman
RR #2, Box 1595RD,
Route 100 South
Waterbury, Vermont 05676-9621
Tel: (800) 800-7760 or (802) 244-7726
Fax: (802) 244-1283
E-mail: grunhaus@aol.com
$$ – $$$$

ABOUT THE B&B

This picture-postcard Austrian-style B&B is tucked away on a secluded hillside in the Green Mountains, perfectly situated for visits to Stowe, Montpelier, Waterbury, and Burlington. Individually decorated guest rooms open onto the carved wood balcony, which offers wonderful views. Help Mark feed the chickens, then enjoy a full breakfast — with selections such as maple-poached pears, apple and cheddar muffins, and ricotta-stuffed French toast — while Chris plays the grand piano. The giant stone fireplace and wood stove in the BYOB pub are favorite gathering places. Nearby activities include spectacular autumn leaf-picking, world-class downhill skiing, golf, boating, bicycling, gliding, canoeing, antique hunting, outlet shopping, and touring Ben & Jerry's ice cream factory. And you can enjoy the B&B's own Jacuzzi, sauna, tennis courts, and cross-country and hiking trails.

SEASON

all year

ACCOMMODATIONS

seven rooms (including one suite)
with private baths;
five rooms with shared baths;
two cabins with private baths

Ferry Point House
Bed & Breakfast
on Lake Winnisquam

Diane and Joe Damato
100 Lower Bay Road
Sanbornton, New Hampshire 03269
Tel: (603) 524-0087
Fax: (603) 524-0959
$$ – $$$

ABOUT THE B&B

This gracious, 175-year-old country Victorian is located on picturesque Lake Winnisquam, in a spot commanding a panoramic view of lake and mountains. The gazebo on the point complements the sandy beach and allows for quiet moments by the water. A 60-foot veranda and all of the rooms are blessed with breathtaking views. Return to the warm, friendly feeling of New England's past with antique furniture, collectibles, and fresh flowers in your room. The lake and surrounding area offer an endless variety of activities, including swimming, fishing, and boating at the inn. Horseback riding, golf, tennis, dinner cruises, scenic train and plane rides, antique shopping, and fine restaurants are all close by. Each morning, you'll be treated to a very special gourmet breakfast with delights such as stuffed French toast, cheese-baked apples, poached pears, and select home-baked breads and muffins.

SEASON

May to November 1

ACCOMMODATIONS

six rooms with private baths

Memère's French Breakfast Crêpes

"This very special and much requested recipe has been in my family for generations. It has taken me years of practice to even come close to the way my grandmother made these crêpes (my mother is still teaching me!). When done to perfection, they should be thin, crisp, and 'melt in your mouth' delicious." — Diane Damato

2 cups all-purpose flour
1 teaspoon baking soda
½ teaspoon salt
3 eggs
1¾ cups milk
Vegetable shortening
Slices of fresh strawberries or raspberries

Warm maple syrup

Note: These crêpes must be cooked in a cast-iron pan.

Combine the flour, baking soda, and salt. In a separate bowl, beat the eggs and milk with a wire whisk and add to the flour mixture. The batter should be smooth and without lumps. Melt 1 tablespoon of shortening in a pan over moderately high heat. When it begins to smoke, it's time to add the batter. Carefully place 2 serving spoons of the batter into the pan in a circular motion. Using the back of the spoon, quickly spread the batter to cover the bottom of the pan and fill in any holes. Flip when the underside browns and the sides begin to curl. Brown the second side and serve immediately. Repeat with the rest of the batter. Garnish with strawberries or raspberries and top with warm maple syrup.
Yield: About 10 crêpes.

Nutty Pumpkin Waffles with Pumpkin-Maple Sauce

2 cups all-purpose flour
2 teaspoons baking powder
1 tablespoon cornstarch
½ teaspoon salt
2 teaspoons ground cinnamon
¼ teaspoon ground ginger
¼ teaspoon grated nutmeg
½ cup solid-packed pumpkin (canned)
2 eggs, separated
1¾ cups milk
2 tablespoons butter or margarine, melted
¼ cup sugar
¾ cup chopped walnuts

Pumpkin-maple sauce (see recipe below)

Combine the flour, baking powder, cornstarch, salt, cinnamon, ginger, and nutmeg in a large bowl. Combine the pumpkin, egg yolks, and milk in a medium bowl and mix well. Add the pumpkin mixture to the dry ingredients, mixing until just moistened. Stir in the melted butter. Beat the egg whites and sugar in a small bowl until soft peaks form. Gently fold the egg whites into the batter.

(continued on next page)

Saltair
Bed and Breakfast

Nancy Saxton and Jan Bartlett
164 South 900 East
Salt Lake City, Utah 84102
Tel: (800) 733-8184 or (801) 533-8184
Fax: (801) 595-0332
$$ – $$$

ABOUT THE B&B

*L*isted on the National Register of Historic Places, this 1903 Victorian house is the oldest continuously operating B&B in Utah and has hosted many dignitaries. The comfortably elegant house is furnished with period antiques, handmade quilts, and highlighted with wood and beveled glass. Room amenities include fresh flowers, saltwater taffy, terry cloth robes, and down comforters. Guests enjoy a warming fire in the parlor, a summer breeze on the front porch swing, or a Salt Lake starlit night in the B&B's hot tub. Breakfast may include cereal and yogurt, fruit, coffee or tea, a hot entrée, and a fruit smoothie. Located in a friendly residential neighborhood, Saltair is one mile west of the University of Utah, the historic downtown Salt Lake area, Temple Square, and the Utah Symphony Concert Hall, and is near Utah Jazz basketball, museums, theaters, and shopping. Seven ski resorts are 35 minutes away, while canyons for hiking and mountain biking are 10 minutes away.

SEASON

all year

ACCOMMODATIONS

two rooms with private baths;
three rooms with shared bath

Bake the waffles on a hot waffle iron according to the manufacturer's directions. Sprinkle walnuts over the baked waffles and serve with pumpkin-maple sauce. *Yield: 5 waffles.*

Pumpkin-maple sauce:
¾ cup solid-packed pumpkin (canned)
1 cup maple syrup
¼ teaspoon ground cinnamon

In a saucepan, heat the pumpkin, maple syrup, and cinnamon until warmed through.

Oat and Green Apple Griddle Cakes

2 large Granny Smith apples, peeled, cored, and cut into ¾ – 1" chunks
⅔ cup large-flake rolled oats
¾ cup water
2 teaspoons canola oil
2 cups buttermilk pancake mix, from scratch or store-bought
   (Krusteaz brand recommended)
¾ cup hazelnut non-dairy creamer
1 egg or 2 egg whites or ¼ cup egg substitute
Strawberry or huckleberry conserve
Non-fat sour cream

Light maple syrup and canola margarine

The night before, microwave the apples in a dish covered with plastic wrap for about 3 minutes or until softened. Leave at room temperature. Drain any remaining liquid just before use.

In the morning, soak the oats in the water for about 15 minutes. Oil and preheat a griddle or large frying pan using 1 teaspoon of the canola oil. Add the pancake mix, creamer, egg, and remaining teaspoon of canola oil to the oats. Mix quickly (if too thick, add more water or creamer). Ladle ⅓ cup of the batter onto the griddle. Place 4 – 5 chunks of apple on top. Cook until bubbles appear. Turn and cook until golden. Repeat with the remaining batter and apple. Serve the pancakes apple side up. Garnish with the fruit conserve and non-fat sour cream. Serve with light maple syrup and canola margarine. *Tip:* To make the recipe lower in sugar and cholesterol, use buttermilk in place of the hazelnut creamer. *Yield: 8 – 10 griddle cakes.*

Berry Patch Inn

Ann M. Caggiano
1150 North Four Winds Road
Coeur d'Alene, Idaho 83814-9734
Tel: (208) 765-4994
Fax: (208) 667-7336
E-mail: Lady_Anne@msn.com
$$$$

ABOUT THE B&B

Hailed as one of the top 20 inns situated in the Rockies by National Geographic Traveler *(March 1997), Berry Patch Inn offers an elegant and restorative mountain chalet retreat. Nestled in a two-acre forest of tall pines, the inn is notable for its eclectic decor and a large living room with beamed ceiling and rock fireplace. Three guest rooms, all with private bath, look out on the forest, wild berry patch, valley, mountain, or waterfall. Ann Caggiano, the world-traveled innkeeper, serves breakfast in the dining room. Here, spectacular views from the big picture window compete with Ann's beautifully presented breakfast creations — emphasizing healthy and low-fat cuisine. This bird watchers' paradise is less than an hour's drive from Spokane International Airport; close to Lake Coeur d'Alene and the Spokane River, for swimming, fishing, lake cruises, and parasailing; and three-and-a-half miles from downtown shopping and dining. A variety of winter sports, including top-rated skiing, are less than an hour's drive away.*

SEASON

all year

ACCOMMODATIONS

three rooms with private baths

Thornrose House at Gypsy Hill

Suzanne and Otis Huston
531 Thornrose Avenue
Staunton, Virginia 24401
Tel: (540) 885-7026
Fax: (540) 885-6458
www.shenwebworks.com:
8001/thornrose
$$

ABOUT THE B&B

Thornrose House is a turn-of-the-century Georgian Revival with a wraparound veranda and nearly one acre of gardens with Greek colonnades. It is adjacent to the 300-acre Gypsy Hill Park with facilities for tennis, golf, swimming, and summer band concerts. Breakfast begins with the house specialty of Bircher muesli, a Swiss concoction of oats, fruit, nuts, and whipped cream. This is followed by an ever-changing menu of hot entrées and fresh baked muffins and breads. Fireplaces in the sitting room and dining room warm you on chilly mornings and winter evenings, while a baby grand piano invites you to share your musical talents. Thornrose House is conveniently located in the heart of the Shenandoah Valley, which offers hiking, biking, antique hunting, historical museums, summer theater, and numerous fine restaurants.

SEASON

all year

ACCOMMODATIONS

five rooms with private baths

Oatmeal Waffles with Spiced Apples

1½ cups all-purpose flour
1 cup quick-cooking rolled oats
1 tablespoon baking powder
½ teaspoon ground cinnamon
¼ teaspoon salt
2 eggs, lightly beaten
1½ cups milk
6 tablespoons butter, melted
2 tablespoons brown sugar
Spiced apples (see recipe below)

In a large mixing bowl, mix the flour, oats, baking powder, cinnamon, and salt. In a small mixing bowl, stir together the eggs, milk, butter, and brown sugar. Add to the flour mixture all at once. Stir just until blended. Pour 1 – 1½ cups batter onto the grid of a preheated, lightly greased waffle iron. When done, remove with a fork. Top with the spiced apples. *Yield: 4 waffles.*

Spiced apples:
2 cooking apples, peeled, cored, and thinly sliced
2 tablespoons butter, melted
¼ cup pecan halves, toasted
1 tablespoon brown sugar
⅛ teaspoon ground cinnamon
⅛ teaspoon grated nutmeg
1 teaspoon vanilla

Cook the apples in the butter in a large skillet over low heat, stirring occasionally until tender. Add the pecans and remaining ingredients, tossing gently. *Yield: 4 servings.*

Oat Pancakes

2 cups all-purpose flour
1 cup large-flake rolled oats
2 teaspoons baking soda
2 teaspoons baking powder
½ teaspoon salt
½ teaspoon ground cinnamon
¼ teaspoon grated nutmeg
4 eggs
¾ cup butter, melted
2 cups buttermilk

Chunky applesauce

Mix the flour, oats, baking soda, baking powder, salt, cinnamon, and nutmeg in a large bowl. Mix the eggs, melted butter, and buttermilk in a small bowl, whisking to blend. Make a well in the center of the dry ingredients and stir in the egg mixture (do not overmix). Spray a skillet or pancake grill with cooking oil spray. Using a ¼ cup measure for each pancake, pour the batter onto the hot grill. Cook until bubbles appear on top and the underside is golden. Turn to brown the other side. Keep the pancakes warm in a 200°F oven. Serve with chunky applesauce, if desired. *Yield: 6 servings.*

Lakeside Farm
Bed and Breakfast

Joy and Glenn Hagen
RR #2, Box 52
Webster, South Dakota
57274-9633
Tel: (605) 486-4430
$

ABOUT THE B&B

More than a century ago, a Norwegian immigrant pioneer established a tree claim on the rugged, beautiful South Dakota prairie. He chose the spot for its fertile soil, gently rolling hills, and proximity to Waubay Lake. Today, this pioneer's grandson, Glenn Hagen, and Glenn's wife Joy own and operate Lakeside Farm. Feel free to explore the grove, barns, and pastures or just relax with a cup of tea in the farmhouse. Enjoy a long, leisurely morning in bed until you're awakened by the tantalizing smell of Joy's home-cooked breakfast. Lakeside Farm is the perfect overnight stop on your way to or from the Black Hills, only a day's drive away. Other things to see and do include Historic Fort Sisseton, Sica Hollow State Park, Waubay National Wildlife Refuge, Native American and pioneer museums, boating, hunting, fishing, rodeo, and bicycling.

SEASON

all year

ACCOMMODATIONS

two rooms with shared bath

Manor House

Diane and Hank Tremblay
PO Box 447
Norfolk, Connecticut 06058
Tel/Fax: (860) 542-5690
$$$$

ABOUT THE B&B

Manor House is a historic 1898 mansion built for the leisure class of an earlier era. Today, it's designated as "Connecticut's most romantic hideaway" (The Discerning Traveler). *Relax in the living room beside the baronial fireplace, retreat to the sun porch to enjoy a book from the inn's library, or take a stroll around the grounds to enjoy the perennial gardens. The inn exudes Victorian elegance, with its Tiffany windows, architectural detail, and antique furnishings. Awake to the wonderful aromas of Manor House's full breakfast, including homemade bread or muffins and honey harvested from the inn's own hives, all served in the elegant dining room. If you have a more romantic breakfast in mind, innkeepers Diane and Hank Tremblay will pamper you with breakfast in bed. Manor House is close to Tanglewood, summer theater, vineyards, and a host of summer and winter activities, including hiking, biking, water sports, and alpine and cross-country skiing.*

SEASON

all year

ACCOMMODATIONS

eight rooms with private baths

Orange Waffles

2 cups all-purpose flour
3 teaspoons baking powder
2 tablespoons sugar
½ teaspoon salt
4 eggs, lightly beaten
1 cup milk
4 tablespoons butter, melted
3 tablespoons grated orange zest

Maple syrup

Sift together the flour, baking powder, sugar, and salt; set aside. Combine the eggs, milk, and butter. Add the orange zest and mix. Add the dry ingredients in two equal parts, beating well after each addition until the batter is smooth. Pour about ¾ – 1 cup of the batter at a time onto a preheated waffle iron, following the manufacturer's directions. Bake until the waffles are golden brown. Serve with maple syrup.
Yield: 8 waffles.

Palisades Fruit Puff Pancakes

6 eggs
1 tablespoon granulated sugar
1 cup all-purpose flour
1 cup milk
¼ teaspoon salt
½ teaspoon vanilla
4 tablespoons butter
Confectioners' sugar

Preheat the oven to 450°F. In a medium bowl, beat the eggs and granulated sugar with an electric mixer on high speed until frothy (about 1 minute). Slowly add the flour, beating on medium speed until blended. Stir in the milk, salt, and vanilla. Melt the butter in 4 (8") ovenproof skillets. Pour the egg mixture into the hot skillets. Bake 12 –15 minutes or until brown and puffed. Remove from the oven and sprinkle with confectioners' sugar. Serve with your favorite filling (see below for suggestions). *Yield: 4 servings.*

Bananas amaretto:
2 tablespoons butter
1 tablespoon light brown sugar
4 firm bananas, sliced
¼ cup amaretto liqueur
Whipped or sour cream
Grated nutmeg

(continued on next page)

Palisades Paradise B&B

Gail Goetz
1200 Palisades Avenue
Redding, California 96003
Tel: (530) 223-5305
$$ – $$$

ABOUT THE B&B

You'll feel you're in paradise when you enjoy the magnificent sunsets over the Sacramento River and breathtaking views of the city and surrounding mountains from this beautiful contemporary home. Housing two rooms with queen-size beds, garden spa, fireplace, wide-screen TV/VCR, and homelike atmosphere, Palisades Paradise is a serene setting for a quiet hideaway, yet conveniently located one mile from shopping and Interstate 5. Visiting Mount Shasta and Mount Lassen are a must, while water-skiing, mountain climbing, and river rafting are nearby for the adventurous at heart. The B&B was established in 1986 and is still owned and operated by Gail Goetz, an early childhood resource specialist.

SEASON

all year

ACCOMMODATIONS

two rooms with shared bath

Melt the butter in a skillet. Add the sugar and sauté the bananas until slightly soft, but not mushy. Gently stir in the liqueur. Fill the puffs with the mixture and top with whipped or sour cream, and a sprinkling of nutmeg.

Assorted fruit:
Fill the puffs with sliced strawberries and kiwi (nice for Christmas!), sliced peaches and blueberries, or canned apples with brown sugar and ground cinnamon. Top with whipped cream or yogurt.

Mandarin orange sauce:
2 tablespoons sugar
1 tablespoon cornstarch
¾ cup water
2 tablespoons frozen orange juice concentrate
11-ounce can mandarin oranges
Whipped cream
Sliced almonds

Combine the sugar and cornstarch in a medium saucepan. Stir in the water and frozen orange juice concentrate. Cook on medium heat, stirring until thick and bubbly. Cook and stir 2 more minutes. Pour into the puffs, top with whipped cream, sprinkle with sliced almonds, and serve. *Tip:* This sauce is also very good over French toast.

Peach French Toast à la Garth

(*Recipe from* Breakfast Inn Bed, Easy and Elegant Recipes from Garth Woodside Mansion.)

29-ounce can sliced peaches
1 cup brown sugar
½ cup butter or margarine
2 tablespoons water
1 loaf French bread, cut into 12 – 14 slices
5 eggs
1½ cups milk
1 tablespoon vanilla

Drain the peaches and reserve the syrup. Heat the sugar and butter on medium-low until melted. Add the water and continue cooking until the sauce becomes thick and foamy. Pour into a 13 x 9" baking dish and cool 10 minutes. Place the peaches on the cooled caramel sauce and cover with the slices of bread, placed close together. In a blender, add the eggs, milk, and vanilla until mixed. Pour over the bread, cover, and refrigerate overnight. Remove from the refrigerator ¾ hour before baking. Preheat the oven to 350°F and bake for 40 minutes. If browning too fast, loosely cover with foil for the last 10 – 15 minutes. Cut around the bread slices, invert onto a plate, and serve with the reserved peach syrup, warmed. *Yield: 12 – 14 servings.*

Garth Woodside Mansion

Diane and Irv Feinberg
RR #3, Box 578
Hannibal, Missouri 63401
Tel: (573) 221-2789
E-mail: Garth@nemonet.com
www.hanmo.com/garth
$$ – $$$

ABOUT THE B&B

Experience affordable elegance in this 1871 Victorian country estate on 39 acres of meadows and woodlands. On the National Register of Historic Places, Garth Woodside Mansion has remained unchanged outside, and graceful arched doors, handsomely decorated rooms featuring original furnishings spanning over 150 years, and magnificent three-story spiral "Flying Staircase" await you inside. You'll enjoy marble fireplaces, canopy beds, your own nightshirt to wear during your stay, an exceptional full breakfast, an afternoon beverage, and more. All rooms are air conditioned and have a private bath. The location is ideal for seeing Mark Twain Country.

SEASON

all year

ACCOMMODATIONS

eight rooms with private baths

Snug Harbor Inn

Laurine "Sis" and Kenneth Hill
1226 West 10th Avenue
Anchorage, Alaska 99501
Tel: (907) 272-6249
Fax: (907) 272-7100
$$

ABOUT THE B&B

*S*nug Harbor Inn offers you *cheerful comfort in a relaxed "home-away-from-home" atmosphere, where absolute privacy is yours. Relax while surrounded by antiques, art, Alaskan artifacts, and period furnishings. The rooms feature handmade quilts and some have their own entrances. At this inn, a fully equipped kitchen, complimentary coffee, tea, and hot chocolate available 24 hours a day, color TV, and complimentary bicycles are at your disposal. The friendly, efficient staff has your every comfort in mind, making Snug Harbor the first choice for the business and pleasure traveler. Located in the heart of Anchorage, Snug Harbor is just four blocks from the central business district, and close to shopping, entertainment, fine dining, and sightseeing. The trail head for Anchorage's extensive bicycle and jogging paths is also nearby.*

SEASON

all year

ACCOMMODATIONS

four rooms with private baths; two rooms with shared bath

Pineapple Upside-Down French Toast

2 tablespoons butter
¼ cup brown sugar
½ cup crushed pineapple
¾ teaspoon ground cinnamon
1 egg
⅔ cup milk
½ teaspoon vanilla
Dash of salt
6 slices raisin bread, cut in ½ diagonally

Heavy cream, maple syrup, or yogurt

Preheat the oven to 400°F. Melt the butter in a 9" cake or pie pan, being careful not to burn it. Spread the brown sugar and pineapple evenly over the bottom of the pan. Sprinkle with the cinnamon. Beat the egg with the milk, vanilla, and salt. Dip the bread into the egg mixture and arrange the cut slices in the pan, overlapping them neatly. Cook uncovered 20 – 25 minutes. Cut into squares and invert onto a plate. Serve with heavy cream, maple syrup, or yogurt. *Yield: 4 – 6 servings.*

Pumpkin Pancakes

2 cups Bisquick baking mix
2 eggs
2 tablespoons vegetable oil
2 tablespoons brown sugar, firmly packed
1 teaspoon vanilla
1 teaspoon ground allspice
12-ounce can evaporated milk
½ cup pumpkin, solidly packed
1 teaspoon ground cinnamon

Butter and Vermont maple syrup

In the order given, mix together the baking mix, eggs, vegetable oil, sugar, vanilla, allspice, milk, pumpkin, and cinnamon. Spoon ¼ cup of the batter onto a hot, greased griddle. When the top side begins to bubble and the underside is brown, flip and cook the other side for 2 minutes. Serve with butter and Vermont maple syrup.
Yield: 18 pancakes.

Red Brook Inn

Ruth Keyes
PO Box 237
Old Mystic, Connecticut 06372
Tel: (860) 572-0349
E-mail: Rkeyes1667@aol.com
$$$$

ABOUT THE B&B

Nestled on a hillside, the Red Brook Inn offers Colonial life at its best. Capturing the spirit and simple pleasures of early New England, two beautifully restored historic buildings offer stone walls, antique-filled rooms, and well-banked fires to keep toes from frosting on chilly nights. Ten guest rooms are decorated with period furnishings, stenciled walls, and canopy beds. Six of the guest rooms have fireplaces and two have whirlpool tubs. A hearty breakfast of home-cooked specialties is served each morning in the Keeping Room. In autumn and winter months, special packages include Colonial dinners cooked over an open hearth. The inn is within minutes of the Mystic Marinelife Aquarium, Old Mystic Village, Mystic Seaport Museum, shops, and two of the world's largest casinos.

SEASON

all year

ACCOMMODATIONS

10 rooms with private baths

Brambly Hedge Cottage

Jacquelyn Smyers
HCR 31, Box 39
Jasper, Arkansas 72641
Tel: 1-800-BRAMBLY or
(501) 446-5849
$$

ABOUT THE B&B

"*Absolutely charming," wrote National Geographic Traveler of this old Ozark mountaintop farmhouse, four miles south of Jasper, Arkansas. A Tennessee guest commented, "The place is uniquely beautiful, the food delicious, and the view inspiring." Three guest rooms with private baths reflect country French elegance in a homestead log cabin. A full breakfast is served on the deck overlooking Buffalo River Valley or behind the screened porch in rocking chairs. You're only minutes from the "Grand Canyon of the Ozarks," challenging-to-easy hiking trails, and canoeing on Buffalo National River. If art is more your style, you'll find the work of true artisans in the Jasper area. For those who wish to sample a night out on the town, Eureka Springs and Branson (Missouri) are nearby. Small group special-interest tours and relaxing massages can be arranged. Hostess Jacquelyn Smyers includes her handmade tatted lace and samovar collection in the decor. She's also a designer, commercial artist, and author of* Come For Tea *and the children's book* The Cloud That Came Into The Cabin *(inspired by the clouds on Sloan Mountain where Brambly Hedge is located).*

SEASON

all year

ACCOMMODATIONS

three rooms with private baths

Rib-Stickin' Pancakes

"These cakes have taste and delightful texture, fill you up, but rest easy in your stomach." — Jacquelyn Smyers

1 cup all-purpose flour
¼ cup white or yellow cornmeal
2 tablespoons wheat germ
2 tablespoons bran
1 scant teaspoon salt
1 tablespoon baking powder
2 eggs
1 cup milk
1 tablespoon vegetable oil

Mix the flour, cornmeal, wheat germ, bran, salt, and baking powder. Add the eggs, milk, and oil and stir, pressing out big lumps. Add a slosh of water to thin the batter so it will pour well. When water drops dance on a hot greased griddle, pour ladles of batter on it and cook until bubbles appear on top and the underside is golden. Turn to brown the other side. With a fork, lift a bit of crust in the middle of each one to be sure it's done. *Yield: 7 pancakes.*

Ricotta-stuffed French Toast

"Our friend Walter used to treat us to this breakfast treat on hiking trips in the mountains." — Christopher Sellers

1 loaf Italian bread, unsliced
8 ounces ricotta cheese
4 eggs
½ cup whipping cream
1 tablespoon vanilla
½ teaspoon grated nutmeg
½ teaspoon ground cinnamon
Confectioners' sugar

Vermont maple syrup

Thinly slice the bread into 24 slices. Spread 12 slices with fresh ricotta cheese, then top with the remaining 12 slices. Beat together the eggs, cream, vanilla, nutmeg, and cinnamon. Dip the cheese sandwiches into the egg mixture. Grill slowly on both sides until browned. Dust with confectioners' sugar and serve with Vermont maple syrup. *Yield: 8 servings.*

Grünberg Haus Bed & Breakfast
Waterbury, Vermont

Grünberg Haus Bed and Breakfast

Christopher Sellers and
Mark Frohman
RR #2, Box 1595RD,
Route 100 South
Waterbury, Vermont 05676-9621
Tel: (800) 800-7760 or (802) 244-7726
Fax: (802) 244-1283
E-mail: grunhaus@aol.com
$$ – $$$$

ABOUT THE B&B

This picture-postcard Austrian-style B&B is tucked away on a secluded hillside in the Green Mountains, perfectly situated for visits to Stowe, Montpelier, Waterbury, and Burlington. Individually decorated guest rooms open onto the carved wood balcony, which offers wonderful views. Help Mark feed the chickens, then enjoy a full breakfast — with selections such as maple-poached pears, apple and cheddar muffins, and ricotta-stuffed French toast — while Chris plays the grand piano. The giant stone fireplace and wood stove in the BYOB pub are favorite gathering places. Nearby activities include spectacular autumn leaf-picking, world-class downhill skiing, golf, boating, bicycling, gliding, canoeing, antique hunting, outlet shopping, and touring Ben & Jerry's ice cream factory. And you can enjoy the B&B's own Jacuzzi, sauna, tennis courts, and cross-country and hiking trails.

SEASON

all year

ACCOMMODATIONS

seven rooms (including one suite)
with private baths;
five rooms with shared baths;
two cabins with private baths

Down the Shore B&B

Annette and Al Bergins
201 Seventh Avenue
Belmar, New Jersey 07719
Tel: (732) 681-9023
Fax: (732) 681-7795
E-mail: Lodgings@cris.com
$$

ABOUT THE B&B

Down the Shore Bed & Breakfast was built specifically to be used as a residence and as a bed and breakfast. There are three guest rooms with a shared guest parlor and a shaded 40-foot front porch. Down the Shore B&B is located one block from the beach and boardwalk. The house may be new but the proprietors are not new to innkeeping. Before moving to Belmar, they operated another bed and breakfast in their lakeside home in Denville, New Jersey. As you can see from the recipe, healthful food is the mainstay of the breakfasts here.

SEASON

all year

ACCOMMODATIONS

one room with private bath;
two rooms with shared bath

Serious Waffles

"These waffles are hearty, but don't have the off-taste you sometimes find with whole grain batters." — *Annette Bergins*

Waffle mix (prepared in bulk; makes about 12 cups):
2 pounds ready-made pancake/waffle mix
1 cup stone-ground cornmeal
1 cup soy flour
½ cup powdered milk
½ cup wheat germ
½ cup whole wheat flour
3 tablespoons baking powder

Batter:
1 cup waffle mix (see recipe above)
1 cup skim milk
1 egg or ¼ cup egg substitute

Combine the pancake mix, cornmeal, soy flour, milk, wheat germ, whole wheat flour, and baking powder and store for immediate and future use (keep about 2 pounds in the pantry and the balance in the freezer). To cook, combine the waffle mix, skim milk, and egg and mix well. Pour ½ of the batter onto the grid of a preheated, lightly greased waffle iron. Bake for about 2 minutes. Repeat with the remaining batter.
Yield: 2 waffles.

Snug Harbor French Toast

10 slices day-old white bread, cut into 1" squares
1 tablespoon ground cinnamon
¼ – ½ cup raisins
12 ounces cream cheese, sliced
1 banana or peach, or 4 slices of pineapple
⅓ cup maple syrup
½ tablespoon vanilla
½ teaspoon grated nutmeg
6 eggs
2 cups milk

Maple syrup or rum raisin ice cream

In a 13 x 8" shallow glass baking dish sprayed with non-stick cooking spray, spread ½ of the bread squares. Dust with a cover of cinnamon and sprinkle the raisins to taste. Distribute the sliced cream cheese to cover the bread completely. Cover the cheese with the remainder of the bread squares, then repeat the distribution of raisins and sprinkle with the remaining cinnamon. Set aside while you blend the liquid portion of this dish.

Combine the fruit, syrup, vanilla, and nutmeg, and purée it. Add the eggs; blend. Add the milk and blend the complete mixture until it becomes as frothy as a thick eggnog. Pour this liquid over the bread and cheese mixture, completely saturating it. Press the bread down with your hands and set it aside for at least 30 minutes, or cover and refrigerate overnight (remove from the refrigerator ¾ hour before baking). Preheat the oven to 375°F. Set the baking dish in a pan of water about ½" deep. Cook 45 – 60 minutes or until a knife inserted into the center comes out clean. Slice and serve hot with maple syrup or rum raisin ice cream.
Yield: 6 – 8 servings.

Snug Harbor Inn

Laurine "Sis" and Kenneth Hill
1226 West 10th Avenue
Anchorage, Alaska 99501
Tel: (907) 272-6249
Fax: (907) 272-7100
$$

ABOUT THE B&B

S nug Harbor Inn offers you cheerful comfort in a relaxed "home-away-from-home" atmosphere, where absolute privacy is yours. Relax while surrounded by antiques, art, Alaskan artifacts, and period furnishings. The rooms feature handmade quilts and some have their own entrances. At this inn, a fully equipped kitchen, complimentary coffee, tea, and hot chocolate available 24 hours a day, color TV, and complimentary bicycles are at your disposal. The friendly, efficient staff has your every comfort in mind, making Snug Harbor the first choice for the business and pleasure traveler. Located in the heart of Anchorage, Snug Harbor is just four blocks from the central business district, and close to shopping, entertainment, fine dining, and sightseeing. The trail head for Anchorage's extensive bicycle and jogging paths is also nearby.

SEASON

all year

ACCOMMODATIONS

four rooms with private baths;
two rooms with shared bath

Turtleback Farm Inn

Susan and William Fletcher
Route 1, Box 650
Eastsound (Orcas Island),
Washington 98245
Tel: (800) 376-4914 or (360) 376-4914
Fax: (360) 376-5329
$$ – $$$$

ABOUT THE B&B

Located on the loveliest of the San Juan Islands, Turtleback Farm Inn is noted for its detail-perfect restoration, elegantly comfortable rooms, glorious setting, and award-winning breakfasts. A short ferry ride from Anacortes, Washington, Orcas Island is a haven for anyone who enjoys spectacular scenery, varied outdoor activities, unique shopping, and superb food. As spring turns into summer, the warm days encourage you to enjoy nature and island life at their best: Flowers are in full bloom, birds flutter, and whales, seals, and porpoises lazily coast through the shimmering waters of the Sound. After a day of hiking, fishing, bicycling, kayaking, sailing, windsurfing, or just reading by the inn's pond, enjoy a relaxing soak in your private bath or a sherry on the deck overlooking the valley below. After a tasty dinner at one of the Island's many fine restaurants, snuggle down under one of the inn's custom-made woolen comforters and peacefully doze off — with visions of the delicious breakfast awaiting you in the morning.

SEASON

all year

ACCOMMODATIONS

11 rooms (including four suites) with private baths

Spiced Oat Waffles

2 cups buttermilk
3 eggs, separated and with whites beaten until they stand in soft peaks
3 tablespoons honey
½ cup butter, melted and cooled
½ cup all-purpose flour
1 cup whole wheat flour
½ cup large-flake rolled oats
1 tablespoon baking powder
1½ teaspoons baking soda
¾ teaspoon salt
¼ teaspoon freshly grated nutmeg
½ cup chopped pecans, toasted

Orange fruit butter (see recipe below)

Blend the buttermilk, egg yolks, honey, and melted butter together in a blender, then transfer to a large bowl. Mix together the flour, oats, baking powder, baking soda, salt, and nutmeg, then add to the buttermilk mixture. Fold in the chopped nuts and egg whites. Bake on a hot waffle iron according to the manufacturer's directions. Serve with the orange fruit butter. *Yield: 4 – 6 waffles.*

Orange fruit butter:
1 tablespoon concentrated orange juice
½ teaspoon grated orange zest
½ cup butter
Honey to taste

Blend the orange juice and zest into the butter, adding honey to taste.

Spicy Apple-Nut Pancakes

1 cup all-purpose flour
¾ cup sugar
1 teaspoon baking powder
¾ teaspoon baking soda
¼ teaspoon salt
½ teaspoon ground cinnamon
¼ teaspoon grated nutmeg
½ teaspoon ground cloves
¼ teaspoon mace
1 egg
1¼ cups buttermilk
4 teaspoons vegetable oil
1 large tart apple (such as Granny Smith)
¾ cup walnuts

Butter or sour cream

Combine the flour, sugar, baking powder, baking soda, salt, and spices, then set aside. In a large bowl, beat the egg. Stir in the buttermilk and oil. Wash and core the apple, then cut it into large pieces and place in a food processor fitted with a steel blade. Add the walnuts to the processor bowl. Pulse several times, leaving the apples and nuts as coarse as possible. Stir the apples and nuts into the egg mixture. Stir the dry ingredients into the egg mixture. Cook the pancakes on a heated, oiled griddle. When brown on the bottom, turn and cook the other side. Serve with butter or sour cream. *Yield: 4 servings.*

Angel Arbor Bed & Breakfast Inn

Marguerite and Dean Swanson
848 Heights Boulevard
Houston, Texas 77007
Tel: (713) 868-4654
Fax: (713) 861-3189
E-mail: b-bhontx@wt.net
www.angelarbor.com
$$ – $$$

ABOUT THE B&B

A few minutes from downtown Houston, this elegant 1920s Georgian-style brick residence graces historic Heights Boulevard with its gazebo-dotted esplanade and walking trail. The first floor boasts an antique-filled parlor, a cozy reading room, a gracious formal dining room, and a sunroom for game playing or casual dining. A wicker-furnished solarium overlooks the backyard garden with its manicured lawn, angel statue, and vine-laden arbor with a tranquil sitting area. Upstairs, three spacious bedrooms, each with an angel-inspired name, feature queen beds and private baths, two with whirlpool tubs for two. A separate outside suite provides seclusion and has its own sitting room and deck. A full delicious breakfast is served daily. Former owners of Durham House B&B, Marguerite and Dean Swanson bring their many years of innkeeping experience to Angel Arbor. The B&B also hosts parties and small meetings, and Marguerite's renowned murder mystery dinner parties.

SEASON

all year

ACCOMMODATIONS

four rooms (including one suite)
with private baths

Thick French Toast with Sautéed Apples

8 medium eggs
1 teaspoon grated nutmeg
½ – ¾ cup half-and-half
12 (1½" thick) slices firm Italian bread
Vegetable oil
4 – 5 tablespoons butter
6 Granny Smith apples, cored, peeled, and thinly sliced
2 tablespoons cinnamon sugar

Whisk together the eggs, nutmeg, and half-and-half until well mixed. Dip the bread slices into the mixture, coat thoroughly, and fry in oil until browned evenly on both sides. Place in the oven to hold on warm while preparing the apples. In a large frying pan, melt the butter on medium heat. Add the apples and raise the heat to medium-high. Gently sauté the apples for about 5 minutes, sprinkle the cinnamon sugar over, and continue to sauté until the apples are just tender (do not overcook). Spoon the apples over the French toast and serve. *Yield: 6 servings.*

Whole Grain No-Cholesterol Pancakes

1 cup whole wheat flour
2 tablespoons baking powder
2 tablespoons sugar
½ teaspoon ground allspice
¼ teaspoon grated nutmeg
2 egg whites, lightly beaten
1 cup skim milk
2 tablespoons canola or vegetable oil

Fresh strawberries

Combine the flour, baking powder, sugar, and spices, then make a well in the center of the mixture. Combine the egg whites, skim milk, and oil. Add to the dry ingredients, stirring just until moistened. Let stand 20 minutes. For each pancake, spoon about 2 tablespoons of the batter onto a moderately hot griddle coated with cooking spray. Turn the pancakes when the tops are covered with bubbles and the edges look cooked. Brown the other side. Garnish with strawberries. *Yield: 8 – 10 pancakes.*

THE MANOR AT TAYLOR'S STORE

The Manor at Taylor's Store B&B Country Inn

Mary Lynn and Lee Tucker
8812 Washington Highway
Smith Mountain Lake,
Virginia 24184
Tel: (540) 721-3951
Fax: (540) 721-5243
E-mail: taylors@symweb.com
www.symweb.com/taylors
$$ – $$$$

ABOUT THE B&B

The Manor at Taylor's Store is an enchanting, historic 120-acre estate in the picturesque foothills of the Blue Ridge Mountains. Guests enjoy luxurious accommodations in the elegant plantation home replete with antiques. Special amenities include a hot tub, exercise room, billiard room, large-screen TV with movies, guest kitchen, and porches and fireplaces throughout. There are six private, spring-fed ponds on the property for swimming, fishing, and canoeing. Nearby, Smith Mountain Lake offers additional recreational opportunities. All guests are treated to a heart-healthy gourmet breakfast in the formal dining room with panoramic views of the countryside. Warm, southern hospitality has made The Manor at Taylor's Store one of the best-known B&B inns in Virginia.

SEASON

all year

ACCOMMODATIONS

seven suites with private baths;
two suites with shared bath;
one cottage for families/groups
with private bath

Quiches, Omelets, Frittatas, & Casseroles

Alpen Rose Baked Eggs

10 eggs, lightly beaten
⅓ cup all-purpose flour
¾ teaspoon baking powder
10 ounces pork breakfast sausage, fried and crumbled
1 pound Monterey Jack cheese, grated
1½ cups cottage cheese
¾ cup sliced mushrooms, sautéed

Preheat the oven to 375°F. Mix the eggs, flour, and baking powder together well. Add the sausage, cheese, and mushrooms to the egg mixture, and beat well. Pour into a greased 13 x 9" glass baking dish. Bake 35 – 40 minutes. *Yield: 10 servings.*

Alpen Rose
Bed & Breakfast

Robin and Rupert Sommerauer
PO Box 769, 244 Forest Trail
Winter Park, Colorado 80482
Tel: (970) 726-5039
Fax: (970) 726-0993
$$ – $$$

ABOUT THE B&B

Hidden in the forest just minutes from downtown Winter Park, the Alpen Rose is a bed and breakfast with Austrian warmth and hospitality. Share Robin and Rupert's love of the mountains by taking in the breathtaking view from the common room, enhanced by aspens, wildflowers, and lofty pines. At Alpen Rose, you'll feel right at home whatever the season — enjoying the spare cozy slippers, lushly quilted beds with down pillows, and steaming outdoor hot tub. What's more, each of the five bedrooms is decorated with treasures brought over from Austria, including traditional featherbeds. A full breakfast featuring homemade yogurt, granola, fresh fruit, freshly baked coffee cake or bread, an egg dish, and a meat dish awaits guests each morning in the sunny common room. Rupert was born in Salzburg, Austria. Robin, an American, met him in Germany after a stint there with Outward Bound.

SEASON

all year

ACCOMMODATIONS

five rooms with private baths

The Marlborough

Al Hammond
320 Woods Hole Road
Woods Hole, Massachusetts 02543
Tel: (508) 548-6218
Fax: (508) 457-7519
$$$

ABOUT THE B&B

The Marlborough is a romantic Cape Cod cottage complete with picket fence, trellis, and garden set up on a hill among the trees. Rooms have private baths and are individually decorated with quilts, coordinated scented linens, and collectibles. Gather for conversation, read, or watch television in the large comfortable parlor. Full gourmet breakfast, including wonderfully brewed coffee and tea, is served outside by the kidney-shaped pool or inside by the fireplace, depending on the season. Informal afternoon tea is served in season, while high tea is served on Sundays in the off-season. Excellent restaurants are nearby, as is Woods Hole Oceanographic Institute, beaches, shopping, bike paths, and ferries to Martha's Vineyard. The Marlborough is a great starting point for day trips to locations all over Cape Cod and the islands, Plymouth, Boston, and Providence. Innkeeper Al Hammond enjoys helping guests get the most out of their visit. A long-time veteran of the foodservice industry, Al enjoys cooking and learning about Cape Cod history.

SEASON

all year

ACCOMMODATIONS

five rooms with private baths

Apple and Brie Omelet Marlborough

1½ tablespoons butter
¼ medium-size Granny Smith apple, peeled and thinly sliced
⅛ teaspoon grated nutmeg
1 teaspoon granulated sugar
1 tablespoon brown sugar
1 tablespoon chopped walnuts
3 eggs
6 (½") cubes Brie cheese

In a heavy skillet, melt ½ tablespoon of the butter. Sauté the apple slices in the butter until slightly translucent, but not mushy. Sprinkle the apples with the nutmeg and granulated sugar. Remove the apples to a side dish to stop the cooking; set aside. Mix together the brown sugar and walnuts; set aside. In an omelet pan or heavy medium skillet, melt the remaining 1 tablespoon butter, heating until bubbly. Break the eggs into a bowl and whisk until foamy. Pour the eggs gently into the bubbling butter. As the eggs begin to set, lift the edges to let the uncooked liquid flood under. When the eggs are almost set, turn the heat off. Put the Brie on one half of the omelet. Top with the sautéed apple slices and fold the omelet in ½. Let sit 3 – 4 minutes to allow the Brie to melt. Remove to a warmed plate and sprinkle with the brown sugar topping.
Yield: 1 serving.

Artichoke Frittata

4 cups frozen artichoke hearts
1 large onion, chopped
12 eggs
2½ cups half-and-half
1 tablespoon Worcestershire sauce
1 tablespoon dry mustard (Coleman's brand recommended)
2 teaspoons seasoning salt
3 sourdough English muffins, broken up
1 pound Monterey Jack cheese, grated
½ cup Italian-style bread crumbs
½ cup grated Parmesan cheese
Paprika or chopped parsley

Preheat the oven to 350°F. Defrost the artichoke hearts. Chop in a blender or Cuisinart. Coat a 13 x 9" pan with nonstick cooking spray and spread with the artichoke hearts. Top with the onion. Blend the eggs with the half-and-half, Worcestershire sauce, mustard, and salt. Pour ½ over the artichokes in the pan. Blend the English muffins into the rest of the egg mixture until smooth. Pour the egg mixture over the ingredients in the pan and add the Monterey Jack cheese. Stir to blend. Top with the Italian bread crumbs and Parmesan cheese. Sprinkle with paprika or chopped parsley as desired. Bake 1 hour and 15 minutes (or until the center is set) on the center rack of the oven. Cool slightly, then cut into squares. *Yield: 30 squares.*

The Babbling Brook Inn

Dan Floyd
1025 Laurel Street
Santa Cruz, California 95060
Tel: (800) 866-1131 or (408) 427-2437
Fax: (408) 458-0989
E-mail: lodging@
babblingbrookinn.com
$$$ – $$$$

ABOUT THE B&B

Cascading waterfalls, a meandering creek, and a romantic gazebo grace an acre of gardens, pines, and redwoods surrounding this secluded inn. Built in 1909 on the foundation of an 1870 tannery, a 1790 grist mill, and a 2,000-year old Indian fishing village, the Babbling Brook features rooms in country French decor, all with private bath, telephone, and television, and most with cozy fireplace, private deck, and outside entrance. Included in your stay is a large, country breakfast and afternoon wine and cheese, where the inn's prize-winning cookies await you on the tea cart in front of a roaring fireplace. Two blocks off Highway 1, the Babbling Brook is within walking distance of the beach, wharf, boardwalk, shops, tennis, running paths, and historic homes. Three golf courses and 200 restaurants are within 15 minutes' drive.

SEASON

all year

ACCOMMODATIONS

12 rooms with private baths

Pickett's Harbor
Bed and Breakfast

Sara and Cooke Goffigon
28288 Nottingham Ridge Lane
Cape Charles, Virginia 23310
Tel: (757) 331-2212
E-mail: pickharb@aol.com
$$ – $$$

ABOUT THE B&B

Chesapeake Bay on Virginia's historic Eastern Shore is home to seagulls, pelicans, sandpipers — and Pickett's Harbor Bed and Breakfast. Enjoy acres of private beach on the southernmost tip of the Delmarva Peninsula. Your hosts Sara and Cooke are descended from the original settlers of the area and, in 1976, built this traditional home by the seashore, complete with high ceilings, fireplaces, antiques, and wooden floorboards made from 200-year-old barns along the James River. Every morning, awake to Sara's full country breakfast where, on any given day, you can sample a fruit cup, juice, paper-thin cured ham, and homemade three-fruit and fig jams (which Sara now sells). Set off on a quiet country lane and surrounded by sea grasses and a pine forest, Pickett's Harbor is marvelously isolated yet close to most attractions on the Eastern Shore, as well as to Norfolk, Hampton, and Virginia Beach.

SEASON

all year

ACCOMMODATIONS

three rooms with private baths; three rooms with shared baths

Asparagus Quiche

10 stalks fresh asparagus, cooked and drained
5 eggs, well beaten
1 cup milk
1 teaspoon salt
2 tablespoons fresh shredded basil
1 cup grated Swiss cheese

Preheat the oven to 350°F. Spray the bottom of a 10" pie plate with nonstick cooking spray. Place the asparagus in the pie plate. Mix the eggs with the milk. Add the salt and basil and pour the mixture over the asparagus. Cover with the cheese. Bake for 30 minutes or until set. Allow to cool slightly before cutting. *Yield: 6 servings.*

Asparagus Strata

"This is our staple during the June asparagus season. Many copies of this recipe go home with our guests." — Larry Fuerst

9 eggs
2 cups milk
1½ cups seasoned bread cubes
1 cup grated low-fat cheddar cheese
1 pound pork breakfast sausage, cooked and drained (optional)
2 cups asparagus, cut into 1" pieces and steamed just until tender
½ cup sliced mushroom
Salt and pepper to taste

Mix the eggs, milk, bread cubes, cheese, sausage (if desired), asparagus, mushrooms, and salt and pepper together. Cover and refrigerate overnight. Remove from the refrigerator ¾ hour before baking. Bake in a greased 13 x 9" baking pan in a preheated 375°F oven for 45 minutes.
Yield: 8 servings.

Hidden Pond Bed & Breakfast

Priscilla and Larry Fuerst
PO Box 461
Fennville, Michigan 49408
Tel: (616) 561-2491
$$$

ABOUT THE B&B

Hidden Pond Bed & Breakfast is set on 28 acres of woods, perfect for bird-watching, hiking, cross-country skiing, or just relaxing in a rowboat on the pond. Guests can enjoy seven entry-level rooms, including bedrooms and baths, living room with fireplace, dining room, library, kitchen, and breakfast porch. Priscilla and Larry, who work for rival airlines, understand the importance of a soothing, calm, and slow-paced overnight stay. They enjoy pleasing guests and creating an atmosphere of quiet elegance. Unwind and take in the sun on the outdoor deck or patio. Turndown service, complimentary soft drinks, tea, hot chocolate, or an evening sherry are offered. Full hot breakfast is served in the sun-washed garden room at your leisure, and features fresh fruit, breads, muffins, and a hot entrée. This lovely retreat is near the beaches of Lake Michigan, the boutiques of Saugatuck, and the winery and cider mill in Fennville.

SEASON

all year

ACCOMMODATIONS

two rooms with private baths

The Summer House

Marjorie and Kevin Huelsman
158 Main Street
Sandwich, Massachusetts 02563
Tel: (800) 241-3609 or (508) 888-4991
E-mail: sumhouse@capecod.net
$$ – $$$

ABOUT THE B&B

The Summer House is an elegant circa 1835 Greek Revival twice featured in Country Living magazine. It was owned by Hiram Dillaway, a prominent mold-maker and colorist at the Boston & Sandwich Glass Factory. Large, sunny bedchambers feature antiques, hand-stitched quilts, and working fireplaces. Stroll to dining, shops, museums, galleries, a pond and gristmill, and a boardwalk to the beach. Bountiful breakfasts change daily and include freshly ground coffee, tea, fruit juice, and fresh fruit served in stemware. Entrées of frittata, stuffed French toast, quiche, or omelets are accompanied by scones, puff pastry, muffins, or fruit cobblers. Dishes are enhanced with vegetables, berries, and herbs from the inn's garden. English-style afternoon tea is served at an umbrella table in the garden. Boston, Newport, Providence, Martha's Vineyard, and Nantucket make pleasant day trips.

SEASON

all year

ACCOMMODATIONS

five rooms with private baths

Avocado, Bacon, and Potato Frittata

1 tablespoon olive oil
1 small onion, chopped
1 small potato, boiled, peeled, and sliced
"Mrs. Dash" mixed seasoning or salt and pepper to taste
2 strips bacon, crisply cooked and crumbled
1 ripe avocado, peeled and sliced
1 green onion, chopped
2 eggs, lightly beaten with 1 tablespoon water
¼ cup grated cheese of your choice

In a large ovenproof nonstick skillet, swirl the olive oil over medium heat. Add the onion, potato, and seasoning. Stir occasionally until the vegetables are browned. Sprinkle the bacon, avocado, and green onion evenly in the pan. Pour in the egg mixture and sprinkle the cheese over the top. Cook until lightly set. Sit the skillet under the broiler on the top rack of the oven for about 1 minute or until the top is set. Remove from the broiler, cut in ½, and slide onto plates. *Tip:* To speed morning preparation, cook the potato and bacon the night before and refrigerate.
Yield: 2 servings.

Baked Cheese Grits Casserole

"This is great for brunch with fruit and biscuits." — Mary Shaw

3 eggs
1 cup milk
1 cup grits, cooked in 4 cups water
6 ounces corn muffin mix
¼ cup butter
1 pound pork breakfast sausage, sautéed and crumbled
½ pound cheddar cheese, grated
Paprika

Fruit and biscuits

Preheat the oven to 325°F. Beat the eggs and milk together. Add the cooked grits, corn muffin mix, and butter and mix. Pour into a greased 15 x 12" casserole. Add the sausage. Sprinkle the top with the cheese and paprika. Bake for about 30 minutes. *Yield: 8 – 10 servings.*

The Shaw House
Bed and Breakfast

Mary and Joe Shaw
613 Cypress Court
Georgetown, South Carolina 29440
Tel: (803) 546-9663
$$

ABOUT THE B&B

The Shaw House Bed and Breakfast is a spacious two-story home in a serene, natural setting. From the glass-walled den, enjoy bird-watching and a beautiful view overlooking miles of marshland formed by four rivers, which converge and flow into the Intercoastal Waterway. Outlined by tall white columns, the wide front porch extends the width of the home and features old-fashioned rockers — ready and waiting for guests who are welcomed as family. All rooms are air conditioned, with private baths and a smattering of antiques. Enjoy a full southern breakfast come morning and bed turn-backs and chocolate come bedtime.

SEASON

all year

ACCOMMODATIONS

three rooms with private baths

Bedford's Covered Bridge Inn

Martha and Greg Lau
RD 2, Box 196
Schellsburg, Pennsylvania 15559
Tel: (814) 733-4093
$$ – $$$

ABOUT THE B&B

Situated near Exit 11 of I-76 (the Pennsylvania Turnpike), Bedford's Covered Bridge Inn borders 4,000-acre Shawnee State Park, a lovely trout stream, and the Colvin covered bridge. From this idyllic location, guests can pursue hiking, biking, fishing, cross-country skiing, birding, and antique hunting right from the inn's door. Nearby swimming and boating on Shawnee Lake, visits to Old Bedford Village and Bedford's historic district, driving tours, downhill skiing at Blue Knob Resort, and tours of Bedford's 14 covered bridges round out the list of local activities. Inside the inn, the Lau's attention to detail creates an atmosphere that is comfortable and inviting. The historic farmhouse (circa 1823) boasts six guest rooms with private baths, traditional and country decor, and memorable breakfasts. "There's no doubt what everyone's favorite activity is," say Martha and Greg, "Sitting on the inn's wrap-around porch and wishing they could live in Bedford County, too!"

SEASON

all year

ACCOMMODATIONS

six rooms with private baths; one cottage for couples or families

Bedford County Breakfast Casserole

2 cups milk
7 eggs
7 slices bread, crusts removed and cubed
1 cup diced ham
⅓ cup finely chopped onion
2 cups grated medium cheddar cheese
1 teaspoon dry mustard
2 tomatoes, thinly sliced
Snipped chives

Combine the milk and eggs and mix well. Fold in the bread, ham, onions, cheese, and mustard and top with the tomatoes and chives. Pour into a greased 13 x 9" pan. Refrigerate overnight. Remove from the refrigerator ¾ hour before baking. Bake on the top rack of a preheated 325°F oven for 1 hour. *Yield: 6 servings.*

Blue Spruce Chilies Rellenos

"My cousin Sonny is a fantastic cook and this was his first published recipe, which appeared in his local paper many years back. I still have the original yellowed article in my recipe box." — Pat O'Brien

1 medium yellow onion, chopped
1 green bell pepper, chopped
3 (8-ounce) cans tomato sauce
2 teaspoons oregano
7-ounce can whole green chilies
3 cups grated Monterey Jack cheese
¼ teaspoon baking powder
¼ cup all-purpose flour
2 eggs, lightly beaten
1 cup milk
1 cup salsa (see recipe on page 352)

Preheat the oven to 375°F. In a medium saucepan, sauté the onion and green pepper until barely tender. Add the tomato sauce and oregano, then bring it to a boil. Keep it warm. Split the chilies, remove any seeds, and stuff with the cheese. Roll them up and place them in a 9 x 7" greased baking pan. Combine the baking powder, flour, eggs, milk, and salsa and pour over the chilies. Sprinkle with any remaining cheese. Bake 35 – 40 minutes. To serve, let the dish set 5 minutes. Lift out each chili, top with sauce, and serve. *Yield: 6 servings.*

Blue Spruce Inn

Pat and Tom O'Brien
2815 Main Street
Soquel, California 95073
Tel: (800) 559-1137 or (408) 464-1137
Fax: (408) 475-0608
E-mail: pobrien@BlueSpruce.com
$$ – $$$$

ABOUT THE B&B

*T*he Blue Spruce Inn welcomes you with the distinct Pacific breeze that freshens the Central Coast hillsides golden with poppies, tempers the heat of the summer sun, and warms the sands during afternoon strolls on winter beaches. The inn is four miles south of Santa Cruz and one mile from Capitola Beach at the northern curve of Monterey Bay. Gracious personal service is the hallmark of this 1875 B&B inn, where beds are graced with Amish quilts and walls hung with original local art that blends the flavor of yesteryear with the luxury of today. There are quiet gardens in which to enjoy the sunshine of Soquel Village, delightful antique shops at the corner of the street, and, a little farther, wineries, gift shops, and regional art displays. Bountiful breakfasts feature fresh fruit, homemade breads, and exceptional entrées. At the end of the day, the hot tub offers welcome respite and, when guests return to their rooms, pillows are fluffed and a special treat awaits.

SEASON

all year

ACCOMMODATIONS

five rooms with private baths

1880 House

Elsie Collins
2 Seafield Lane, PO Box 648
Westhampton Beach,
New York 11978
Tel: (800) 346-3290 or (516) 288-1559
Fax: (516) 288-7696
$$$ – $$$$

ABOUT THE B&B

Tucked away in the village of Westhampton Beach stands 1880 House, a bed and breakfast country retreat that's the perfect place for a romantic hideaway, a weekend of privacy, or just a change of pace from city life. Only 90 minutes from Manhattan, 1880 House is ideally situated on Westhampton Beach's exclusive Seafield Lane. Amenities include a swimming pool and tennis court and you're only a short, brisk walk away from the ocean beach. Long a popular summer resort area, the Hamptons will more than satisfy your penchant for antique hunting, and also offer many outstanding restaurants and shops. Indoor tennis facilities are available locally and Guerney's International Health Spa and the scenic area of Montauk Point are nearby. 1880 House is not just a rural retreat but a home lovingly preserved by Mrs. Elsie Collins and filled with her antiques and personal touches.

SEASON

all year

ACCOMMODATIONS

three suites with private baths

Breakfast Casserole

1 pound pork breakfast sausage
½ pound sharp cheddar cheese, grated
½ teaspoon dry mustard
½ teaspoon paprika
1 teaspoon salt
1 cup sour cream
10 – 16 eggs (depending on desired number of servings)

Preheat the oven to 325°F. Cook and crumble the sausage in a large skillet, then drain. Spray a 2 or 3 quart dish with nonstick cooking spray. Put ½ of the grated cheese on the bottom of the dish. Mix the mustard, paprika, and salt with the sour cream, mix in the sausage, then spread this mixture over the grated cheese in the dish. Beat the eggs and pour them over the mixture in the dish. Sprinkle the remaining grated cheese on top. Bake 25 – 30 minutes or until set. *Yield: 6 – 14 servings.*

Broccoli, Ham, and Swiss Cheese Quiche

Crust:
9" unbaked pie shell
1 teaspoon all-purpose flour

Filling:
1 cup milk
4 eggs, lightly beaten
¼ teaspoon dry mustard
Pinch of freshly ground black pepper
1 cup cubed cooked ham
1½ cups grated Swiss cheese
1 cup broccoli florets
1 tablespoon chopped onion

Preheat the oven to 350°F. Line a 9" pie pan with the unbaked pie crust. In a bowl, combine the milk, eggs, dry mustard, and pepper. Set aside to let rest. Layer the ham, cheese, broccoli, and onion in the pie crust and pour the milk mixture over top. Bake 40 – 50 minutes or until a knife inserted in the quiche's center comes out clean. Let stand about 5 minutes before cutting and serving. *Yield: 6 – 8 servings.*

Bishopsgate Inn

Colin, Jane, Colin, Jr.,
and Lisa Kagel
7 Norwich Road
East Haddam, Connecticut 06423
Tel: (860) 873-1677
Fax: (860) 873-3898
$$$ – $$$$

ABOUT THE B&B

Built in 1818 by Horace Heyden, a merchant and shipbuilder, this Colonial home welcomes guests seeking gracious hospitality and well-appointed accommodation in a secluded setting. The inn offers six guest rooms, including four with open fireplaces and a suite with a sauna. Tastefully furnished, each floor of the inn has its own sitting area for conversation, reading, and other restful pursuits. Known for its excellent kitchen, Bishopsgate offers ample breakfasts and, if desired, specially arranged candlelight dinners. The Kagels maintain an up-to-date library of local offerings and can help you plan your visit to the area: everything from the Goodspeed Opera House's renowned musical productions, the Historical Society Museum, Gillette Castle and Devil's Hopyard state parks, and cruises and canoe trips on the Connecticut River. Historic Essex, with its beautiful harbor, wonderful old houses, and intriguing shops, is just a few minutes' drive away.

SEASON

all year

ACCOMMODATIONS

six rooms (including one suite) with private baths

Durbin Street Inn B&B

Sherry and Don Frigon
843 South Durbin Street
Casper, Wyoming 82601
Tel: (307) 577-5774
Fax: (307) 266-5441
E-mail: Dfrigon@trib.com
$$

ABOUT THE B&B

Built in 1917, Durbin Street Inn is a large two-story American foursquare located in Casper's historic district. The inn prides itself on good food and a friendly atmosphere. Choose from four large non-smoking guest rooms with shared baths. Each room has queen-size or double beds, robes, and one has a fireplace. Or, you can choose the non-smoking guest room with private bath, small sitting room, and refrigerator. Awake to a full country breakfast where scrambled eggs, bacon, sausage, hash browns, fruit juice, homemade jams, and such specialties as honey-wheat pancakes, biscuits and gravy, scones, brunch omelet torte, spicy sausage and potatoes, and roast beef hash are served family-style. After breakfast, gather in the common room by the fireplace, or enjoy the deck, patio, and flower and vegetable gardens. Nearby are walking, hiking, cycling trails, river rafting and canoeing, golfing, swimming, fishing, skiing, shopping, covered wagon and horseback trips along the Oregon Trail, museums, historic sites, Fort Casper, Independence Rock, Devil's Gate, and Hell's Half Acre.

SEASON

all year

ACCOMMODATIONS

four rooms with shared baths;
one room with private bath

Brunch Omelet Torte

"This do-ahead recipe requires some time to prepare, but is sensational for a special breakfast or brunch." — Sherry Frigon

2 sheets of frozen puff pastry, thawed

Potatoes:
¼ cup butter or margarine
6 medium new red potatoes, sliced ⅛" thick (about 3 cups)
1 cup thinly sliced onion, separated into rings
¼ teaspoon salt
¼ teaspoon pepper

Omelet:
2 tablespoons butter or margarine
6 eggs
¼ cup chopped fresh parsley
⅛ tablespoon salt
⅛ teaspoon pepper
2 tablespoons water

(continued on next page)

Filling:
½ pound thinly sliced cooked ham or your favorite deli meat
2 cups grated cheddar cheese

1 egg lightly mixed with 1 tablespoon water

On a lightly floured surface, roll each sheet of puff pastry into a 12" square. Lay 1 sheet into a lightly greased 10" pie pan, and set aside.

To make the potatoes: In a large skillet, melt the butter until sizzling. Add the potatoes, onion, salt, and pepper. Cover and cook over medium-high heat, turning occasionally until the potatoes are lightly browned and crisply tender (approximately 12 – 15 minutes). Set aside.

To make the omelets: Clean the skillet and melt 1 tablespoon of the butter in it until sizzling. Meanwhile, in a small bowl, stir together the eggs, parsley, salt, pepper, and water. Pour ½ of the omelet mixture (¾ cup) into the skillet with the sizzling butter. Cook over medium heat. As the omelet sets, lift it slightly with a spatula to allow the uncooked portion to flow underneath. Continue cooking until set (2 – 3 minutes). Slide the omelet onto a cookie sheet. Repeat with the remaining 1 table-spoon butter and omelet mixture.

To assemble: Layer the ingredients into the pie pan with the puff pastry in the following order: 1 omelet, ½ of the ham, ½ of the fried potatoes, ½ of the grated cheese, the remaining potatoes, ham, cheese, and omelet. Top with the remaining sheet of puff pastry. Press together the edges of both sheets of puff pastry to form a rim. Trim off the excess puff pastry. Crimp or flute the edges of the puff pastry. Cover and refrigerate over-night or preheat the oven to 375°F. Brush the egg and water glaze over the puff pastry. Bake 30 – 35 minutes or until golden brown. Let stand 5 minutes; cut into wedges. If the torte is refrigerated overnight, let it stand at room temperature 30 minutes before baking as directed above. *Yield: 8 servings.*

The Quail's Nest Bed and Breakfast

Nancy and Gregory Diaz
PO Box 221, Main Street
Danby, Vermont 05739
Tel: (802) 293-5099
Fax: (802) 293-6300
E-mail: Quails_Nest@
compuserve.com
$$

ABOUT THE B&B

A circa 1835 country inn, The Quail's Nest is located just off Route 7 in Danby, Vermont — a quiet and picturesque town reminiscent of the last century. The inn's six rooms are wrapped in the warmth of handmade quilts, and a delightful home-cooked breakfast will tempt you out of those quilts each morning! To the east of the inn is the magnificent Green Mountains National Forest, which boasts some of the finest swimming, hiking, fishing, hunting, and skiing in Vermont. Located 13 miles to the south, Manchester, Vermont, features factory outlet shopping, while crafts and antiques can be purchased right in the heart of Danby. A wide variety of restaurants to satisfy every palate are either a short drive or walk away.

SEASON

all year

ACCOMMODATIONS

four rooms with private baths; two rooms with shared bath

Cheddar Cheese Pie

"This recipe was given to me by my cousin and very special friend, Diana M. Spiller. It is rich in flavor and a favorite of all who try it." — Nancy Diaz

9" unbaked pie shell, chilled
4 eggs
1 cup heavy cream
1 cup milk
½ teaspoon salt
⅛ teaspoon hot pepper sauce (such as Tabasco)
1 cup grated Vermont cheddar cheese

Preheat the oven to 450°F. Prick the pie shell with a fork, then bake 10 minutes or until lightly browned. Reduce the oven to 325°F. In a medium bowl, beat the eggs, cream, milk, salt, and hot pepper sauce together. Spread the cheese over the bottom of the pie shell. Pour in the egg mixture and bake 45 minutes or until a knife inserted in the center comes out clean. *Yield: 6 servings.*

Chicken Quiche

Rice crust:
1 cube chicken bouillon
1 cup boiling water
1 cup instant rice (such as Minute brand rice)
1 egg, lightly beaten
1 cup Parmesan cheese

Filling:
2 cubes chicken bouillon
2 cups boiling water
3 cups diced cooked chicken
1 cup chopped green bell pepper
¾ cup chopped onion
3 cups grated cheddar cheese
9 extra-large eggs
1 tablespoon Tabasco sauce
1 teaspoon garlic salt
1 teaspoon black pepper

(continued on next page)

Bed & Breakfast at Sills Inn

Tony Sills and Glenn Blind
270 Montgomery Avenue
Versailles, Kentucky 40383
Tel (800) 526-9801 or (606) 873-4478
Fax: (606) 873-7099
E-mail: SillsInn@aol.com
$$ – $$$$

ABOUT THE B&B

Guests are treated to true southern hospitality as soon as they step into this restored 1911, three-story Victorian inn in downtown Versailles — the center of bluegrass horse country and just seven minutes west of Lexington Airport/ Keeneland Racetrack and 10 minutes from the Lexington area. Each of the 12 accommodations is distinctively decorated and has its own private bath, including nine suites with double Jacuzzis. A full gourmet breakfast is served on the sun porch, complete with china, crystal, and linen. Guests are also treated to freshly baked chocolate-chip cookies, refreshments, and popcorn anytime they're in need of a snack. The pampering continues as guests choose from the inn's restaurant menu book, have dinner reservations made for them, and are given a map highlighting their way to the restaurant.

SEASON

all year

ACCOMMODATIONS

12 rooms (including nine suites)
with private baths

Preheat the oven to 325°F.

To prepare the rice crust: Mix the bouillon with the boiling water until dissolved. Mix with the rice and set aside until set. Once set, add the egg and cheese and mix together well. Pat down in a deep-dish pie pan generously sprayed with nonstick cooking spray. Set aside.

To prepare the filling: Mix the bouillon with the boiling water until dissolved. Combine the chicken, green peppers, and onions, then add the bouillon mixture, mixing well. Microwave on high for 6 minutes. Drain and cool (so the cheese won't melt when added). Mix in the cheese and pour over the rice crust. Beat the eggs, Tabasco, garlic salt, and pepper together. Mix carefully with the chicken filling in the pan. Push the filling away from the sides of the pie pan, creating space for the egg mixture to pool (this will help reduce overflow during cooking). Place the pie pan on a foil-covered cookie sheet, and cover and tent the entire cookie sheet (including the pie pan) with foil.

Bake for 1 hour and 45 minutes or until the egg mixture sets. Let cool before cutting. *Tip:* Individual slices reheat well in the microwave oven. *Yield: 8 servings.*

Coach's Quiche

"Several years ago, the folks in the school where I taught decided we'd put together a cookbook, and that's where this recipe is from. By now, the cookbook is well worn and more than a bit stained, but I still keep it around as a memory of good friends." — Marie Gery

9" unbaked pie shell
10 ounces frozen chopped spinach
1 medium onion, minced
¼ cup butter
5 eggs, separated
1 cup milk or half-and-half
8 ounces cream cheese, at room temperature
¾ cup bread crumbs
1 cup grated Parmesan cheese
1 large can mushroom pieces and stems
1 teaspoon chopped tarragon leaves
Salt and pepper to taste

Preheat the oven to 400°F. Have the unbaked pie shell ready before beginning to prepare the quiche batter. Cook the spinach according to package directions; drain well. Sauté the onion in butter until translucent. Beat the egg yolks until slightly thickened and paler yellow.

(continued on next page)

Martin Oaks
Bed & Breakfast

Marie and Frank Gery
PO Box 207, 107 First Street
Dundas, Minnesota 55019
Tel: (507) 645-4644
$$

ABOUT THE B&B

In 1869, the Archibald Brothers had this home built as a wedding present for their sister, Sarah Etta Archibald. Now listed on the National Register of Historic Places, Martin Oaks, the Archibald-Martin House, and the Carriage House occupy half a city block. Located in historic Dundas Village, Martin Oaks transports guests to an era where elegant women and fine gentlemen enjoyed good conversation and classical music, and savored elegant foods served on fine china. Two charming bedrooms filled with antiques offer the opportunity for a memorable, quiet evening. Recently featured in Minnesota Monthly Magazine, Martin Oaks is less than five minutes away from Northfield, Carleton, and St. Olaf colleges, and is near superb shopping and bookstore browsing, fine antique hunting on and off Division Street, golfing, hiking, and cross-country skiing. Minneapolis, St. Paul, and the Mall of America are within a 40-minute drive.

SEASON

April 1 to December 31

ACCOMMODATIONS

two rooms with shared baths

Add the milk, cream cheese, bread crumbs, and Parmesan cheese, and beat well. Add the cooked spinach, onion, mushrooms, tarragon, and salt and pepper. Wash the beaters, then beat the egg whites until they stand in soft peaks. Fold the egg whites into the above mixture and pour into the pie shell. Bake until the top is brown (about 15 – 20 minutes). Reduce the heat to 350°F and bake until a knife blade inserted in the center comes out clean (about 45 minutes – 1 hour). *Yield: 6 – 8 servings.*

Corn Quiche

(Recipe from Breakfast at Nine, Tea at Four: Favorite Recipes from Cape May's Mainstay Inn.*)*

3 eggs
¼" slice of onion
1 tablespoon sugar
1 tablespoon all-purpose flour
1 teaspoon salt
3 tablespoons butter, melted
1⅓ cups half-and-half, scalded
2 cups uncooked fresh corn, or frozen, thawed
9" unbaked pie shell
Fresh parsley
Peach half
Fresh strawberries

Preheat the oven to 375°F. In a food processor, combine the eggs, onion, sugar, flour, and salt. Add the butter and half-and-half and blend. Fold in the corn. Turn the mixture into the pie shell and bake for 45 minutes or until slightly puffed up and lightly browned. Cut into wedges and serve immediately, garnished with fresh parsley, a peach half, and fresh strawberries. **Yield: 6 – 8 servings.**

The Mainstay Inn

Sue and Tom Carroll
635 Columbia Avenue
Cape May, New Jersey 08204
Tel: (609) 884-8690
$$$ – $$$$

ABOUT THE B&B

According to the Washington Post, "The jewel of them all has got to be the Mainstay." Built by a pair of wealthy gamblers in 1872, this elegant and exclusive club-house is now among the premier B&B inns in the country. The Mainstay now comprises three historic buildings on one of the most beautiful streets of the historic Cape May district. Guests enjoy 16 antique-filled rooms and suites (some with fireplaces and whirlpool baths), three parlors, spacious gardens, and rocker-filled verandas. Breakfast and afternoon tea are served daily. Beautiful beaches, historic attractions, biking, birding, golf, and tennis are all available in Cape May, a National Historic Landmark community.

SEASON

all year

ACCOMMODATIONS

16 rooms (including seven suites) with private baths

The Babbling Brook Inn

Dan Floyd
1025 Laurel Street
Santa Cruz, California 95060
Tel: (800) 866-1131 or (408) 427-2437
Fax: (408) 458-0989
E-mail: lodging@
babblingbrookinn.com
$$$ – $$$$

ABOUT THE B&B

Cascading waterfalls, a meandering creek, and a romantic gazebo grace an acre of gardens, pines, and redwoods surrounding this secluded inn. Built in 1909 on the foundation of an 1870 tannery, a 1790 grist mill, and a 2,000-year old Indian fishing village, the Babbling Brook features rooms in country French decor, all with private bath, telephone, and television, and most with cozy fireplace, private deck, and outside entrance. Included in your stay is a large, country breakfast and afternoon wine and cheese, where the inn's prize-winning cookies await you on the tea cart in front of a roaring fireplace. Two blocks off Highway 1, the Babbling Brook is within walking distance of the beach, wharf, boardwalk, shops, tennis, running paths, and historic homes. Three golf courses and 200 restaurants are within 15 minutes' drive.

SEASON

all year

ACCOMMODATIONS

12 rooms with private baths

Cottage Cheese Delight

1 cup milk
1 cup all-purpose flour
2 cups low-fat cottage cheese
6 eggs
½ cup butter, melted
1 pound Monterey Jack cheese, grated
Bread crumbs
Sour cream
Fruit conserve or fresh fruit of your choice

Preheat the oven to 350°F. Blend the milk, flour, cottage cheese, eggs, and butter. Grease an 8 x 8" or 9 x 9" pan and sprinkle with the grated cheese. Pour the milk mixture over and dust with the crumbs. Bake 45 minutes. Cut into squares and top with the sour cream and fruit conserve or fresh fruit. *Tip:* If doubling the recipe, bake in a 13 x 9" pan for 1 hour and 20 minutes. You can bake it a day ahead, then reheat the individual slices in a microwave oven (1 minute on high per square). *Yield: 12 – 16 servings.*

Country Quiche

"At our B&B, we have fresh eggs from our chicken flock and also grow a large garden, so this quiche recipe is really homemade."
— Sharleen Bergum

12 strips bacon
4 eggs, lightly beaten
2 cups half-and-half
9" baked pie shell
1½ cups grated Swiss cheese
⅓ cup diced onion, sautéed
½ cup chopped broccoli or spinach

Fry the bacon crisp and cut it into bite-sized pieces. Mix the eggs and half-and-half together. Line the pie crust with the cheese, then add the bacon, vegetables, and finally the egg mixture. Bake in a preheated 425°F oven for 15 minutes, then reduce to 300°F for 30 minutes or when a knife inserted in the center comes out clean. Let stand 10 minutes, then serve.
Yield: 6 servings.

Rockinghorse Bed & Breakfast

Sharleen and Jerry Bergum
RR #1, Box 133
Whitewood, South Dakota 57793
Tel: (605) 269-2625
$$

ABOUT THE B&B

A cedar clapboard-sided house built in 1914 to accommodate local timber teams, Rockinghorse was moved to its present location by Sharleen and Jerry, who have lovingly restored the interior. Handsome wood floors, columns, and trims, along with antiques, country charm decor, and the original stairway grace the home. Rockinghorse is situated in the rustic Black Hills, where you can watch deer graze nearby and wild turkeys strut across the valley. Listen to the sounds of coyotes in the evening while a rooster's crow awakens you in the morning. You can also pet a bunny, ride the horse-drawn wagon, or have wood/fiber artist Sharleen help you master the spinning wheel. A gift shop is also on the premises. The B&B is near historic Deadwood, the world renowned Passion Play, the scenic Spearfish Canyon route, and a one-hour drive from Mount Rushmore. Full breakfast includes fresh fruit (in season), homemade breads, blueberry pancakes, and special egg-cheese dishes.

SEASON

all year

ACCOMMODATIONS

three rooms with private baths

Dreams of Yesteryear Bed and Breakfast

Bonnie and Bill Maher
1100 Brawley Street
Stevens Point, Wisconsin 54481
Tel: (715) 341-4525
Fax: (715) 344-3047
$$ – $$$$

ABOUT THE B&B

This elegant, turn-of-the-century Victorian Queen Anne was home to three generations of the Jensen family before being purchased in 1987 and restored by current owners Bonnie and Bill Maher. An article Bonnie wrote about the restoration was featured in the Winter 1991 issue of Victorian Homes magazine. In 1990, after giving many tours, the Mahers opened their home as the Dreams of Yesteryear Bed and Breakfast. Listed on the National Register of Historic Places, Dreams of Yesteryear is located three blocks from historic downtown Stevens Point, two blocks from the Wisconsin River and Green Circle jogging, hiking, biking trails, a half mile from the University of Wisconsin, and near wonderful restaurants, theaters, and antique shops. Your visit includes a gourmet breakfast, warm hospitality, and wonderful memories.

SEASON

all year

ACCOMMODATIONS

two suites with private baths;
two rooms with shared bath

Crustless Quiche

½ cup butter
½ cup all-purpose flour
6 eggs, lightly beaten
1 cup milk
1 pound Monterey Jack cheese, cubed
3 ounces cream cheese, softened
2 cups cottage cheese
1 teaspoon baking powder
1 teaspoon salt
1 teaspoon sugar

Preheat the oven to 350°F. Melt the butter in a small saucepan. Add the flour and cook until smooth. Add the eggs and beat. Add the milk, cheese, baking powder, salt, and sugar and stir until well blended. Pour in a well-greased 13 x 9" pan. Bake uncovered for 45 minutes. *Tip:* This recipe can be used as a breakfast dish or cut into small pieces as an hors d'oeuvre. *Yield: 12 servings.*

Eggs St. Moritz

½ pound Swiss cheese (or Jarlsberg or Havarti or Edam), grated
2 tablespoons white Worcestershire sauce
½ cup heavy cream
12 eggs, well beaten
2 sprinkles of snipped fresh dill

Preheat the oven to 350°F. Spread the grated cheese in the bottom of a greased 13 x 9" pan. Whip the Worcestershire sauce into the cream, then divide into 2 equal portions of ¼ cup each. Pour one ¼ cup of cream immediately into the pan and reserve the rest. Beat the eggs and pour over the cheese and cream in the pan. Pour the second ¼ cup of cream over the top of the eggs. Sprinkle with the dill and bake 35 – 45 minutes until the eggs are set and the top is golden and puffy. Garnish with more fresh dill. *Tip:* This dish can be served right from the pan on a buffet or cut into squares and served on individual plates. *Yield: 9 – 12 servings.*

Ashling Cottage

Goodi and Jack Stewart
106 Sussex Avenue
Spring Lake, New Jersey 07762
Tel: (888) ASHLING
Fax: (732) 974-0831
E-mail: Ashling@lonekeep.com
$$$ – $$$$

ABOUT THE B&B

For generations, rambling Victorian homes have fronted the spring-fed lakes from which Spring Lake, New Jersey, gets its name. Tree-lined walkways surround the lakes, and wooden foot bridges connect grassy areas of park. Sun, sand, surf, and serenity in equal measure — Spring Lake offers all this and Ashling Cottage, too. Since 1877, the visiting gentry have enjoyed sumptuous breakfasts on the porches of this lovely and intimate seaside inn, overlooking both ocean and lake. Today, the tradition continues with casual hospitality and personal attention offered for your vacationing pleasure. While leisure activities abound (such as golf, tennis, biking, horseback riding, and sightseeing in nearby New York and Philadelphia), the most delightful feature of this inn and this town is the guilt-free ability to do absolutely nothing!

SEASON

May to October

ACCOMMODATIONS

eight rooms with private baths;
two rooms with shared bath

Calmar Guesthouse
Bed & Breakfast

Lucille B. Kruse
103 West North Street
Calmar, Iowa 52132
Tel: (319) 562-3851
$$

ABOUT THE B&B

Open since 1986, the Calmar Guesthouse is a beautiful, remodeled Victorian home with warm hospitality, good food, and quiet elegance. The house features stained glass windows, refinished wood, handmade quilts, crafts, antiques, and queen-size beds. Breakfast is served in the formal dining room, with candles and music. Nearby activities include a bike trail, golf, tennis, outdoor swimming, canoeing, trout fishing, and more. Local places of interest include Billy Brothers world famous carved-wood clocks, the Norwegian Museum, the Laura Ingalls Museum, the World's Smallest Church, the Little Brown Church in the Vale (the inspiration for the song), the two-mile underground Niagara Cave, Spook Cave, and many beautiful parks.

SEASON

all year

ACCOMMODATIONS

five rooms with shared baths

Famous Guesthouse Quiche

"This basic quiche can be used with other ingredients or vegetables of your choice. I get the best results by leaving it simple and tasty."
— Lucille Kruse

White bread slices
1 cup grated cheddar cheese
¾ cup cubed ham
6 eggs
1 cup milk
¼ cup chopped green and red bell pepper
Snipped chives

Preheat the oven to 350°F. Grease a standard quiche pan. Line the bottom with bread slices. Cover with the cheese. Sprinkle the ham over the cheese. Beat the eggs and add the milk, then pour this over the bread, cheese, and ham in the pan. Sprinkle with the chopped peppers and chives. Bake 30 – 35 minutes. Serve hot. *Yield: 6 servings.*

Farmer's Frittata

10 strips bacon, chopped
½ cup diced onion
3 medium potatoes, cooked with skins on and diced
11 eggs
1¼ cups milk
1 teaspoon salt
¼ teaspoon pepper
4 ounces cheddar cheese, grated
4 ounces Swiss cheese, grated

Preheat the oven to 350°F. Sauté the bacon and onions. Drain the fat. Put the bacon mixture in the bottom of a greased 10" quiche pan. Sprinkle the diced potatoes over. Beat the eggs and milk, then add the salt and pepper. Pour over the potato mixture. Sprinkle the cheese over the top. Bake 1 hour and 15 minutes. *Yield: 6 servings.*

La Corsette Maison Inn

Kay Owen
629 1st Avenue East
Newton, Iowa 50208
Tel: (515) 792-6833
$$ – $$$$

ABOUT THE B&B

To spend the night at the Maison Inn is to be the personal house guest of Kay Owen, and to enjoy charming French bedchambers, down-filled pillows, and beckoning hearths. Kay lives in this opulent, mission-style mansion built in 1909 by early Iowa state senator August Bergman. Here amid the charm of the original mission oak woodwork, art nouveau stained glass windows, brass light fixtures, and even some of the original furnishings, Kay operates the highly acclaimed La Corsette restaurant, considered a unique dining experience by gourmets nationwide. The Maison Inn is a delightful extension of that experience. Choose from seven distinctive accommodations (some with double whirlpools and fireplaces), including the penthouse, where you'll be nudged awake in the morning by a rainbow of sunlight coming through the mass of beveled glass windows. In the morning, be prepared for a delectable breakfast served in the gracious tradition of La Corsette.

SEASON

all year

ACCOMMODATIONS

seven rooms (including two suites) with private baths

7 Gables Inn

Leicha and Paul Welton
PO Box 80488
Fairbanks, Alaska 99708
Tel: (907) 479-0751
Fax: (907) 479-2229
E-mail: gables7@alaska.net
www.alaska.net/~gables7
$$ – $$$

ABOUT THE B&B

This 10,000 square foot Tudor-style house is located within walking distance of the University of Alaska Fairbanks campus, which is probably why 7 Gables began as a fraternity house. Its convenient location (between the airport and train station) is further enhanced by being right in the middle of a number of major attractions in the area: Riverboat Discovery, Pump House Restaurant, Cripple Creek Resort, University Museum, and Alaskaland. You enter the B&B through a floral solarium into a foyer with antique stained glass and an indoor waterfall. Other features include cathedral ceilings, wine cellar, and wedding chapel. Some additional amenities include laundry facilities, Jacuzzis, in-room cable TV and phones, canoes, bikes, gourmet breakfasts, luggage or game storage, and library collection. Leicha enjoys cooking, music, hosting parties, and learning foreign languages, while Paul collects books and manages the inn's marketing and maintenance.

SEASON

all year

ACCOMMODATIONS

12 rooms with private baths

Gables Frittata

½ pound pork breakfast sausage
2 cups grated zucchini
2 green onions, chopped
½ teaspoon oregano
½ teaspoon basil
1 tablespoon (packaged) powdered Italian salad dressing mix
6 eggs
½ cup whipping cream
4 ounces cream cheese, softened
1 cup grated mozzarella cheese
1 cup grated cheddar cheese

Preheat the oven to 325°F. Brown and crumble the sausage and drain on a paper towel. Place the sausage in an 8" quiche pan or pie plate. Spread the zucchini and onions over the sausage, and sprinkle with the oregano, basil, and powdered salad dressing mix. Beat the eggs with the whipping cream and pour over the ingredients in the pan. Cut the cream cheese into cubes and sprinkle evenly over the top. Cover with the mozzarella and cheddar cheese. Bake for 45 minutes or until set.
Yield: 6 servings.

Hash Brown Casserole

2½ cups frozen hash brown potatoes, skillet-cooked
½ cup chopped broccoli
½ cup chopped tomato (or mild salsa)
2 tablespoons chopped onion
Salt and pepper to taste
Milk
6 eggs (or enough to cover casserole), lightly beaten
1 cup grated cheddar cheese
1 cup grated mozzarella cheese

Preheat the oven to 350°F. Spray a 13 x 9" pan with nonstick cooking spray. Layer the potatoes, broccoli, tomato, and onion. Sprinkle with salt and pepper. Add a small amount of milk to the eggs. Pour just enough to cover the layered ingredients in the pan. Cook for 30 minutes or until the eggs are done. Remove from the oven. Add the grated cheese and return to the oven long enough for the cheese to melt. Cut into squares and serve hot. *Tip:* For variety, try adding 2 slices ham, chopped, or 2 sausages, cooked and crumbled, to the layered ingredients. *Yield: 6 servings.*

Day Dreams Country Inn

Joyce and Bob Guerrera
2720 Colonial Drive
Pigeon Forge, Tennessee 37863
Tel: (800) 377-1469 or (423) 428-0370
Fax: (423) 428-2622
E-mail: daydreams@Sprynet.com
$$ – $$$

ABOUT THE B&B

*D*elight in the true country charm of this antique-filled, two-story log home with its six uniquely decorated bedrooms. Enjoy an evening by the cozy fireplace or day dream on the front porch to the soothing sound of Mill Creek dancing by. Take a leisurely stroll around the three acres and enjoy the innumerable willows, hemlocks, and redbuds, or any of the beautiful gardens. Treat your taste buds to the inn's bountiful country breakfast each morning. Perfect for family reunions and retreats, the inn is situated within minutes of the Pigeon Forge trolley and many action-packed attractions, including Dollywood, factory outlet shopping, horseback riding, golf, evening shows, and dinner theater.

SEASON

all year

ACCOMMODATIONS

six rooms with private baths

King-Keith House Bed & Breakfast

Jan and Windell Keith
889 Edgewood Avenue NE
Atlanta, Georgia 30307
Tel: (800) 728-3879 or (404) 688-7330
Fax: (404) 584-0730
E-mail: KingKeith@travelbase.com
$$ – $$$

ABOUT THE B&B

*S*outhern hospitality is alive and well at the King-Keith House. Located in a National Register of Historic Places neighborhood, which includes the home of the founder of Coca-Cola, this Queen Anne B&B is one of the most photographed houses in Atlanta. Built in 1890 by the local hardware magnate, George E. King, it boasts 12-foot ceilings, carved fireplaces, and elegant public spaces, one of which showcases a baby grand piano. Guest rooms are furnished with period antiques and elegant accessories and have access to a private upstairs porch. A gourmet breakfast is served around a large oak table and may include orange French toast, blueberry multi-grain pancakes, homemade breads and coffee cakes, and fruit. The architect owner and his wife enjoy old home restoration, antique hunting, decorating, gardening, and cooking. King-Keith House is within walking distance of the Little Five Pointe commercial district, and is close to Atlanta's most popular in-town shopping, restaurant, and theater areas.

SEASON

all year

ACCOMMODATIONS

four rooms (including one suite)
with private baths;
two rooms with shared bath

Hearty Breakfast Quiche

2 (9") unbaked pie shells
1 tablespoon olive oil
4 tablespoons butter
4 cloves garlic, finely chopped
1 large sweet onion (such as Vidalia), chopped
1 pound sweet Italian-style turkey sausage, casing removed
½ red and ½ green bell pepper, chopped
10 – 12 medium-sized mushrooms, sliced
10 ounces frozen chopped spinach, cooked and drained well
1 teaspoon Italian seasoning mix or 3 teaspoons chopped fresh herbs
    (such as rosemary, thyme, basil, and oregano)
½ teaspoon grated nutmeg
1 teaspoon salt
1 teaspoon pepper
12 eggs
2 cups heavy cream (or substitute with a mixture of 1 cup cream cheese
    and 1 cup half-and-half or whole milk)
¾ cup grated Parmesan cheese
4 cups grated Swiss cheese or a combination of Swiss, provolone,
    Asiago, white cheddar, and Romano
1 tomato, thinly sliced

1 – 2 cups peach salsa (salsa mixed with some mashed peaches)

With 1 pie shell, line the bottom and part way up the sides of a 10" springform pan. Cut the remaining pie shell into 4 strips and finish lining the sides of the pan, coming slightly over the rim. Press the crusts together to form 1 crust.

(continued on next page)

Preheat the oven to 400°F. In a large frying pan, heat the oil and butter. Sauté the garlic, onion, and sausage (chopping up the sausage as it cooks). Add the peppers, then add the mushrooms, spinach, and seasonings, tossing to mix together for 1 minute. Set aside. In a large bowl, beat the eggs until light and fluffy. Add the cream and mix well. Fold in the cheese by hand, followed by the vegetable and meat mixture. Pour into the springform pan. Arrange the tomato slices on top. Place the pan on a large cookie sheet on a rack in the lower third of the oven. Bake 1 – 1½ hours or until set and browned (cover with foil if the top is browning too quickly). Serve with a dollop of peach salsa, which can be made by mixing a good quality salsa with some mashed peaches. *Yield: 12 servings.*

The Parson's House

Sandy and Harold Richardson
638 Forest Avenue
Crete, Nebraska 68333
Tel: (402) 826-2634
$

ABOUT THE B&B

Laze on the porch swing of this 11-room, foursquare-style house built at the turn of the century. The inside of The Parson's House is equally relaxing, and has been refinished and furnished mostly in antiques. Doane College and its beautiful campus is located just one block away. Lincoln, the state capital and home of the University of Nebraska and the Lied Center for the Performing Arts, is 25 miles away. Host Harold, a Baptist minister with a local UCC church, also runs a remodeling business, while hostess Sandy manages real estate rentals as well as the bed and breakfast. Together, they'll make your stay as comfortable and relaxing as possible, and make you feel like The Parson's House is your "home away from home." A full breakfast is served in the formal dining room.

SEASON

all year

ACCOMMODATIONS

two rooms with shared bath

He-Man Omelet

6 ounces frozen hash brown potatoes, thawed
4 eggs
⅓ cup water
¼ teaspoon salt
Dash of onion powder
Dash of garlic powder
4 – 8 drops hot sauce (such as Tabasco)
1 cup chopped ham
½ cup grated sharp cheddar cheese
Chopped chives or green onion or parsley

Fry the hash brown potatoes until crisp and browned. Combine the eggs, water, salt, onion powder, garlic powder, and hot sauce and pour over the potatoes in the frying pan. Add the chopped ham. Cover and cook until firm. Lift the potatoes once or twice and tilt the pan so the liquid egg mixture can run under to cook. Add the grated cheese and let melt. Serve garnished with chopped chives, green onion, or parsley.
Yield: 2 servings.

Impossible Pie

"We serve this dish on Sunday mornings alongside baked tomatoes, a variety of homemade muffins, fruit compotes, and blackberry-cherry cobbler. Folks leave the table very happy and satisfied."
— *Dorsey Allison Comer*

1 pound pork breakfast sausage, browned, crumbled, and drained
⅓ cup chopped red onion (or Vidalia onion when in season)
½ cup sliced mushroom
1 cup mixture of fresh French sorrel, basil, and parsley, chopped
12 ounces mozzarella cheese, grated
1 cup biscuit mix
4 eggs
2 cups milk
Paprika to taste

Preheat the oven to 400°F. Layer the sausage, onion, mushrooms, and herbs in a deep glass pie dish. Top with the mozzarella cheese. Beat the biscuit mix, eggs, and milk with a hand beater until smooth. Pour over the layered ingredients, then sprinkle with paprika. Bake for about 45 minutes or until set. Let stand about 5 minutes before serving.
Yield: 6 servings.

Sleepy Hollow Farm Bed & Breakfast

Beverley Allison and
Dorsey Allison Comer
16280 Blue Ridge Turnpike
Gordonsville, Virginia 22942
Tel: (800) 215-4804 or (540) 832-5555
Fax: (540) 832-2515
$$ – $$$$

ABOUT THE B&B

A long the scenic and historic byway of Virginia Route 231, a red mailbox signals your arrival at Sleepy Hollow Farm. If you miss the mailbox, look for a green barn with a very red roof, a gazebo, a pond, and a brick house snoozing under trees in a sleepy hollow. Generations of farm families have lived here since the late 1700s, and today Sleepy Hollow Farm attracts a wide spectrum of guests, including many international sojourners. Memories to take home with you include the "Dolley Madison hospitality" of innkeepers Beverley Allison and Dorsey Allison Comer, the farm's pure spring water, and the commanding landscapes of surrounding horse, cattle, and sheep farms. And, unlike many B&Bs, this one is equipped to handle children!

SEASON

all year

ACCOMMODATIONS

four rooms (including one suite)
with private baths;
guest cottage with two suites
and private baths

Hidden Pond
Bed & Breakfast

Priscilla and Larry Fuerst
PO Box 461
Fennville, Michigan 49408
Tel: (616) 561-2491
$$$

ABOUT THE B&B

Hidden Pond Bed & Breakfast is set on 28 acres of woods, perfect for bird-watching, hiking, cross-country skiing, or just relaxing in a rowboat on the pond. Guests can enjoy seven entry-level rooms, including bedrooms and baths, living room with fireplace, dining room, library, kitchen, and breakfast porch. Priscilla and Larry, who work for rival airlines, understand the importance of a soothing, calm, and slow-paced overnight stay. They enjoy pleasing guests and creating an atmosphere of quiet elegance. Unwind and take in the sun on the outdoor deck or patio. Turndown service, complimentary soft drinks, tea, hot chocolate, or an evening sherry are offered. Full hot breakfast is served in the sun-washed garden room at your leisure, and features fresh fruit, breads, muffins, and a hot entrée. This lovely retreat is near the beaches of Lake Michigan, the boutiques of Saugatuck, and the winery and cider mill in Fennville.

SEASON

all year

ACCOMMODATIONS

two rooms with private baths

Michigan Week Eggs

"This recipe goes back 35 years, originating from a family friend who gave it to my parents, who gave it to me." — Larry Fuerst

¼ cup sherry
2 (10¾-ounce) cans cream of chicken soup
½ pound mushrooms, sliced
5 – 6 tablespoons butter
12 eggs, lightly beaten
¾ pound Romano cheese, grated

Preheat the oven to 350°F. Add the sherry to the chicken soup. Sauté the mushrooms in the butter. Soft scramble the eggs and set aside. Put ¾ of the soup mixture on the bottom of a 13 x 9" pan. Add ½ the cheese, all the eggs, then the mushrooms. Cover with the remaining soup and finish with the rest of the cheese. Bake 40 – 45 minutes. *Yield: 4 – 6 servings.*

Oven Omelet

¼ cup butter
18 eggs
1 cup sour cream
1 cup milk
2 teaspoons salt
¼ teaspoon pepper
¼ cup chopped green onion

Preheat the oven to 325°F. Melt the butter in a 12 x 9" pan in the oven — watching closely so as not to burn the butter. Beat the eggs, sour cream, milk, salt, and pepper in a bowl. Add the green onions and pour into the pan with the butter. Bake for 35 minutes until set but still moist.
Yield: 8 – 10 servings.

The Hen-Apple Bed and Breakfast

Flo and Harold Eckert
409 South Lingle Avenue
Palmyra, Pennsylvania 17078
Tel: (717) 838-8282
$$

ABOUT THE B&B

Built around 1825, the Hen-Apple is an intimate and fully restored bed and breakfast filled to the brim with everything country and old-fashioned. It offers a relaxed atmosphere with six air conditioned guest rooms (each with private bath), a porch filled with rockers, a screened porch for warm weather dining, a herb garden, lots of flowers, and a shady retreat in the orchard. The Hen-Apple's well-rounded breakfasts are something to remember — especially the cinnamon French toast. Tea is served in the afternoon. Just two miles from Hershey, Pennsylvania, Palmyra is an antique lover's dream. In addition, wineries, shopping outlets, Hershey attractions, the riverboat, and horse racing are nearby. Your hosts, Flo and Harold Eckert, love going to flea markets and auctions, and enjoy reading, gardening, and music. Flo is also a Christmas enthusiast so, come the merry season, the B&B sports a tree in just about every room and an impressive Santa collection.

SEASON

all year

ACCOMMODATIONS

six rooms with private baths

Harbour Woods

Christine and Joe Titka
PO Box 1214
Southwest Harbor, Maine
04679-1214
Tel: (207) 244-5388
Fax: (207) 244-7156
E-mail: harbourwoods@acadia.net
$$ – $$$

ABOUT THE B&B

*C*hristine and Joe welcome you to their gracious 1800s Maine farmhouse across the street from the Great Harbor Marina. Harbour Woods offers an intimate social setting accented by family keepsakes, antiques, flowers, and softly glowing oil lamps. What's more, the warm tones and subtle designs of the wall coverings create an atmosphere of casual elegance. Each morning, a candlelight breakfast becomes a dining experience of the finest kind. Listen to soft music and enjoy a variety of coffees, teas, juices, in-season fruit, home-baked breads, muffins, and entrées of the day, which are imaginatively prepared and presented. A cookie jar and tea for the munchies and a refrigerator stocked with complimentary soft drinks are always available. Guest rooms are distinctively decorated and feature queen-size beds, crackling fireplaces, evening mints and candy, telephones, and private baths with luxurious towels and a selection of rich soaps. And, of course, you may privately reserve the B&B's indoor spa, which awaits to refresh and relax you after a full day of activities in Acadia National Park.

SEASON

all year

ACCOMMODATIONS

three rooms with private baths

Puffy Cheesy Strata

Crustless white bread slices (enough to make 2 layers covering the bottom of a 13 x 9" pan)
½ pound white sharp cheddar cheese, grated
¾ pound and a sprinkle of Monterey Jack cheese, grated
8 eggs
2½ cups milk
Fresh chopped parsley

Place 1 layer of bread in a 13 x 9" nonstick baking pan. Combine the grated cheddar and ¾ pound of the grated Monterey Jack cheese, then sprinkle ⅓ of the cheese mixture evenly on top of the bread. Add a second layer of bread. Blend together the eggs and milk. Pour evenly over the bread slices. Top with the remaining ⅔ of the cheese mixture. Cover and refrigerate overnight, allowing the bread slices to soak up the liquid. Remove from the refrigerator ¾ hour before baking. Bake, covered, in a preheated 350°F oven approximately 35 – 40 minutes, taking the cover off halfway through. When done, the cheese should be puffy and just starting to turn light brown. Cut into 6 – 8 pieces and garnish with a sprinkle of Monterey Jack cheese and fresh parsley. *Yield: 6 – 8 servings.*

Sausage Delights

1 cup biscuit mix
⅓ cup milk
2 tablespoons mayonnaise
1 pound bulk pork breakfast sausage
1 large onion, chopped
1 egg
4-ounce can chopped green chilies, drained
2 cups grated medium cheddar cheese

Preheat the oven to 350°F. Combine the biscuit mix, milk, and mayonnaise and spread evenly over the bottom of a greased and floured 13 x 9" pan. Brown the sausage and onion and drain well. Spread the mixture evenly over the dough mixture. Combine the egg, chilies, and cheese well and spread over the top. Bake 25 – 35 minutes. Let cool for 10 minutes and serve warm. *Yield: 6 – 8 servings.*

Snug Harbor Inn

Laurine "Sis" and Kenneth Hill
1226 West 10th Avenue
Anchorage, Alaska 99501
Tel: (907) 272-6249
Fax: (907) 272-7100
$$

ABOUT THE B & B

S nug Harbor Inn offers you cheerful comfort in a relaxed "home away from home" atmosphere, where absolute privacy is yours. Relax while surrounded by antiques, art, Alaskan artifacts, and period furnishings. The rooms feature handmade quilts and some have their own entrances. At this inn, a fully equipped kitchen, complimentary coffee, tea, and hot chocolate available 24 hours a day, color TV, and complimentary bicycles are at your disposal. The friendly, efficient staff has your every comfort in mind, making Snug Harbor the first choice for the business and pleasure traveler. Located in the heart of Anchorage, Snug Harbor is just four blocks from the central business district, and close to shopping, entertainment, fine dining, and sightseeing. The trail head for Anchorage's extensive bicycle and jogging paths is also nearby.

SEASON

all year

ACCOMMODATIONS

four rooms with private baths;
two rooms with shared bath

"An Elegant Victorian Mansion" Bed & Breakfast Inn

Lily and Doug Vieyra
1406 "C" Street
Eureka, California 95501
Tel: (707) 444-3144
Fax: (707) 442-5594
www.bnbcity.com/inn/20016
$$$ – $$$$

ABOUT THE B&B

Featured in many newspapers and magazines — not to mention on television and radio — this restored national historic landmark offers prestigious and luxurious accommodations. Spirited and eclectic innkeepers provide lavish hospitality in the splendor of a meticulously restored 1888 Victorian masterpiece, complete with original family antique furnishings. The inviting guest rooms offer both graceful refinement and modern-day comfort, individually decorated with Victorian elegance. Guests enjoy gourmet breakfasts and a heavenly night's sleep on top-quality mattresses, as well as secured parking and laundry service. Located in a quiet, historic residential neighborhood overlooking the city and Humboldt Bay, the non-smoking inn is near carriage rides, bay cruises, restaurants, and the theater, and is just minutes from giant redwood parks, coastal beaches, ocean charters, and horseback riding.

SEASON

all year

ACCOMMODATIONS

two rooms (including one suite) with private baths; two rooms with shared bath

Spinach-Soufflé Quiche

9" unbaked pie shell
5 ounces frozen spinach soufflé (Stouffer's brand recommended)
3 strips bacon, cooked
5 ounces Swiss cheese, grated
5 ounces cheddar cheese, grated
3 tablespoons grated Parmesan cheese
4 eggs
1½ cups half-and-half
Dash of salt
⅛ teaspoon cayenne pepper
¼ teaspoon grated nutmeg or to taste
Paprika (optional)

Preheat the oven to 375°F. Arrange the unbaked pie shell in a 10" quiche dish. Cut the frozen spinach in 1" cubes and place on top of the shell. Crumble the bacon and sprinkle over the spinach. Sprinkle the grated cheese over the bacon. In a separate bowl, beat the eggs, then add the half-and-half, salt, pepper, and nutmeg. Pour this mixture over the cheese in the quiche dish. Sprinkle with the paprika (if wished) and bake for 40 minutes or until the center is well set. Cool 5 minutes before cutting into serving pieces. *Yield: 6 – 8 servings.*

Strawberry Omelet

3 eggs, separated and with whites at room temperature
3 tablespoons sugar
1 tablespoon rum
Pinch of salt
Strawberry butter (see recipe below)

2 tablespoons sour cream
2 strawberries, sliced

Preheat the oven to 350°F. Butter a large ovenproof skillet or 10" omelet pan. Beat the yolks with 1 tablespoon of the sugar and the rum. Add a pinch of salt to the egg whites and beat until frothy. Gradually add the remaining 2 tablespoons sugar to the egg whites and beat until soft peaks form. Fold this mixture into the yolk mixture. Pour into the prepared skillet and bake 20 minutes. Spread the strawberry butter on ½ of the omelet and fold over. Serve with the sour cream and sliced strawberries. *Yield: 2 servings.*

Strawberry butter:
½ cup butter
½ cup strawberry jam
2 teaspoons lemon juice

Whip the butter, then add the jam and lemon juice. Whip until smooth; refrigerate. *Yield: About 1 cup.*

Buttonwood Inn

Liz Oehser
50 Admiral Road
Franklin, North Carolina 28734
Tel: (704) 369-8985
$$

ABOUT THE B&B

This small mountain bed and breakfast with a cozy home atmosphere awaits your visit. Sleep in chenille- or quilt-covered antique beds surrounded by country furnishings, collectibles, and crafts. Two rooms on the first floor each have a double and twin bed, while the two rooms on the second floor each have a double bed. Breakfast delights include artichoke quiche, sausage apple ring filled with puffy scrambled egg, Dutch babies with raspberry sauce, stuffed French toast, blintz soufflé, muffins, and cinnamon scones with homemade lemon butter. After breakfast, enjoy gem mining, hiking, horseback riding, water rafting, golf, or tennis. Stay long enough to tour the Biltmore Estate in nearby Asheville, drive through the Smokey Mountain Parkway to Cherokee Indian Reservation, or "shop till you drop" in Gatlinburg. Hospitality, comfort, and delightful breakfasts are this inn's priorities.

SEASON

April to December 15

ACCOMMODATIONS

four rooms with private baths

The Reeds
Bed & Breakfast

Jackie and Charles Reed
PO Box 12011
Washington, DC 20005
Tel: (202) 328-3510
Fax: (202) 332-3885
$$ – $$$$

ABOUT THE B&B

Rated "highest quality" and "best value" by Frommer's Washington DC Guidebook, *The Reeds Bed & Breakfast is housed in a 100-year-old Victorian in downtown historic Washington that has been carefully and extensively restored by its current owners. The exterior features landscaping, gardens, a terrace, and fountains, while the interior is graced with original wood paneling, stained glass, chandeliers, art nouveau, and Victorian antiques and furnishings — including a player piano. Guest rooms range from spacious one- and two-bedded rooms, some with fireplaces and canopy beds, to a one-bedroom apartment with laundry facilities. The Reeds Bed & Breakfast is ten blocks from the White House, and near bus and subway lines. Host Jackie has studied interior design and was involved in real estate development, while Charles is an attorney, a former Fulbright Fellow and law clerk to Supreme Court Justice Tom Clark, and is a partner in a real estate development and syndication firm.*

SEASON

all year

ACCOMMODATIONS

four rooms with private baths;
two rooms with shared bath;
one-bedroom apartment

Sunrise Frittata

1 cup frozen hash brown potatoes
1 tablespoon vegetable oil
½ pound pork breakfast sausage
½ cup chopped onion
½ cup chopped green bell pepper
½ cup chopped red bell pepper
½ cup chopped zucchini
6 slices American cheese, diced
½ cup grated cheddar cheese
¼ cup milk
15 – 18 eggs, lightly beaten
1 tomato, thinly sliced
Grated Parmesan cheese
Chopped fresh parsley

Salsa (see recipe on page 352)

In a large ovenproof frying pan, sauté the potatoes in the vegetable oil until browned; set aside. Cook the sausage and crumble; set aside. Lightly brown the onion, peppers, and zucchini; set aside. Preheat the oven to 350°F. Return the potatoes to the pan. Add the sausage, browned vegetables, American and cheddar cheese, and milk to the eggs, mixing to blend all of the ingredients. Pour over the potatoes in the pan and cook for about 10 minutes over medium heat to cook the bottom of the frittata. Place the pan in the middle of the oven and cook for 15 – 25 minutes or until the center is set. Place the tomato slices over the frittata and sprinkle with Parmesan cheese and parsley. Slice and serve immediately with salsa on the side. *Yield: 8 large servings or 12 small servings.*

Tex-Mex Eggs

"Light, delicious, and different, this recipe originates from a southwestern B&B." — Carole Seaman

6 eggs, lightly beaten
½ cup half-and-half
¼ teaspoon salt
⅛ teaspoon pepper
4-ounce can chopped green chilies, drained
1 cup grated cheddar cheese

Preheat the oven to 325°F. Lightly oil a 9" square baking pan. Beat the eggs with the half-and-half, salt, and pepper. Mix in the chilies. Put the cheese in the bottom of the pan and pour the egg mixture over it. Bake for 25 minutes or until set. *Yield: 6 servings.*

Custer Mansion B&B

Carole and Mill Seaman
35 Centennial Drive
Custer, South Dakota 57730
Tel: (605) 673-3333
$$ – $$$

ABOUT THE B&B

This unusual 1891 Victorian Gothic home is now on the National Register of Historic Places. Antique light fixtures, ceiling fans, door transoms, stained glass windows, and gingerbread accents help preserve Custer Mansion's turn-of-the-century mood. Bedrooms, including one family suite and two honeymoon/anniversary suites, are individually decorated in country and Victorian flavor and are named for songs. Delicious home-cooked breakfasts are served in the spacious dining room, with an adjacent butler pantry used for serving juice, coffee, and tea. The one-acre yard offers plenty of room for outdoor relaxing and features a shaded patio near a natural rocky hillside. Custer Mansion is located near Mount Rushmore, Crazy Horse Memorial, Custer State Park, and many other attractions. Nearby activities include swimming, hiking, fishing, golfing, and hiking in the beautiful Black Hills. Mill, a retired school administrator, and Carole, mother of six and grandmother of 15, specialize in western hospitality and delicious food.

SEASON

all year

ACCOMMODATIONS

five rooms (including three suites)
with private baths

The Degas House

David Villarrubia
2306 Esplanade Avenue
New Orleans, Louisiana 70119
Tel: (800) 755-6730 or (504) 821-5009
Fax: (504) 821-0870
E-mail: degas@bellsouth.net
www.degashouse.com
$$$$

ABOUT THE B&B

Listed on the National Register of Historic Places and included in Fodor's The South's Best Bed and Breakfasts, *The Degas House is where Edgar Degas, the renowned French Impressionist, made his home from 1872 – 73, during which he painted 17 works. Today, B&B guests admire reproductions of his work found throughout the house. Seven guest rooms are located on the top two floors. Back in 1872, guests would have heard music flowing up from the two formal parlors below. The rooms have much the same flavor as they did when Degas lived in the house, corresponding to the colors shown in his paintings of the house or those mentioned in correspondence. Breakfast is served in what was Degas's studio. Specialties such as Estelle's Spinach Quiche and Uncle Michel's Creole Quiche are named after Degas family members. The Degas House is five minutes from the French Quarter.*

SEASON

all year

ACCOMMODATIONS

seven rooms with private baths

Uncle Michel's Creole Quiche

"Uncle Michel was Edgar Degas's American mother's brother. He was heir to his father's successful cotton business and presided over an extensive household of 18 people when Degas came to visit for six months." — David Villarrubia

1 small onion, finely diced
1 tablespoon olive oil
1 tablespoon butter
2 new red potatoes, unpeeled and coarsely chopped
1 green bell pepper, diced
1 clove garlic, minced
1 tablespoon dried parsley
Salt and cayenne pepper to taste
2 tomatoes, diced
4 eggs, lightly beaten
1½ cups half-and-half
1½ cups grated Monterey Jack cheese
9" baked pie shell

Preheat the oven to 350°F. Sauté the onion in the oil and butter for 2 minutes. Add the potato and cook until it is slightly browned.

(continued on next page)

Add the green pepper, garlic, parsley, salt, and cayenne. Add the tomato and allow the mixture to simmer on low heat, stirring occasionally, for 15 minutes or until the pepper is tender. In the meantime, beat the eggs and half-and-half for 1 minute and set aside. Remove the cooked vegetable mixture from the heat and fold in 1 cup of the Monterey Jack cheese. Pour into the pie shell. Pour the egg mixture over and top with the remaining cheese. Bake 30 – 35 minutes or until a knife inserted in the center comes out moist with no liquid sticking to it. Serve warm or at room temperature. *Yield: 6 servings.*

Grünberg Haus
Bed and Breakfast

Christopher Sellers and
Mark Frohman
RR #2, Box 1595RD,
Route 100 South
Waterbury, Vermont 05676-9621
Tel: (800) 800-7760 or (802) 244-7726
Fax: (802) 244-1283
E-mail: grunhaus@aol.com
$$ – $$$$

ABOUT THE B&B

This picture-postcard Austrian-style B&B is tucked away on a secluded hillside in the Green Mountains, perfectly situated for visits to Stowe, Montpelier, Waterbury, and Burlington. Individually decorated guest rooms open onto the carved wood balcony, which offers wonderful views. Help Mark feed the chickens, then enjoy a full breakfast — with selections such as maple-poached pears, apple and cheddar muffins, and ricotta-stuffed French toast — while Chris plays the grand piano. The giant stone fireplace and wood stove in the BYOB pub are favorite gathering places. Nearby activities include spectacular autumn leaf-picking, world-class downhill skiing, golf, boating, bicycling, gliding, canoeing, antique hunting, outlet shopping, and touring Ben & Jerry's ice cream factory. And you can enjoy the B&B's own Jacuzzi, sauna, tennis courts, and cross-country and hiking trails.

SEASON

all year

ACCOMMODATIONS

seven rooms (including one suite)
with private baths;
five rooms with shared baths;
two cabins with private baths

Vermont Cheddar Pie

"Eggs gathered each morning from Mark's chickens make this a special dish at the Grünberg Haus." — Christopher Sellers

2½ cups diced parboiled potato
½ cup chopped onion
1 teaspoon seasoned pepper
½ teaspoon garlic powder
⅓ cup chopped steamed spinach
⅓ cup crumbled feta cheese
¼ cup freshly grated Romano cheese
1 cup grated white cheddar cheese
2 eggs
½ cup low-fat milk
Dried parsley flakes
Paprika

Preheat the oven to 350°F. Grease a 10" glass pie plate. Combine the potatoes and ½ the onions, and press into a pie plate as a crust. Sprinkle with the pepper and garlic powder. Carefully put a layer each of spinach and crumbled feta cheese on top of the crust, then top with the Romano, then the cheddar cheese. Combine the eggs and milk and beat them together lightly; pour carefully over the cheese. To garnish the pie, make a small circle with the remaining ¼ cup onions in the center of the pie, sprinkle the parsley flakes in a larger circle around the onions, and sprinkle the paprika in a larger circle around the parsley flake circle. Bake for 1 hour or until set. *Yield: 6 servings.*

Grünberg Haus Bed & Breakfast
Waterbury, Vermont

Zucchini Frittata

½ tablespoon olive oil
1 teaspoon butter
½ cup grated zucchini
Sprinkle of salt
House of Tsang Mongolian Fire Oil*
4 eggs, lightly beaten
½ cup grated Monterey Jack cheese
2 tablespoons mild or hot salsa

*Available in Asian markets, Mongolian Fire Oil is more flavorful than hot so don't let the name scare you — this dish won't be the same without it so try not to omit it. You'll also find yourself using it to perk up lots of other dishes.

Heat the olive oil and butter in a medium ovenproof skillet until the butter is melted. Cover the bottom of the pan with the grated zucchini. Sprinkle with the salt and 5 – 6 shakes of the Fire Oil. Add the eggs to the pan; don't stir. Cook the mixture on low heat until ¾ set. Sprinkle the cheese over the eggs and place under a preheated broiler until the eggs puff and the cheese is golden. Cut in ½ and put on individual plates with a tablespoon of salsa on each. *Yield: 2 servings.*

Hutton House

Loretta Murray and Dean Ahren
PO Box 88, Route 250/219
Huttonsville, West Virginia 26273
Tel: (304) 335-6701
$$

ABOUT THE B&B

Majestically situated above the tiny town of Huttonsville, this meticulously restored turn-of-the-century Queen Anne Victorian commands a broad view of the Tygart River Valley and the Laurel Mountains. Hutton House, which is listed in the National Register of Historic Places, features original oak woodwork, ornate windows, a three-story turret, arched pocket doors, wraparound porch, and a winding staircase. Antiques abound, and each of the guest rooms is furnished in its own individual style. Breakfast is a time to get to know your hosts and the other guests, while enjoying a variety of pancake, French toast, and egg dishes along with fresh fruit, crème brûlée, sorbet, or even porridge. Guests can then relax on the porch, play games on the lawn, or take a leisurely hike on the trail behind the house. Nearby attractions include Cass Railroad, National Radio Observatory, underground caverns, and rock climbing.

SEASON

all year

ACCOMMODATIONS

six rooms with private baths

Egg, Meat, & Fish Main Dishes

Austrian Skillet Florentine

6 thick strips bacon
4 – 6 large potatoes, scrubbed, peeled, and diced
10 ounces frozen chopped spinach
Hollandaise sauce mix (or see recipe on page 330)
6 eggs

In a large frying pan, fry the bacon until crisp; drain and reserve the bacon drippings for the potatoes. Fry the potatoes in the bacon drippings. Place in a warm oven, then prepare the frozen spinach according to package directions, drain off excess liquid, and keep warm. Prepare the hollandaise sauce according to the package directions and keep warm while preparing the poached (or over easy or sunny side up) eggs. To serve, place a generous portion of the potato mixture on each plate, top with a few spoonfuls of spinach, place an egg on top, and drizzle with hollandaise sauce. *Yield: 6 servings.*

Doelling Haus

Carol and David Doelling
4817 Towne South
St. Louis, Missouri 63128
Tel: (314) 894-6796
$$

ABOUT THE B&B

Rediscover old-world hospitality at Doelling Haus, where you'll delight in beautiful rooms reminiscent of a European country home decorated with German antiques and collectibles, handed down from the hosts' families and gathered during their travels. Hearty full breakfasts include German and Austrian delicacies, and homemade truffles await beside your bed. Many points of interest are nearby, including the famous Arch monument, Grant's Farm, the historic settlement of Kimmswick, recreational areas, malls, and fine restaurants. Carol will direct you to wonderful shops for antique hunting and David, who owns a sports memorabilia store, will gladly show off his old baseball card collection. Come experience "Gemutlichkeit" (a sense of well-being) at Doelling Haus.

SEASON

all year

ACCOMMODATIONS

one room with private bath;
one room with shared bath

**The Hen-Apple
Bed and Breakfast**

Flo and Harold Eckert
409 South Lingle Avenue
Palmyra, Pennsylvania 17078
Tel: (717) 838-8282
$$

ABOUT THE B&B

Built around 1825, the Hen-Apple is an intimate and fully restored bed and breakfast filled to the brim with everything country and old-fashioned. It offers a relaxed atmosphere with six air conditioned guest rooms (each with private bath), a porch filled with rockers, a screened porch for warm weather dining, a herb garden, lots of flowers, and a shady retreat in the orchard. The Hen-Apple's well-rounded breakfasts are something to remember — especially the cinnamon French toast. Tea is served in the afternoon. Just two miles from Hershey, Pennsylvania, Palmyra is an antique lover's dream. In addition, wineries, shopping outlets, Hershey attractions, the riverboat, and horse racing are nearby. Your hosts, Flo and Harold Eckert, love going to flea markets and auctions, and enjoy reading, gardening, and music. Flo is also a Christmas enthusiast so, come the merry season, the B&B sports a tree in just about every room and an impressive Santa collection.

SEASON

all year

ACCOMMODATIONS

six rooms with private baths

Bacon and Cheese Breakfast Pizza

Pastry for 1 single-crust pie (9")
½ pound bacon, cooked and crumbled
2 cups grated mozzarella or cheddar cheese
4 eggs
1½ cups sour cream
2 tablespoons chopped fresh parsley

Preheat the oven to 425°F. Roll the pastry to fit into a 12" pizza pan, then bake for 5 minutes. Sprinkle the bacon and cheese evenly over the crust. Beat the eggs, sour cream, and parsley in a bowl until smooth. Pour over the pizza. Bake 20 – 25 minutes or until the pizza is puffy and lightly browned. *Yield: 6 servings as a main dish, 18 as an appetizer.*

Bauernfrühstuck – Farmer's Breakfast

"This Bavarian dish is traditionally served at supper, which is considered the small meal of the day. You'll discover that this dish makes a hearty breakfast and that it's not just for farmers anymore!" — *Carol Doelling*

6 thick strips bacon
4 – 6 large boiling potatoes, scrubbed, peeled, and diced small
3 whole chicken breasts, cooked
Salt and pepper to taste
½ teaspoon paprika
6 eggs

Preheat the oven to 200°F. In a large frying pan, fry the bacon until crisp; drain and reserve the bacon drippings for the potatoes. Fry the potatoes in the bacon drippings. While the potatoes are cooking, dice the chicken breasts into small pieces. Add the chicken to the potatoes and finish cooking until the potatoes are lightly browned and soft throughout. Crumble the bacon and add to the potato mixture. Season the mixture with salt and pepper to taste. Sprinkle with approximately ¼ teaspoon of the paprika and toss. Place the potato mixture in the oven to keep warm. Poach eggs or prepare over easy or sunny side up. To serve, place a generous portion of potato mixture on each plate and top with an egg. Sprinkle with a dash of paprika. *Yield: 6 servings.*

Doelling Haus

Carol and David Doelling
4817 Towne South
St. Louis, Missouri 63128
Tel: (314) 894-6796
$$

ABOUT THE B&B

Rediscover old-world hospitality at Doelling Haus, where you'll delight in beautiful rooms reminiscent of a European country home decorated with German antiques and collectibles, handed down from the hosts' families and gathered during their travels. Hearty full breakfasts include German and Austrian delicacies, and homemade truffles await beside your bed. Many points of interest are nearby, including the famous Arch monument, Grant's Farm, the historic settlement of Kimmswick, recreational areas, malls, and fine restaurants. Carol will direct you to wonderful shops for antique hunting and David, who owns a sports memorabilia store, will gladly show off his old baseball card collection. Come experience "Gemutlichkeit" (a sense of well-being) at Doelling Haus.

SEASON

all year

ACCOMMODATIONS

one room with private bath;
one room with shared bath

The Mellon Patch Inn

Andrea and Arthur Mellon
3601 North A-1-A,
North Hutchinson Island
Fort Pierce, Florida 34949
Tel: (800) 656-7824 or (561) 461-5231
Fax: (561) 464-6463
www.sunet.net/mlnptch
$$ – $$$

ABOUT THE B&B

North Hutchinson Island is a barrier island on the Atlantic Ocean with a beach that, according to a recent University of Maryland study, is one of the most beautiful stretches of sand in the United States. In this idyllic setting you'll find The Mellon Patch Inn, a newly constructed Florida-style home designed specifically as a B&B. Each room is individually decorated with hand-painted walls and furniture done by a local artist. Choose from the exotic Tropical Paradise Room, the charm of the Patchwork Quilt Room, the tranquility of the Seaside Serenity Room, or the warmth of the Santa Fe Sunset Room. All rooms have air conditioning, television, private bath, and a water view. The Mellon Patch serves a full gourmet breakfast. Along with tennis, beach activities, sportfishing, and boating, guests have use of the inn's canoe to explore Florida's waterways. The Mellon Patch Inn is a quarter mile from the Jack Island Nature Preserve and the Pepper Park fishing docks.

SEASON

all year

ACCOMMODATIONS

four rooms with private baths

Blintz Soufflé with Fruit Topping

"In a pinch, you can simply top this soufflé with sliced strawberries mixed with a small amount of orange marmalade. Any way you top it, this soufflé is loved by all!" — Andrea Mellon

1 pound cottage cheese
3 ounces cream cheese, softened
¼ cup butter or margarine, melted
⅓ cup sugar
½ cup all-purpose flour
3 eggs
½ teaspoon lemon juice
¼ teaspoon baking powder
½ teaspoon ground cinnamon

Fruit topping (see recipe below) or sliced strawberries mixed with a small amount of orange marmalade

Preheat the oven to 350°F. Grease an 8" square baking pan. Combine the cheese, butter, and sugar in a medium bowl. Add the flour, eggs, lemon juice, and baking powder and stir well. Spoon into the prepared pan and sprinkle with the cinnamon. Bake 45 minutes or until the edges turn light brown and the top is springy to the touch. Cut into squares and serve with the fruit topping. *Yield: 4 servings.*

(continued on next page)

Fruit topping:
1 cup frozen blueberries, raspberries, cherries, or peaches, thawed
    and drained
¼ cup orange juice
1 tablespoon honey
1 tablespoon cornstarch dissolved in 1 tablespoon cold water

Combine the fruit, orange juice, honey, and cornstarch mixture in
a saucepan and cook until the color becomes clear and the topping
thickens.

Bridgeford House

Denise and Michael McDonald
263 Spring Street
Eureka Springs, Arkansas 72632
Tel: (501) 253-7853
Fax: (501) 253-5497
E-mail: EurekaBnB@aol.com
$$ – $$$

ABOUT THE B&B

*I*n the heart of Eureka Springs's historic district, Bridgeford House is an 1884 Queen Anne/Eastlake-style Victorian delight. Outside, you'll find shady porches that invite you to pull up a wicker chair and enjoy the panorama of horse-drawn carriages and Victorian homes that is uniquely Spring Street. Yet Bridgeford House is far enough away from downtown that it affords you the luxury of a peaceful and quiet stay. Select from four distinct accommodations: a two-room suite or three large, comfortable bedrooms. From your private entrance, you'll step into rooms tastefully filled with antique furnishings. Your comfortable bedroom and large modern bathroom offer a variety of distinctive touches that let you know you are indeed a special guest — things like fresh hot coffee in your room, color TV, and air conditioning. The large gourmet breakfast is just the right send-off for a pleasant day in one of America's most charming and unusual cities. Denise and Michael are full-time innkeepers and can devote their full attention to all of your needs.

SEASON

all year

ACCOMMODATIONS

four rooms (including one suite)
with private baths

Bridgeford Eggs

10¾-ounce can cream of chicken soup
10¾-ounce can cream of mushroom soup
1 cup mayonnaise
2 teaspoons fruit juice
¼ cup golden sherry
¼ cup milk
12 eggs, hard boiled
Rice or English muffins

Preheat the oven to 350°F. Mix the chicken soup, mushroom soup, mayonnaise, juice, sherry, and milk together. Cover the bottom of a 13 x 9" glass baking dish with ⅓ of the liquid mixture. Chop up the eggs and place in the dish. Cover with the rest of the sauce. Bake for 20 minutes. Serve over rice or a split English muffin. *Tip:* This dish can be prepared the night before and baked in the morning. *Yield: 10 servings.*

Brunch Enchiladas

"My mother gave me this recipe many years ago — it's now my most asked-for recipe. I don't know where she got it, but it's definitely a part of our family history. My mother's family were early settlers in Santa Barbara, California, and my great-grandfather is even buried in Santa Barbara Mission." — Pat O'Brien

2 cups finely chopped cooked ham
½ cup sliced green onion
½ cup finely chopped green bell pepper
2½ cups grated cheddar cheese
8 (7" diameter) flour tortillas
4 eggs, lightly beaten
2 cups light cream or milk
1 tablespoon all-purpose flour
¼ teaspoon salt (optional)
¼ teaspoon garlic powder
Few drops of hot pepper sauce (such as Tabasco)
Avocado slices
Fresh salsa
Sour cream

Mexican corn muffins (see page 68)
Shrimp gazpacho (see page 42)

(continued on next page)

Blue Spruce Inn

Pat and Tom O'Brien
2815 Main Street
Soquel, California 95073
Tel: (800) 559-1137 or (408) 464-1137
Fax: (408) 475-0608
E-mail: pobrien@BlueSpruce.com
$$ – $$$$

ABOUT THE B&B

The Blue Spruce Inn welcomes you with the distinct Pacific breeze that freshens the Central Coast hillsides golden with poppies, tempers the heat of the summer sun, and warms the sands during afternoon strolls on winter beaches. The inn is four miles south of Santa Cruz and one mile from Capitola Beach at the northern curve of Monterey Bay. Gracious personal service is the hallmark of this 1875 B&B inn, where beds are graced with Amish quilts and walls hung with original local art that blends the flavor of yesteryear with the luxury of today. There are quiet gardens in which to enjoy the sunshine of Soquel Village, delightful antique shops at the corner of the street, and, a little farther, wineries, gift shops, and regional art displays. Bountiful breakfasts feature fresh fruit, homemade breads, and exceptional entrées. At the end of the day, the hot tub offers welcome respite and, when guests return to their rooms, pillows are fluffed and a special treat awaits.

SEASON

all year

ACCOMMODATIONS

five rooms with private baths

In a bowl, combine the ham, onion, and green pepper. Place ⅓ cup of this mixture and 3 tablespoons of the cheese at one end of a tortilla. Roll up. Repeat with the rest. Arrange the tortillas seam-side down in a greased 12 x 7½ x 2" ovenproof casserole dish. Combine the eggs, cream, flour, salt, garlic powder, and hot pepper sauce. Pour over the tortillas.

Cover and refrigerate several hours or overnight. Remove from the refrigerator ¾ hour before baking. Preheat the oven to 350°F and bake 45 – 60 minutes or until set. Sprinkle with the remaining cheese. Bake 3 minutes more until the cheese melts, then let stand 10 minutes. Garnish with avocado slices, salsa, and sour cream. For a wonderful mix of textures and temperatures, serve this entrée with spicy Mexican corn muffins and chilled shrimp gazpacho. *Yield: 8 servings.*

Variations: Try whole wheat flour tortillas and use cooked ground turkey or chicken in place of the ham.

Cheddar Creamed Eggs on Toast

4 strips bacon
1 medium onion, chopped
1½ cups sharp cheddar cheese
3 generous tablespoons all-purpose flour
1½ cups milk
6 eggs, hard boiled and sliced
Toast

Brown the bacon; crumble it and reserve. Drain most of the drippings from the skillet. Sauté the onion in the remaining drippings. Combine the cheese and flour and add to the onion in the skillet. Add the milk and stir on medium heat until the mixture thickens. Fold in the eggs and crumbled bacon. Serve over toast. *Yield: 4 servings.*

Bedford's Covered Bridge Inn

Martha and Greg Lau
RD 2, Box 196
Schellsburg, Pennsylvania 15559
Tel: (814) 733-4093
$$ – $$$

ABOUT THE B&B

Situated near Exit 11 of I-76 (the Pennsylvania Turnpike), Bedford's Covered Bridge Inn borders 4,000-acre Shawnee State Park, a lovely trout stream, and the Colvin covered bridge. From this idyllic location, guests can pursue hiking, biking, fishing, cross-country skiing, birding, and antique hunting right from the inn's door. Nearby swimming and boating on Shawnee Lake, visits to Old Bedford Village and Bedford's historic district, driving tours, downhill skiing at Blue Knob Resort, and tours of Bedford's 14 covered bridges round out the list of local activities. Inside the inn, the Lau's attention to detail creates an atmosphere that is comfortable and inviting. The historic farmhouse (circa 1823) boasts six guest rooms with private baths, traditional and country decor, and memorable breakfasts. "There's no doubt what everyone's favorite activity is," say Martha and Greg, "Sitting on the inn's wraparound porch and wishing they could live in Bedford County, too!"

SEASON

all year

ACCOMMODATIONS

six rooms with private baths;
one cottage for couples or families

Faye and Wayne Payne
20 Rose Lane
Ashville, Alabama 35953
Tel: (205) 594-4366
$ – $$

ABOUT THE B&B

Built in 1890, this spacious three-story bed and breakfast is located in the center of quaint Ashville, Alabama. Listed on the National Register of Historic Places, the house is resplendent with Victorian elegance. Features such as wraparound porches, balconies, stained glass windows, carved mantles, winding stairs, and period furniture make Roses and Lace an excellent example of the area's craftsmanship and architectural integrity. Come and relax, walk to town and shop for antiques, or shop at the famed Boaz outlet city, just 30 minutes away.

SEASON

all year

ACCOMMODATIONS

three rooms with private baths;
two rooms with shared bath

Chicken Crêpes

Crêpes:
1 cup all-purpose flour
¼ teaspoon baking powder
¼ teaspoon salt
1¼ cups milk
1 egg
1 tablespoon margarine, melted
1 tablespoon butter

Chicken filling:
3 tablespoons margarine
3 tablespoons all-purpose flour
½ teaspoon salt
2 cups chicken broth
1½ cups chopped cooked chicken
⅔ cup chopped apple
½ cup chopped celery
2 tablespoons chopped or grated onion

(continued on next page)

To make the crêpes: Sift together the flour, baking powder, and salt. Stir in the milk, egg, and margarine and beat until smooth. Heat the butter in a medium skillet until bubbly. For each crêpe, pour ¼ cup batter into the skillet. Immediately rotate the skillet until the thin batter covers the bottom like a film. Cook until the crêpe turns light brown. Using a wide spatula, run it around the edges and flip. Cook the other side. Repeat with the remaining batter. Let the crêpes cool, then stack with waxed paper between each crêpe. *Tip:* The crêpes can be made in advance and warmed up the next day.

To make the filling: Preheat the oven to 350°F. Heat the margarine over low heat until melted. Blend in the flour and salt. Cook low, stirring constantly, until the mixture is smooth and bubbly. Remove from heat. Stir in the broth and heat to boiling, stirring constantly. Continue boiling and stirring for 1 minute. In a separate bowl, mix the chicken, apple, celery, onions, and ¾ cup chicken broth mixture. Place a scant ½ cup of chicken mixture in the center of each crêpe; roll up. Place crêpes seam side down in an ungreased baking dish. Pour the remaining chicken broth mixture over the crêpes. Bake uncovered until hot (about 20 minutes). *Yield: 4 servings.*

Alexander Hamilton House

Barbara Notarius and Brenda Barta
49 Van Wyck Street
Croton-on-Hudson, New York
10520
Tel: (914) 271-6737
Fax: (914) 271-3927
E-mail: ALEXHMLTNHS@ aol.com
www.AlexanderHamiltonHouse.com
$$$ – $$$$

ABOUT THE B&B

The Alexander Hamilton House (circa 1889) is a sprawling Victorian home situated on a cliff overlooking the Hudson River. Grounds include a mini orchard and in-ground pool. The home has many period antiques and collections and offers a queen-bedded suite with a fireplace in the living room; a double-bedded suite with fireplace and a small sitting room; and a bridal chamber with king-size bed, Jacuzzi, entertainment center, pink marble fireplace, and sky-lights. A one-bedroom apartment is also available with a double bed, living room/kitchen, private bath, and sepa-rate entrance. Nearby attractions include West Point, the Sleepy Hollow Restorations, Lyndhurst Mansion, Boscobel (a fabulous Federal-period restoration), the Rockefeller mansion, hiking, biking, sailing, and New York City (under an hour away by train or car).

SEASON

all year

ACCOMMODATIONS

seven rooms (including three suites) with private baths

Coddled Eggs

1 strip bacon, cooked and crumbled
2 tablespoons grated cheddar cheese
2 tablespoons grated mozzarella cheese
1 egg

Fresh bread

Spray the inside of a medium egg coddler with nonstick cooking spray. Sprinkle the crumbled bacon in the bottom. Add 1 tablespoon of the cheddar and the mozzarella cheese, break in the egg, and add the remaining cheese. Screw on the top of the coddler and drop it gently into boiling water to cover. Boil for 10 minutes and serve with fresh bread. *Yield: 1 serving.*

Cornmeal Soufflé

3 tablespoons butter
2 tablespoons chopped green onion
¼ cup cornmeal
½ teaspoon oregano
1¼ cups milk
¾ cup grated Monterey Jack cheese
4 eggs, separated

Preheat the oven to 350°F. Melt the butter in a medium saucepan. Sauté the onions. Add the cornmeal and oregano. Add the milk to make a sauce. Add the cheese, then the egg yolks. Stir to blend. Beat the egg whites until they stand in soft peaks. Fold into the cornmeal mixture. Pour into 2 (2-cup) soufflé dishes. Set in a pan of water, and bake for 45 minutes. *Yield: 4 servings.*

The Heirloom

Melisande Hubbs and Patricia Cross
214 Shakeley Lane
Ione, California 95640
Tel: (209) 274-4468
$$ – $$$

ABOUT THE B&B

*D*own a country lane to an expansive English romantic garden is a touch of the old south. The Heirloom is a brick, two-story southern antebellum home, circa 1863, located in the heart of California gold country. It was built by Virginians who came to California during the Gold Rush to be merchants in Ione, the supply center of the mining camps of Amador County. Sweet magnolias, wisteria, hammocks, croquet, verandas, cozy fireplaces, and heirloom antiques (including a historic piano) await you, not to mention a royal breakfast and gracious hospitality. Near the inn are over 20 wineries, Gold Rush historical points, museums, and nature walks, and opportunities for gourmet dining, gold panning, gliding, and hiking.

SEASON

all year

ACCOMMODATIONS

four rooms with private baths;
two rooms with shared bath

Creamed Beef on Toast

"When I was in the military service, my favorite breakfast was what they called S-O-S. I've worked with the basic recipe over the years and came up with this winner." — Bob Martz

1 pound ground round beef
1 teaspoon dried basil
1 teaspoon dried oregano
1 teaspoon dried thyme
Salt and pepper to taste
4 tablespoons chopped onion
5 tablespoons margarine
3 tablespoons all-purpose flour
2 cups hot milk
1 tablespoon sherry or cognac
Toast or biscuits

In a heavy large skillet, cook the ground round with the basil, oregano, thyme, and salt and pepper. Remove the meat mixture from the skillet. In the same skillet, sauté the onion in margarine until transparent (about 8 minutes). Add the flour, stirring with a wooden spoon for about 1 minute. Add the hot milk all at once, stirring constantly with a wire whisk until thickened. Remove from the heat, stir in the sherry, and add the meat mixture. Serve over toast or biscuits. *Tip:* For a healthier meal, use non-fat milk and no-cholesterol margarine. *Yield: 4 servings.*

Creamed Eggs with Smoked Salmon in Puff Pastry

4 unbaked puff pastry shells
8 eggs
2 tablespoons butter
4 – 6 tablespoons chopped smoked salmon (or diced ham)
2 tablespoons each chopped red and green bell peppers
2 tablespoons sour cream
Hollandaise sauce mix (or see recipe on page 330)
Chopped parsley or paprika

Fresh fruit

Bake the puff pastry shells according to the package directions. Let them cool.

Beat the eggs until light and fluffy. In a frying pan, melt the butter, then add the salmon and peppers. Sauté until just barely limp. Add the eggs, cooking and stirring until almost done. Add the sour cream, and stir. Do not let the eggs get too dry; remove them from the heat while still creamy. Spoon the mixture into each pastry shell, allowing some of the egg mixture to overflow onto the plate. Cover with 2 – 3 tablespoons of hollandaise sauce, then sprinkle with the parsley or paprika. Serve with fresh fruit in season (melon is excellent). *Yield: 4 servings.*

"An Elegant Victorian Mansion" Bed & Breakfast Inn

Lily and Doug Vieyra
1406 "C" Street
Eureka, California 95501
Tel: (707) 444-3144
Fax: (707) 442-5594
www.bnbcity.com/inns/20016
$$$ – $$$$

ABOUT THE B&B

Featured in many newspapers and magazines — not to mention on television and radio — this restored national historic landmark offers prestigious and luxurious accommodations. Spirited and eclectic innkeepers provide lavish hospitality in the splendor of a meticulously restored 1888 Victorian masterpiece, complete with original family antique furnishings. The inviting guest rooms offer both graceful refinement and modern-day comfort, individually decorated with Victorian elegance. Guests enjoy gourmet breakfasts and a heavenly night's sleep on top-quality mattresses, as well as secured parking and laundry service. Located in a quiet, historic residential neighborhood overlooking the city and Humboldt Bay, the non-smoking inn is near carriage rides, bay cruises, restaurants, and the theater, and is just minutes from giant redwood parks, coastal beaches, ocean charters, and horseback riding.

SEASON

all year

ACCOMMODATIONS

two rooms (including one suite)
with private baths;
two rooms with shared bath

High Meadows Inn

Peter Sushka and Mary Jae Abbitt
High Meadows Lane, Route 4, Box 6
Scottsville, Virginia 24590
Tel: (800) 232-1832 or (804) 286-2218
Fax: (804) 286-2124
E-mail: peterhmi@aol.com
www.highmeadows.com
$$ – $$$$

ABOUT THE B&B

As Virginia's only inn that is on the National Register of Historic Homes and has a Renaissance farm vineyard, High Meadows offers a rare opportunity to experience 170 years of architectural history and 10 years of new viticultural growth. High Meadows is a grand house, where guests are welcomed with champagne and stay in rooms furnished with period antiques and art, each with private bath. The innkeepers' many special touches and attention to detail make your visit one to be remembered. Enjoy the simplicity of nature on the 50 surrounding acres of gardens, footpaths, forests, and ponds. Owner/chef Peter Sushka ensures that dining at High Meadows is just as pleasurable as lodging there. Start with a breakfast of fresh orange juice, a variety of homemade breads, muffins, and scones, fresh fruit, gourmet egg dishes, and coffee or tea. End your day with a multi-course dinner, offering distinctive northern European and Mediterranean dishes.

SEASON

all year

ACCOMMODATIONS

14 rooms (including four suites) with private baths

Easiest Turkey Timbales

(Recipe from The Best of High Meadows — A Selected Recipe Collection.*)*

2 ounces turkey (or ham or chicken), cubed
2 ounces sharp cheddar cheese, grated
2 – 3 eggs
½ cup milk
2 tablespoons chopped green onion
½ teaspoon paprika
½ teaspoon white pepper
1 teaspoon grated Parmesan cheese

Preheat the oven to 375°F. Lightly grease 2 (6-ounce) custard cups and place the cubed meat and grated cheese on the bottom of each cup. Mix the eggs, milk, green onions, paprika, and pepper, and pour ½ into each custard cup (on top of the meat and cheese). Top with the Parmesan cheese and bake for 30 minutes. Serve hot. *Yield: 2 servings.*

Eggs Benedict Caledonia

2 English muffins, split
Butter or margarine
4 slices Canadian bacon or ham, cooked
4 eggs, poached (whites set with yolks liquid)
Hollandaise sauce mix
3 tablespoons lemon juice

Toast or broil the muffin halves and spread with the butter. Top with the slices of Canadian bacon or ham, then keep warm in a 160°F oven. Place the poached eggs on the muffins. Prepare the hollandaise sauce mix using 3 tablespoons of lemon juice instead of water. Cover the eggs with sauce. Garnish as desired. *Yield: 2 servings.*

Caledonia Farm — 1812

Phil Irwin
47 Dearing Road
Flint Hill, Virginia 22627
Tel: (800) BNB-1812 or
(540) 675-3693
Fax: (540) 675-3696
$$ – $$$$

ABOUT THE B&B

With Virginia's Blue Ridge Mountains as a backdrop, Caledonia Farm offers its guests a beautiful setting amid scenic pasturelands surrounded by stone fences. The farm's Federal-style house and companion summer kitchen were completed in 1812. Restoration was completed in 1965, with the original two-foot-thick stone walls and 32-foot-long beams remaining intact along with the original mantels, paneled windows, and wide pine floors. The winter kitchen's huge fireplace provides a delightful atmosphere during cool seasons while three porches offer a variety of views in the warmer months. Guest rooms are air conditioned, and have working fireplaces, individual heat control, and fine double beds. The B&B is called Caledonia (the mythological name for Scotland) to honor the original immigrants to this magnificent area.

SEASON

all year

ACCOMMODATIONS

two suites with private baths;
two rooms with shared bath

The Old Powder House Inn

Eunice and Al Howes
38 Cordova Street
St. Augustine, Florida 32084
Tel: (800) 447-4149
Fax: (904) 825-0143
E-mail: ahowes@aug.com
www.oldcity.com/powderhouse
$$$

ABOUT THE B&B

The Old Powder House Inn stands on the ground where, in the late 18th century, a powder house once stood, used by Spanish soldiers at nearby fort Castillo de San Marcos. Today, it's a charming turn-of-the-century Victorian inn. Lace curtains and hardwood floors adorn antique-filled rooms. Leave your cares behind as you relax on the veranda or sit by the fountain in the courtyard. The inn is located in the historic district steps away from quaint shops and landmarks of the nation's oldest city. Choose from one of eight distinctive rooms, each with private bath. The romantic Queen Anne's Lace, for example, features a queen-size pedestal bed with lace canopy, while Memories features its own Jacuzzi tub. Enjoy a gourmet breakfast in the formal dining room, where stuffed pears, granola, chocolate-chip muffins, and soufflés may be part of the morning menu. Join other guests and innkeepers Eunice and Al Howes for afternoon tea or evening wine with hors d'oeuvres.

SEASON

all year

ACCOMMODATIONS

eight rooms (including two suites)
with private baths

Eggs in Snow

2 slices bread
Butter
Pinch of grated nutmeg
Salt and pepper to taste
2 eggs, separated
Grated cheese of your choice

Toast the bread on 1 side. Turn and toast the underside very lightly. Butter the lightly toasted side; keep hot. Add the seasonings to the egg whites and beat until they stand in soft peaks. Spread over the buttered toast. Make a slight indentation in the middle of each piece of toast and drop in an egg yolk. Sprinkle with cheese and place under a hot broiler for a few minutes until the egg yolk has partially set. Serve immediately. *Yield: 2 servings.*

Eggs Neptune

8 eggs
4 English muffins, split
4 ounces crab meat (snow, king, or lobster meat), cooked
Hollandaise sauce (see recipe below)
Fresh snipped dill

Poach the eggs, then put in a bowl with ice water (they will keep overnight in the refrigerator). Toast the muffins. Warm the crab meat in the microwave oven or by placing in hot water for a few minutes, then squeezing out the excess water. Place the crab meat on the muffins. Top with the eggs heated in hot water for 2 minutes, and garnish with the hollandaise sauce and fresh dill. *Yield: 4 servings.*

Hollandaise sauce:
2 egg yolks
1 tablespoon warm water
Juice of ¼ lemon
½ cup butter
Dash of cayenne pepper

Mix the egg yolks, water, and lemon juice and whip for 2 minutes with a wire whisk. In a double boiler, melt the butter. Put aside and keep warm, but not hot. Put the egg mixture in a bowl and set on top of the double boiler. Whip constantly with a wire whisk and add the butter in a steady, very slow stream (otherwise the egg mixture will break). The sauce is ready when it reaches the consistency of thick molasses. Add the cayenne pepper and mix.

Glynn House Victorian Inn

Betsy and Karol Paterman
43 Highland Street, PO Box 719
Ashland, New Hampshire 03217
Tel: (800) 637-9599 or (603) 968-3775
E-mail: glynnhse@lr.net
www.nettx.com/glynnhouse.html
$$ – $$$

ABOUT THE B&B

Come enjoy the gracious elegance of this beautifully restored 1890 Queen Anne home — from the cupola of the inn's tower and gingerbread wraparound veranda to the carved oak foyer and pocket doors. Each of the beautifully appointed bedrooms has its own distinctive mood, distinguished by unique interior design, period furniture, the fragrance of fresh flowers, and soft, fluffy robes. A memorable full breakfast is served in the dining room, consisting perhaps of eggs Benedict or eggs Neptune, Belgian waffles, thick French toast, ambrosia, juice, and the specialty of the house — strudel. After breakfast, take a walk or boat ride around famous Squam Lake (where the movie On Golden Pond was filmed) just a few minutes away, and enjoy all that the Lakes Region and White Mountains have to offer. Allow Betsy and Karol to provide hospitality with a warm smile and make you feel as though you're part of their family.

SEASON

all year

ACCOMMODATIONS

eight rooms with private baths

The Voss Inn

Frankee and Bruce Muller
319 South Willson
Bozeman, Montana 59715
Tel: (406) 587-0982
Fax: (406) 585-2964
www.wtp.net/go/vossinn
$$$

ABOUT THE B&B

Built in 1883 by a prominent journalist and mining engineer named Mat Alderson, The Voss Inn is an elegant brick Victorian with a spacious front porch overlooking an English cottage perennial garden. The six guest rooms and the guest parlor are furnished with Victorian antiques. Guests eat a full gourmet breakfast in their rooms or family-style in the guest parlor. The antique radiator bun warmer is a star attraction of the upstairs buffet area where guests help themselves to an elegant fruit plate, freshly baked muffins or cinnamon rolls, and their choice of an egg/meat dish served in individual ramekins or hot or cold cereal. Afternoon tea is served daily, featuring a variety of freshly baked desserts and tea sandwiches. Owners Frankee and Bruce Muller previously operated a photographic safari camp in the African country of Botswana. Their special interests include wildlife, fly fishing, skiing, golf, and, of course, gourmet cooking — all of which can be enjoyed to the utmost in Bozeman. The Voss Inn is located three blocks from historic downtown Bozeman and is within walking distance of shops and dining.

SEASON

all year

ACCOMMODATIONS

six rooms with private baths

Eggs with Potatoes and Cheese Sauce

Potatoes:
3 large russet potatoes, scrubbed and washed
1 small onion, chopped
4 sprigs parsley, chopped
½ cup butter, melted
Salt and pepper to taste

Cheese sauce:
½ cup butter
½ cup all-purpose flour
¾ teaspoon salt
¼ teaspoon pepper
¾ teaspoon dry mustard
3 cups milk
1 pound medium cheddar cheese, grated

8 eggs
8 thick strips bacon, cooked crisp and crumbled

(continued on next page)

To prepare the potatoes: Grate the potatoes directly into a bowl of cold salted water. Let stand 5 minutes. Drain, rinse, and pat dry with paper towels. Mix with the chopped onion, parsley, melted butter, and salt and pepper. Bake in a greased 13 x 8" glass baking dish at 400°F until brown and crispy (about 1 hour).

To prepare the cheese sauce: Melt the butter in a large saucepan over medium heat. Add the flour and stir vigorously, then add the salt, pepper, and mustard powder while still stirring. Stir for 2 minutes. Add 1 cup of the milk slowly while stirring constantly (adding more milk as necessary to keep the mixture from thickening too much). Add the cheese to the mixture and reduce the heat to medium-low. Let the cheese melt completely, stirring constantly, and add as much of the remaining milk as needed to thin the sauce slightly.

To assemble: Preheat the oven to 350°F. Spray 8 (8-ounce) ramekins with nonstick cooking spray. Place a handful (approximately ½ cup) of potatoes in the bottom of each ramekin. Top the potatoes with ⅓ cup of the cheese sauce, making a well in the center with the back of a spoon. Break an egg in the center. Top with the crumbled bacon. Bake for 25 minutes or until the egg white is fully cooked and the yolk is still soft. *Yield: 8 servings.*

Golden Maple Inn

Jo and Dick Wall
Wolcott Village, Vermont
05680-0035
Tel: (800) 639-5234 or (802) 888-6614
Fax: (802) 888-6614
E-mail: GoldnMaple@aol.com
$$

ABOUT THE B&B

O riginally the home of prominent mill owner H.B. Bundy, this historic 1865 B&B is nestled alongside northern Vermont's Lamoille River — famous for excellent trout fishing and quiet canoeing. Guests can read or doze in the library, put together puzzles in the parlor, or listen to the gurgle of the river from the comfort of an Adirondack chair. Jo and Dick's delightful candlelit breakfasts include fresh-ground coffees, teas, juice, fresh fruit in season, homemade granola, and a scrumptious daily specialty entrée, all prepared in their country kitchen from only the finest local ingredients. To complete the day, teas and sweets are served to guests each evening in the library and parlor. Country walks, trout fishing, canoeing, biking, and back-country skiing are all available right from the inn. Golden Maple is located near the historic Fisher Covered Railroad Bridge, Bread & Puppet Museum, Cabot Creamery, Ben & Jerry's Ice Cream Factory, and the shops of Stowe Village.

SEASON

all year

ACCOMMODATIONS

four rooms (including two suites) with private baths

Festive Holiday Eggs

"A very old Wall family recipe traditionally served on Christmas morning." — Dick Wall

12 eggs
8 strips maple-smoked bacon
Garlic salt
Seasoned pepper
Crushed red pepper flakes
Chopped parsley

Preheat the oven to 325°F. Grease a 12-cup shallow muffin pan. Cut the bacon crosswise into 1" squares and place 5 squares evenly around the edge of each muffin cup, keeping ½ the bacon inside and ½ outside each cup. Break 1 egg into each cup. Add a dash of seasonings (to taste) onto each egg. Bake for 25 minutes. Carefully loosen the baked eggs from the cups with a sharp knife and lift with a tablespoon onto paper towels to blot. Serve hot. *Yield: 6 servings.*

Feta, Phyllo, and Spinach Croustade

½ cup finely chopped onion
3 tablespoons butter and 2 tablespoons butter, melted
8 sheets frozen phyllo dough (17 x 12" rectangles), thawed
10 ounces frozen chopped spinach, thawed and squeezed dry
3 tablespoons all-purpose flour
¼ teaspoon tarragon
⅛ teaspoon pepper
1 cup milk
2 eggs
1 cup creamed cottage cheese
½ cup feta cheese, crumbled

Preheat the oven to 350°F. In a large nonstick skillet, sauté the onion in the 3 tablespoons of butter until tender. Add the spinach, breaking it up with a fork. Stir in the flour, tarragon, and pepper; add the milk. Cook, stirring on low heat until thick and bubbly. Lightly beat the eggs and add to the skillet in a folding motion. When the eggs have set, fold in the cheese. Turn to the lowest heat and assemble the phyllo dough as follows.

(continued on next page)

The Summer House

Marjorie and Kevin Huelsman
158 Main Street
Sandwich, Massachusetts 02563
Tel: (800) 241-3609 or (508) 888-4991
E-mail: sumhouse@capecod.net
$$ – $$$

ABOUT THE B&B

The Summer House is an elegant circa 1835 Greek Revival twice featured in Country Living magazine. It was owned by Hiram Dillaway, a prominent mold-maker and colorist at the Boston & Sandwich Glass Factory. Large, sunny bedchambers feature antiques, hand-stitched quilts, and working fireplaces. Stroll to dining, shops, museums, galleries, a pond and gristmill, and a boardwalk to the beach. Bountiful breakfasts change daily and include freshly ground coffee, tea, fruit juice, and fresh fruit served in stemware. Entrées of frittata, stuffed French toast, quiche, or omelets are accompanied by scones, puff pastry, muffins, or fruit cobblers. Dishes are enhanced with vegetables, berries, and herbs from the inn's garden. English-style afternoon tea is served at an umbrella table in the garden. Boston, Newport, Providence, Martha's Vineyard, and Nantucket make pleasant day trips.

SEASON

all year

ACCOMMODATIONS

five rooms with private baths

Place a large nonstick pizza pan in the middle of your counter. Carefully remove the phyllo dough from the carton and unfold. Take 1 sheet and fold it in thirds lengthwise. Place one end of the folded sheet in the center of the pizza pan, extending the other end out over the side of the pan. Repeat with the 7 remaining sheets, arranging them in a spoke fashion evenly around the pan. (The inner ends of each sheet should overlap in the center of the pan and should be about 3" apart at the outer ends of each spoke.)

Spread the filling in an 8" circle in the center of the phyllo dough. Lift the end of 1 phyllo strip and gently bunch it together and place it on top of the filling. Repeat with the other 7 strips, leaving a 3" circle of the filling exposed in the center. Drizzle with the 2 tablespoons of melted butter and bake on the middle rack for about 15 minutes or until the dough is golden brown. Cut into 8 wedges and serve immediately.
Yield: 8 servings.

Gujarati Indian Eggs with Broiled Tomato

2 eggs, lightly beaten
1 tablespoon water
1 teaspoon masala mix*
1 tablespoon butter
1 tomato, cut into ½" slices
Sprinkle of grated Parmesan cheese
Sprinkle of lemon pepper
Chopped parsley
Asian chili sauce (optionally diluted with a light tomato sauce)

Masala mix can be purchased in gourmet food shops or you can make your own: mix equal parts ground coriander, cumin, turmeric, mild chili powder, and 3 parts mild curry powder.

Combine the eggs, water, and masala mix, and cook in a buttered frying pan as either scrambled eggs or an omelet. Cover the tomatoes with the cheese and broil in the oven for a few minutes until done. Sprinkle the cooked tomatoes with lemon pepper, and serve with the eggs. Garnish with the parsley and some chili sauce. *Yield: 1 serving.*

Chalet Kilauea — The Inn at Volcano

Lisha and Brian Crawford
Box 998, Wright Road
Volcano, Hawaii 96785
Tel: (808) 967-7786
Fax: (808) 967-8660
E-mail: Reservations@
Volcano-Hawaii.com
$$$$

ABOUT THE B&B

Explore treasures from around the world at Chalet Kilauea, a lush Hawaiian haven nestled in Volcano Village. Owners Lisha and Brian Crawford are international travelers who know the art of hospitality. At the inn, choose from superior rooms inspired by Oriental, African, or European themes, or the Treehouse Suite, with most featuring marble Jacuzzis. Tempt your appetite with a candlelit, two-course gourmet breakfast featuring local and international cuisine. Luxuriate in the Jacuzzi, relax by the fireplace, peruse the library, or wander in the garden. The spacious vacation homes are particularly suited for families, larger parties, and those seeking complete privacy. All offer a full kitchen and include afternoon tea and use of the Jacuzzi. Near the inn, you'll find Hawaii Volcanoes National Park, Black Sand Beach, and the city of Hilo with all its splendors. Opportunities abound for lava viewing, hiking, biking, golfing, swimming, bird watching, exploring, and just plain unwinding!

SEASON

all year

ACCOMMODATIONS

six rooms with private baths;
six vacation homes

Carrington's Bluff B&B

Lisa and Edward Mugford
1900 David Street
Austin, Texas 78705
Tel: (800) 871-8908 or (512) 479-0638
Fax: (512) 476-4769
$$$

ABOUT THE B&B

The setting is Shoal Creek Bluff and an 1877 Texas farmhouse nestled in the arms of a 500-year-old oak tree. Today, Carrington's Bluff B&B offers Texas hospitality to make your stay delightful. Upon arrival, you'll find yourself surrounded by rooms filled with English and American antiques, handmade quilts, and the sweet smell of potpourri. The 35-foot front porch beckons you to sit among the plants and flowers and enjoy the gentle breezes with your morning coffee or afternoon tea. The smell of fresh-brewed gourmet coffee invites you to a breakfast that begins with fresh fruit and homemade granola served on fine English china. Homemade muffins or breads and a house specialty ensure you won't go away hungry. Carrington's Bluff is near the University of Texas and the State Capital grounds, just minutes from parks, hiking and biking trails, shopping, and wonderful restaurants.

SEASON

all year

ACCOMMODATIONS

eight rooms with private baths

Ham and Swiss-stuffed Puff Pastry

(Recipe from What's Cooking at Carrington's Bluff.*)*

1 package (2 sheets) frozen puff pastry, thawed
1 teaspoon Dijon mustard
8 – 10 slices ham
8 – 10 slices Swiss cheese
1 egg, lightly beaten
1 tablespoon light cream

Preheat the oven to 400°F. Unfold the puff pastry. Spread the mustard over 1 sheet of the puff pastry. Cover with a layer of ham then a layer of cheese, alternating until all is used. Cover with the other sheet of puff pastry. Whip together the eggs and cream. Brush the edges of the pastry with the egg mixture. Seal with a fork. Cut slits in the top with a sharp knife. Bake 15 – 20 minutes or until golden brown and puffed.
Yield: 8 servings.

Hawaiian-style Croute Fromage

1 thick slice bread
1 teaspoon mayonnaise
⅛ cup grated cheddar cheese
⅛ cup grated Monterey Jack cheese
1 slice tomato
1 tablespoon sweet Thai chili sauce mixed with guava jelly or
    rice vinegar
1 teaspoon chopped macadamia nuts
3 slivers green onion

Lightly toast or grill the bread on both sides. Spread one side with the mayonnaise. Sprinkle with the cheese and place under the broiler until the cheese melts (do not brown). Add the tomato slice and sauce, and return to the broiler to brown the top. Garnish with the nuts and green onion. *Yield: 1 serving.*

Chalet Kilauea — The Inn at Volcano

Lisha and Brian Crawford
Box 998, Wright Road
Volcano, Hawaii 96785
Tel: (808) 967-7786
Fax: (808) 967-8660
E-mail: Reservations@
Volcano-Hawaii.com
$$$$

ABOUT THE B&B

*E*xplore treasures from around the world at Chalet Kilauea, a lush Hawaiian haven nestled in Volcano Village. Owners Lisha and Brian Crawford are international travelers who know the art of hospitality. At the inn, choose from superior rooms inspired by Oriental, African, or European themes, or the Treehouse Suite, with most featuring marble Jacuzzis. Tempt your appetite with a candlelit, two-course gourmet breakfast featuring local and international cuisine. Luxuriate in the Jacuzzi, relax by the fireplace, peruse the library, or wander in the garden. The spacious vacation homes are particularly suited for families, larger parties, and those seeking complete privacy. All offer a full kitchen and include afternoon tea and use of the Jacuzzi. Near the inn, you'll find Hawaii Volcanoes National Park, Black Sand Beach, and the city of Hilo with all its splendors. Opportunities abound for lava viewing, hiking, biking, golfing, swimming, bird watching, exploring, and just plain unwinding!

SEASON

all year

ACCOMMODATIONS

six rooms with private baths;
six vacation homes

The Heirloom

Melisande Hubbs and Patricia Cross
214 Shakeley Lane
Ione, California 95640
Tel: (209) 274-4468
$$ – $$$

ABOUT THE B&B

Down a country lane to an expansive English romantic garden is a touch of the old south. The Heirloom is a brick, two-story southern antebellum home, circa 1863, located in the heart of California gold country. It was built by Virginians who came to California during the Gold Rush to be merchants in Ione, the supply center of the mining camps of Amador County. Sweet magnolias, wisteria, hammocks, croquet, verandas, cozy fireplaces, and heirloom antiques (including a historic piano) await you, not to mention a royal breakfast and gracious hospitality. Near the inn are over 20 wineries, Gold Rush historical points, museums, and nature walks, and opportunities for gourmet dining, gold panning, gliding, and hiking.

SEASON

all year

ACCOMMODATIONS

four rooms with private baths; two rooms with shared bath

Heart-Healthy Spinach Soufflé

4 tablespoons butter or margarine
2 green onions, chopped
2 cubes chicken bouillon
2 tablespoons all-purpose flour
½ teaspoon salt
½ teaspoon pepper
Dash of grated nutmeg
2 cups milk
1 cup grated Swiss cheese
20 ounces frozen spinach, cooked and squeezed dry
8 egg whites

Preheat the oven to 350°F. Melt the butter in a large saucepan. Sauté the green onions. Add the bouillon cubes. Add the flour and seasonings, and mix well. Add the milk to make a sauce. When slightly thickened, add the cheese. Heat until the cheese is melted and mixed in well. Add the spinach. Beat the egg whites until they stand in soft peaks. Fold into the spinach mixture. Pour into an ungreased soufflé dish or individual dishes. Place in a water bath. Bake 40 – 50 minutes. *Yield: 6 servings.*

Huevos Rancheros

(*Recipe from* A Baker's Dozen Breakfast Favorites.)

"The green chili stew is great by itself or on top of most anything. We especially like it with our huevos rancheros." — *Susan Vernon*

Butter
4 blue or yellow corn tortillas
1⅓ cups cooked pinto beans, warmed
4 eggs, poached
¾ cup grated Monterey Jack or mild cheddar cheese
1 cup green chili stew (see recipe below)
4 strips bacon, cooked well done and crumbled
Sour cream

Melt some butter in a skillet and lightly cook the tortillas to soften. Assemble in equal quantities on each of 4 warmed plates: a tortilla on the bottom, beans spread on the tortilla, a poached egg, grated cheese, green chili stew, and crumbled bacon. Top with a dollop of sour cream.
Yield: 4 servings.

Green chili stew:
1 pound ground pork
3 cloves garlic, crushed
6 tablespoons all-purpose flour
2 pounds mild green chilies, freshly roasted, peeled, and chopped or
    2 (16-ounce) cans chopped green chilies
2 teaspoons ground cumin
Salt to taste

(continued on next page)

Casa de las Chimeneas
Bed & Breakfast Inn

Susan Vernon
Box 5303, 405 Cordoba Road
Taos, New Mexico 87571
Tel: (505) 758-4777
Fax: (505) 758-3976
E-mail: casa@newmex.com
$$$$

ABOUT THE B&B

Written up by many magazines, newspapers, and guidebooks over the years, Casa de las Chimeneas (House of Chimneys Inn) has earned an enviable reputation for luxurious accommodations and delicious breakfast fare. Only a short walk from Taos's historic plaza, this hacienda-style B&B is set off from the town by seven-foot adobe walls. The grounds of this oasis are adorned with lovingly tended gardens, featuring more than 2,400 bulbs and countless perennials. Each guest room features a pueblo-style fireplace, private bath, and a private entrance, plus special attention to detail — such as lace-trimmed linens and hand-painted bathroom tiles. Common areas feature regional art, tiled hearths, French doors, and traditional ceiling beams (called "vigas"). The Southwestern influence is also felt at the Casa's breakfast table, where house specialties include huevos rancheros with green chili stew and blue corn pancakes with fresh berries. Innkeeper Susan Vernon is an avid gardener and enjoys sharing her love of horticulture.

SEASON

all year

ACCOMMODATIONS

six rooms (including one suite)
with private baths

Brown the ground pork. Drain the fat into a large pot. Sauté the garlic in the fat. Add the flour and stir until the mixture is brown. Add the green chilies, pork, cumin, and salt. Add water to cover. Cook at least 30 minutes or until hot and bubbling. *Tip:* This stew freezes well. *Yield: 6 – 7 cups.*

Italian Eggs with Asparagus and Smoked Ham

¼ cup butter
1 cup sliced mushrooms
¼ pound smoked ham, cubed
1 clove garlic, chopped
⅓ medium green bell pepper, chopped
½ pound asparagus, chopped
8 eggs
1 tablespoon minced fresh basil
½ teaspoon dried oregano
Pinch of salt and pepper
⅓ teaspoon crushed red pepper (optional)
4 ounces cream cheese
4 ounces mozzarella cheese, grated
¼ cup grated Parmesan cheese

In a large skillet, heat ½ of the butter. Add the mushrooms, ham, garlic, and green pepper. Sauté over medium heat until the vegetables are tender. Remove with a slotted spoon and set aside. Blanch the asparagus until crisp tender. Whisk together the eggs, herbs, and seasonings. Add the cream cheese in small pieces. Just before serving, heat the remaining butter in a skillet and add the egg mixture, folding with a spatula to blend the cream cheese. When the eggs are half set, add the vegetable mixture, mozzarella, Parmesan, and drained asparagus. Continue to cook gently, folding with a spatula until the eggs are just done. Serve immediately. *Yield: 8 servings.*

Glynn House
Victorian Inn

Betsy and Karol Paterman
43 Highland Street, PO Box 719
Ashland, New Hampshire 03217
Tel: (800) 637-9599 or (603) 968-3775
E-mail: glynnhse@lr.net
www.nettx.com/glynnhouse.html
$$ – $$$

ABOUT THE B&B

*C*ome enjoy the gracious elegance of this beautifully restored 1890 Queen Anne home — from the cupola of the inn's tower and gingerbread wraparound veranda to the carved oak foyer and pocket doors. Each of the beautifully appointed bedrooms has its own distinctive mood, distinguished by unique interior design, period furniture, the fragrance of fresh flowers, and soft, fluffy robes. A memorable full breakfast is served in the dining room, consisting perhaps of eggs Benedict or eggs Neptune, Belgian waffles, thick French toast, ambrosia, juice, and the specialty of the house — strudel. After breakfast, take a walk or boat ride around famous Squam Lake (where the movie On Golden Pond was filmed) just a few minutes away, and enjoy all that the Lakes Region and White Mountains have to offer. Allow Betsy and Karol to provide hospitality with a warm smile and make you feel as though you're part of their family.

SEASON

all year

ACCOMMODATIONS

eight rooms with private baths

Al Hammond
320 Woods Hole Road
Woods Hole, Massachusetts 02543
Tel: (508) 548-6218
Fax: (508) 457-7519
$$$

ABOUT THE B&B

The Marlborough is a romantic Cape Cod cottage complete with picket fence, trellis, and garden set up on a hill among the trees. Rooms have private baths and are individually decorated with quilts, coordinated scented linens, and collectibles. Gather for conversation, read, or watch television in the large comfortable parlor. Full gourmet breakfast, including wonderfully brewed coffee and tea, is served outside by the kidney-shaped pool or inside by the fireplace, depending on the season. Informal afternoon tea is served in season, while high tea is served on Sundays in the off-season. Excellent restaurants are nearby, as is Woods Hole Oceanographic Institute, beaches, shopping, bike paths, and ferries to Martha's Vineyard. The Marlborough is a great starting point for day trips to locations all over Cape Cod and the islands, Plymouth, Boston, and Providence. Innkeeper Al Hammond enjoys helping guests get the most out of their visit. A long-time veteran of the foodservice industry, Al enjoys cooking and learning about Cape Cod history.

SEASON

all year

ACCOMMODATIONS

five rooms with private baths

Marlborough Egg-stuffed Bakers

6 large baking potatoes, scrubbed
½ cup butter, melted
12 eggs, lightly beaten
2 cups chopped broccoli, cooked and drained
2 tablespoons diced green onion or snipped chives
1½ cups grated Monterey Jack cheese

Warm corn muffins (see recipe on page 64)

Bake the potatoes in a preheated 400°F oven 45 – 60 minutes. Test with a fork for doneness (the potatoes should be cooked, but firm). Cool slightly. Cut the potatoes in ½ lengthwise. Run a knife around the inside edge of each potato, about ¼" inside the skin to loosen the pulp, and then scoop out the pulp with a spoon, leaving a potato shell (save the potato pulp for home fries or hash). Using a pastry brush, brush some of the melted butter inside and on the outside of the potato shells. Put the shells back into the oven on a cookie sheet for 15 minutes to brown slightly.

(continued on next page)

Meanwhile, pour the remaining butter into a heavy skillet and heat until bubbly. Add the eggs and stir until firm but not dry. Turn off the heat. Add the broccoli and green onions. When the potato shells have browned, remove from the oven and fill with the egg mixture, dividing it equally between the 12 potato halves. Top with the grated cheese and place under a broiler until the cheese is bubbly. Serve hot with warm corn muffins. *Tips:* Egg substitute can be used in place of the eggs, margarine in place of the butter, and low-sodium/low-fat cheese in place of the regular cheese for a heart-healthy entrée. The potatoes can be prepared a day ahead and kept covered with foil and refrigerated. They need only be browned and stuffed before serving. *Yield: 6 servings.*

7 Gables Inn

Leicha and Paul Welton
PO Box 80488
Fairbanks, Alaska 99708
Tel: (907) 479-0751
Fax: (907) 479-2229
E-mail: gables7@alaska.net
www.alaska.net/~gables7
$$ – $$$

ABOUT THE B&B

This 10,000 square foot Tudor-style house is located within walking distance of the University of Alaska Fairbanks campus, which is probably why 7 Gables began as a fraternity house. Its convenient location (between the airport and train station) is further enhanced by being right in the middle of a number of major attractions in the area: Riverboat Discovery, Pump House Restaurant, Cripple Creek Resort, University Museum, and Alaskaland. You enter the B&B through a floral solarium into a foyer with antique stained glass and an indoor waterfall. Other features include cathedral ceilings, wine cellar, and wedding chapel. Some additional amenities include laundry facilities, Jacuzzis, in-room cable TV and phones, canoes, bikes, gourmet breakfasts, luggage or game storage, and library collection. Leicha enjoys cooking, music, hosting parties, and learning foreign languages, while Paul collects books and manages the inn's marketing and maintenance.

SEASON

all year

ACCOMMODATIONS

12 rooms with private baths

McKinley Breakfast

"This recipe is jokingly called the 'McKinley Breakfast' (after the mountain), because of the peaks of the sandwich. It's an easy dish to fix and an interesting twist on the traditional ham and egg breakfast." — Leicha Welton

1 cup chopped ham
1 cup grated cheddar cheese
1 tablespoon Dijon mustard
¼ cup mayonnaise
6 slices whole wheat bread
3 eggs
1½ cups milk

In a medium bowl, combine the ham, cheese, mustard, and mayonnaise. Make 3 sandwiches with this ham mixture. Cut each sandwich diagonally into 4 triangular pieces. Place the sandwich pieces with their points sticking up (like mountain peaks) in a glass baking dish sprayed with nonstick cooking spray. In another bowl, combine the eggs and milk. Pour over the sandwich pieces, making sure that the mixture soaks the bread. Refrigerate overnight. Remove from the refrigerator ¾ hour before baking. Bake in a preheated 325°F oven for 40 minutes.
Yield: 6 servings.

Ozarks Eggs Benedict

"This long time holiday breakfast favorite of my mom's family looks beautiful, tastes great, and warmly satisfies. It's also the easiest breakfast I know to make!" — Jacquelyn Smyers

2 eggs, hard boiled and with the eggs and whites separated
2 tablespoons butter
2 tablespoons all-purpose flour
¼ teaspoon salt
¼ teaspoon pepper
1 cup milk
¼ – ½ cup cubed ham, crumbled crisp bacon, or cooked pork breakfast
    sausage bits (optional)
4 slices toast
Mint sprigs

Grate the egg yolks into a dish and cut the whites into medium chunks in another dish. Melt the butter over low heat. Add the flour, stir to blend, then add the salt and pepper. Add the milk all at once, stirring well. Continue to stir over medium heat until the sauce bubbles and gets thick. Add the meat if wished. Remove from the heat; add egg white chunks. Place 2 pieces of toast on each of 2 plates. Spoon the sauce across both slices and top with the grated egg yolk. Garnish with the mint sprigs. *Tip:* If the sauce needs to be warmed in the microwave oven, be careful not to overdo it or the egg whites will become terribly tough. *Yield: 2 servings.*

Brambly Hedge Cottage

Jacquelyn Smyers
HCR 31, Box 39
Jasper, Arkansas 72641
Tel: 1-800-BRAMBLY or
(501) 446-5849
$$

ABOUT THE B&B

"*A*bsolutely charming," wrote National Geographic Traveler *of this old Ozark mountaintop farmhouse, four miles south of Jasper, Arkansas. A Tennessee guest commented, "The place is uniquely beautiful, the food delicious, and the view inspiring." Three guest rooms with private baths reflect country French elegance in a homestead log cabin. A full breakfast is served on the deck overlooking Buffalo River Valley or behind the screened porch in rocking chairs. You're only minutes from the "Grand Canyon of the Ozarks," challenging-to-easy hiking trails, and canoeing on Buffalo National River. If art is more your style, you'll find the work of true artisans in the Jasper area. For those who wish to sample a night out on the town, Eureka Springs and Branson (Missouri) are nearby. Small group special-interest tours and relaxing massages can be arranged. Hostess Jacquelyn Smyers includes her hand-made tatted lace and samovar collection in the decor. She's also a designer, commercial artist, and author of* Come For Tea *and the children's book* The Cloud That Came Into The Cabin *(inspired by the clouds on Sloan Mountain where Brambly Hedge is located).*

SEASON

all year

ACCOMMODATIONS

three rooms with private baths

Turtleback Farm Inn

Susan and William Fletcher
Route 1, Box 650
Eastsound (Orcas Island),
Washington 98245
Tel: (800) 376-4914 or (360) 376-4914
Fax: (360) 376-5329
$$ – $$$$

ABOUT THE B&B

Located on the loveliest of the San Juan Islands, Turtleback Farm Inn is noted for its detail-perfect restoration, elegantly comfortable rooms, glorious setting, and award-winning breakfasts. A short ferry ride from Anacortes, Washington, Orcas Island is a haven for anyone who enjoys spectacular scenery, varied outdoor activities, unique shopping, and superb food. As spring turns into summer, the warm days encourage you to enjoy nature and island life at their best: Flowers are in full bloom, birds flutter, and whales, seals, and porpoises lazily coast through the shimmering waters of the Sound. After a day of hiking, fishing, bicycling, kayaking, sailing, windsurfing, or just reading by the inn's pond, enjoy a relaxing soak in your private bath or a sherry on the deck overlooking the valley below. After a tasty dinner at one of the Island's many fine restaurants, snuggle down under one of the inn's custom-made woolen comforters and peacefully doze off — with visions of the delicious breakfast awaiting you in the morning.

SEASON

all year

ACCOMMODATIONS

11 rooms (including four suites)
with private baths

Picture-Perfect Breakfast Pizza

1 red bell pepper, thinly sliced
1 yellow bell pepper, thinly sliced
1 green bell pepper, thinly sliced
1 medium onion, thinly sliced
1 cup diced ham
1½ tablespoons butter

Dough:
2 cups all-purpose flour
1 tablespoon baking powder
Pinch of salt
½ cup butter, cold, cut into bits
1 cup half-and-half

6 medium eggs
2 cups grated cheese (raw milk cheddar or any medium to sharp cheese)

(continued on next page)

Sauté the peppers, onion, and ham in the butter in a skillet until the peppers and the onion become soft. Set aside.

Preheat the oven to 425°F. In the work bowl of a food processor (using the steel blade), blend the dough's flour, baking powder, and salt with the butter until the mixture resembles coarse meal. Add the half-and-half through the feed tube and blend briefly until the dough begins to gather into a ball. Remove the dough and pat into a round on a floured board. Let rest a few minutes, then divide into 6 equal pieces. Roll each piece on the floured board into an 8" round. Pinch the outside edge up into a ½" rim around each circle. (The diameter of each round will now be a little over 5".)

Transfer each round to a buttered cookie sheet, top with the pepper mixture, leaving a well in the center. Break an egg into each center and top with about ⅓ cup grated cheese. Bake 15 minutes or until the eggs are set, then serve immediately. *Yield: 6 servings.*

The Oval Door

Judith McLane and Dianne Feist
988 Lawrence Street
Eugene, Oregon 97401
Tel: (800) 882-3160 or (541) 683-3160
Fax: (541) 485-5339
$$ – $$$

ABOUT THE B&B

This early 20th-century farmhouse-style home with a two-sided wraparound porch is actually newly built, yet its vintage 1920s design fits into the neighborhood so well that people are surprised to learn it was built circa 1990! Each of the four spacious guest rooms features a private bath. In addition, guests can enjoy the Tub Room — a whirlpool bath for two, with bubbles, candles, and music. Newly decorated and inviting, the common living room has a fireplace and the library offers comfortable chairs for watching TV, using the VCR, or browsing through the travel books. Located just three blocks from the city's center, it's an easy walk to the Hult Center for the Performing Arts, many of Eugene's fine restaurants and shops, and a short drive to the University of Oregon. Guests enjoy a full breakfast served in the dining room. Extra touches include terry robes, Perrier, and candies.

SEASON

all year

ACCOMMODATIONS

four rooms with private baths

Popeye's Morning

2 (10-ounce) cans cream of potato soup
2 cups sour cream
40 ounces frozen chopped spinach
8 eggs
1 cup grated Monterey Jack cheese

Preheat the oven to 325°F. Mix the soup and sour cream. Defrost the spinach in the microwave oven; squeeze well to drain excess liquid. Add to the soup mixture, mixing well. Divide equally into 8 individual au gratin dishes sprayed with nonstick cooking spray. Make an indentation in the middle of each dish and break an egg into the space. Sprinkle with the grated cheese. Bake 25 – 30 minutes or until the eggs are set and the spinach is bubbly. *Yield: 8 servings.*

The Oval Door Bed & Breakfast Inn

Saffron Cream Eggs

2 cups heavy cream
¼ cup butter (do not use salted)
½ cup grated sharp cheddar cheese
½ teaspoon white pepper
½ teaspoon cayenne pepper
½ teaspoon paprika
½ teaspoon ground cinnamon
½ teaspoon seasoned salt
⅛ teaspoon powdered saffron
12 eggs, lightly beaten
¼ cup pecans

In a skillet, heat the cream and butter to make a base sauce, then add the cheese. Let thicken. Blend in the seasonings, then pour the eggs gently into the sauce and soft scramble. Sprinkle the pecans on top before serving. *Yield: 6 servings.*

Saltair Bed and Breakfast

Nancy Saxton and Jan Bartlett
164 South 900 East
Salt Lake City, Utah 84102
Tel: (800) 733-8184 or (801) 533-8184
Fax: (801) 595-0332
$$ – $$$

ABOUT THE B&B

*L*isted on the National Register *of Historic Places, this 1903 Victorian house is the oldest continuously operating B&B in Utah and has hosted many dignitaries. The comfortably elegant house is furnished with period antiques, handmade quilts, and highlighted with wood and beveled glass. Room amenities include fresh flowers, saltwater taffy, terry cloth robes, and down comforters. Guests enjoy a warming fire in the parlor, a summer breeze on the front porch swing, or a Salt Lake starlit night in the B&B's hot tub. Breakfast may include cereal and yogurt, fruit, coffee or tea, a hot entrée, and a fruit smoothie. Located in a friendly residential neighborhood, Saltair is one mile west of the University of Utah, the historic downtown Salt Lake area, Temple Square, and the Utah Symphony Concert Hall, and is near Utah Jazz basketball, museums, theaters, and shopping. Seven ski resorts are 35 minutes away, while canyons for hiking and mountain biking are 10 minutes away.*

SEASON

all year

ACCOMMODATIONS

two rooms with private baths;
three rooms with shared bath

Hoyt House
Bed and Breakfast

Rita and John Kovacevich
804 Atlantic Avenue
Amelia Island, Florida 32034
Tel: (800) 432-2085 or (904) 277-4300
Fax: (904) 277-9626
E-mail: hoythouse@
b&b.net-magic.net
www.hoythouse.com
$$$ – $$$$

ABOUT THE B&B

Stroll up the brick path, enter through the double Yankee doors, and pass into the elegance and charm of a home from a bygone era. Built in 1905 using only the finest materials and craftsmen, Hoyt House is an example of Queen Anne-style architecture that demonstrates an attention to detail and quality that is rare. Guest chambers, some with fireplaces, are each unique in style, blending antique furnishings, current reproductions, custom-designed window treatments, and inspiring colors. Breakfast begins with a beautiful table setting, fresh flowers, china, European-sized silverware, and fine table linens, and includes juice, fresh fruit, coffee, tea, homemade baked specialties, plus a gourmet breakfast entrée. Located in the heart of the downtown historic district, Hoyt House is steps away from shops, fine antique emporiums, the Museum of History, and many excellent restaurants. Amelia Island is home to golf, tennis, sportfishing, horseback riding, historic Fort Clinch, and miles of endless beach.

SEASON

all year

ACCOMMODATIONS

nine rooms with private baths

Salsa and Cheddar Eggs

"A quick and easy dish that never fails to please."
— *Rita and John Kovacevich*

6 eggs, well beaten
2 tablespoons water
½ cup salsa (see recipe below)
½ cup grated cheddar cheese
3 English muffins
Butter
Hot sauce to taste, such as Tabasco (optional)
Paprika to taste

Cooked bacon or sausage

In a large bowl, lightly beat the eggs, water, salsa, and cheddar cheese together. Spray 4 microwave-safe soufflé dishes with nonstick cooking spray. Distribute the egg mixture evenly among the dishes. Cover with plastic wrap and cook 2 at a time in the microwave on ¾ power for about 7 minutes or until set, turning once or twice. Split, toast, butter, then halve the English muffins. Place 3 halves on a plate then invert the soufflé dish over them — the egg should fall out of the dish. Top with some hot sauce, if desired, and garnish with paprika. Serve with cooked bacon or sausage. *Yield: 4 servings.*

(continued on next page)

Hoyt House salsa:
½ cup chopped onion
1 green bell pepper, finely chopped
1 clove garlic, minced
Olive oil
1 tomato, chopped
4-ounce can green chilies, chopped
¼ teaspoon dried oregano
⅛ teaspoon salt
8-ounce can tomato sauce

Sauté the onion, green pepper, and garlic in the oil. Combine this vegetable mixture with the tomato, chilies, oregano, and salt in a blender or food processor. Blend for 2 or 3 seconds. Add the tomato sauce and mix well.

Hutton House

Loretta Murray and Dean Ahren
PO Box 88, Route 250/219
Huttonsville, West Virginia 26273
Tel: (304) 335-6701
$$

ABOUT THE B&B

Majestically situated above the tiny town of Huttonsville, this meticulously restored turn-of-the-century Queen Anne Victorian commands a broad view of the Tygart River Valley and the Laurel Mountains. Hutton House, which is listed in the National Register of Historic Places, features original oak woodwork, ornate windows, a three-story turret, arched pocket doors, wraparound porch, and a winding staircase. Antiques abound, and each of the guest rooms is furnished in its own individual style. Breakfast is a time to get to know your hosts and the other guests, while enjoying a variety of pancake, French toast, and egg dishes along with fresh fruit, crème brûlée, sorbet, or even porridge. Guests can then relax on the porch, play games on the lawn, or take a leisurely hike on the trail behind the house. Nearby attractions include Cass Railroad, National Radio Observatory, underground caverns, and rock climbing.

SEASON

all year

ACCOMMODATIONS

six rooms with private baths

Sausage Madeira

10 – 12" hot Italian sausage
¼ cup Madeira wine
2 tablespoons butter
1 – 2 carrots, thinly sliced
½ medium onion (preferably sweet), thinly sliced

Fry the sausage thoroughly and let brown on all sides; set aside. Pour the sausage oil off of the pan. Deglaze the pan with the wine and butter, and cook until bubbly. Add the carrot and onion to the pan and cook until the carrots are soft but crisp and the onion is becoming translucent. Slice the sausage and add to the pan, and heat all together. Serve immediately. *Yield: 2 servings.*

Sausage Strudel

3 pounds bulk sage sausage
2 onions, chopped
3 pounds mushrooms, sliced
1½ cups cream cheese
20 leaves phyllo dough (5 per strudel)
½ cup butter, melted

Preheat the oven to 400°F. Fry the sausage and put in a large bowl. Fry the onions and mushrooms until just dry. Add to the bowl. Mix in the cream cheese. Layer 5 phyllo leaves with the butter and roll with ¼ of the sausage mixture. Repeat with the remaining phyllo leaves. Brush with butter before baking. Bake for 25 minutes. *Yield: 4 strudels, serving 20.*

The Rosewood Mansion Inn

Lynn and David Hausner
54 North Hood Street
Peru, Indiana 46970
Tel: (765) 472-7051
Fax: (765) 474-5575
E-mail: rosewood@netusa1.net
$$

ABOUT THE B&B

Built by Elbert Shirk in 1872, The Rosewood Mansion Inn is a lovely Victorian home situated near downtown Peru, Indiana. The mansion has 19 rooms, including 11 bedrooms, each with private bath. As a welcome change from impersonal hotel or motel accommodations, the inn offers the warmth and friendliness of home, coupled with the privacy and elegance of a fine hotel — a combination that makes for a truly unique experience. Enjoy the warmth of the oak-paneled library, the splendor of the three-story staircase with stained glass windows, the elegance of the Victorian parlor, and the comfort and charm of your room. Consider Rosewood Mansion for your next romantic getaway, anniversary, party, business meeting, or corporate retreat. Nearby points of interest include Mississinewa Reservoir (featuring boating, fishing, hiking, picnicking, and water-skiing), Miami County Museum, International Circus Hall of Fame, Cole Porter's home and burial site, tennis, golf, and antique shops.

SEASON

all year

ACCOMMODATIONS

11 rooms with private baths

The Ancient Pines B&B

Genevieve Simmens
2015 Parley Street
Nauvoo, Illinois 62354
Tel: (217) 453-2767

$

ABOUT THE B&B

Surrounded by 140-year-old evergreens, this turn-of-the-century home features exquisite exterior brick detailing, stained glass windows, and etched glass front door — all part of the original construction. Pressed tin ceilings, carved woodwork, an open staircase, claw-foot tubs, and lovingly decorated bedrooms grace the interior. You can relax on the front veranda and watch the workers at the nearby winery or find seclusion on the side porch. There are herb and flower gardens to wander in, a lawn for croquet, and a library for playing chess or music. When the day is done, you'll drift off in clean, comfortable beds, lulled to sleep by the whispering pines, then awake to the smell of baking bread. A heart-healthy menu can be provided upon request.

SEASON

all year

ACCOMMODATIONS

three rooms with shared baths

Scrambled Eggs with Ham and Onions

1 tablespoon butter
1 medium onion, thinly sliced
8 ounces ham, cubed
8 eggs, lightly beaten
¼ cup milk

Melt the butter in a skillet. Add the onion and sauté for 5 minutes. Add the ham and cook 5 minutes, stirring constantly. Combine the eggs with the milk, then add to the skillet. Cook, stirring, until done but still soft (do not brown). *Yield: 6 servings.*

Southwestern Eggs Fiesta

12 eggs
3 (6" diameter) flour tortillas
6 ounces cheddar cheese, sliced
Crumbled cooked bacon or bacon bits
Chopped cilantro (also known as coriander)
Sour cream
Mild salsa
Parsley

Preheat the oven to 375°F. Grease 6 individual (5 – 8 ounce) soufflé dishes with nonstick cooking spray and break 2 eggs into each dish. Slice the tortillas in ½ and place around the insides of the soufflé dishes (a ½ tortilla per dish), with the rounded edge sticking up out of the dish. Top with a slice of cheddar cheese and sprinkle with bacon and a dash of cilantro. Bake for 30 minutes or until the eggs are set, the cheese is melted, and the tortilla is slightly brown. Top with a dab of sour cream and a teaspoon of mild salsa. Sprinkle a dash of cilantro on top and serve on a plate. Garnish with parsley. *Yield: 6 servings.*

Holden House — 1902 Bed & Breakfast Inn

Sallie and Welling Clark
1102 West Pikes Peak Avenue
Colorado Springs, Colorado 80904
Tel: (719) 471-3980
Fax: (719) 471-4740
E-mail: HoldenHouse@
worldnet.att.net
www.bbonline.com/co/holden/
$$$

ABOUT THE B&B

Experience the romance of the past with the comforts of today at Holden House — 1902 Bed & Breakfast Inn. This storybook Victorian and carriage house filled with antiques and family heirlooms is located in a residential area near the historic district and central to the Pikes Peak region. Enjoy the front parlor, living room with a fireplace and wingback chairs, or the wide veranda with mountain views. Immaculate suites boast queen-size beds, down pillows, private baths, tubs for two, and fireplaces. Enjoy complimentary refreshments, homemade cookies, and friendly resident cats Mingtoy and Muffin.

SEASON

all year

ACCOMMODATIONS

five suites with private baths

Durbin Street Inn B&B

Sherry and Don Frigon
843 South Durbin Street
Casper, Wyoming 82601
Tel: (307) 577-5774
Fax: (307) 266-5441
E-mail: Dfrigon@trib.com
$$

ABOUT THE B&B

Built in 1917, Durbin Street Inn *is a large two-story American foursquare located in Casper's historic district. The inn prides itself on good food and a friendly atmosphere. Choose from four large non-smoking guest rooms with shared baths. Each room has queen-size or double beds, robes, and one has a fireplace. Or, you can choose the non-smoking guest room with private bath, small sitting room, and refrigerator. Awake to a full country breakfast where scrambled eggs, bacon, sausage, hash browns, fruit juice, homemade jams, and such specialties as honey-wheat pancakes, biscuits and gravy, scones, brunch omelet torte, spicy sausage and potatoes, and roast beef hash are served family-style. After breakfast, gather in the common room by the fireplace, or enjoy the deck, patio, and flower and vegetable gardens. Nearby are walking, hiking, cycling trails, river rafting and canoeing, golfing, swimming, fishing, skiing, shopping, covered wagon and horseback trips along the Oregon Trail, museums, historic sites, Fort Casper, Independence Rock, Devil's Gate, and Hell's Half Acre.*

SEASON

all year

ACCOMMODATIONS

four rooms with shared baths;
one room with private bath

Spicy Sausage and Potatoes

1½ pounds (about 6 links) mild Italian sausage, cut into 1" pieces and
    marinated overnight in ½ cup Chianti wine
10 small new red potatoes, quartered
½ teaspoon pepper
½ teaspoon thyme
1 clove garlic, minced
1 red onion, sliced ⅛" thick (about 1 cup)
1 green bell pepper, cut into 1" pieces
¼ cup chopped fresh parsley

Scrambled eggs, sliced tomatoes, and wheat scones or cornbread

In a large skillet, combine the sausage, potatoes, pepper, thyme, and garlic. Cook over medium-high heat, stirring occasionally until the potatoes are browned (10 – 12 minutes). Reduce the heat to medium-low. Cover and cook until the potatoes are tender (8 – 10 minutes). Stir in the onion, green pepper, and parsley. Continue cooking, uncovered, until the vegetables are crisply tender (4 – 5 minutes). Serve with scrambled eggs, fresh garden tomatoes in season, sliced, and wheat scones or cornbread. *Yield: 6 servings.*

Sunday Soufflé

5 – 6 slices French bread, cubed
2 cups grated cheddar cheese
½ cup cubed ham or bulk pork breakfast sausage (optional)
4 eggs
1 teaspoon Worcestershire sauce
2 cups milk

Cover the bottom of a buttered 1½-quart baking dish with ½ of the bread cubes. Alternate layers of bread and cheese (and ham if you wish), ending with a top layer of cheese. Combine the eggs, Worcestershire sauce, and milk until well blended and pour over the dry mixture. Refrigerate overnight. Remove from the refrigerator ¾ hour before baking. Bake in a preheated 350°F oven for 1 hour or until golden brown. *Yield: 6 – 8 servings.*

Snug Harbor Inn

Laurine "Sis" and Kenneth Hill
1226 West 10th Avenue
Anchorage, Alaska 99501
Tel: (907) 272-6249
Fax: (907) 272-7100
$$

ABOUT THE B & B

S *nug Harbor Inn offers you cheerful comfort in a relaxed "home away from home" atmosphere, where absolute privacy is yours. Relax while surrounded by antiques, art, Alaskan artifacts, and period furnishings. The rooms feature handmade quilts and some have their own entrances. At this inn, a fully equipped kitchen, complimentary coffee, tea, and hot chocolate available 24 hours a day, color TV, and complimentary bicycles are at your disposal. The friendly, efficient staff has your every comfort in mind, making Snug Harbor the first choice for the business and pleasure traveler. Located in the heart of Anchorage, Snug Harbor is just four blocks from the central business district, and close to shopping, entertainment, fine dining, and sightseeing. The trail head for Anchorage's extensive bicycle and jogging paths is also nearby.*

SEASON

all year

ACCOMMODATIONS

four rooms with private baths;
two rooms with shared bath

1880 House

Elsie Collins
2 Seafield Lane, PO Box 648
Westhampton Beach,
New York 11978
Tel: (800) 346-3290 or (516) 288-1559
Fax: (516) 288-7696
$$$ – $$$$

ABOUT THE B&B

Tucked away in the village of Westhampton Beach stands 1880 House, a bed and breakfast country retreat that's the perfect place for a romantic hideaway, a weekend of privacy, or just a change of pace from city life. Only 90 minutes from Manhattan, 1880 House is ideally situated on Westhampton Beach's exclusive Seafield Lane. Amenities include a swimming pool and tennis court and you're only a short, brisk walk away from the ocean beach. Long a popular summer resort area, the Hamptons will more than satisfy your penchant for antique hunting, and also offer many outstanding restaurants and shops. Indoor tennis facilities are available locally and Guerney's International Health Spa and the scenic area of Montauk Point are nearby. 1880 House is not just a rural retreat but a home lovingly preserved by Mrs. Elsie Collins and filled with her antiques and personal touches.

SEASON

all year

ACCOMMODATIONS

three suites with private baths

Turkey Sausage Soufflé

1 pound turkey sausage
8-ounce can sliced mushrooms
2 large onions, sliced
16 slices whole wheat bread, crusts removed
1 pound sharp cheddar cheese, grated
5 eggs
2 cups milk
¼ teaspoon grated nutmeg
1 teaspoon dry mustard

Cook the sausage in a large skillet. When cooked, drain, crumble, and set aside. Sauté the mushrooms and onions together, then add to the sausage. Butter a 13 x 9" soufflé baking dish. Line the bottom with the bread. Layer ½ of the sausage mixture over the bread, then layer ½ of the grated cheese over the sausage mixture. Again, layer the bread, the rest of the sausage mixture, and the rest of the cheese, ending with a last layer of bread. Beat together the eggs, milk, nutmeg, and mustard, then pour over the bread in the dish. Refrigerate for 24 hours. Remove from the refrigerator ¾ hour before baking. Bake in a preheated 350°F oven for 1 hour or until a knife inserted in the center comes out clean.
Yield: 12 – 16 servings.

Vegetable-Cheese Soufflé

Roux:
¼ cup butter or margarine
¼ cup all-purpose flour
½ teaspoon salt
Dash of cayenne pepper
1 cup milk

8 ounces sharp cheddar cheese, grated
3 egg yolks
6 – 8 mushrooms, sliced
2 tablespoons diced red bell pepper
½ cup diced broccoli or asparagus tips
2 teaspoons olive oil
6 egg whites

Preheat the oven to 400°F. To make the roux: Melt the butter, then blend in the flour, salt, and cayenne pepper. Add the milk all at once. Cook over medium heat until the mixture thickens and bubbles. Remove from the heat.

Add the cheese, and stir until melted. Beat the egg yolks in a separate bowl until slightly thickened and paler yellow. Slowly add to the cheese mixture, stirring constantly. Reserve, cover, and keep warm. Sauté the mushrooms, red pepper, and broccoli in the olive oil, and reserve. Beat the egg whites until they stand in soft peaks. In a mixing bowl, add the cheese mixture to the vegetables and fold in the egg whites. Pour into an ungreased soufflé dish or 6 individual ramekins. Bake in a hot water bath 15 – 20 minutes or until the puffed "top hat" is lightly browned. Serve immediately. *Yield: 6 servings.*

Blue Harbor House, A Village Inn

Jody Schmoll and Dennis Hayden
67 Elm Street
Camden, Maine 04843-1904
Tel: (800) 248-3196 or (207) 236-3196
Fax: (207) 236-6523
E-mail: balidog@midcoast.com
www.blueharborhouse.com
$$$ – $$$$

ABOUT THE B&B

A classic village inn on the Maine Coast, the Blue Harbor House welcomes guests to relax in a restored 1810 Cape where yesterday's charms blend perfectly with today's comforts. The beautiful town of Camden, renowned for its spectacular setting where the mountains meet the sea, is just outside the door. The inn's bright and inviting guest rooms surround you with country antiques and hand-fashioned quilts — several even have canopy beds and whirlpool tubs. Breakfasts feature such specialties as lobster quiche, cheese soufflé, and blueberry pancakes with blueberry butter. As for dinner, guests can arrange to have a romantic candle-lit affair or an old-fashioned down-east lobster feed.

SEASON

all year

ACCOMMODATIONS

eight rooms with private baths; two carriage-house suites with private baths

The Manor at Taylor's Store
B&B Country Inn

Mary Lynn and Lee Tucker
Box 510,
8812 Washington Highway
Smith Mountain Lake,
Virginia 24184
Tel: (540) 721-3951
Fax: (540) 721-5243
E-mail: taylors@symweb.com
www.symweb.com/taylors
$$ – $$$$

ABOUT THE B&B

The Manor at Taylor's Store is an enchanting, historic 120-acre estate in the picturesque foothills of the Blue Ridge Mountains. Guests enjoy luxurious accommodations in the elegant plantation home replete with antiques. Special amenities include a hot tub, exercise room, billiard room, large-screen TV with movies, guest kitchen, and porches and fireplaces throughout. There are six private, spring-fed ponds on the property for swimming, fishing, and canoeing. Nearby, Smith Mountain Lake offers additional recreational opportunities. All guests are treated to a heart-healthy gourmet breakfast in the formal dining room with panoramic views of the countryside. Warm, southern hospitality has made The Manor at Taylor's Store one of the best-known B&B inns in Virginia.

SEASON

all year

ACCOMMODATIONS

seven suites with private baths;
two suites with shared bath;
one cottage for families/groups
with private bath

Virginia Ham Breakfast Soufflé

1 pound Virginia ham sausage or turkey sausage
4 green onions, chopped
1 – 2 cloves garlic, minced
16 ounces egg substitute
1 cup skim milk
¼ teaspoon salt
¼ teaspoon cayenne pepper
¾ teaspoon powdered mustard
½ cup grated sharp cheddar cheese
6 slices whole wheat bread, cubed

Cook the sausage, onions, and garlic in a large skillet until the sausage is browned; stir until the sausage crumbles. Drain the grease from the pan. Drain the sausage mixture well. Set aside. Combine the egg substitute and the milk, salt, cayenne, and mustard in a large bowl. Stir in the sausage mixture, cheese, and bread cubes. Spoon into 10 (6-ounce) ramekins or custard cups coated with cooking spray, then cover and chill overnight. Remove from the refrigerator ¾ hour before baking. Preheat the oven to 350°F. Bake uncovered for 30 minutes or until set. Serve immediately. *Yield: 10 servings.*

THE MANOR AT
TAYLOR'S
STORE

Zucchini-Turkey Sausage Split

1 pound zucchini, finely chopped
1 onion, chopped
14 ounces salsa
1 pound cheddar cheese, grated
1 cup mayonnaise
½ cup grated Parmesan cheese
1 pound turkey sausage, cooked and crumbled
2 eggs, lightly beaten
¼ cup chopped fresh parsley
2 cups bread or cracker crumbs
Salt and pepper
1 teaspoon oregano or chopped fresh herbs to taste
English muffin halves or corn biscuits

Mix the zucchini, onion, salsa, cheddar cheese, mayonnaise, Parmesan cheese, sausage, eggs, parsley, bread crumbs, salt and pepper, and oregano together. Spoon the mixture over split English muffins or corn biscuits. Broil until golden and serve hot. *Yield: 12 – 24 servings (more as hors d'oeuvres).*

The Babbling Brook Inn

Dan Floyd
1025 Laurel Street
Santa Cruz, California 95060
Tel: (800) 866-1131 or (408) 427-2437
Fax: (408) 458-0989
E-mail: lodging@
babblingbrookinn.com
$$$ – $$$$

ABOUT THE B&B

Cascading waterfalls, a meandering creek, and a romantic gazebo grace an acre of gardens, pines, and redwoods surrounding this secluded inn. Built in 1909 on the foundation of an 1870 tannery, a 1790 grist mill, and a 2,000-year old Indian fishing village, the Babbling Brook features rooms in country French decor, all with private bath, telephone, and television, and most with cozy fireplace, private deck, and outside entrance. Included in your stay is a large, country breakfast and afternoon wine and cheese, where the inn's prize-winning cookies await you on the tea cart in front of a roaring fireplace. Two blocks off Highway 1, the Babbling Brook is within walking distance of the beach, wharf, boardwalk, shops, tennis, running paths, and historic homes. Three golf courses and 200 restaurants are within 15 minutes' drive.

SEASON

all year

ACCOMMODATIONS

12 rooms with private baths

Spreads & Toppings

Apple Butter

(Recipe from What's Cooking at Carrington's Bluff.)

2 cups unsweetened applesauce
½ cup sugar
1 teaspoon ground cinnamon
¼ teaspoon ground allspice
Pinch of ground ginger
Pinch of ground cloves

Pear bread (see recipe on page 102)

In a saucepan, combine the applesauce, sugar, cinnamon, allspice, ginger, and cloves and bring to a boil. Reduce the heat and simmer for 1 hour. Cool. *Tip:* This butter is great served on pear bread. *Yield: 2½ cups.*

Carrington's Bluff B&B

Lisa and Edward Mugford
1900 David Street
Austin, Texas 78705
Tel: (800) 871-8908 or (512) 479-0638
Fax: (512) 476-4769
$$$

ABOUT THE B&B

The setting is Shoal Creek Bluff and an 1877 Texas farmhouse nestled in the arms of a 500-year-old oak tree. Today, Carrington's Bluff B&B offers Texas hospitality to make your stay delightful. Upon arrival, you'll find yourself surrounded by rooms filled with English and American antiques, handmade quilts, and the sweet smell of potpourri. The 35-foot front porch beckons you to sit among the plants and flowers and enjoy the gentle breezes with your morning coffee or afternoon tea. The smell of fresh-brewed gourmet coffee invites you to a breakfast that begins with fresh fruit and homemade granola served on fine English china. Homemade muffins or breads and a house specialty ensure you won't go away hungry. Carrington's Bluff is near the University of Texas and the State Capital grounds, just minutes from parks, hiking and biking trails, shopping, and wonderful restaurants.

SEASON

all year

ACCOMMODATIONS

eight rooms with private baths

Brambly Hedge Cottage

Jacquelyn Smyers
HCR 31, Box 39
Jasper, Arkansas 72641
Tel: 1-800-BRAMBLY or
(501) 446-5849
$$

ABOUT THE B&B

"*Absolutely charming,*" *wrote* National Geographic Traveler *of this old Ozark mountaintop farmhouse, four miles south of Jasper, Arkansas. A Tennessee guest commented, "The place is uniquely beautiful, the food delicious, and the view inspiring." Three guest rooms with private baths reflect country French elegance in a homestead log cabin. A full breakfast is served on the deck overlooking Buffalo River Valley or behind the screened porch in rocking chairs. You're only minutes from the "Grand Canyon of the Ozarks," challenging-to-easy hiking trails, and canoeing on Buffalo National River. If art is more your style, you'll find the work of true artisans in the Jasper area. For those who wish to sample a night out on the town, Eureka Springs and Branson (Missouri) are nearby. Small group special-interest tours and relaxing massages can be arranged. Hostess Jacquelyn Smyers includes her hand-made tatted lace and samovar collection in the decor. She's also a designer, commercial artist, and author of* Come For Tea *and the children's book* The Cloud That Came Into The Cabin *(inspired by the clouds on Sloan Mountain where Brambly Hedge is located).*

SEASON

all year

ACCOMMODATIONS

three rooms with private baths

Apricot-Date Fruit Spread

"Guests appreciate a really good sugarless spread for toast or pancakes." — Jacquelyn Smyers

⅓ – ½ cup dried apricots*
4 – 5 pitted dates
Water to cover

Toast or pancakes

*Canned apricots that are water-packed and slightly drained work fine in a pinch and don't need to be microwaved.

Put the dried apricots into a 2-cup glass measuring cup. Add the dates. Add water to cover. Cook in the microwave oven until the water boils and the fruit is steamed and softened. Insert a small electric drink mixer into the measuring cup and purée the fruit. Add more water, if needed, to make a spreadable consistency. *Tip:* Add more dates for a sweeter spread. *Yield: 1 generous cup.*

Blueberry-Cranberry Compote

½ cup fresh blueberries
½ cup fresh cranberries
½ cup sugar (or more if desired)
¼ cup port
¼ cup orange juice
Grated zest of 1 orange
Cornstarch (if necessary)

Waffles

In a medium saucepan, combine the berries, sugar, port, orange juice, and zest and simmer for ½ hour. Thicken with a little cornstarch if necessary. Serve warm with waffles. *Yield: About 1 cup.*

The Parsonage Inn

Elizabeth and Ian Browne
202 Main Street
East Orleans, Massachusetts 02643
Tel: (508) 255-8217
Fax: (508) 255-8216
$$$

ABOUT THE B&B

Dating back to around 1770, The Parsonage Inn was a vicarage in the 1880s and is now a romantic inn. Despite having been remodeled over the years, the house still retains the feeling of historic old Cape Cod. Each of the eight guest rooms (with its own private bath) is uniquely decorated with country antiques, quilts, stenciling, and fresh flowers. A delicious breakfast of waffles, French toast, crêpes, scones, muffins, and fresh fruit is served in the dining room or on the brick patio (a popular gathering place for guests). The Parsonage Inn is conveniently located close to Cape Cod's main attractions — Nauset Beach, the National Seashore, and the many bike paths that crisscross the Cape — and is within walking distance of fine restaurants and antique stores. Both innkeepers were born in England; Elizabeth was raised in Kenya and is a pianist and piano teacher, while Ian is an accountant and former medical group executive.

SEASON

all year

ACCOMMODATIONS

eight rooms with private baths

Volden Farm
Bed and Breakfast

JoAnne and Jim Wold
RR #2, Box 50
Luverne, North Dakota 58056
Tel: (701) 769-2275
$$ – $$$

ABOUT THE B&B

After living all over the world, JoAnne and Jim Wold settled "where we belong — on the wide open prairie of North Dakota." Here, they opened Volden Farm, a B&B with an old-world atmosphere, thanks to the Russian and Norwegian decor and collectibles, which reflect the hosts' heritage and interests. Part of the home was built in 1926, comprising the parlor, music room, library, and two guest bedrooms. A new addition was built in 1978 to include a fireplace and dining area overlooking miles of tranquil prairie land. Bedrooms are filled with family heirloom quilts and one-of-a-kind antiques. Also available is a separate small house called the Law Office — with a bath, limited kitchen facilities, and fabulous view — where Jim used to have his office. The Scandinavian breakfast takes advantage of fresh ingredients from the farm and garden. After breakfast, guests can wander through 300 acres of fields, woods, hills, coulees, and virgin prairie. JoAnne and Jim take pleasure in reading, gardening, singing, and raising animals.

SEASON

all year

ACCOMMODATIONS

two rooms with shared bath
in main house;
two rooms with shared bath
in private cottage

Chocolate-Peanut Butter Topping

4 squares semisweet chocolate
4 tablespoons honey
4 tablespoons chunky peanut butter

Fresh fruit or ice cream

Place all the ingredients in a microwave-safe dish and microwave on high power for 3 minutes. Stir and pour over fresh fruit or ice cream.
Yield: About 1 cup.

Crimson Sauce

1¼ cups sugar
6 tablespoons cornstarch
3 cups water
12-ounce can frozen cranberry juice concentrate
16 ounces frozen blueberries
2 pinches of ground cloves
1 teaspoon ground cinnamon

Pancakes, waffles, or ice cream

Combine the sugar and cornstarch in a large saucepan. Add the water, cranberry juice, blueberries, cloves, and cinnamon and stir often over medium heat until slightly thickened. Serve over pancakes, waffles, or ice cream. *Yield: 12 servings.*

Bedford's Covered Bridge Inn

Martha and Greg Lau
RD 2, Box 196
Schellsburg, Pennsylvania 15559
Tel: (814) 733-4093
$$ – $$$

ABOUT THE B&B

*S*ituated near Exit 11 of I-76 (the Pennsylvania Turnpike), Bedford's Covered Bridge Inn borders 4,000-acre Shawnee State Park, a lovely trout stream, and the Colvin covered bridge. From this idyllic location, guests can pursue hiking, biking, fishing, cross-country skiing, birding, and antique hunting right from the inn's door. Nearby swimming and boating on Shawnee Lake, visits to Old Bedford Village and Bedford's historic district, driving tours, downhill skiing at Blue Knob Resort, and tours of Bedford's 14 covered bridges round out the list of local activities. Inside the inn, the Lau's attention to detail creates an atmosphere that is comfortable and inviting. The historic farmhouse (circa 1823) boasts six guest rooms with private baths, traditional and country decor, and memorable breakfasts. "There's no doubt what everyone's favorite activity is," say Greg and Martha, "Sitting on the inn's wrap-around porch and wishing they could live in Bedford County, too!"

SEASON

all year

ACCOMMODATIONS

six rooms with private baths;
one cottage for couples or families

Carrington's Bluff B&B

Lisa and Edward Mugford
1900 David Street
Austin, Texas 78705
Tel: (800) 871-8908 or (512) 479-0638
Fax: (512) 476-4769
$$$

ABOUT THE B&B

The setting is Shoal Creek Bluff and an 1877 Texas farmhouse nestled in the arms of a 500-year-old oak tree. Today, Carrington's Bluff B&B offers Texas hospitality to make your stay delightful. Upon arrival, you'll find yourself surrounded by rooms filled with English and American antiques, handmade quilts, and the sweet smell of potpourri. The 35-foot front porch beckons you to sit among the plants and flowers and enjoy the gentle breezes with your morning coffee or afternoon tea. The smell of fresh-brewed gourmet coffee invites you to a breakfast that begins with fresh fruit and homemade granola served on fine English china. Homemade muffins or breads and a house specialty ensure you won't go away hungry. Carrington's Bluff is near the University of Texas and the State Capital grounds, just minutes from parks, hiking and biking trails, shopping, and wonderful restaurants.

SEASON

all year

ACCOMMODATIONS

eight rooms with private baths

Devonshire Cream

(Recipe from What's Cooking at Carrington's Bluff.*)*

8 ounces sour cream
½ cup confectioners' sugar
1½ teaspoons vanilla
1 cup whipping cream

Fresh fruit or breakfast breads

Whip the sour cream, sugar, vanilla, and whipping cream together and refrigerate. Serve on fresh fruit or breakfast breads. *Yield: 2 cups.*

Fresh Berry Syrup

"We often serve this with French toast that's stuffed with the same fruit as the syrup." — Muffy Vhay

1¼ cups juice from your choice of strawberries, blueberries, blackberries, elderberries, or raspberries
1½ cups sugar
¼ cup white corn syrup
1 tablespoon lemon juice

Fruit-stuffed French toast

Note: Adapt the basic recipe to the amount of juice you have. Don't make more than you can fit in a water-bath canner in 1 load.

Extract the juice (as for jelly making) from the fruit by bringing the fruit to a boil and simmering until soupy. Strain through a jelly bag (if the fruit is dry, add up to ½ cup water for each cup of fruit). Or, use a steam extractor and follow the manufacturer's directions. Combine the juice with the sugar, corn syrup, and lemon juice in a large, heavy kettle. Bring to a rolling boil and boil for 1 minute. Remove it from the heat, skim off any foam, and pour into hot, sterile canning jars. Seal the jars with 2-piece canning lids, and process in a boiling water bath for 10 minutes (add 10 minutes more if you're over 5,000 feet altitude). Store in a cool, dark, dry place. Discard if mold develops. Refrigerate after opening. Multiply the recipe for the amount of syrup required. *Yield: 1¼ pints.*

Deer Run Ranch Bed and Breakfast

Muffy and David Vhay
5440 Eastlake Boulevard
Washoe Valley,
Carson City, Nevada 89704
Tel: (702) 882-3643
$$$

ABOUT THE B&B

Relax and unwind on 200 of the most beautiful acres in western Nevada. This working alfalfa ranch is located just eight miles north of Carson City and 22 miles south of Reno, Nevada. Watch the deer in the fields, enjoy the smell of western sage, and listen for the night cry of coyotes. This architect-designed western ranch house, shaded by tall cottonwood trees, overlooks a pond, Washoe Valley, and the Sierra Nevada Mountains to the west. Two comfortable guest rooms have queen-size beds, private baths, window seats, spectacular views, and lots of privacy. Both guest rooms share the sitting room with a wood-burning stove, dining area, guest refrigerator, TV/VCR, and other amenities. The owners' pottery studio and woodshop are also on the premises. Full ranch breakfasts include house specialties and fresh fruit and vegetables from the garden. Recreation at the ranch includes swimming, horseshoes, hiking, biking, and ice skating on the pond in winter. Deer Run is conveniently located near golf, skiing, casinos and show theaters, and many excellent restaurants.

SEASON

all year

ACCOMMODATIONS

two rooms with private baths

Thistle Hill
Bed & Breakfast

Mary and Dave Hendricks
Route 1, Box 93
Wakeeney, Kansas 67672-9736
Tel: (785) 743-2644
$$

ABOUT THE B&B

Described as "an oasis on the prairie" by its guests, Thistle Hill Bed & Breakfast is a convenient, secluded cedar farm home located halfway between Kansas City and Denver, Colorado. Thistle Hill is surrounded by native prairie, 60 acres of wildflower-prairie restoration, and cottage-style flower and herb gardens. Accommodations range from the spacious Oak Room with a rustic queen-sized bed crafted of antique hedge fence posts, the Sunflower Room with a handmade Kansas sunflower quilt, and the Prairie Room honoring family members who were pioneers of the area. After being awakened by the rooster's crow, feast on a hearty country breakfast of fragrant homemade muffins or hot cakes made from freshly ground Kansas wheat, along with an egg dish, fresh fruit and juice, and gourmet coffee or herbal tea. Thistle Hill is located close to Castle Rock, Cedar Bluff Reservoir, the Cottonwood Ranch, and Sternberg Museum.

SEASON

all year

ACCOMMODATIONS

three rooms with private baths

Herb Garden Syrup

1½ – 2 cups garden fresh cinnamon basil (available from a herb farm)
5 cups water
4 cups sugar
5 teaspoons lemon juice

Featherweight whole wheat pancakes (see recipe on page 238)

Gather the cinnamon basil from the garden after the dew has dried but before the sun is hot. Wash several times in a large basin of water. Shake off the excess water and chop the basil leaves into large pieces. Boil the water in a non-metallic pan and add the basil leaves. Bring to another boil, remove from heat, and cover. Let set for 20 minutes to infuse the flavor. Strain into a large bowl, discarding the basil leaves. Rinse the pan and return the infusion to it. Add the sugar and lemon juice and simmer slowly, stirring frequently, until the sugar is dissolved and the syrup thickens slightly. Serve warm with the featherweight whole wheat pancakes. Store in the refrigerator for up to 2 months. *Yield: 6 cups.*

Honey-Orange Sauce

(Recipe from Breakfast Inn Bed, Easy and Elegant Recipes from Garth Woodside Mansion.)

2 cups honey
4 teaspoons grated orange zest
½ cup orange juice
4 teaspoons Grand Marnier or Triple Sec

Sliced oranges or apples

Warm the honey, orange zest, orange juice, and liqueur in a saucepan and serve over sliced oranges or apples. Store in the refrigerator.
Yield: About 2¾ cups.

Garth Woodside Mansion

Diane and Irv Feinberg
RR #3, Box 578
Hannibal, Missouri 63401
Tel: (573) 221-2789
E-mail: Garth@nemonet.com
www.hanmo.com/garth
$$ – $$$

ABOUT THE B&B

Experience affordable elegance in this 1871 Victorian country estate on 39 acres of meadows and woodlands. On the National Register of Historic Places, Garth Woodside Mansion has remained unchanged outside, and graceful arched doors, handsomely decorated rooms featuring original furnishings spanning over 150 years, and magnificent three-story spiral "Flying Staircase" await you inside. You'll enjoy marble fireplaces, canopy beds, your own nightshirt to wear during your stay, an exceptional full breakfast, an afternoon beverage, and more. All rooms are air conditioned and have a private bath. The location is ideal for seeing Mark Twain Country.

SEASON

all year

ACCOMMODATIONS

eight rooms with private baths

Manor House

Diane and Hank Tremblay
PO Box 447
Norfolk, Connecticut 06058
Tel/Fax: (860) 542-5690
$$$$

ABOUT THE B&B

Manor House is a historic 1898 mansion built for the leisure class of an earlier era. Today, it's designated as "Connecticut's most romantic hideaway" (The Discerning Traveler). Relax in the living room beside the baronial fireplace, retreat to the sun porch to enjoy a book from the inn's library, or take a stroll around the grounds to enjoy the perennial gardens. The inn exudes Victorian elegance, with its Tiffany windows, architectural detail, and antique furnishings. Awake to the wonderful aromas of Manor House's full breakfast, including homemade bread or muffins and honey harvested from the inn's own hives, all served in the elegant dining room. If you have a more romantic breakfast in mind, innkeepers Diane and Hank Tremblay will pamper you with breakfast in bed. Manor House is close to Tanglewood, summer theater, vineyards, and a host of summer and winter activities, including hiking, biking, water sports, and alpine and cross-country skiing.

SEASON

all year

ACCOMMODATIONS

eight rooms with private baths

Lemon-Chive Sauce

"This is delicious served over poached eggs on English muffins."
— Diane Tremblay

⅓ cup butter
2 tablespoons finely chopped chives
1 tablespoon lemon juice
1 teaspoon grated lemon zest
½ teaspoon salt
Dash of pepper

Poached eggs on English muffins

Melt the butter and add the chives, lemon juice, zest, salt, and pepper, beating thoroughly. Serve the sauce hot. *Yield: ½ cup.*

Macadamia-Cranberry Conserve

"This conserve makes a special gift for Christmas. It's also great with my toasted Pilialoha grain bread." — Machiko Heyde

2 oranges
2 cups water
12 ounces fresh cranberries
5½ cups sugar
3 ounces liquid fruit pectin
1 cup unsalted chopped macadamia nuts or walnuts

Pilialoha grain bread (see recipe on page 104)

Peel the oranges, trim away the inner white part (pith) from the peels, and cut the peels into very thin strips. Mix the peels and water in a Dutch oven. Bring to boiling; reduce heat. Cover and simmer 10 minutes. Chop the orange segments and add them, along with the cranberries and sugar, to the peel and water mixture. Bring to a full rolling boil over high heat, stirring constantly. Add the fruit pectin and stir well into the fruit mixture. Boil 1 minute, stirring constantly. Remove from heat. Add the chopped macadamia nuts. Ladle into hot, sterilized jars, filling to within ⅛" of tops. Wipe rims and seal completely. Store in a cool, dark, dry place. Discard if mold develops. *Yield: 6 (8-ounce) jars.*

Pilialoha Bed & Breakfast Cottage

Machiko and Bill Heyde
2512 Kaupakulua Road
Haiku, Maui, Hawaii 96708-6024
Tel: (808) 572-1440
Fax: (808) 572-4612
E-mail: heyde@mauigateway.com
www.mauigateway.com/~heyde
$$$

ABOUT THE B&B

Located in cool upcountry Maui, this quiet cottage sits on lush pasture land, surrounded by a rose and flower garden and overlooking a eucalyptus grove. Only 20 minutes from Kahului Airport and less than five minutes from Makawao town, Pilialoha is also close to Haleakala National Park, the quaint town of Hana, and other points of interest. This private cottage is furnished with a full kitchen (stocked with gourmet coffees and teas), cable TV and a VCR, phone, washer/dryer, picnic coolers, beach chairs, mats and towels, snorkel gear, as well as informative books and videos. It's most comfortable for two people but will accommodate up to five. Freshly baked bread or muffins, fruit, and juice are brought to the cottage daily. Your hosts Machiko (an artist) and Bill (a self-employed computer technician) live on the same property and are available to provide visitor information during your stay.

SEASON

all year

ACCOMMODATIONS

one fully furnished cottage
with private bath

The Georges

Marie and Carolyn George
57759 874th Road
Dixon, Nebraska 68732-9728
Tel: (402) 584-2625
E-mail: DixonMom@aol.com
$

ABOUT THE B&B

Look past the large grove of trees and you'll discover The Georges, a large remodeled, air conditioned farmhouse designed to comfortably accommodate the travel needs of a large family. Your stay includes a hearty breakfast featuring homemade jellies and jams, while other meals can be arranged. Bunking at The Georges offers you the opportunity to see a modern farming operation firsthand, including the planting and harvesting of corn, soybeans, and alfalfa. You'll also hear the chickens clucking and make the acquaintance of several farm cats. During the warm season, you can hike, bird-watch, relax with a book in a quiet spot, or visit county fairs and local festivals. In the fall, pheasant hunting season is in its prime and, depending on the winter snowfall, you can choose from sledding, hiking, cross-country skiing, or ice skating on farm ponds.

SEASON

all year

ACCOMMODATIONS

five rooms with shared baths

Muskmelon Jam

"This recipe has been a family favorite since my mother whipped up the first batch over 50 years ago. It's wonderful served on toast, biscuits, yogurt, or ice cream." — Marie George

1 quart just-ripe muskmelons, peeled, seeded, and chopped into ½" or
    smaller cubes (don't substitute honeydew for muskmelon)
2 tablespoons lemon juice
⅛ teaspoon ground cinnamon
1 cup sugar

Toast, biscuits, yogurt, or ice cream

Place the fruit in a heavy kettle, then let stand a few minutes until it begins to form its own juice. Add the lemon juice and heat carefully to avoid scorching. Simmer until soft and juicy, then add the cinnamon and sugar. Continue simmering until no longer runny, stirring occasionally to prevent scorching. Seal in pint jars or refrigerate until used. *Tips:* Since this jam has a low sugar content, it won't keep more than a few days — even with refrigeration. If multiplying the recipe, don't cook more than 3 quarts of fruit at a time. *Yield: About 4 cups.*

No-Cholesterol Tofu Whipped Cream

"This recipe is excellent for people watching their sugar intake."
— *Barbara Gavron*

1 cup tofu (about 8 ounces)
6 tablespoons rice syrup*
1 tablespoon vegetable oil or nut butter
Pinch of sea salt
3 tablespoons agar-agar flakes**
½ cup apple juice
1 teaspoon vanilla

Rice syrup is made from brown rice and is used as a natural sweetener instead of sugar. You can find it in health food stores.

**Agar-agar is an unflavored, gelatinous product made from seaweed that's high in protein. You can find it in health food stores.*

Drop the tofu into boiling, salted water. Remove it from the heat and let it sit 2 – 3 minutes. Drain. Squeeze out any liquid. Blend the tofu, rice syrup, oil, and sea salt together until creamy. Set aside. Combine the agar-agar with the apple juice and bring to a boil. Lower the heat and simmer until the agar-agar dissolves. Remove from the heat. Add the vanilla to the tofu mixture. Beat with a wire whisk or electric mixer until smooth and creamy. Set aside to gel. When the mixture has almost set, beat again. Set aside for a few hours to mellow. Chill if not using immediately. To freshen, beat again before using. *Yield: 1¼ cups.*

Singleton House

Barbara Gavron
11 Singleton
Eureka Springs, Arkansas 72632
Tel: (800) 833-3394 or (501) 253-9111
$$ – $$$

ABOUT THE B&B

Singleton House is an old-fashioned place with a touch of magic. Sheltering a hidden enchanted garden on a hillside in Eureka Spring's historic district, this 1890s Victorian home is whimsically decorated with an eclectic collection of cherished antiques and unexpected treasures. Light and airy guest rooms are furnished with romantic touches and homey comforts. In addition, a honeymoon cottage with a Jacuzzi for two is located in a separate wooded location. Enjoy a full breakfast served on the balcony overlooking the fantasy wildflower garden, winding stone paths, and a lily-filled goldfish pond. Browse through the small nature library and identify the feathered inhabitants of some 50 bird-houses scattered over the grounds. A short stroll down a scenic wooded foot-path leads to shops and cafes. For would-be B&Bers, your host offers an apprenticeship program with hands-on training for anyone wanting to try on the innkeeper's hat before taking the plunge!

SEASON

all year

ACCOMMODATIONS

five rooms (including one suite)
with private baths;
one honeymoon cottage
with private bath

Berry Patch Inn

Ann M. Caggiano
1150 North Four Winds Road
Coeur d'Alene, Idaho 83814-9734
Tel: (208) 765-4994
Fax: (208) 667-7336
E-mail: Lady_Anne@msn.com
$$$$

ABOUT THE B&B

Hailed as one of the top 20 inns situated in the Rockies by National Geographic Traveler (*March 1997*), *Berry Patch Inn offers an elegant and restorative mountain chalet retreat. Nestled in a two-acre forest of tall pines, the inn is notable for its eclectic decor and a large living room with beamed ceiling and rock fireplace. Three guest rooms, all with private bath, look out on the forest, wild berry patch, valley, mountain, or waterfall. Ann Caggiano, the world-traveled innkeeper, serves breakfast in the dining room. Here, spectacular views from the big picture window compete with Ann's beautifully presented breakfast creations — emphasizing healthy and low-fat cuisine. This bird watchers' paradise is less than an hour's drive from Spokane International Airport; close to Lake Coeur d'Alene and the Spokane River, for swimming, fishing, lake cruises, and parasailing; and three-and-a-half miles from downtown shopping and dining. A variety of winter sports, including top-rated skiing, are less than an hour's drive away.*

SEASON

all year

ACCOMMODATIONS

three rooms with private baths

Poppy Seed Dressing

"This dressing is extremely low in fat and sugar." — *Ann Caggiano*

1 pound low-fat sour cream substitute (IMO brand recommended)
⅓ pound non-fat vanilla frozen yogurt
1 packet sugar substitute (such as Equal brand)
2 tablespoons poppy seeds

Fruit or cold fruit soups

Place the sour cream substitute, frozen yogurt, sugar substitute, and poppy seeds in a bowl and blend well using an electric beater (this will take about 10 minutes). Use as a topping for a variety of fruit and for cold fruit soups, elegantly garnished with a sprinkle of poppy seed and a sprig of mint. *Tip:* The dressing will keep for at least 1 week stored in a container with a tight-fitting lid in the refrigerator. ***Yield: About 3 cups.***

Raspberry-Rhubarb Compote

1 pound fresh rhubarb, chopped
10 ounces frozen raspberries
½ cup sugar

Waffles or biscuits

Combine the rhubarb, raspberries, and sugar and cook until the rhubarb is tender. Use as a topping on waffles or biscuits. Refrigerate covered or freeze for later use. *Yield: 4 cups.*

The Blushing Rosé B&B

Ellen and Bucky Laufersweiler
11 William Street
Hammondsport, New York
14840
Tel: (607) 569-3402
Fax: (607) 569-3483
$$

ABOUT THE B&B

In the heart of the wine country, The Blushing Rosé is a pleasant hideaway for honeymooners, anniversary couples, and romantic trysters alike. Whether you spend your day driving, hiking, biking, or just plain relaxing, The Blushing Rosé is the ideal haven at which to end your day. Arise to the wonderful aroma of fresh-baked granola and whole grain bread, and begin your day with a special breakfast. The inn itself has an ambiance of cozy, 19th-century America. There are four spacious guest rooms each with a sitting area and private bath. Air conditioning and ceiling fans are among some of the amenities offered. This B&B is located on the southern tip of Keuka Lake, one of New York's famous Finger Lakes.

SEASON

May 1 to November 30

ACCOMMODATIONS

four rooms with private baths

The Inn
On Golden Pond

Bonnie and Bill Webb
PO Box 680, Route 3
Holderness, New Hampshire 03245
Tel: (603) 968-7269
Fax: (603) 968-9226
E-mail: innongp@lr.net
$$$

ABOUT THE B&B

In 1984, Bonnie and Bill Webb left their desk jobs in southern California to establish The Inn On Golden Pond, an 1879 Colonial home located near Squam Lake, setting for the classic film On Golden Pond. *Ideal in all seasons, this central area of New Hampshire offers hiking, bicycling, golfing, water activities, skiing, and skating. The inn is known for its refreshingly friendly yet professional atmosphere. Rooms are individually decorated in traditional country style, featuring hardwood floors, braided rugs, country curtains, and bedspreads. There are seven spacious guest rooms and one extra-large suite, all with private baths. Morning is a treat as Bonnie makes all the breads, muffins, coffee cakes, and her special rhubarb jam. A full breakfast is offered each day featuring regional favorites, such as baked French toast and apple pancakes.*

SEASON

all year

ACCOMMODATIONS

eight rooms (including one suite) with private baths

Rhubarb Jam

"This jam makes its appearance every morning on the breakfast tables. Guests especially enjoy it with my homemade white bread. The rhubarb is grown in the inn's backyard." — Bonnie Webb

6 cups chopped rhubarb
5 cups sugar
20-ounce can crushed pineapple
6-ounce box strawberry Jell-O

In a large pot, bring the rhubarb, sugar, and pineapple to a boil. Boil for 2 minutes. Add the Jell-O and stir well. Pour into sterilized jars and top with paraffin wax. Store in a cool, dark, dry place. Discard if mold develops. *Yield: 8 (8-ounce) jars.*

Rhubarb Sauce

4 cups chopped rhubarb
¼ cup water
1 cup sugar

Waffles or biscuits

Cook the rhubarb in the water until tender. Add the sugar and stir until dissolved. Use as a topping on waffles or biscuits. Keep refrigerated.
Yield: 8 servings.

The Blushing Rosé B&B

Ellen and Bucky Laufersweiler
11 William Street
Hammondsport, New York
14840
Tel: (607) 569-3402
Fax: (607) 569-3483
$$

ABOUT THE B&B

*I*n the heart of the wine country, The Blushing Rosé is a pleasant hideaway for honeymooners, anniversary couples, and romantic trysters alike. Whether you spend your day driving, hiking, biking, or just plain relaxing, The Blushing Rosé is the ideal haven at which to end your day. Arise to the wonderful aroma of fresh-baked granola and whole grain bread, and begin your day with a special breakfast. The inn itself has an ambiance of cozy, 19th-century America. There are four spacious guest rooms each with a sitting area and private bath. Air conditioning and ceiling fans are among some of the amenities offered. This B&B is located on the southern tip of Keuka Lake, one of New York's famous Finger Lakes.

SEASON

May 1 to November 30

ACCOMMODATIONS

four rooms with private baths

The Mainstay Inn

Sue and Tom Carroll
635 Columbia Avenue
Cape May, New Jersey 08204
Tel: (609) 884-8690
$$$ – $$$$

ABOUT THE B&B

According to the Washington Post, *"The jewel of them all has got to be the Mainstay."* Built by a pair of wealthy gamblers in 1872, this elegant and exclusive clubhouse is now among the premier B&B inns in the country. The Mainstay now comprises three historic buildings on one of the most beautiful streets of the historic Cape May district. Guests enjoy 16 antique-filled rooms and suites (some with fireplaces and whirlpool baths), three parlors, spacious gardens, and rocker-filled verandas. Breakfast and afternoon tea are served daily. Beautiful beaches, historic attractions, biking, birding, golf, and tennis are all available in Cape May, a National Historic Landmark community.

SEASON

all year

ACCOMMODATIONS

16 rooms (including seven suites) with private baths

Spicy Apple Syrup

(*Recipe from* Breakfast at Nine, Tea at Four: Favorite Recipes from Cape May's Mainstay Inn.)

1 cup applesauce
10-ounce jar apple jelly
½ teaspoon ground cinnamon
⅛ teaspoon ground cloves
Dash of salt

Pancakes or French toast

Combine the applesauce, apple jelly, cinnamon, cloves, and salt. Cook over medium heat, stirring constantly until the jelly is melted and the syrup is hot. Serve with pancakes or French toast. *Yield: 2 cups.*

Strawberry Butter

½ cup butter
8 ounces cream cheese
¼ cup honey
½ cup mashed strawberries or blueberries

Muffins, waffles, pancakes, or whole grain bread

Combine the butter, cream cheese, honey, and berries. Store in a covered container in the refrigerator. Best served with muffins, waffles, pancakes, or whole grain bread. *Yield: 2 cups.*

The Blushing Rosé B&B

Ellen and Bucky Laufersweiler
11 William Street
Hammondsport, New York
14840
Tel: (607) 569-3402
Fax: (607) 569-3483
$$

ABOUT THE B&B

*I*n the heart of the wine country, *The Blushing Rosé is a pleasant hideaway for honeymooners, anniversary couples, and romantic trysters alike. Whether you spend your day driving, hiking, biking, or just plain relaxing, The Blushing Rosé is the ideal haven at which to end your day. Arise to the wonderful aroma of fresh-baked granola and whole grain bread, and begin your day with a special breakfast. The inn itself has an ambiance of cozy, 19th-century America. There are four spacious guest rooms each with a sitting area and private bath. Air conditioning and ceiling fans are among some of the amenities offered. This B&B is located on the southern tip of Keuka Lake, one of New York's famous Finger Lakes.*

SEASON

May 1 to November 30

ACCOMMODATIONS

four rooms with private baths

New Berne House Inn

Marcia Drum and Howard Bronson
709 Broad Street
New Bern, North Carolina 28560
Tel: (800) 842-7688 or (919) 636-2250
$$

ABOUT THE B&B

New Berne House Inn is centrally located in the Colonial town of New Bern and within comfortable walking distance of numerous historic sights, highlighted by Tryon Palace and its formal gardens, only one block away. Quaint shops, fine restaurants, and historic buildings are all in the neighborhood. New Berne House's seven guest rooms feature queen- and king-size beds, antiques and collectibles, private baths, and telephones and clock radios, along with other amenities to pamper guests. A full breakfast is served in the dining room from 8:00 to 9:00 am, but coffee is available as early as 6:30 am. Throughout the day, guests are invited to join the innkeepers in the library or parlor for light refreshments, television, and good conversation. Two weekends each month are reserved for a "juicy" who-done-it mystery package, which blends in nicely with the inn's two haunted rooms (where "odd occurrences" have been reported over the years!).

SEASON

all year

ACCOMMODATIONS

seven rooms with private baths

Whipped Fruit Butter

"We used to call this Strawberry Butter . . . that was before we tried blueberries, peaches, applesauce, maple syrup, and orange marmalade!" — Marcia Drum

1 cup butter
1 cup strawberries, washed and hulled

Pancakes, waffles, French toast, toasted English muffins, or scones

Let the butter stand at room temperature until it is soft enough to spread. Put the butter in a bowl with the berries and beat it with an electric mixer at medium-high speed until the berries are absorbed and the mixture is fluffy. Heap into a serving bowl and serve at room temperature with pancakes, waffles, French toast, toasted English muffins, or scones.
Yield: 2 cups.

Index

of

Recipes

Notes

$\mathcal{R}$ise & $\mathcal{D}$ine books make unique gifts!

Purchase through a bookstore or mail form with payment to one of the following addresses.

USA:
Callawind Publications Inc.
2083 Hempstead Turnpike, Suite 355
East Meadow, New York 11554-1730

Canada:
Callawind Publications Inc.
3383 Sources Boulevard, Suite 205
Dollard-des-Ormeaux, Quebec H9B 1Z8

You may return books *in original condition* at any time for a full refund on the purchase price.

Qty	Description	Total
	Rise & Dine America: Savory Secrets from America's Bed & Breakfast Inns (second edition) @ US$16.95 / C$21.95 **each**	
	Rise & Dine Canada: Savory Secrets from Canada's Bed & Breakfast Inns @ US$14.95 / C$19.95 **each**	
	Shipping: Surface mail @ US$4.95 / C$5.95 **for 1 book** and US$0.80 / C$1.00 **for each additional book** (2 – 4 weeks delivery)	
	7% goods and services tax (GST) for Canadian orders only	
	Prices subject to change without notice.	_____

Name _____ Tel. _____

Address _____

City _____ State/Prov. _____ Zip/Postal code_____

Payment enclosed (payable to Callawind Publications): ❑ *Check* ❑ *Money order*

To help us better understand our readers, kindly provide the following information:

Where did you first see this book? _____

Are you buying it for yourself or as a gift? _____

Comments about the book _____

Questions? Call: (514) 685-9109 / Fax: (514) 685-7055 / E-mail: info@callawind.com

Metric Equivalents

Volume

1 teaspoon = 5 milliliters
1 tablespoon = 15 milliliters
¼ cup = 60 milliliters
⅓ cup = 80 milliliters
½ cup = 120 milliliters
⅔ cup = 160 milliliters
1 cup = 230 milliliters

Weight

1 ounce = 28 grams
1 pound = 454 grams

Oven Temperatures

300°F = 150°C
325°F = 165°C
350°F = 175°C
375°F = 190°C
400°F = 200°C
425°F = 220°C
450°F = 230°C
475°F = 245°C

General Formula for Metric Conversion

Ounces to grams: multiply ounce figure by 28.35

Pounds to grams: multiply pound figure by 453.59

Pounds to kilograms: multiply pound figure by 0.45

Ounces to milliliters: multiply ounce figure by 30

Cups to liters: multiply cup figure by 0.24

Fahrenheit to Celsius: subtract 32 from the Fahrenheit figure, multiply by 5, then divide by 9

Inches to centimeters: multiply inch figure by 2.54